INFOCULTURE

INFOCULTURE

THE SMITHSONIAN BOOK OF INFORMATION AGE INVENTIONS

STEVEN LUBAR

HOUGHTON MIFFLIN COMPANY

BOSTON   NEW YORK

1993

FOR LISA

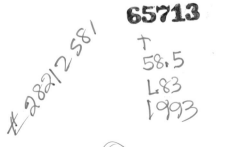
For information about permission to reproduce selections from this book, write
to Permissions, Houghton Mifflin Company, 222 Berkeley Street, Boston,
Massachusetts 02116.

Library of Congress Cataloging-in-Publication Data
Lubar, Steven D.
    InfoCulture : the Smithsonian book of the inventions of the
Information Age / Steven Lubar.
        p.   cm.
Based on an exhibit at the Smithsonian Institution's National
Museum of American History.
    Includes bibliographical references and index.
    ISBN 0-395-57042-5
    1. Information technology — History.   2. National Museum of
American History (U.S.) — Exhibitions.   I. National Museum
of American History (U.S.)   II. Title.
T58.5.L83   1993   93-4815
303.48'33 — dc20   CIP

The author gratefully acknowledges permission to quote from: "The Distance Fiend,"
by A. H. Folwell, reprinted by permission, copyright 1925, 1953 The New Yorker
Magazine, Inc. "Song of Reproduction," by Michael Flanders, reprinted by permission
of Claudia Flanders. "Stereophonic Sound," by Cole Porter, reprinted by permission of
Robert H. Montgomery, Jr., The Cole Porter Musical and Literary Property Trust,
Copyright © 1955 by Cole Porter, copyright renewed. "DEPRIVACY," by Felicia
Lamport, reprinted by permission of the author.

Drawings by Chris Costello.

I N F O C U L T U R E
A C K N O W L E D G M E N T S

The materials gathered for the "Information Age" exhibit at the Smithsonian Institution's National Museum of American History provided the foundation for this book. My thanks to all of the people who chose artifacts, collected information, and wrote labels for that exhibit: David Allison, Nance Briscoe, Betsy Burstein, Paul Ceruzzi, Jon Eklund, Bernard Finn, Louis Hutchins, Peggy A. Kidwell, Peter Liebhold, Marie Mattson, Jacqueline McGlade, Uta C. Merzbach, Nat Pendleton, Victoria Pinpin, Steven Schloss, Ann Seeger, Elliot Sivowitch, Susan Smulyan, Carlene Stephens, Peter Vogt, Deborah Warner, and Michael R. Williams.

Many of these people, and many others, have helped as I've gone over the same ground for this book. Some read chapters and gave me suggestions on what to include and how to include it: my thanks to David Allison, Paul Ceruzzi, Jon Eklund, Bernard Finn, Robert Friedel, Elizabeth Harris, Paul Israel, Richard John, Peggy A. Kidwell, Peter Liebhold, Barbara Lubar, Kenneth Lubar, William Lubar, Jim Miller, Jeff Rosenwald, Elliot Sivowitch, Carlene Stephens, Paul Theerman, Lisa Thoerle, and JoAnne Yates. Others have offered advice and information: my thanks to Dwight Bowers, Nance Briscoe, Bridget Burke, Jonathan Coopersmith, Peter Fannon, Ken Haase, Tomás Lozano-Pérez, Charles McGovern, Beth Parkhurst, Rodris Roth, and Helena Wright. Special thanks to Susan Smulyan, who has given good advice throughout.

Several researchers have helped gather material for the book: Jim Cullen, Kathleen Franz, and Michael Kucher. Thanks again.

This book depends on some of the technology it discusses; the members of the history of computers and history of technology newsgroups on the Internet (SHOTHC-L@SIVM.SI.EDU and HTECH-L@SIVM.SI.EDV) have been very helpful.

The drawings in this book are the work of Chris Costello. For assistance with them, and for helping to find photographs and getting permission to use them, my thanks to Laura Kreiss, Betsy Burstein, and Michael Kucher. The Smithsonian Office of Printing and Photographic Services has, as always, been helpful in many ways. Thanks also to the many individuals, firms, libraries, museums, and archives that provided pictures for the book.

The National Museum of American History branch of the Smithsonian

Institution Libraries, a treasure trove of information, has proven ideally suited to this work. Interlibrary loan has brought in even more. Jim Roan has been of invaluable assistance in getting the books I need, and calling useful books and articles to my attention. Bridget Burke has been an exemplary reference librarian, helping me find answers to many obscure questions.

Thanks also to Carlene Stephens, Ed Ezell, and Art Molella, at the Museum of American History, for allowing me time to work on this book.

The book is based on the work of many historians, in a wide range of specialties, and it is a pleasure to acknowledge my indebtedness to their research and interpretations. All errors are, of course, my own responsibility.

INFOCULTURE
CONTENTS

America was already an information culture in 1903 when Charles Dana Gibson drew this cartoon of a businessman hard at work while on vacation. Information machines have come to shape American society. We've all come to depend on them in almost every aspect of our lives.

INFOCULTURE
INTRODUCTION

I N 1903 CHARLES DANA GIBSON DREW A CARTOON lampooning the new Information Age. The caption reads: "Mr. A Merger Hogg is taking a few days much-needed rest at his country home." He is clearly doing no such thing. Mr. Merger Hogg — his name reflects the merger mania at the turn of the century; today he'd be doing leveraged buyouts on Wall Street — is surrounded by information machines. A newspaper and stock ticker brings him information from markets around the world. Two telegraph messengers have fallen asleep on a bench, exhausted from their efforts. His son, or perhaps his office assistant, is on the telephone, relaying orders to buy or sell, or perhaps sending instructions to his subordinates back at the office. His wife — or is it his secretary? — sits at a typewriter, ready to take down memos or letters. And all of this on his vacation!

Mr. Hogg no doubt told his friends that he couldn't live without his telegraph and typewriter, that he couldn't bear to be without his links to the information that formed so large a piece of his world. He stands near the beginning of a new age in which information drives society and business and, as the cartoon makes clear, people's lives. He's "modern" in a way that people before him were not. For we too are surrounded by information machines, and linked to the world around us by communications machines. Like Mr. Hogg, we see the world through our information and communications machines. Like him, we are afloat in a world of information.

Our machines are different, at least in outward appearance. I am writing this book on a Macintosh computer, a machine that replaces the gears and levers of a typewriter with a microprocessor, electronic circuitry, software, and a display screen. On the floor is a modem, which lets my computer talk to other computers over the phone lines. There are some 20 million people on the Internet whom I could reach via modem if I knew their electronic-mail address. I check my E-mail; I'm carrying on several electronic conversations about the book, and about other topics. I check a few bulletin boards (there are tens of thousands I might look in on; I keep up to date with a half dozen), looking for interesting information about computers and communications that might enliven the story, and keep it current. Occasionally I broadcast requests for information: Does anyone know about early word processing, for example, or the history of "open" software?

1

On top of the modem sits the telephone, and that, too, ties me in to an information network. There are more than 500 million phones in the world, and if I knew the number and were willing to pay the bill, I could reach any of them. And as I work, I almost always have the radio on, picking a station from dozens of possibilities of broadcast entertainment and news. There is an astonishing electronic information infrastructure surrounding me — surrounding us all.

But the electronic part of the information infrastructure is only a tiny fraction of what's available to me. Every morning the newspaper is thrown into the driveway. The paper is an amazing achievement, more than one hundred pages of news, data, photographs, and advertisements pulled over electronic threads from around the world, processed, organized, and delivered. Every day at about noon the mailman brings mail to the box at the end of the driveway. It has been collected, sorted, moved, and delivered: a traditional information stream, but an important one.

Behind me as I sit in my office is a wall of books. Each of them has its own story — each one written, edited, designed, printed, distributed. The author of each has spent months or years collecting information through all of the channels mentioned here, and more, deciding what's important, and figuring out how best to state the facts, and how to make the case for his or her interpretation of them. Many of the books are checked out of the library — an enormously effective information distribution mechanism, every bit as impressive an achievement as the most modern computer network. Some have been obtained through interlibrary loan, a system that moves thousands of books around the country every day.

I swim in an ocean of information. But my information infrastructure is shallow compared to some. The modern equivalent of Mr. Hogg — a bond trader, say — has a phone to each ear; there might be an open line to Tokyo, another to London. Three computer terminals and a TV set tuned to CNN sit in front of her. The computers not only keep track of her trades but advise her when and what to buy and sell. In her car she has a cellular phone and a fax machine. A satellite paging system means that she can always receive an important message, that she's never out of touch. Stock prices, transmitted on a special radio band, are available at the touch of a button. Next to the alarm clock on her bedside table sits a computer with a modem so that she can get the prices on the Tokyo exchange at any hour of the night. The modern trader is a cyborg, a combination of machine and person. Tied to the world by electronic threads, she sees the world as information. The money she trades exists merely as electronic information. It's real only because we all believe it is. It has value only because we trust the information machines that keep track of it.

The bond trader's information infrastructure, impressive as it is, makes up only a small part of what's available. She's just one of many types of information cyborg. The computer hacker, spending his nights glued to the screen as he travels through cyberspace, has a different sort of information world. An air-traffic controller or Aegis missile system operator receives *all* his or her information filtered through a technological system; the raw sensory data of radar beams are interpreted by computers before appearing as glowing spots on cathode-ray tubes. Even the couch potato, sitting at home with eighty-four channels of cable TV to choose from, a few hundred CDs to listen to, a rack of videos to watch or Nintendo games to play, and stacks of junk mail on the table — junk mail he gets because a computer has pulled his name out of a data bank — is more tied into the information age than he might imagine.

Today, with information machines so widespread, and communications networks bringing news and data from around the world, we're *all* driven by information machinery. Like Mr. Hogg, we can't get away from our information. Like the currency trader, we're afraid to go to sleep at night, for fear of missing something on the news, something halfway around the world that might affect our business or our lives — or just something that we're afraid of not knowing about even though it doesn't really affect us at all. We're all like the Aegis missile system operator; our lives are dependent on our information machines. And like the couch potato, we can't escape, even if we might like to. We are all cyborgs. Mark Alan Stamaty, in a cartoon published in 1991, sums up the Information Age: "Information Is Power."

We are surrounded by new machines, new devices, new technologies that let us — or make us — deal with more information than ever before. We are also surrounded by new economic and social and cultural systems which support and make possible these machines, and which, in turn, are supported by them. Together our information culture and our information machines shape the way we live, work, and play, and change the way we think about the world around us. No aspect of our lives remains untouched. But we shape the machines, too, deciding

Mark Alan Stamaty's 1991 "Washingtoon" shows an information culture different only in degree from Charles Dana Gibson's 1903 view.

what we want to use and how we use it. We change along with the machines, and they change along with us.

TECHNOLOGY AND INFOCULTURE

I call this new world of information, communications, and entertainment machines an information culture. I use the term "information culture" because these machines, and the social structures that they are part of, have come to define our culture, at least as much as ethnicity, race, or geography. How we feel about the world around us, about one another, even about ourselves has been changed by these machines and the way we've chosen to use them.

Our tools help to shape what we see when we look around us. Information machines are new, sometimes better, always different tools for seeing. What we hear when we talk to one another is determined by what other noises are present, and information machines can create a cacophony, or sometimes a new silence. Information machines and organizations make it easier to focus on some things, certain kinds of data, and harder to focus on others. For most Americans, starting in the mid-nineteenth century, what we see, hear, and think about, and how we understand it, is in part shaped by the way we use information machines.

What are the outlines of our information culture? It's a culture that likes speed, exactness, and continuous novelty. It's a culture with a strong desire for control, though also with room for dissent. Its ideology is democratic — it looks to its new machines as encouraging democracy — but it also tends toward bureaucracy and rules. It's a society in which computer hackers or radio amateurs can be heroes, but which is driven toward increasingly large data banks and stricter rules about data. Our information culture prizes the appearance of choice in entertainment, but limits that choice by making entertainment expensive, and judging it by its profitability. For the most part, it's a white middle-class male corporate culture, though also a culture that occasionally allows people from the geographic, racial, or class margins of society to gain a new influence. America's information culture is a culture of fragmentation within centralization, a culture of freedom within control.

How did this all happen? In part, that's a story of technological history: new communications and entertainment machines such as the telegraph and telephone and television, and new information processing machinery such as the adding machine and the computer. In part — just as important a part — it's business history, the story of new ways of organizing work or of processing the flow of information necessary to make sense of a factory or store or market. And it can be looked at in another way: it's part of our social and cultural history — the story of new ways of organizing our lives to deal with information in ever-increasing amounts. We invent new organizations to make the best use of information.

It is often tempting to try to say which came first, the technology or the social and business organization or the cultural changes; but history doesn't work that way. All these things happen together, each incremental change allowing, suggesting, and making possible others. Social changes support new technologies, just as new technologies support social changes.

Oftentimes, new technologies find a small niche that supports them until wider applications find them useful. These niches can be in the military, which is willing to pay for technology others can't afford (computers in the early days, for example), or in entertainment, which often supports peculiar technologies before they achieve wider use. (Computer games, one of the first applications of the personal computer, and the wireless, adopted by amateurs, are good examples.) But sometimes the cost-is-no-object, high-reliability demands of military projects, or the time-is-no-object style of those who enjoy playing with technology, whether amateur radio operators or computer hackers, mean that technology developed for specialized audiences must be drastically reshaped for a mass market.

Much technology is adopted to fit a niche that has already been created. For example, cheap portraits, made by using mechanical systems, were popular before photography. The new photographic art was quickly accepted because it didn't seem all that different from what was already familiar. Newspapers had grown in size before the steam press was adopted; the steam press made it easier to meet already existing needs. So technologies often come along to fill a need, rather than create it — though they sometimes do that, too.

New forms of communications are one element in the creation of the American information culture. The communications revolution was not just technological but also social and cultural. Technologically, a key event was the application of electricity to communications. With the invention of the telegraph in the 1830s, electricity made instantaneous communications possible. Instantaneous communications in turn meant a vast increase in the usefulness — and thus the quantity — of information. (It's important to note, though, that the telegraph added to an already impressive communications system based on the postal system.) New communications technology increased its users' power to control activities at a distance.

It also redefined our ideas about community, even as those ideas determined how we used new communications technologies. Communications historian James Carey has suggested that communications has a ritual purpose in addition to its role in sending messages, that some communications is directed "not toward the extension of messages in space but toward the maintenance of society in time; not the act of imparting information but the representation of shared beliefs." Communications of this sort allows "the construction and maintenance of an ordered, meaningful cultural world that can serve as a control and container for human action." Communications, in this sense, serves as "a symbolic process whereby reality is produced, maintained, repaired, and transformed."[1] Letters from children give way to collect phone calls, and soon to faxes and E-mail, but all these forms serve to maintain personal connections. Communication is a form of interaction that creates and re-creates our social and cultural world.

A second element of our information culture is the organizations that process information, communicate it, and use it for control. These began to grow in size and scale and complexity at about the same time that electrical communications began. Military forces, government bureaucracies, and business firms found that there were advantages to increased internal control, to hierarchies of managers whose job it was to process information.

In part this came about because new technologies — the manufacturing technologies of the Industrial Revolution and the transportation technologies of the railroad — showed the advantages for large-scale enterprises. It also occurred because of new cultural ideas about class, gender, and race, and a feeling, widespread among the upper classes, especially in the second half of the nineteenth century, that things were out of control, that society was getting too complicated, too messy, and that new methods of organization and control were needed.

Both governments and business organizations found advantages to using more and more information to control their operations, and were willing to pay for the technology that allowed them to increase that control. They used information to manage their machinery and workers; to increase efficiency; to grow in size; to provide more services; and, most important, to earn larger profits. They used the new communications technology, and also a vast new set of social and technical innovations, to process their information. These included everything from the railroad timetable, and the system of rules required to enforce it, to new kinds of filing cabinets, to the computer. The new technology made possible new bureaucracies, just as the new bureaucracies made new technologies usable.

A third element of the information culture is found on the consumer side of the industrial economy. Not just at work, but also at home, Americans found new uses for information technology. They used it for entertainment. The technology of the record player, say, could be used for office dictating machines, or it could be used to play music. Telephones and telegraphs could be used for relaying business information or for exchanging personal messages. Radio waves could be used for emergency messages to ships at sea or to broadcast music and news to a mass audience.

Consumers — especially middle-class customers, workers in the new bureaucracies — eagerly adopted this entertainment and communications technology, for it fit well with the ongoing traditions of mass entertainment as well as newer beliefs about culture as a commodity. Consumers and marketers would find ways to use the technologies, and read new meanings into it. These ideas — about community defined as communications, about the lack of real communications despite all of the new machines, about the place of the individual in a country so taken with bureaucracy, mass communications, and entertainment — not only were shaped by the new machines but helped to shape the way they were used.

The technologies of the second half of the twentieth century — the computer, the television, and all of the digital miscegenations of communications and computation — came into a society and culture already shaped by bureaucracy and mass communications. According to the cultural historian Raymond Williams, a new communications system never creates a new society or new social conditions. The decisive and earlier transformation of industrial production, and its new social forms, which had grown out of a long history of capital accumulation and working technical improvements, created new needs but also new possibilities, and the communications systems, down to television, were their intrinsic outcome.[2]

The technological base for the computer came from the electronics invented for communications, especially radio and telephony, before and during World War II. But its social base — equally important for allowing computers to spread, in the course of fifty years, from a few military installations to 100 million desktops around the world — came from the business and social organization that had existed for more than a century. It was easy for organizations to adopt the computer; it fit in with social and business structures and cultural predispositions.

Television took its business structure from radio, from the complex system of advertising revenues and networks that had been established, in hard-fought battles, in the 1920s. It drew from a long tradition of mass entertainment, from vaudeville to movies to newspapers. Raymond Williams uses television as an example of the ways in which technologies are developed. They come into being, he insists, because they meet the needs of society. If it weren't for television, we would "still be manipulated or mindlessly entertained, but in some other way and perhaps less powerfully."[3] Technologies, he reminds us, are symptoms of social processes, not their causes. Williams restores intention to the process of research and development. Technologies were developed with certain purposes and practices in mind.

The same is true of the technologies of today and tomorrow. Videodisks, video games, multimedia, electronic mail, all partake of their social and cultural settings. Technologies may occasionally (though rarely) be all new, revolutionary; but the uses to which they are put never are. People use machines in ways in which they have become accustomed to using them, or to using their predecessors. This means not that things don't change — entrepreneurs are always finding new markets, new ways to sell, new arguments to convince, and society and culture are always changing in response to new technologies — but rather that technological change and social and cultural change go together. Change is mutual. To predict our future, we must know about not only our technological possibilities but also our social and cultural trajectories.

WHAT'S COVERED AND HOW

This book examines some of these new technologies and some of the ways they were put to work, how people used them, and what people thought about them. It starts with printed books and the postal system, the information machines of the eighteenth century; moves on to the beginning of electrical communications with Morse's invention of the telegraph in 1838; and comes right up to the present day to look at the vast proliferation of computers, fax machines, satellite links, and digital phone systems.

The book is organized by technology, but (for the most part) by enduser technology rather than the technology inside the machines. The inside technology is covered where it was first or most widely used. So the invention, early history, and technology of the vacuum tube is discussed in the chapter on wireless telegraphy, the transistor in the chapter on radio, the integrated circuit under computers, and so on.

The topics covered are, for the most part, those that have affected daily life, the average man's and woman's activities. Computers, for example, have found use everywhere, so much so that it's impossible to keep track of all their applications. I've focused on the applications that affect our day-to-day life —

word processing or computer games, say, rather than the use of computers in science. I consider the telegraph as it was used in business rather than as it was used in war — though I discuss wartime uses, too, when they are particularly important. Television has found no end of uses other than as a means of providing news and entertainment, but it's as news and entertainment that it affects most people, and so that is what I've focused on.

This book is intended for people who look around them and ask, How did the world get to be this way? I answer that question by looking at history. Who invented the machines? What did they have in mind? Who put the machines to use, and what were their goals? How has the history of the use of machines shaped the machines, and shaped the way we use them today? How has that history shaped us individually, as members of communities, and as a nation?

The technologies and the people who use them change together. It's not always easy to tell which changes come first, the technical ones or the social and cultural ones — or, more accurately, how the changes happen together, interactively, simultaneously, synergistically. That's one of the questions that is most interesting. Culture prepares the way for changes in technology just as technology prepares the way for changes in culture.

I don't try to tell every bit of the technological history of each of the machines of the Information Age. Rather, I have selected the bits of history that are most interesting, or revealing, or important, those that tell us something of the way our information culture developed. That is, I focus on the stories that were important in their own day, in their own right. I have also included, of course, stories about the old technologies that turned out to be "right," that turned out to be on the path to the present. But I've tried to put these into their historical setting. Picking them out and holding them up as technological triumphs leads to a backward kind of history. It suggests a predetermined path of technological and social development toward a predetermined end. It's not useful for understanding the past, and it's a misleading way of understanding the present. We have to follow the roads that turned out to be dead ends as well as those that turned out to be superhighways to the present.

There is one road that I have not followed. There are obviously many ways we get information that don't include computers or telephones, or any machine at all. Bill McKibben made this point wonderfully well in *The Age of Missing Information*:

> We believe that we live in the "age of information," that there has been an information "explosion," an information "revolution." While in a certain narrow sense this is the case, in many important ways just the opposite is true. . . . Our society is moving steadily from natural sources of information toward electronic ones, from the mountain and the field toward the television; this great transition is very nearly complete. And so we need to understand the two extremes. One is the target of our drift. The other an anchor that might tug us gently back, a source of information that once spoke clearly to us and now hardly even whispers.[4]

McKibben is absolutely right: in gaining our new technological world, we have lost an older, quieter one. It has become easier for us to learn from machines than from nature. I agree with McKibben that the world we have lost is an appealing one with much that we should keep alive, or at least whose heritage we should treasure. But this book, unlike McKibben's, is about the new world of information, not the old.

That is, it's about *technologically mediated information* — the information that comes to us through machines. So it's not, for example, about people talking to one another, or the thinking that goes on inside one's head. Only when some machine is involved — from a book to a telephone to a computer — is it considered here. There are limits, of course. I don't include, for example, music made by using traditional instruments, though of course that is a technology; I do include recorded music, as well as electronically amplified music.

The reason I limit the book this way is that machines are increasingly important; for better or worse, information machines have come more and more to define our culture and shape our future. We should understand where the Information Age is headed — understand its history — as we are engulfed in its currents. Focusing on information machines allows me to concentrate on the way new machines are put to use, the way that people adopt them, fitting them into their old patterns, and sometimes changing the way they live and work in order to use them. And since information machines are changing ever more rapidly, it is important to understand the process of change, adoption, and adaptation.

There are political reasons, too, for focusing on information machines. Decisions tend to get made when new machines become available, and new information machines can define our choices. For example, when fiber-optic technology makes possible a new information infrastructure, business and government stop to consider the investment. Or when computer storage technology makes possible bigger data banks, businesses look for ways to use them, and the government looks for legal ways to define their use or prevent their abuse. All too often it's exciting new machines that get the attention, when low-tech solutions offer cheaper, better answers to problems. Government planners worried about education tend to look at the number of computers in the classroom rather than the number of teachers or the number of textbooks. It's more exciting — more cutting edge — to build high-speed digital data communications systems than to, say, spend the same money on books for libraries, or to keep libraries open longer hours. We would do well to understand the attraction of new technologies, how they have been used before, and how they are likely to be used again.

AMERICA'S INFORMATION CULTURE

Looking over the whole course of the Information Age, we see some themes that stand out, some problems that have over and over again become apparent, and that have been solved or resolved in similar ways. There are patterns in our use of information machines. These are the motifs of our information culture — ideas that continue to determine how we adopt and use new information machines, and that determine our future just as much as new technologies.

Perhaps the most striking thing is the astonishing weight of expectations that information technologies carry. Whether making predictions about the telegraph or the personal computer, supporters of the technology have suggested that it would go a long way toward ushering in the millennium. James Carey calls this "the rhetoric of the electrical sublime." Throughout American history, he finds, we have mythologized "electrical techniques as the motive force of desired social change, the key to re-creation of a humane community, the means for returning to a cherished naturalistic bliss." Every technological advance in communications, writes historian Daniel Czitrom, has generated a "religiously inflected rhetoric celebrating moral, political, and social improvements."[5]

One particular sort of moral improvement has been at the top of the list. New information machines from the printing press to the personal computer have been proclaimed particularly "democratic" technologies, allowing the individual increased power and autonomy. Perhaps these new machines have been so eagerly greeted because information holds a privileged position in our society; we believe that information means knowledge and knowledge means freedom. Perhaps it's because we believe in equality of access to information, part of an egalitarian ideal about the possibilities of success in America.

In a peculiarly American way we have often sought technical solutions to social problems. Indeed, more than anything else, this tendency defines American information culture. Whether the problem is the war in Vietnam or children watching too much television, we look for a new gadget to solve the problem: the electronic battlefield, or a TV locking device. And so we attach an enormous importance to new machines, especially information machines, layering them with all of our hopes and dreams. Every new invention that promises to make it easier to communicate or to process information has been greeted with enormous enthusiasm, and the most hopeful predictions.

Information technology can be a strong centrifugal force, giving power to the individual. Some technologies release potent democratic energies. Whether rock 'n' roll or desktop publishing, new technologies let people into the mainstream of the information culture before they're part of mainstream society. The cultural historian Jim Cullen points out that black American musicians from blues to rap have used technology "to innovate for themselves culturally and emancipate themselves economically."[6] Machines can be used to fight tyranny: the fax was a tool of the student revolt in China in 1989, the Xerox machine of the Solidarity labor movement in Poland.

But the technology can also have strong centralizing tendencies. Information machines, like most machines, are used to support existing social structures. The history of the introduction of new information technology shows a continual disjuncture between the democratic hopes and the commercial facts. One of the inventors of the radio was horrified to see the commercial uses to which it was put. The personal computer, which many had hoped would serve as a tool of personal liberation, found its first major use in manipulating financial information, and before long it was just another business tool. Like most technologies, information technologies are shaped to fit into the social relations of the times, which often means that they become part of the commercial and industrial world. The computer, according to computer scientist and philosopher Joseph Weizenbaum, arrived just in time "to save — and to save very nearly intact, indeed, to entrench and stabilize — social and political structures that otherwise might have been either radically renovated or allowed to totter under the demands that were sure to be made on them."[7] Technologies of communications and information processing, rather than being technologies of freedom, all too often became technologies of control.

"We'll all be happy then," a 1911 prediction.

The reason why information technology has both centrifugal and centralizing tendencies is that our society itself has both of those tendencies. A theme that appears throughout the history of the Information Age is the constant effect of social needs and desires and cultural predilections on the technology. The technology reflects the society and culture that use it.

As I have said, technologies are often adopted because they fit into the existing society and culture. Movies fit nicely with vaudeville shows. Television fit into preexisting beliefs about entertainment and the role of family life. The transistor radio confirmed and extended changes already under way in the manner in which people used their radios. Photography was accepted easily because there was already a tradition of inexpensive portraiture. Perhaps most important, the computer fit into an extensive system of accounting and control that had been in existence for more than a century.

This is not to say that the technology wasn't changed by its adopters. Early European telegraphs used printing receivers while American telegraph systems used "sounders," receivers that simply clicked out the incoming messages for the telegrapher to write down. This was a result, in part, of the low density of the American telegraph network; more expensive printing telegraphs required too much capital investment. The rise of network radio came about partly because advertisers wanted a national market, and because of a struggle for control between telephone and radio companies. The cash register took its present shape because store owners distrusted cashiers. Every information technology was affected by its users, shaped by its role in society.

But technology also helps shape the culture and society around it. The historian Warren Sussman suggests that the American "culture of abundance" was a consequence of the communications revolution. Industrial technology may have made more goods available, but information technology made possible the consumer culture that came to define America. Perhaps no previous culture, he writes, was as significantly shaped by the available communications technology. The new machines allowed the creation of new cultural forms, new organizations, and a new social order.

In part because of the contradictory ways information machines are used, America's information culture has developed in surprising, unpredictable ways. Machines created for one purpose — often military or business purposes — have found much wider use in other fields. The invention of the tape recorder, for example, had an enormous impact on the sorts of music that were recorded and became popular, and, along with the invention of the transistor radio, helped to bring about rock 'n' roll and the youth movement of the 1960s. The invention of the typewriter, originally conceived as a tool for authors writing books and preachers preparing sermons, became primarily a business tool and, along with other office machines that helped subdivide office work, had a large effect on the employment of women, and on the relationships of men and women in the workplace. Managers in the 1960s thought that introducing robotics into factories would mean that they could hire unskilled workers, or none at all; instead, they found themselves more dependent on workers with a wider range of skills. Early computers, first built for breaking codes, calculating trajectories of artillery shells, and guiding anti-aircraft guns, evolved into general-purpose machines that sit on millions of office desks, changing the nature of work and thought in ways we are only beginning to see.

But perhaps the most important theme, though occasionally the hardest to discern, is the close connection between us and our information machines. More than any other technology, information machines reflect our lives and shape our thoughts. All machines intermediate between us and nature and other people; they change the way we deal with the world. Information machines do that and more: they change the way we think about the world and about ourselves.

By helping us gather information, analyze and understand it, control it, and use it to control other people and our environment, the machines of the Information Age change the way we deal with the world around us. J. David Bolter, a philosopher who has called the computer the "defining technology" of our culture, suggests that "the scientist or philosopher who works with such electronic tools will think in different ways from those who have worked at ordinary desks with paper and pencil, with stylus and parchment, or with papyrus. He will choose different problems and be satisfied with different solutions." Moreover, Bolter continues, "by promising (or threatening) to replace man, the computer is giving us a new definition of man, as an 'information processor,' and of nature, as 'information to be processed.' "[8] Whether or not this is true is open to argument, as is whether or not this trend is good or appropriate. But for better or worse, we have found a new and powerful way to think of the world around us.

New machines are not accepted because they are, in some abstract sense, "better." They're accepted because they fill the needs of some individual or group; and they are fought by people who feel that their economic or intellectual interests are at stake. Those with an interest in the phonograph, for example, were opposed to the radio, and did their best to keep it from "stealing" their market. They wouldn't allow records to be played on the air, and tried to keep recording stars from singing before radio microphones. Likewise, movie moguls at first tried to keep television from showing movies.

Almost every new information technology has been opposed as an intellectual and moral step backward by those with an investment in the status quo. The production of cheap chromolithographs to hang on living room walls caused intellectuals to worry about the decline of American art. First picture books, then movies, and then television, it was feared, would corrupt American youth. Calculators would ruin children's math skills. The same fears are heard again and again.

And on occasion, the fears of entrenched interests have been justified. New technology has sometimes allowed powerless groups to gain power. Telegraphs, telephones, and E-mail permit individuals far from the center of the action to enjoy influence. It's often the young who are the first to adopt new machines. The young amateur radio enthusiast or computer hacker gained new prestige when he could run the machine and his parents couldn't.

It has come to seem that the world around us is a world of information. Information has also come to seem the key to power and truth. And so we become dependent on our information machines, perhaps even addicted to them. Thoreau poked fun at this even before the Civil War: "Hardly a man takes his

A new authority, 1924.

half hour's nap after dinner," he wrote, "but when he wakes he holds up his head and asks 'What's the news?'"[9] Today we need more and more news. We must run faster and faster just to stay in place. We need not just CNN but Headline News, too.

Samuel F. B. Morse said in 1832, when the idea of the electrical telegraph had just occurred to him, "I see no reason why intelligence might not be instantaneously transmitted by electricity to any distance."[10] But the amount of information we want to send has increased enormously, often more quickly than our technological ability to send it. It's a close race between capacity and demand. We are spoiled by our capabilities, and as the price of information goes down, so too, it sometimes seems, does its value. The business executive of 1880 was content to send a carefully considered telegram of a few words. By 1920 he or she might think that the same message required a ten-minute telephone call. Today the message might seem to require a video conference. A telegram might be a few hundred bits of data; a telephone call roughly a million; a video link perhaps 10 billion bits. What seems, from a distance, to be almost identical *information* might require billions of times more *data*. New capacity brings new demand, and new demand requires new capacity. We tend to fill our communications channels, and push against their edges. Whether more information — let alone greater wisdom — flows over the wire is a different, and more difficult, question.

The flip side of information dependence is information overload. Edward Tenner, a historian of information, writes, "The real pitfall is not to overvalue or undervalue information, or the amount of information available, but to be mesmerized and anesthetized by it."[11] Too much information makes it harder to pick out the right information, or the most useful information; it can be worse than not enough information. Henry James worried about this when he wrote in the late 1890s, "We may have been great fools to develop the post office, to invent the newspaper and the railway; but the harm is done — it will be our children who will see it; we have created a Frankenstein monster at whom our simplicity can only gape."[12] New means of communication and new information machines do not always bring new discernment. John Updike put it thus: "Ever more informational technique, ever more inane information."[13]

There's another pitfall, too. Every new communications technology has been greeted with fear that it will, in fact, make real communication — people knowing one another — more difficult. People lose their true character when they are surrounded by too much information. Public communications make private communications impossible. One English writer complained of the speed-up of information and its concomitant declining quality in 1889: "All men are compelled to think of all things, at the same time, on imperfect information, made with too little interval for reflection. . . . The constant diffusion of statements in snippets, the constant excitements of feeling unjustified by fact, the constant formation of hasty or erroneous opinions, must in the end, one would think, deteriorate the intelligence of all to whom the telegraph appeals."[14] New information machines provide us with new ways of understanding, but also new ways of misunderstanding. As Lewis Mumford warned in 1934: "Against the convenience of instantaneous communication is the fact that the great economical abstractions of writing, reading, and drawing, the media of reflective thought and deliberate action, will be weakened."[15]

We are the inheritors of a culture that has responded in certain ways to information technology. American culture has been shaped by information machines and will continue to be shaped by them. For almost every new way of putting information to work, we can find precedents in the way Americans have used it before. Not only do the technologies of information build upon past technologies — the movie projector on the record player, or television on radio — but the way we use those machines builds on our past use of information machines, too.

Terrors of the telephone: the orator of the future, as seen in 1877.

So as we look forward to virtual reality, say, it is useful to think about the ways that Americans first adopted the telegraph or the wireless or the fax machine. As we look forward to the rewiring of the country with fiber optics, we should consider the way that the country was first wired with telegraph cable, then telephone, then microwaves. Ever faster computers should set us thinking about how increased computer power has been used in the past. New forms of entertainment and new ways of waging war have led the way toward new technologies in the past; so are they likely to in the future. As new technologies, unimagined today, come into existence, it's worth considering how the new technologies of the past muscled their way past older ones, pushing them aside but at the same time finding valuable symbiotic relationships.

The lessons aren't obvious. But information machines are part of our society, our information culture, and to understand them, and how they will be used in the future, we must understand the trajectory of our information culture.

FOR FURTHER READING

There are books on every aspect of information technology, and on American culture. Some thoughtful books that give a general overview of American information culture include James R. Beniger, *The Control Revolution: Technological and Economic Origins of the Information Society* (1986); J. David Bolter, *Turing's Man: Western Culture in the Computer Age* (1984); James W. Carey, *Communication as Culture: Essays on Media and Society* (1988); Daniel J. Czitrom, *Media and the American Mind from Morse to McLuhan* (1982); Bill McKibben, *The Age of Missing Information* (1992); Vincent Mosco, *The Pay-Per Society: Computers and Communications in the Information Age: Essays in Critical Theory and Public Policy* (1989); Joseph

Weizenbaum, *Computer Power and Human Reason: From Judgment to Calculation* (1976); and Raymond Williams, *Television: Technology and Cultural Form* (1975).

NOTES

1. James W. Carey, *Communication as Culture: Essays on Media and Society* (1989), pp. 18–19, 23.
2. Raymond Williams, *Television: Technology and Cultural Form* (1975), p. 19.
3. Williams, *Television*, p. 12.
4. Bill McKibben, *The Age of Missing Information* (1992), pp. 9–10.
5. Carey, *Communication as Culture*, pp. 115 and 123, and Daniel Czitrom, "Communication Studies as American Studies," *American Quarterly* (December 1990): 679.
6. Jim Cullen, letter to author, August 5, 1992.
7. Joseph Weizenbaum, *Computer Power and Human Reason: From Judgment to Calculation* (1976), pp. 28–29.
8. J. David Bolter, *Turing's Man: Western Culture in the Computer Age* (1984), pp. 7–8 and 13.
9. Quoted in McKibben, *The Age of Missing Information*, p. 166.
10. Quoted in Carleton Mabee, *The American Leonardo: A Life of Samuel F. B. Morse* (1943), p. 149.
11. Edward Tenner, "The Impending Information Implosion," *Harvard Magazine* (November-December 1991): 34.
12. Quoted in Neil Harris, *The Land of Contrasts, 1880–1901* (1970), p. 22.
13. John Updike, *Roger's Version* (1986), p. 110.
14. *Spectator,* November 9, 1889, pp. 631–632, quoted in Daniel J. Czitrom, *Media and the American Mind from Morse to McLuhan* (1982), p. 19.
15. Lewis Mumford, *Technics and Civilization* (1934), p. 240.

The value of information depends on its time and place. People who need information have always been willing to pay dearly for recent news that might mean victory in war or profit in trade.

With the invention of the telegraph, and its successors from the telephone to electronic mail, more information can now travel faster, more cheaply, and to more people. What has made this possible is not just new technology but also an enormous investment in the communications infrastructure — new wires,

COMMUNICATION

new switching systems — and new business and personal systems for putting ever more information to use.

New systems of communications have transformed American society. They have changed the way we work and redefined the way we think about our communities. By making it easier to talk to one another, communications technologies have sometimes reinforced, and sometimes destroyed, the culture that produced them.

Newspapers and magazines and books — words printed on paper — are the media for much of our news and entertainment, and have been for centuries. Here, in "Newsboy selling New York *Herald*," by James Henry Cafferty, an 1857 painting, the newsboy stands in front of a wall plastered with printed advertisements — common sights in American cities by the mid-nineteenth century.

COMMUNICATION
WORDS

IN 1836 THE *PHILADELPHIA PUBLIC LEDGER* AN-
nounced: "In the cities of New York and Brooklyn, containing together a population of 300,000, the daily circulation of the penny papers is
not less than SEVENTY THOUSAND. This is nearly sufficient to
place a newspaper in the hands of every man in the two cities, and even
every boy old enough to read. These papers are to be found in every street, land
and alley; in every hotel, tavern, counting house, ship and store. Almost every
porter and dray-man, when not engaged in his occupation, may be seen with a
paper in his hands."[1] By the 1830s the newspaper had become, as James Gordon Bennett, publisher of the *New York Herald* put it, exaggerating just a bit,
"the great organ and pivot of government, society, commerce, finance, religion,
and all human civilization."[2]

Bennett was perhaps the first philosopher of the Information Age, one
of the first men to trumpet the power of information. He wrote: "Books have
had their day — the theaters have had their day — the temple of religion has had
its day. A newspaper can be made to take the lead of all these in the great movements of human thought and of human civilization. A newspaper can send more
souls to Heaven, and save more from Hell, than all the churches or chapels in
New York — besides making money at the same time."[3]

Bennett, like so many others of his time, believed that the increase of information brought with it a moral benefit. More information, more communication, would make America more democratic, more virtuous, more *American*.
Samuel Bowles, editor of the *Springfield* (Mass.) *Republican,* expressed similar
thoughts:

> The brilliant mission of the newspaper is . . . to be, the high prince of His-
> tory, the vitalizer of Society, the world's great informer, the earth's high
> censor, the medium of public thought and opinion, and the circulating life
> blood of the whole human mind. It is the great enemy of tyrants, and the
> right arm of liberty, and is destined, more than any other agency, to melt
> and mould the jarring and contending nations of the world into that one
> great brotherhood which, through the long centuries, has been the ideal of
> the Christian and the philanthropist.[4]

Bennett and Bowles wrote at the beginning of the flood of technological innovations that helped make the newspapers, and the information they

spread, a central element in American culture. Over the next fifty years, faster printing presses, cheaper paper, and new machines to set type would change the publishing business in ways Bennett could not imagine. But he might not be too surprised, for he could look back at a long period of history in which written communications had come to be increasingly fundamental.

DEMOCRATIC READING

Even in the seventeenth century the literacy rate in English North America was high, compared to that of European countries. John Adams wrote, "A native American who cannot read and write is as rare as a comet or any earthquake"[5] — true, but only if he was restricting his thoughts to white men. Some 60 percent of white adult males in the British colonies could read in 1650, 70 percent in 1710, and 90 percent in 1790; probably fewer could write. The white female literacy rate was lower, about 30 percent in 1650, 40 percent in 1710, and 50 percent in 1790. (It's probable that a higher percentage of women than this could read; these figures are based on the ability to write.) Few African Americans could read or write, and in fact most slaves were forbidden to learn. Throughout the century before Bennett's comments, schooling had become more common, more books were being published, and the speed of communications had increased. Richard D. Brown, a historian of this communications revolution, has called these related changes "a self-intensifying spiral of growth in the production, distribution, and consumption of print."[6]

Horn books like this seventeenth-century example were used to teach children to read. They were called horn books because the single page of paper was protected by a transparent sheet of horn.

Books were published in the English colonies starting in 1639, when the first printing press was established in Cambridge, Massachusetts. Early books included an almanac and a book of Psalms. The most popular American book was the *New England Primer,* a textbook giving instruction in reading and religion, first published in 1690. It was reprinted in many editions, and by 1830 between 6 and 8 million copies had been sold.

The first daily newspaper in the colonies, the *Boston News-Letter,* was founded in 1704. Its circulation was a few hundred. Like most colonial newspapers it was designed to increase communications between Great Britain and the colonies. These early papers covered mostly European affairs, and were aimed at merchants and other members of the gentry. The postal system in the colonies, reorganized in 1711 under British imperial control, served the same audience, and carried similar news. The long-distance communications that early newspapers and the postal system made possible were important only to those engaged in trade beyond their local community, a small portion of the population.

Most people got the information they needed from their immediate surroundings. What they learned was mostly local, which was appropriate. Farmers predicted the next day's weather by looking at the sky, not at a newspaper. Prices for most goods and services were locally set, often in terms of labor or in barter for other goods; communities were in large part self-contained. Information about the world beyond the local community came by word of mouth, from talking to neighbors or travelers passing through, or by visiting other towns or cities. Even big-city merchants got most of their information from friends and acquaintances they met in coffeehouses and taverns.

Not until after the Revolution did many people come to believe that wide circulation of information was a good thing. Improved communications throughout the United States became, for some, a philosophical underpinning of the new nation. Some of the authors of the Constitution were convinced that better communications was the key to creating a democracy in a country the size of the United States. One reason the new country put so much effort into "internal improvements" — roads, canals, and railroads — was the feeling that improved transportation would mean improved communications. And improved communications would allow an ever larger country to remain a democracy. It would hold the country together and help to create a virtuous, public-spirited citizenry. Better communications would mean better community. Thomas Jefferson wrote, "New channels of communication will be opened between the states, the lines of separation will disappear, their interests will be identified, and their union cemented by new and indestructible ties."[7] Benjamin Rush, a Philadelphia physician and writer, called newspapers the "sentinels of our liberties." "Information," declared *New-York Magazine* in 1790, was the mainspring of the Revolution. Let all citizens be enlightened by reading magazines and "oppression must cease. . . . Those institutions are the most effectual guards to public liberty which diffuse the rudiments of literature among a people."[8]

And yet there was a strong individualist, anticommunications feeling, too. Robert Wiebe has described the America of the early nineteenth century as a "segmented society," in which each community felt it had to run on its own track — interested in what went on elsewhere, because it might represent competition, but wanting to preserve differences. Each community, he writes, "presumed to choose its own route and seek its own objectives without interference from any other."[9] James Madison, in the *Federalist,* suggested that poor communications, not good communications, would preserve the country by making a national faction impossible.

Before the Revolution few people read newspapers. The *Pennsylvania Evening Post* started in 1783 with a circulation of only 2,500. In an average year between 1764 and 1794, only 500 advertisers bought space in Philadelphia newspapers. But after the Revolution, newspapers increased their circulation, not only in numbers but also in area covered. The first national paper — national in the sense that many newspapers copied its news — was the *National Intelligencer and Washington Advertiser,* started in 1800. Noah Webster wrote in 1793, "In no Country on earth, not even in Great-Britain, are Newspapers so generally circulated among the body of the people, as in America."[10]

Newspapers and magazines were read by people from all levels of society. The *New-York Magazine,* a typically eclectic publication founded in 1790, included articles on manners and morals, politics and government, fiction, humor, and poetry. It had 370 subscribers, according to its first issue. David Paul Nord, a historian who tracked down information about these subscribers, discovered that about half of them were professionals and merchants, and about half shopkeepers, artisans, and unskilled workers. The magazine was rather expensive — $2.25 a year at a time when a workingman earned about $150 a year.

The government took seriously the notion that informed citizens were essential to democracy. The postal system was a key element in keeping citizens informed; an 1832 report called the postal system "one of the most effective instruments of civilization."[11] Postage rates were very low for newspapers, low enough that after reading a paper some people mailed it on to friends or relatives. And postage was free for newspaper exchanges between editors — one of the main ways that they got nonlocal news for their papers. The number of newspapers expanded, too. In 1790 there were 92 newspapers; in 1800, 242. In 1833, newspapers accounted for 90 percent of the mail carried by the U.S. Post Office.

Presses were cheap, and easy to move. Alexis de Tocqueville wrote in his *Democracy in America* in 1835: "It is owing to the laws of the Union that there are no licenses to be granted to printers. . . . The consequence is that nothing is easier than to set up a newspaper, as a small number of subscribers suffices to defray the expenses. Hence the number of periodical and semi-periodical publications in the United States is almost incredibly large. . . . In America there is scarcely a hamlet that has not its newspaper."[12] These early papers, in addition to their practical role in conveying news, served as a key element in the forma-

A small printing shop circa 1840.

tion of local and national communities. St. Louis's first newspaper, for example, was published in 1808, when that town had a population of less than 1,500.

Most early newspapers were party papers; that is, they reflected the views of one political party, without any attempt at "objectivity." You subscribed to the paper that presented views you agreed with. De Tocqueville described these rough-and-tumble newspapers: "The characteristics of the American journalist consist in an open and coarse appeal to the passions of his readers; he abandons principle to assail the characters of individuals, to track them into private life and disclose all their weaknesses and vices." Whether despite or because of this, Tocqueville continued, "when many organs of the press adopt the same line of conduct, their influence in the long run becomes irresistible, and public opinion, perpetually assailed from the same side, eventually yields to the attack. In the United States each separate journal exercises but little authority; but the power of the periodical press is second only to that of the people."[13]

This situation began to change in the 1830s with the "penny press." This was a new kind of newspaper, aimed at the rising middle class of skilled craftsmen, merchants, and tradesmen. These papers took advantage of new technologies to change the very nature of the newspaper. They aimed at "objectivity," and, even more important, at a vast readership. Bennett's *New York Herald* had sales of 77,000 by the Civil War, the *New York Tribune* sales of over 200,000.

Mass circulation changed the nature of the newspaper. Or perhaps as the nature of the newspaper changed, its circulation increased. New technology, in fact, came along after the renaissance of the newspaper. The *New York Sun* was the first "penny paper," featuring sensational stories aimed at a mass audience. Founded in 1833, it specialized in "human interest" stories, especially sex and crime — the *National Enquirer* of its day. It stretched the limit of its hand presses with its 10,000 copies a day. (When a series of stories announcing the discovery of life on the moon appeared, it sold 20,000 copies in a day; by then it had switched to a steam-powered press.) Benjamin Day, its publisher, bragged about its power: "Since the *Sun* began to shine upon the citizens of New York, there has been a great and decided change in the condition of the laboring classes, and the mechanics. Now every individual, from the rich aristocrat who lolls in his carriage to the humble laborer who wields a broom in the streets, reads the *Sun*; nor can even a boy be found in New York City or the neighboring country who will not know in the course of the day what is promulgated in the *Sun* in the morning."[14] Between 1828 and 1840 the number of daily newspapers doubled from 852 to 1,631 and total circulation increased from 68 million to 195 million. More daily newspapers were printed in the United States than in the rest of the world.

These penny papers made objectivity their claim. Editors wrote that, unlike the elite press of the first years of the republic, their paper was "true," not biased. They even claimed a new "photographic realism" on the basis of the pictures they printed. James Gordon Bennett, in the first issue of the *New York Herald* in 1835, gave as the paper's credo: "We shall endeavor to record facts on every public and proper subject, stripped of verbiage and coloring." Another editor, Isaac Pray, suggested that a reporter should be a mere machine, repeating the facts of the news, the truth.

Not everyone agreed with the self-promoting claims of the press. James Fenimore Cooper wrote in *The American Democrat* (1838): "If newspapers are

The press room of the *New York Tribune,* 1861. The *Tribune,* edited by Horace Greeley, was one of the most powerful newspapers in the country.

useful in overthrowing tyrants, it is only to establish a tyranny of their own. The press tyrannizes over publick men, letters, the arts, the stage and even over private life. Under the pretense of protecting publick morals, it is corrupting them to the core, and under the semblance of maintaining liberty, it is gradually establishing a despotism as ruthless, as grasping, and one that is quite as vulgar as that of any christian state known."[15] Cooper was protesting the new power of the press, calling into question its attacks on the old order. "Objectivity" can be, in its own way, a form of bias.

New technology was one key to these newspapers. A steam-powered printing press patented by Frederick Koenig in 1813 was put to use by the *Times* of London in 1814. It used two rotating cylinders to print 1,100 sheets per hour, about four times as fast as the old hand press. Richard Hoe, a New York machinist, built a kind of press, called a rotary press, which put the type, too, on a cylinder instead of on a flat bed. The *New York Herald* installed a Hoe press in 1849 that could print 12,000 impressions per hour. By 1860 presses could print 20,000 impressions per hour. Stereotypes — cast replicas of the type that fit on the cylinders, solving the problem of type flying into the press, as well as freeing up type for the next day's paper or the next book — were adapted to these presses in 1854. Faster printing and more copies sold meant a cheaper newspaper. In the 1830s most newspapers cost about six cents a copy, about the cost of a pint of whiskey. By the 1850s newspapers were being sold for a penny apiece. Overall, it has been calculated, between 1820 and 1860 printing productivity increased by a factor of one hundred.

Postal reforms in the 1840s and 1850s reduced postal rates, not only making possible the extended friendships by letter that were so much a part of Victorian culture but also opening the mails for widespread distribution of magazines and newspapers. (Postage was free for local distribution.) *Harpers' Monthly*, founded in 1850, had a circulation of 200,000 by 1860. *Godey's Lady's Book* and *Peterson's*, both aimed at women, had circulations of over 150,000. Religious journals and newspapers proliferated. Specialized journals helped spread news of technological innovation and science: *Scientific American*, founded in 1845, had a circulation of 30,000 copies a week in 1859, at least in part because it promised that the way to wealth was through learning about science and invention, and the way to do that was by reading *Scientific American.*

New technology also made possible a new range of stories, and a new timeliness. These papers competed not only for stories from around the nation and around the world but also for speed. Some papers even hired agents to meet ships fifty miles offshore and send back news by carrier pigeon! The telegraph fit nicely into this pattern, and so newspapers were quick to adopt it. Press lords were among the early investors in telegraph companies. Samuel Bowles, editor of the *Springfield Republican*, wrote in 1851: "The increase of facilities for the transmission of news brought in a new era. The railroad car, the steamboat, and the magnetic telegraph, have made neighborhood among widely dissevered States. . . . These active and almost miraculous agencies have brought the whole world in contact."[16]

The telegraph helped change the idea of news, made possible modern methods of gathering news, and helped changed the way news was presented. It changed the form of the newspaper story. Stories sent over the telegraph wire at so much per word offered less room for opinion, and journalists transmitting news over the sometimes unreliable telegraph put the key facts of a story into a short paragraph at the head of the story. One writer in 1877 gave the telegraph credit for the compactness of modern journalism. The telegraph required short, pithy paragraphs, he wrote; it was responsible for the breaks and new headings that made a newspaper page look like a checkerboard.

The cost of telegraphing the news led to the formation of a telegraphic news organization, the Associated Press. Organized in 1848 by six New York newspapers, and joined with the Telegraph and General News Association in 1851, the Associated Press represented 500 daily journals in North America, Europe, and Asia by 1877. A writer in that year called it the "focal point through which the telegraph has become the newsgatherer of the world. . . . The current history of the world is written on the instant by skillful hands, gathered, exchanged by telegraph, and published daily." In 1860 the AP spent over $200,000 on gathering news. (See TELEGRAPH.)

Books as well as newspapers and magazines found new audiences in the nineteenth century. Between 1820 and 1849 some 25,000 titles were pub-

Newspaper reading became a community ritual, as shown here in Richard Caton Woodville's 1848 "War News from Mexico."

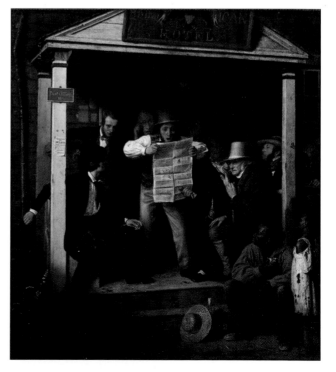

J. P. Jewett built this "tasteful, elegant and convenient" book-store in Boston in 1854 with the profits he earned from publishing *Uncle Tom's Cabin*.

lished in the United States. And some of them sold very well indeed. In the years before 1860, Americans bought more than 800,000 copies of Washington Irving's books, more than a million copies of T. S. Arthur's, and over 30 million copies of Webster's dictionary. The best seller of the day was Harriet Beecher Stowe's *Uncle Tom's Cabin*, which sold some 300,000 copies the first year it was published.

Because popular access to information about government activities was presumed to be a right of the citizens of a democracy, even governments got into the printing business. Between 1790 and 1840 federal and state governments accounted for 30 percent of all imprints in the United States. In the 1830s the American Tract Society produced five pages of religious information each year for every American. The American Sunday-School Union printed over 6 million books. Books became cheaper and more diverse. Bookstores and publishers came to pride themselves on the quantity and diversity of their publications. People owned more books.

The way people used books changed, too. In the eighteenth century most people had owned only a few books, usually just the Bible and a religious tract or two. They read these books repeatedly. Reading like this was more a devotional or ritualistic function than an informative one. It was, historians have noted, a basically conservative style of reading. After about 1800 or so the way people used books changed. Not only did more people read, but the purpose of

reading changed. People began to read for information and for entertainment, as well as ritual. Historians of reading call this a change from "intensive" to "extensive" reading, even "promiscuous" reading. A survey of Ohio book owners before the Civil War found that about 70 percent of those who owned books owned three or more.

In part this increase in book publishing stemmed from technological change. The Foudrinier and Gilpin paper making machines greatly reduced the cost of paper. Steam presses vastly reduced the amount of labor needed to print books. Folding and binding was partially automated. These innovations cut the average price of a book in half, to about a dollar in 1850 — perhaps a day's wage to an typical workingman. Many books cost only twenty-five to fifty cents. New technology also made it easier to read: better lamps, improved eyeglasses, more common after 1833, and even the railroad, which gave travelers new leisure time, helped promote reading.

Cities and states began to create public libraries in the 1840s. These public libraries joined private subscription libraries, some of which dated back to the 1730s, and libraries at colleges and theological schools, and rental libraries, which started in the 1760s. Public libraries, supported by tax dollars, and often tied to schools, were advocated by labor unions, among other groups, and came to be considered an important part of public education. George Ticknor, a founder of the Boston Public Library, wrote in 1852 that the new library would encourage democracy, morality, and upward mobility by bringing books "into the homes of the young; into poor families; into cheap boarding houses; in short, wherever they will be most like to affect life and raise personal character."[17] In 1850, according to the Census, there was a library for every 600 free adults in the United States, one library book for every two people. (Most of these libraries were in the East, especially in New York and Massachusetts.) Books available in libraries supplemented books at home. In the 1840s and 1850s, according to a

The post office delivered an enormous amount of mail. In the 1880s, when this picture was drawn, some 4 billion pieces of mail moved through the postal system. Post offices were more than just places where mail was delivered. They were community centers, too, and places where the news of the day was discussed.

study of two Ohio counties, about one half of all households owned books; 80 percent of the households owned religious books, 54 percent schoolbooks, 15 percent practical books, and 8 percent classics.

Cheaper printing and rising literacy rates brought new kinds of publications for new audiences. There were books aimed at every segment of the population: children's literature, dime novels for workingmen, and romances for women, as well as scientific books and textbooks. (Starting in the 1840s, and increasing during the Civil War, there was also pornography, and a flurry of newspaper articles denouncing it.) In short, American literature had become, as Walt Whitman wrote in *Democratic Vistas* in 1871, "drawn out not for a single class alone, or for the parlors or lecture rooms, but with an eye to practical life, the west, the working man, the facts of farm and jackplane and engineers, and the broad range of the women also of the middle and working strata."[18]

New technology and a larger market brought about by improved transportation meant not only an increased diversity of books but also larger printings, cheaper publications, and wider distribution — the rise of a national print culture. Books were printed in New York, Philadelphia, and Boston and distributed throughout the country.

And yet the variety of reading materials could serve to separate communities, too. In the years before the Civil War, as the country was pulling itself apart into separate pieces, publishers were leading the charge in all directions. The American Antislavery Society waged a "postal campaign" in 1835, flooding the mails with its publications, which led to riots at some Southern post offices. Each side of every argument had its own newspaper or magazine. There were labor newspapers, radical Republican newspapers, abolitionist papers, and proslavery newspapers. The editor of a San Francisco newspaper, writing in 1858, recalled the papers of that city: "We have gone through the long list of periodicals started in San Francisco within the last eleven years. They number 132 in all. . . . The papers have been printed in six different languages, have represented nine different nationalities . . . have preached eight different forms of religion, and have been the organs of seven distinct political parties. Most of these papers expired within a twelve-month after they started, and only twenty-six survive."[19]

Richard D. Brown, a historian of information, writes: "Where printing had once been an instrument of cultural cohesion, it had now become a principal agent of fragmentation and competition."[20] Printing, like other communications technologies, would have both centralizing and centrifugal forces throughout American history, tending to reinforce existing communities and, all too often, widen the differences between communities.

In the last third of the nineteenth century, newspaper, book, and magazine publishing boomed. It was a golden age for journalism in the United States. New technologies, including cheaper paper production from wood pulp, faster presses, new ways to set type, and cheaper transportation, meant greatly reduced prices for newspapers, magazines, and books, and helped make possible the mass-circulation literature of the late nineteenth century. Printing and publishing became a major industry. The 1880 Census of Manufacturing counted some 3,500 printing and publishing establishments (one fourth of them in New York), employing more than 56,000 men, women, and children, and producing some $90 million worth of books and other printed materials a year.

In 1850 there had been 254 newspapers in the United States, with a total circulation of 758,000. In 1909 there were 2,600 daily newspapers, 520 Sunday newspapers, and 15,000 weekly newspapers. Total circulation was almost 80 million. There were papers of every description, for every ethnic group and every political party. Between 1870 and 1900 the number of copies of newspapers sold each day increased tenfold. The number of magazines doubled every ten years after the Civil War, reaching 5,500 by 1900. A change in American copyright law in 1891 helped the American book industry boom and brought forth a new flowering of books by Americans. In 1869 some 2,600 titles were published in the United States; in 1900, more than 6,300 titles.

The big newspapers were bigger and more important than ever. The turn of the twentieth century saw the beginning of the era of the press baron. Joseph Pulitzer, William Randolph Hearst, and E. W. Scripps built newspaper empires that made them key players in national politics. Newspaper chains came to control more and more papers — from 10 percent in 1910 to 40 percent by 1935.

Printers from the time of Gutenberg took about one minute to set a line of type. It was a job that required a great deal of skill and many inventors tried to automate it. The first commercially successful machine in this field was the Linotype machine, invented by Ottmar Mergenthaler in Baltimore in 1885. It could produce five lines per minute — about 6,000 characters per hour — and was quickly adopted. Mark Twain, who lost a great deal of money investing in an automatic typesetting machine, suggested its value when he wrote that a Linotype "could work like six men and do everything but drink, swear, and go out on strike." By the end of the century 3,000 Linotype machines were in use around the world. Some typesetters got jobs as Linotype machine operators. Many typefounders went out of business.

The Linotype has a keyboard similar to a typewriter keyboard. When a letter is pressed, a mold, or "matrix," of that letter falls into place. When an entire line of matrices is complete, molten lead is poured into them, producing a solid line of new type. These lines, called "slugs," are automatically arranged in columns as they are made. These columns of type are then removed from the machine and laid out into the newspaper pages. After printing, the used slugs are remelted.

The Monotype, invented in 1887 by Tolbert Lanston of Troy, Ohio, competed with the Linotype. It cast letters separately, not as a slug, and the type could be rearranged and reused after its initial use. It produced higher quality type and — most important for what was to come — it was controlled by a punched paper tape.

The newsroom of the *Baltimore Sun*, circa 1914. Newspaper reporting and editing was labor-intensive work.

The classic reporter, from *Okay, America,* a 1932 film directed by Tay Garnett. The tools of the trade were the beat-up manual typewriter, the telephone, and a bottle of whiskey.

A magazine stand in Windsor Locks, Connecticut, in 1939. By the late nineteenth century, magazines were cheap, easily available, and widely read.

These papers had enormous circulation, some of them more than 200,000, a circulation made possible by continuing improvements in the speed of presses. Newspapers tended to run more syndicated features and less local news. Increasingly the chain newspapers defined the news. Hearst's famous reply to Frederic Remington, his newspaper artist in Cuba, sums up the power of these papers. When Remington cabled in early 1897 that there was no war, Hearst cabled back: "Please remain. You furnish the pictures, and I'll furnish the war" — which is exactly what he did.[21] Newspapers had reached a new level of power.

Nationwide magazines also boomed at the turn of the century. Made possible in part by new printing techniques, the expansion of the postal system and cheaper postal rates — but mostly by a huge expansion of advertising — magazines such as *Cosmopolitan*, *Munsey's Magazine*, and *McClure's* reached a mass audience. *Ladies' Home Journal* was the first magazine to sell more than 1 million copies, in 1903. By 1920 there were fourteen others with circulations over a million. Magazines served as a form of nationwide culture. In 1926 the post office delivered almost 5 billion pieces of second-class mail, mostly magazines and newspapers.

Some people thought favorably of the new power and ubiquity of the press. In 1910 Senator Albert J. Beveridge called the muckraking newspapers a "people's literature" that amounted to "almost a mental and moral revolution."[22] And in 1927 John Dewey echoed Thomas Jefferson's thoughts of some 150 years earlier when he suggested that the popular press was a key element that united Americans, an essential element of American democracy.

But not everyone agreed. The democratization of the newspaper and the book — the appeal to a mass market, the stooping to the lowest common denominator to boost sales — was greeted with a mixed reaction. One American, looking back at the good old days, complained that the telegraph had "transformed journalism from what it once was, the periodical expression of the thought of the time . . . into an agency for collecting, condensing, and assimilating the trivialities of the entire human existence."[23] Sherwood Anderson's

Winesburg, Ohio (1919) is in part a lament for the loss of innocence that new communications brings:

> In the last fifty years a vast change has taken place in the lives of our people. A revolution has in fact taken place. . . . Books, badly imagined and written though they may be in the hurry of our times, are in every household, magazines circulate by the millions of copies, newspapers are everywhere. In our day a farmer standing by the stove in the store in his village has his mind filled to overflowing with the words of other men. The newspapers and magazines have pumped him full. Much of the old brutal ignorance that had in it also a kind of beautiful childlike innocence is gone forever.[24]

George Beard, an American doctor and social critic, listed the telegraph and the newspaper among the five causes of "nervousness," a disease he thought characterized Americans at the end of the nineteenth century: "Our morning newspaper, that we read with our breakfast, has the history of the sorrows of the whole world for a day; and a nature but moderately sympathetic is robbed thereby, consciously or unconsciously, of more or less nervous strength."[25]

But, in fact, few people read very much. In 1919 a survey found that while 95 percent of the white urban population bought newspapers, fewer than half bought magazines, and only 15 percent bought books. In 1929, according to Department of Commerce figures, the average adult spent about $10 a year on newspapers and magazines and $4 a year on books. Some 10,000 books were published in 1929, and the total number of copies printed was about 214 million — fewer than two books per person on average.

Literacy and reading were key elements of the welfare work movement in American industry at the beginning of the twentieth century. This poster dates from 1921.

WORDS AT WORK

Alongside the presses and the Linotypes of the newspaper, magazine, and book publishers was another information industry. Business offices depended on words, too. How they communicated those words changed over time, but their importance never varied.

In 1760 John Rowe was a wealthy Boston merchant. He owned a good bit of real estate and several ships, and made his living in trade, both overseas and inland. Information about prices, and about events that might affect prices, was essential to him. And so he spent much of his time gathering that information. Talking to people was one way to get information. Tuesday evenings he met with the Posee Club, a group of friends. The next day he'd meet the Wednesday Club. He also belonged to the Charitable Society, the St. John's Masonic lodge, and church groups. During the day Rowe would make the rounds of the wharves, stopping at coffeehouses and talking to everyone he met. Letters were

Develop the Power that is within you

Get ahead. Books are free at your Public Library

The children's room of the Brooklyn Public Library, about the turn of the century. More and larger libraries helped to make books accessible. Starting at the end of the nineteenth century, Andrew Carnegie provided funds to establish almost 1,700 community libraries in the United States. By 1910, there were over 10,000 town and city libraries with over 1,000 volumes. Libraries were a key element of the Progressive agenda that held that upward mobility was available to all.

another way. Rowe had an extensive circle of correspondents, and was an avid reader of newspapers. The historian Richard Brown, who analyzed Rowe's diary, concludes that "to succeed as a merchant, access to current information was as much a necessity as capital, credit, or the ability to calculate."[26]

The Post Office Act of 1792, recognizing the importance of communications for both business and politics, called for the expansion of the postal system without worry about cost. Before Independence there were only about sixty-five post offices in what would be the United States — one for every 40,000 people. These were mostly in port towns, and merchants were their main users. Postal rates were high. After the Revolution the postal system expanded, a reflection of the general belief in the value of the dissemination of information. In 1800 there were 903 post offices. By 1820 the postal system had expanded to 4,500 post offices; by 1840 to almost 13,500; and to almost 29,000 by the beginning of the Civil War. In 1860 there was one post office for every 1,100 people. Improved transportation — better roads and canals and railroads — meant that mail and news could pass from one end of the country to the other in days, not weeks. Lower costs meant that information could move more easily.

As business organizations expanded, the desire to have information available wherever and whenever it was wanted fueled the demand for new communications technologies and broader channels of information flow. Thomas

Companies specializing in credit reporting began to appear in the 1840s, among the very first businesses whose only product was information. Firms doing business with nearby companies hadn't needed formal information-gathering systems; personal relationships and mutual trust were enough. But when the circle of commerce widened in the mid-nineteenth century, it became important to find out about customers before granting them credit. In 1848 the Mercantile Agency (shown here in 1841), the largest credit-reporting firm, answered 5,000 inquiries daily. It employed hundreds of reporters to report on the creditworthiness of businesses, and kept track of the information in a series of thousands of notebooks.

Cochran, a business historian, found that new systems of communication were the most important factors in American economic development.

In the first half of the nineteenth century an increasing volume of trade and better and faster systems of communications and transportation — especially the railroad and the telegraph — changed the structure of the merchant's world. As the size of markets grew because of improved transportation, specialization became increasingly profitable. Middlemen of all kinds — factors, jobbers, and brokers — who were experts in certain crops, or certain markets, began to emerge. They took advantage of their specialized knowledge and superior sources of information to earn greater profits for their clients — and for themselves.

By 1840 or so, merchants and manufacturers were at the center of an information web. They dealt with banks, which allocated credit and collected funds; with other manufacturers; with purchasers; with other merchants, both specialists and generalists; and with insurance firms, which tried to determine risks based on information gathered from earlier experiences. These specialized firms lowered the cost of information, and thus helped the economy grow.

There were important changes inside business firms, too. Growing businesses needed to keep up with new technology. Clerks switched from the quill pen to the steel pen after about 1840. Before about 1850 most letters were copied by hand. After that date many firms adopted the "letter press" system. They would copy correspondence by putting it, with the ink still wet, into a bound volume of tissue paper, and squeezing it with a letter press to copy the ink onto the tissue paper. The letter press books served as a chronological file; they were also indexed by correspondent. Stationery stores sold special preindexed volumes for this purpose. Incoming correspondence would be filed separately. (See BEFORE COMPUTERS.)

The clerks who ran offices in the early nineteenth century were men who aspired to rise in business. An 1841 article described them: "The majority of clerks are young men who have hopes and prospects of business before them. . . . A

One of the earliest commercial typewriters, manufactured at the gun works of E. Remington & Sons in 1873. It was mounted on a sewing machine stand, with a treadle to operate the carriage return.

good clerk feels that he has an interest in the credit and success of his employer beyond the amount of his salary. . . . He feels that he too, by his assiduity and fidelity has added something to his capital — something to his future prospects."[27] Larger business offices demanded more clerks, and so increasingly men did not see clerking as a step on the path to upward mobility. During the Civil War, when there was a labor shortage, women filled vacancies as clerks and copyists. Without better options elsewhere, they worked for lower pay than men would, and without the promise of promotion.

The typewriter, invented by Christopher Sholes in 1867 and introduced into widespread use by the Remington Company in the late 1870s, fit well into the dramatic changes in the social structure of the office that were already under way. Although its inventor had thought that court reporters and "literary men" — authors and ministers — would be its main users, it found its widest use in business. At first typewritten correspondence was considered rude and impersonal, but by 1890 handwritten letters stood out as old-fashioned, even unbusinesslike. By 1886 some 50,000 typewriters had been sold. The *Pensman's Art Journal* noted the new competition in 1887: "Five years ago the type writer was simply a mechanical curiosity. Today its monotonous click can be heard in almost every well regulated business establishment in the country. A great revolution is taking place, and the type writer is at the bottom of it."[28] The typewriter was faster, allowed easier production of copies, and made possible a division of labor, increasing efficiency.

The typewriter almost immediately became a woman's machine, but it played only a minor role in the feminization of office work. The growing number of educated women looking for work in the late 1800s was a more important factor, as were managerial decisions to establish a division of labor in clerical work. Women who acquired the specialized skill needed to run the machine fit neatly into the new subdivided structure of work. Because it was a new machine, with no tradition of either a male or a female operator, the typewriter allowed women to come into the office without appearing to take over men's work. By 1920 office work was being done largely by women. Women office workers were, for the most part, young, unmarried, and living with their families. Most were from lower-middle-class backgrounds. They were under strict supervision at work, and were usually expected to quit when they got married.

The typewriter was soon joined in the office by other specialized communications machines. Thomas Edison's dictating machine allowed the replacement of skilled stenographers by lower-paid typists. (One 1911 study found that using the machines doubled the number of letters typists could produce, to between 60 and 80 per day. The average cost came down from 5.2 cents to 2.7 cents.) (See RECORDED SOUND.) New copying machines, too, found their way into the office. The mimeograph machine, first used with Edison's 1876 "electric pen," and then with other ways of creating masters, made it easy and cheap

Sales Department
General Office
Swift & Company

F.R.237

to send out many copies. Photographic devices made it possible to copy letters after they had been typed. Even simple technologies such as the preprinted form (one of the favorites of progressive managers starting in the 1870s and 1880s) and carbon paper (widely adopted in the early twentieth century) helped organize the collection and flow of information.

A large office, circa 1910.

The technologies of the early years of the twentieth century, joined by the Xerox machine in the 1960s, were the material basis for American industry through the 1970s. It was the paper office that the new technology of computers and electronics was first to supplement, and then, everyone predicted, replace. But this paper office continued strong. Even in 1992 American businesses generated more than 2.5 trillion pieces of paper a year.

THE ELECTRONIC WORD

The new technology of electronics and the computer which would change the office and office work was first introduced in the 1950s. Over the course of the next few decades it would change the newspaper business, too, and the way that authors wrote books. First would come new machines for putting words on paper, and then new ways to eliminate paper altogether.

Word processing began in computer centers. Computer programmers wrote their programs on computers, using primitive "editors" that allowed them to move and delete words. If you could write programs using these "editors," why not use them to write the documentation for the programs, too, or any written document? Perhaps the first "word processor" was the Lincoln Writer, on

MIT Lincoln Laboratories' TX-2 computer, in the 1950s. Both IBM and Digital Equipment Corporation (DEC) introduced text editors in the early 1960s. IBM claimed that its program, Text-90, was the first commercial computer program that could manipulate text. (One major innovation: it could deal with lower-case letters!) DEC's program had a more honest name: it was called Expensive Typewriter, one of a series of "expensive" programs for the PDP-1, including Expensive Tape Recorder and Expensive Desk Calculator.

In the 1960s and 1970s computers began to find wider use as "expensive typewriters." IBM introduced its Magnetic Tape Selectric Typewriter (MTST) in 1964. This was a typewriter with a memory unit on the side. It recorded each keystroke onto magnetic tape to reduce the repetitive work of typing many similar letters. The next step was a "smart" typewriter that would be useful for one-of-a-kind letters, and by the early 1970s there were more than a dozen companies offering text-editing typewriters. IBM had originally expected to sell some 6,000 MTSTs; it sold many more. By 1973 there were more than 100,000 word processors in American offices. Over the next few years there would be enormous competition, and enormous improvements: display screens, better editing systems, and, most important, a computer.

Starting in the mid-1970s small computers were sold specifically for word processing. One of the first was DEC's DS310, based on the PDP-8 computer; it cost $16,000. When personal computers were introduced in the late 1970s, they took over the word processing market. Word processing was the application that led many people to buy their own personal computer. The first computerized word processor was introduced by Wang Laboratories in 1976. An Wang, president of the company, recalled: "People saw text editing done on a screen, and they thought it was magic."[29] Even at $30,000 each, word processors sold like hotcakes.

The xerographic machine, the first important new office machine since the dictaphone, entered the office in the 1960s. Chester Carlson, a physicist, invented the electrophotographic process in 1938. In his work at a patent firm he had to make a lot of copies, and he was convinced there had to be an easier way than the photographic process used there. He persuaded the Batelle Memorial Institute, a private research organization, to continue his work. In 1945, officials from the Haloid Company, a distributor of photographic supplies, saw Batelle's machine and invested some $75 million in further development. On March 1, 1960, Haloid shipped the first Xerox machine, the Model 914. It was an immediate success. In 1961 Haloid's sales were $61 million; by 1968 they had hit $1.125 billion and the company had changed its name to Xerox. In 1966 offices made over 14 billion copies.

Shown is the Model 613 copier, introduced in 1963.

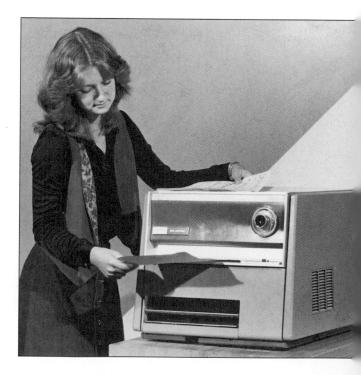

These devices promised to change the very nature of the office. In the late 1970s manufacturers of office automation equipment suggested that the nirvana of a "paperless office" was just around the corner. (The basis for the continuing call for the paperless office is clear from one statistic: a 1975 Stanford Research Institute study found that business and government used some 800 billion pieces of paper each year.) To get there, office automation consultants proposed that offices be restructured to allow the best use of the new technology. Businesses, they urged, should eliminate the long tradition of an individual secretary for each executive. They called this the "divorce" of the executive and his (or, less commonly, her) secretary. In the office of 1985, one company predicted in 1978, "there are no secretaries. You receive services from a pool shared by several managers in your group; we call this pool the Administrative Support Center. Within the Support Center, there are Administrative Support Specialists, Information Storage/Retrieval Specialists and Word Processing Specialists."[30] This specialization and division of labor would increase efficiency, advocates claimed, and would allow closer supervision of the work — especially given the potential of the machines to measure work by counting keystrokes. It also tended to decrease the range of a worker's skills, and to increase managerial control.

Problems with this vision surfaced immediately. Managers resisted losing their secretaries, who were status symbols. And many secretaries resisted their reassignment to typing pools, where the work was less interesting. A 1982 study revealed the problem: "Interviews with typists indicated that the change from copy typing to word processing had reduced task variety, meaning and contribution [and] control over work scheduling." Managers, by contrast, "felt that closer control over typing work would increase productivity. The new work organization achieved this control, but appeared to restrict the typists' ability to exploit fully the potential benefits of the new technology."[31]

As the price of word processors fell, and as they were replaced by more versatile personal computers — some 10 million personal computers were in use in offices by 1985 — a new strategy was tried. The machines were treated like typewriters, and given to each secretary. This vastly increased the amount of text output — so much for the fantasy of the "paperless office" — and also the number of secretaries. But it also revealed a way out, in some offices, as secretaries were replaced by the new machines. Managers were given their own personal computer, and expected to do their own typing. As one manager interviewed by journalist Barbara Garson put it: "A secretary is superfluous and, even worse, gets in the way. . . . For the manager who isn't afraid of it, the computer means greater and greater control over his or her life. It means the security of less and less dependency on other people. . . . By 1990 the traditional secretary will be obsolete."[32] But the predictions of the end of the "traditional secretary," like so many predictions about computers, was based on a strictly technological logic, considering people only as information processors. Like the repeated predictions of the "paperless office," the date projected for the prediction kept moving further into the future. (See COMPUTERS and BEYOND TELEPHONES.)

Not just offices but also publishers took advantage of the new technology. Electronic communications and computers as well as innovations in typesetting and printing helped make it possible for newspapers to increase efficiency, decrease costs, and reach their readers better. In the 1960s and 1970s newspapers underwent three technological revolutions — in typesetting, printing, and editing.

The earliest revolution was in typesetting. In the 1950s newspapers began to connect paper-tape readers to their Linotype machines, and to feed them with paper tape punched with stories taken directly from the newswire machines — eliminating the traditional retyping — and with locally written stories. In the 1960s at some papers a computer was introduced into the system to handle hyphenation and spacing. These systems could set up to fourteen lines of text per minute, a significant increase from the five lines per minute of the traditional Linotype operator.

But Linotypes themselves were soon to be replaced. The Linotype machine required a skilled operator, and had fundamental speed limits. It was replaced by phototypesetting systems that used mechanical and optical devices to project the images of letters onto photosensitive paper. The paper was developed, the columns of "type" were cut up and pasted together to form each page, and the pages were photographically copied onto printing plates.

Then in the 1960s electronics began to change phototypesetting. Michael Barnett at MIT built the first computer-driven typesetter in 1961. Cathode-ray tubes were used to "print" the letters onto the paper. Magnetic tape replaced punched paper tape to drive the machines. In the 1970s the first laser typesetting machines were introduced. These stored the letter images digitally instead of photographically. In the mid-1960s photocomposition systems could set eighty lines per minute; in the mid-1970s, 150 to 175 lines per minute.

The typesetting revolution was complemented by a printing revolution — almost every newspaper in the United States switched to web offset printing presses in the 1960s and 1970s — and then by a computer revolution. In the mid-1970s many newspapers adopted computers that allowed reporters to type their stories directly into a video display terminal and see the material in its column format. This made writing and rewriting faster and easier, and made it possible to fit copy easily and accurately to available space. Some newspapers found a 20 to 30 percent increase in writers' efficiency. Most reporters loved the new machines. Nan Robertson, a reporter for the *New York Times*, told an interviewer: "The computer made it infinitely easier. And now I'm absolutely addicted. The computer has liberated us."[33]

A push of a button would transmit the story from the reporter to the editor, who would edit it, and push another button to transmit it to a typesetting machine. The typeset copy would then be transmitted electronically to a printing plant, and the paper printed. (Computerized page-layout systems that allowed the entire page to be designed by computer came in the 1980s.) The key here was that the article was typed only once; there was no waiting for type to be reset, corrected, and re-proofread. The stories could even be stored electronically for easy future reference, and for resale.

The computer made it possible for the reporter to do the job of the typesetter in addition to his or her own job. Newspapers could save one third of their labor costs with the new technology. Linotype operators struck many papers in an attempt to keep their jobs, but the new technology had made them obsolete. In 1973, when the *Washington Post* introduced computerized typesetting and its Linotype operators went on strike, twenty-five managers took over 125 Linotype operators' jobs. By the mid-1980s almost every newspaper in the United States had switched to computer typesetting. The number of Linotype operators in New York City fell from 8,000 in 1968 to 3,800 in 1978, and to zero a few years later.

The introduction of the computer eventually changed the nature of the newspaper business. It tended to return control of the paper to the editorial department from the production department, which had gained power as the final arbiter of what could be done. It extended deadlines, making it possible to print late-breaking news. It made it much easier to originate stories from outside bureaus, which could be sent over phone lines. Papers could be printed in several versions, each focused on a particular area or market. And papers could be transmitted by satellite to printing plants across the country, making possible nationwide papers such as the *Wall Street Journal* and *USA Today*. The London-based *Financial Times* became a global newspaper.

The new technology also opened the door to abuses. It became very easy simply to reprint press releases that arrived in computer-ready form. The typesetter had been cut out of the loop; why not the journalist as well? One side effect of the elimination of Linotype operators was a dramatic rise in the number of typos in newspapers: they had been silently correcting the copy as they worked!

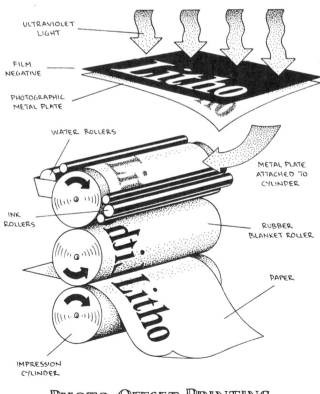

The first step in modern lithographic printing is to produce a photographic printing plate. A negative film of the image to be printed is put on top of the plate and exposed to ultraviolet light. Where the light hits the plate — where there are letters or images — it is exposed, and when the plate is developed the areas that were not exposed are washed away. The areas that were exposed are "fixed" so that ink will stick to them.

These plates are put onto the plate cylinder of a press. In offset printing, the words to be printed are transferred from the plate first to a rubber roller and then to the paper. To print in color four separate plates are made, one for each of the three primary colors and black that make up the image.

PHOTO-OFFSET PRINTING

This technology allowed big newspapers to get bigger, with more pages and larger circulation. In 1990 there were 1,600 daily papers. Only fifteen companies were responsible for the majority of daily newspapers, and few cities had more than one daily paper. Smaller weekly newspapers also flourished. Small and medium-sized suburban papers took advantage of the new technology, and increasing suburban populations, to publish local news and advertisements. Many cities gained new "underground" weeklies. Total daily circulation was as high as ever, over 60 million. In the 1980s almost 75 percent of adults read a newspaper every day. More money was spent on advertising in daily newspapers than in any other medium: in 1987 over one fourth of all advertising expenditures went to newspapers, almost $30 billion.

Magazine and book publishing changed in similar ways. As with the newspaper business, the big publishers got bigger. Six major corporations accounted for many of the 11,000 commercial magazines published in 1990, and for a large part of the circulation. (One company, Time Warner, accounted for one third of the revenue and 40 percent of the profits of all American magazines.) But there were also enormous numbers of smaller magazines, including over 110,000 scientific and technical journals published worldwide in 1990. Thousands of very small magazines, using desktop publishing and cheap offset printing or xerography, filled the bottom of the market. The costs of entry into magazine publishing were very low.

Similar trends were apparent in book publishing. The big firms got bigger in an orgy of corporate takeovers in the 1980s. But small-press publishing soared in the 1960s and 1970s, too, because of the lower costs of production. In 1958, 1,000 publishers had issued 13,500 titles. In 1985 there were over 15,000 publishers, who issued over 50,000 titles. In 1979 U.S. book industry revenues were $7.2 billion, not including textbooks.

Modern newsrooms are all-electronic. At the *Los Angeles Times,* in 1990, there were 1,200 terminals used by 1,500 people. Each day, as many as 25,000 electronic mail messages move through the network, as well as hundreds of stories. Over 100,000 stories were stored on-line, and many millions more were accessible through phone lines to other information databases.

Reporters were among the first users of laptop computers. They could write stories on location and transfer them over the phone lines directly to the editing room. The first widely popular portable was the Radio Shack Model 100, introduced in 1983. It included a built-in modem.

Spending on newspapers and magazines rose to a peak of about $75 per person each year in the mid-1950s, then declined to about $60 in 1988 — a decline reflecting the increasing importance of radio and television as a source of news. (These figures are in constant 1982 dollars.) The percentage of the public buying magazines peaked in 1960 at 62 percent, then fell to 45 percent in the 1980s as some national magazines, even several with circulations in the millions, lost advertising to television, became unprofitable, and ceased publication.

Expenditures on books increased from a low of about $14 per person in 1934 until they reached a maximum of about $40 per year around 1980, and then began to decline. (Some of the increase was due to the popularity of the Book-of-the-Month Club, founded in 1926, and even more to the invention of the modern paperback book in 1939.) Reading expenditures as a percentage of total expenditures declined from a peak of about 1.6 percent in the late 1940s to about half of that by 1985. Reading expenses counted for more than 30 percent of entertainment costs in the late 1940s, and less than 10 percent in 1985. Words on paper lost ground to the electronic media, which went from almost nothing in the 1920s to about 28 percent of entertainment spending by the 1980s, a steady rise that started after World War II.

In the 1970s only 50 percent of families bought any sort of reading material regularly. A 1961 study of Baltimore residents found that 76 percent of households contained books (96 percent of the respondents had a TV set). In 1983 only 70 percent of the American public said they read a newspaper regularly, and older people tended to read more newspapers than younger people. Today roughly 25 percent of the public claim to read books regularly, a figure that has remained unchanged from 1930 to the present. In one 1947 survey 74 percent of respondents said they hadn't read one book in the previous month.

DESKTOP PUBLISHING AND BEYOND

In the 1980s, with the spread of the personal computer, almost everyone who wrote began to use a word processor. Some authors spent more time arguing about which computer was fastest and which program was easiest to use, or most powerful, than they did writing. For a while it was a fad to list hardware and software in the acknowledgments of a book.

Writing on the computer is in fact easier in some ways: it's easier to edit, it's easier to revise, it's easier to make a page look good. But, as many teachers of writing have found, computer-aided writing can be sloppier because using the computer encourages minor, point-by-point revisions, not rethinking; and it can lead to lazy recopying, cutting and pasting what's available electronically. Of course, this may not be bad. John C. Dvorak, a computer magazine columnist, suggests that we should stop considering sacrosanct "drudgelike intellectual pursuits" such as spelling and writing. "Papers composed of cut-and-paste excerpts from online services and CD-ROMs are the future," he continues, calling the result not plagiarism but the essential new skill of "knowledge mining."[34]

The new technology brings new tradeoffs and possibilities not only to writing but to presentation, too. It's possible to spend endless time on making a page look good rather than writing it well. Standards rise as the technology to

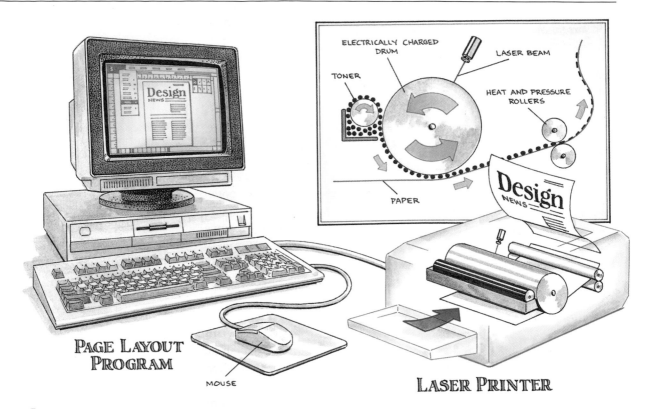

ELECTRICALLY CHARGED DRUM

LASER BEAM

TONER

HEAT AND PRESSURE ROLLERS

PAPER

PAGE LAYOUT PROGRAM

MOUSE

LASER PRINTER

Desktop publishing incorporates all of the elements of layout and printing into a series of electronic processes.

Layout takes place on the computer screen. Words are "imported" from a word processing program. Drawings are scanned from photographs or drawings, or drawn on the screen. They are combined using a page-layout program, which makes it easy for the designer to manipulate the elements of design, making each page look good but also keeping a consistency of design throughout the publication. The program then sends the description of the page to the laser printer.

A laser printer is a xerographic printer — with a few changes. In a regular xerographic printer, the image of a page is projected onto the charged surface of a drum coated with a photoconductive material, usually selenium. Selenium holds an electrostatic charge in the dark, but loses it in the light. Dark areas of the material being copied remain charged, but where the image is light the charge disappears. When toner powder is sprinkled on the drum it sticks to the charged areas but not the uncharged ones, so when the toner is transferred from the drum to a sheet of paper, the original image is reproduced. Finally, the paper is heated to fuse the toner to the paper. A laser printer differs in that the image is drawn onto the photoconductive drum by a laser. Software directs the laser over the drum, turning it on and off in a pattern of more than 300 dots to an inch, to reproduce the image drawn on the computer screen.

meet them becomes available. Overelaborate design, electronic delivery of text, and interactivity can overwhelm ideas. It can focus attention on the medium rather than the message.

In the late 1980s the publishing business underwent another electronics revolution: desktop publishing. Desktop publishing required new hardware (a fast, smart, versatile, high-resolution printer) and new software (in addition to word processing software, a page-description language and a program that allowed the user to design the page on the computer screen). Desktop publishing required better-quality output than the modified typewriters and "dot matrix" printers connected to most PCs. The laser printer, originally invented for high-speed computer output, proved to be the solution. Laser printers used the same principle of printing as the Xerox machine, except that instead of optics focusing the image of the original on the light-sensitive drum, the computer drove a laser that "exposed" the drum. The first practical laser printers were invented at the Xerox Palo Alto Research Center (PARC) in the early 1970s for use with the bit-mapped displays of the Alto computer. The first "personal" laser printer was the Apple LaserWriter, introduced in 1985. "Personal" here was a bit of a reach on Apple's part; it cost $7,000, more than the Macintosh computer it was attached to.

The next breakthrough was in software: a "page-description language," invented by John Warnock and Martin Newell at PARC. The first language was called JaM; it metamorphosed into Interpress, which was used on Xerox laser printers, and became PostScript, developed by Warnock after he founded Adobe Systems, Inc., in 1982. These languages allowed the computer to store the information about how to form each letter not as a series of dots but rather as a mathematical description, a series of curves. These descriptions could be mathematically manipulated to form letters of any size, and at any location or angle on the page. PostScript could also describe images other than letters. (See PICTURES.)

The final step in desktop publishing was a program that allowed the user to describe the page on the screen and translate the image to a PostScript file that would be sent to the printer. Paul Brainerd and a group of engineers at Aldus wrote the first desktop publishing software, called PageMaker. Now, with computer editing, desktop publishing software, and a laser printer, anyone with a personal computer could produce typeset output, more cheaply than ever before. The low price meant that anyone could be a graphic designer. Desktop publishing was the breakthrough application for the Macintosh, and it made the founders of Aldus and Adobe rich. (It also produced a glut of badly designed, ugly pages with too many fonts, as the technology made it possible for the first time for people without graphics training to become graphic designers.)

Almost every newspaper, magazine, and book publisher adopted the new technology. By 1990 there were very few publishers that did not use computers throughout their operations, from writing to editing to design to typesetting to printing. But in the 1990s the final result — words on paper — was up against new competitors that cut out printing on paper and gave consumers the information in electronic form instead. Some of the new systems delivered information electronically, over the phone lines, on radio or TV, or from computer databases on CD-ROM. Businesses did their best to eliminate paperwork, including some 800 billion forms a year, by switching to electronic systems. (See BEYOND TELEPHONES.) New technologies changed the very form of the book. Some people predicted the end of the printed word and its replacement by the electronic media. Christopher Evans, in his 1979 book *The Micro Millennium*, foresaw "the death of the book": "The 1980s will see the book as we know it . . . begin a slow but steady slide into oblivion."[35]

It seemed that if the book couldn't beat the electronic media, it might join them. The electronic book had possibilities far beyond the simple printed page. "Interactive" was one buzzword, "hypertext" another. In a hypertext document, viewed on a computer screen, a reader can select a word and jump from there to other parts of the text: a definition, a comment from another reader, or more information on related topics. The earliest proposal for this kind of document appeared in an article by Vannevar Bush in the *Atlantic Monthly* in 1945. The mind, he wrote, "snaps instantly [from one idea] to the next that is suggested by the association of thoughts, in accordance with some intricate web of trails carried by the cells of the brain." Why not a mechanical system that would work the same way? He proposed a device he called the Memex, "in which an individual stores his books, records, and communications, and which is mechanized so that it may be consulted with exceeding speed and flexibility. It is an enlarged intimate supplement to his memory."

Bush envisioned a mechanical system, some sort of elaborate microfilm reader. But computers made the idea workable. In the mid-1960s Douglas Engelbart at the Stanford Research Institute built the first hypertext system. Englebart had read Bush's *Atlantic Monthly* article and was immediately taken with it. Englebart's name for his group at SRI gives an idea of what he wanted to do: he called it the Augmented Human Intellect Research Center. His program, called Augment, allowed the electronic linking together of documents on many computers by keywords. At about the same time, Theodor H. Nelson suggested the power of a universe of linked documents, annotated by readers and available to all. In his 1965 *Literary Machines* he coined the word "hypertext": "By 'hypertext' I mean *nonsequential writing* — text that branches and allows choices to the reader, best read at an interactive screen. As popularly conceived, this is a series of text chunks connected by links which offer the reader different pathways."[36]

The text exists only in electronic form, infinitely variable and, in some hypertext systems, constantly changing. There have been several experiments with hypertext systems, but whether or not a hypertext document is easier to read, or easier to learn from, than a printed book is not yet clear. It allows greater freedom to explore the text, perhaps, but by weakening the narrative it tends to lessen the voice of the author. It becomes harder to make, or follow, arguments when there's no single narrative path. Its supporters see it as the successor to the book, a revolution as important as the invention of printing. George P. Landow writes in his 1992 *Hypertext*: "Electronic text processing marks the next major shift in information technology after the development of the printed book. It promises (or threatens) to produce effects on our culture, particularly on our literature, education, criticism and scholarship, just as radical as those produced by Gutenberg's movable type."[37]

The written word has been around for a long time and survived many changes. Books, magazines, and newspapers have existed in something like their modern state for the last hundred years. The written word has proved to be a flexible, enormously powerful medium. And there are more words around now than ever before; one study estimates that Americans consume some 7 trillion words a day. The delivery vehicle may change, but words will survive, prosper, and even remain central in the age of electronic information.

FOR FURTHER READING

On literacy, see Carl F. Kaestle, Helen Damon Moore, et al., *Literacy in the United States: Readers and Reading since 1880* (1991). The March 1988 issue of *American Quarterly* was devoted to articles on the history of reading. For the way in which printed words fit into the larger picture of information, see Richard D. Brown, *Knowledge Is Power: The Diffusion of Information in Early America, 1700–1865* (1989); and William J. Gilmore, *Reading Becomes a Necessity of Life: Material and Cultural Life in Rural New England, 1780–1835* (1989).

On newspapers, see Dan Schiller, *Objectivity and the News: The Public and the Rise of Commercial Journalism* (1981); Edwin and Michael Emery, *The Press and America: An Interpretive History of the Mass Media*, 5th ed. (1984); and Michael Schudson, *Discovering the News: A Social History of American Newspapers* (1978). On magazines, see Frank Luther Mott, *A History of American Magazines*, 5 vols. (1930–1968). The *Proceedings* of the American Antiquarian Society for 1991 includes a special issue on the history of the newspaper.

On book publishing see Hellmut Lehmann-Haupt with Lawrence C. Wroth and Rollo G. Silver, *The Book in America: A History of the Making and Selling of Books in the United States,* 2d ed. (1952); and John Tebbel, *A History of Book Publishing in the United States,* 5 vols. (1972–1981). For an example of the ways that books informed popular culture, see Michael Denning, *Mechanic Accents: Dime Novels and Working-Class Culture in America* (1987).

Library history has its own literature. For an overview, see Jesse Shera, *Foundations of the American Public Libary: The Origins of the Public Library Movement in New England* (1949); and Sidney Ditzion, *Arsenals of a Democratic Culture: A Social History of the American Public Library Movement in New England and the Middle States from 1850–1900* (1947). A history of the way librarians thought about their work, along with a good bit of information about what the public wanted to read, can be found in Dee Garrison, *Apostles of Culture: The Public Librarian and American Society, 1876–1920* (1979).

The history of the recent technology of writing and publishing is nowhere fully described; for parts of the story, see Ernest C. Hynds, *American Newspapers in the 1970s* (1975); and John J. Simon, Jr., *From Sand to Circuits and Other Inquiries* (1986).

The best description of the effects of new technology in the office in the nineteenth century is JoAnne Yates, *Control through Communication: The Rise of System in American Management* (1989). See also Olivier Zunz, *Making America Corporate, 1870–1920* (1990), for the human side of the corporate revolution. On the importance of communications to business in the nineteenth century, see Thomas C. Cochran, *Frontiers of Change: Early Industrialism in America* (1981).

The history of office work has received a good bit of study lately. On office workers of the nineteenth and early twentieth centuries, a good source is Sharon Hartman Strom, *Beyond the Typewriter: Gender, Class, and the Origins of Modern American Office Work, 1900–1930* (1992).

There's much recent writing on the possibilities of electronic texts. See Stewart Brand, *The Media Lab: Inventing the Future at MIT* (1987); George P. Landow, *Hypertext: The Convergence of Contemporary Critical Theory and Technology* (1992); J. David

Bolter, *Writing Space: The Computer, Hypertext, and the History of Literacy* (1990); James M. Nyce and Paul D. Kahn, eds., *From Memex to Hypertext: Vannevar Bush and the Mind's Machine* (1991); and Louis Reynolds and Steven J. Derose, "Electronic Books," in *BYTE* (June 1992): 263–268.

NOTES

1. Quoted in Dan Schiller, *Objectivity and the News: The Public and the Rise of Commercial Journalism* (1981), p. 17.

2. Quoted in Oliver Carlson, *The Man Who Made News: James Gordon Bennett* (1942), p. 396.

3. James Gordon Bennett, "Editorial," *New York Herald*, August 19, 1836; quoted in Peter C. Marzio, *The Men and Machines of American Journalism* (1973), p. 74.

4. *Springfield* (Mass.) *Republican*, January 4, 1851; quoted in Marzio, *Men and Machines*, p. 54.

5. Quoted in Cathy Davidson, "Toward a History of Books," *American Quarterly* (March 1988): 10.

6. Richard D. Brown, "From Cohesion to Competition," in *Printing and Society in Early America*, ed. William L. Joyce et al. (1993), p. 305.

7. Thomas Jefferson, *Writings* (1854), vol. 8, p. 11; quoted in James W. Carey, *Communications as Culture: Essays on Media and Society* (1989), p. 7.

8. *New York Magazine* (January 1790): 24–25; quoted in David Paul Nord, "A Republican Literature: A Study of Magazine Readers and Reading in Late Eighteenth-Century New York," *American Quarterly* (March 1988): 58.

9. Robert H. Wiebe, *The Segmented Society: An Introduction to the Meaning of America* (1975; reprint 1979), p. 19.

10. Noah Webster, "The Editors' Address to the Public," *American Minerva*, December 9, 1793: 1.

11. Francis Lieber, *Encyclopedia Americana* (1832); quoted in Richard John, "Concept of a Communications Revolution," unpublished paper, p. 6.

12. Alexis de Tocqueville, *Democracy in America* (1835; Henry Reeve Text as revised by Francis Bowen, ed. Phillips Bradley, 1945), pp. 193–194.

13. Tocqueville, *Democracy in America*, p. 195.

14. Quoted in Marzio, *Men and Machines*, p. 44.

15. Bennett quoted in Mitchell Stephens, *A History of News: From Drum to Satellite* (1988), p. 226; James Fenimore Cooper, *The American Democrat* (1838; reprint 1969), p. 183; quoted in Michael Schudson, *Discovering the News: A Social History of American Newspapers* (1978), p. 13.

16. *Springfield* (Mass.) *Republican*, January 4, 1851; quoted in Marzio, *Men and Machines*, p. 54.

17. Quoted in Evelyn Geller, *Forbidden Books in American Public Libraries, 1846–1939* (1984), p. 10.

18. Quoted in Daniel J. Czitrom, *Media and the American Mind from Morse to McLuhan* (1982), p. 37.

19. Edward C. Kemble, *A History of California Newspapers, 1846–1858* (1858); quoted in Jeremy Tunstall, *The Media Are American* (1977), p. 28.

20. Brown, "From Cohesion to Competition," p. 308.

21. Quoted in Schudson, *Discovering the News*, p. 62.

22. Quoted in Thomas C. Leonard, "Magazines and Newspapers," in *The Reader's Companion to American History*, ed. Eric Foner and John A. Garraty, p. 691.

23. W. J. Stillman, "Journalism and Literature," *Atlantic Monthly* (November 1991): 694; quoted in Czitrom, *Media and the American Mind*, p. 19.

24. Sherwood Anderson, *Winesburg, Ohio* (1919); quoted in Warren I. Sussman, "Culture and Communications," in *Culture as History: The Transformation of American Society in the Twentieth Century* (1984), p. 260.

25. Quoted in Czitrom, *Media and the American Mind*, p. 20.

26. Richard D. Brown, *Knowledge Is Power: The Diffusion of Information in Early America, 1700–1865* (1989), p. 112.

27. *Hunt's Merchants' Magazine*; quoted in Olivier Zunz, *Making America Corporate, 1870–1920* (1990), p. 106.

28. Quoted in JoAnne Yates, *Control through Communication: The Rise of System in American Management* (1989), p. 41.

29. Quoted in Douglas K. Smith and Robert C. Alexander, *Fumbling the Future: How Xerox Invented, Then Ignored, the First Personal Computer* (1988), p. 176.

30. Datapro Research Corporation, "Evolving Office of the Future," *Office Automation Solutions Workbook* (June 1978); quoted in Barbara Garson, *The Electronic Sweatshop: How Computers Are Transforming the Office of the Future into the Factory of the Past* (1988), p. 177.

31. David A. Buchanan and David Boddy, "Advanced Technology and the Quality of Working Life: The Effects of Word Processing on Video Typists," *Journal of Occupational Psychology*, no. 1 (1982): 1; quoted in Harley Shaiken, *Work Transformed: Automation and Labor in the Computer Age* (1985), p. 267.

32. Garson, *The Electronic Sweatshop*, p. 202.

33. Quoted in Carla Marie Rupp, "The Times Goes Computer," in *Digital Deli,* ed. Steve Ditlea (1984): 171.

34. John C. Dvorak, "The Welcome Death of Old Skills," *DEC Professional* (July 1992): 112.

35. Christopher Evans, *The Micro Millennium* (1979), p. 115.

36. Theodor H. Nelson, *Literary Machines* (1981), p. 2; quoted in George P. Landow, *Hypertext: The Convergence of Contemporary Critical Theory and Technology* (1992), p. 4.

37. Landow, *Hypertext*, p. 19.

The smallest News and Post Card Stand in New Orleans, La., 103 Royal St.

In the nineteenth century the processes of producing and reproducing images were mechanized and industrialized, and there was an explosion of images that were put to use in all sorts of new ways. Today, we are so surrounded by images that we often don't even see them. Our newspapers and magazines are packed with full-color images. Our photo albums are filled with the photographs we take — some 41 million a day in the United States. We send postcards instead of writing letters when we travel. The standards of images set by photographs and other means of mechanical image-making in the nineteenth century shape our modern world of images — a world that is being redefined, once again, by the computer.

COMMUNICATION
PICTURES

ONE OF THE FIRST DESCRIPTIONS OF PHOTO-graphs in this country appeared in the *Knickerbocker,* a New York magazine, in 1839. The article had a tone of wonder, of amazement, as it reported: "We . . . have no hesitation in avowing that they [the photographs] are the most remarkable object of curiosity and admiration, in the arts, that we ever beheld. Their ex-quisite perfection almost transcends the bounds of sober belief."[1] Right from the beginning, photography was accepted as objective. Edgar Allan Poe vouched for the "truthfulness" of photographic images when he wrote in 1840: "In truth the daguerreotype plate is infinitely more accurate than any painting by human hands. . . . The closest scrutiny of the photographic draw-ing discloses only a more absolute truth, more perfect identity of aspect with the thing represented."[2] In 1842 the U.S. Congress accepted daguerreotypes as "undeniably accurate evidence" in a U.S.-Canadian border dispute.[3] Tech-nological representation always seems more true than any mere human inter-pretation.

Because of their apparent truth, photographs, and pictures made with newer technologies from chromolithography to the computer, have been in-vested with great authority. They have been produced in enormous numbers, serving both as personal keepsakes and as public landmarks, and used to sell everything from westward expansion to oatmeal. There have been many gener-ations of image technology since the invention of photography, and all of them have inherited its power.

PHOTOGRAPHY

Photography combined the camera obscura, an old device used by artists to trace images, with the newly discovered chemistry of the effects of light on silver salts. The first person to take a photograph was Joseph-Nicéphore Niépce, in 1824. He set up a partnership with L. J. M. Daguerre, who in 1837 invented a much-improved process, using a copper plate coated with silver io-dide. At about the same time, in England, William Henry Fox Talbot found a

51

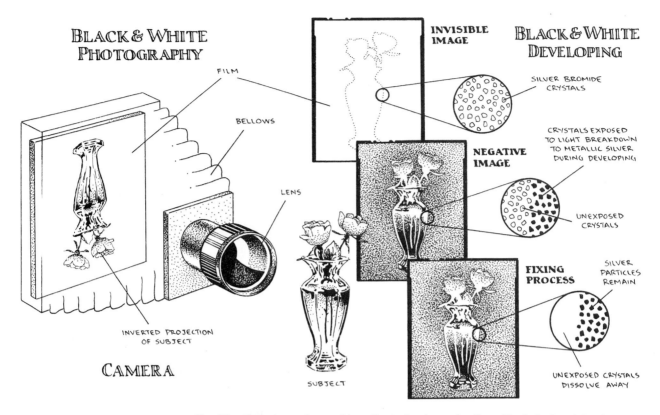

BLACK & WHITE PHOTOGRAPHY

FILM
BELLOWS
LENS
INVERTED PROJECTION OF SUBJECT
CAMERA
SUBJECT

INVISIBLE IMAGE

NEGATIVE IMAGE

BLACK & WHITE DEVELOPING

SILVER BROMIDE CRYSTALS

CRYSTALS EXPOSED TO LIGHT BREAKDOWN TO METALLIC SILVER DURING DEVELOPING

UNEXPOSED CRYSTALS

FIXING PROCESS

SILVER PARTICLES REMAIN

UNEXPOSED CRYSTALS DISSOLVE AWAY

Traditional photography combines the technology of optics with photochemistry. Lenses focus light onto film — originally glass, later paper and celluloid plastic. The film is coated with a light-sensitive chemical compound, usually silver salts. When exposed to light these salts break down into metallic silver, registering the image on the film. The film is then developed, which completes the chemical reaction, making the silver-coated areas of the film black. The film is then "fixed," and the unexposed silver salts washed away. The result is a negative of the original image, which is then printed on paper in much the same way as the film was exposed.

way to produce a negative picture using transparent paper coated with silver salts. Its advantage was that it could be copied.

Samuel Morse was one of the first American photographers. Morse met Daguerre in Paris, and was so fascinated by the new art that he put aside his desperate efforts to improve the telegraph to experiment with it. Others were taken with it, too. Within a few years photography was all the rage throughout the country. "It is hard to find the man who has not gone through the 'operator's' hands from once to half-a-dozen times, or who has not the shadowy faces of his wife and children done up in purple morocco and velvet, together or singly, among his household treasurers," wrote *Godey's Lady's Book,* one of the most popular magazines of the day, in 1845.[4] In 1850 Americans bought some 3 million daguerreotypes. In 1853 there were one hundred daguerreotypists in New York City, charging an average of $2.50 for a portrait.

Photography fit nicely into American culture. It arrived at a time when increased industrialization and improved transportation were bringing great mobility in the United States. People wanted keepsakes of distant family and friends. Even before the day of the photograph, there were many itinerant portrait painters in the United States, who traveled from town to town drawing portraits for a few dollars. The drawings (silhouettes, cut from paper, were also popular) were formulaic, and quite cheap. Some itinerant artists used mechanical devices to help speed up the process of production; few drawings took more than fifteen minutes. The quick sketches were very popular, often finding a place on parlor walls.

In a few short years many of the portraitists had become photographers, and they had been joined by many others who saw the demand for images as a way of making money. Photography won easy acceptance because it was based on earlier ways of seeing, and of representing vision. Rudolph Arnheim, in *Art and Visual Perception,* points to a Western "preference for mechanical reproduction and geometrical constructs in place of creative imagery."[5] "Photographs, film, and video cameras are merely devices for recording . . . this long-established, predetermined way of seeing," writes John Armes, a philosopher of images.[6]

Photographs found use everywhere. According to John Berger, a historian of photography: "Within a mere thirty years of its invention as a gadget for an elite, photography was being used for police filing, war reporting, military reconnaissance, pornography, encyclopedic documentation, family albums, postcards, anthropological records . . . sentimental moralising, inquisitive probing . . . aesthetic effects, news reporting and formal portraiture."[7] In 1846 *Living Age* magazine looked into this future, and found it a mixed blessing: "For our own part we are unable to conceive any limits to the progress of this art. On the contrary, it tasks the imagination to conjecture what it will not accomplish. . . . A man cannot make a proposal or a lady decline one — a steam boiler cannot explode, or an ambitious river overflow its banks — a gardener cannot elope with an heiress, or a reverend bishop commit an indiscretion, but straightway, an officious daguerreotype will proclaim the whole affair to the world."[8] And as photography continued to improve, with faster exposures and more sensitive plates, the prediction came true. Photography affected every aspect of private and public life.

The next photographic fad was the *carte de visite,* or "card photograph." These were small photographs, reproduced very cheaply and in large numbers. As early as 1860 they were available at twenty-five photographs for a dollar. They were sent to friends and collected in albums. The Civil War spurred the demand, as every mother wanted a photograph of her son as he headed off to war. They were made in the millions, and not just of ordinary people, but also of art objects, racehorses, celebrities, and the like. The *cartes de visite,* albumin prints, were joined by other photographic processes, especially the tintype, in the 1860s. Photographers set up in army camps to take pictures of soldiers to send to the folks back home. Tintypes and *cartes de visite,* stored in photo albums, became

A daguerreotype camera from about 1850.

a fixture in every middle-class home in the 1860s. They were brought out on special occasions, when guests visited, or when viewing the photograph might give solace or pleasure.

But there were also photographs that were less personal, that were purchased for entertainment and education. Starting in the 1850s, stereographs — two photographs mounted side by side which, when viewed in a special viewer, gave a three-dimensional image — became wildly popular. There were stereograph views of everything: tourist attractions, landscapes, furniture. One British firm sold a million views in 1862. Almost every household had a stereoscope. The views seemed almost real to the Victorians. Hermann von Helmholtz, the German scientist, wrote: "These stereoscopic photographs are so true to nature and so lifelike in their portrayal of material things, that after viewing such a picture and recognizing in it some object like a house, for instance, we get the impression, when we actually do see the object, that we have already seen it before."[9] Oliver Wendell Holmes urged communities to set up libraries of stereographs, as a way of teaching students and those unable to travel about the world around them.

Other photographs were shown in public galleries. During the Civil War, photographers visited camps and battlefields to record the war in progress. Mathew Brady, one of the premier photographic entrepreneurs of the day, sold photographs of generals to the public, and exhibited photographs of battle scenes in his galleries. Viewers of the photographs found them painfully realistic. Oliver Wendell Holmes wrote: "It was so nearly like visiting the battlefield to look over these views, that all of the emotions excited by the actual sight of the stained and sordid scene, strewed with rags and wrecks, came back to us, and we buried them in the recesses of our cabinet as we would have buried the mutilated remains of the dead they too vividly represented."[10]

Photography was a primary means of reporting the opening of the American West. Pictures taken in the 1860s by Carleton E. Watkins, William Henry Jackson, and Timothy O'Sullivan, among others, shaped Easterners' views of the frontier. These photographs portrayed the West as immense, deserted, virgin, and open for exploitation. (Some were produced for the railroad companies, eager to open up the territory around the new tracks.) These photographic images, like all photographic images, were carefully composed, but were thought to be pure and true. They were a fine sales tool.

Photography redefined American painting. Thomas Cole, one of the greatest American painters of the day, wrote that photography would produce "a great revolution in the pictorial arts. . . . It will have the effect of annihilating the false lying artists who of late have deluged the world with their production — those things called views — purporting to be sketched on the spot."[11] The art historian Elizabeth Lindquist-Cock suggests that photography set "the permissible levels of verisimilitude by which both portrait and landscape painter were to judge their success." Portrait painting changed, too, to more static poses, a subdued range of hues, harsh lighting, a lack of plastic quality, and "most of all, an objectivity approaching the objectivity of the camera's lens."[12] Eventually, painters would rebel against the verisimilitude that photography made so easy, moving toward a modernist, subjective approach. A German expressionist manifesto of 1907 put it thus: "Today, photography takes over exact representation. Thus painting, relieved from this task, gains its former freedom of action."[13]

PRINTED PICTURES

Magazines and newspapers eagerly adopted photographs. The more images journals ran, the more popular they were. The first picture magazine was Herbert Ingram's *Illustrated London News,* in 1842. In the United States the first newspaper whose appeal was mainly pictorial was Frank Leslie's *Illustrated Newspaper,* started in 1855. Close behind was *Harper's Weekly,* in 1857. All were immediate successes.

At first these newspapers were illustrated by woodcuts. The drawings were often labeled "drawn by our artists on the spot," but in fact were usually done from photographs. The image would be sketched onto the woodblock, and then a skilled engraver would cut away the wood between the lines. To speed up the process, sometimes the block was cut into pieces, each piece given to a different engraver. It was then bolted back together. To print a large number of newspapers, the block was pressed into clay or wax. Molten type metal was poured in it, producing a "stereotype." This allowed the paper to be printed on several presses at once, using several stereotypes.

There were many improvements in this process over the next few years. One way to cut out some of the handwork was to treat the woodblock with a photographic emulsion and print a photograph directly onto it. The wood engraver would just follow the image. Methods using other materials were also tried. It was possible, for example, to photograph onto a properly treated sheet of zinc, which could be processed directly onto a printing plate. The problem with all of these methods was that they could reproduce only black and white images, and only lines. They couldn't reproduce the grays of a photograph.

In the 1870s the first techniques for printing these intermediate tones were developed: the Woodburytype and the Albertype. But these early methods were difficult and found use only in expensive books. Many inventors tried to develop cheaper techniques for producing printing blocks by purely photographic methods. The Zincograph, first practical in the 1880s, allowed photoengraving. Even more important was the halftone, invented by a Cornell professor, Frederick E. Ives. The halftone technique allowed printers to reproduce the grays of a photograph by purely mechanical means. It made its first newspaper appearance in the *New York World* in 1883. Max and Louis Levy of Philadelphia patented the modern method in 1893.

Photographs reproduced by halftone were soon found everywhere. Sunday supplements, heavily illustrated, were introduced in 1896. By 1900 halftones were common in magazines and newspapers. In 1899, according to one survey, almost 90 percent of the illustrations in magazines were reproduced from photographs, only 10 percent from drawings. Neil Harris, a cultural historian, describes the halftone effect as "an iconographical revolution of the first order," ranking it an innovation in printing second in importance only to the invention of movable type.[14] Because the halftone looked like a photograph, it was more powerful, more true, or at least more easily believed, than the engravings it replaced.

Photographs made an enormous difference in journalism. Printed photographs made possible photojournalism, that is, stories told entirely in pictures. It also brought complaints against the abuses it was prone to; it was easy to fake photographs, to misrepresent news, under the cover of photographic truth. It

Photographs were engraved for reproduction in magazines. The artists at *Harper's Weekly* took this photograph of the battlefield at Antietam and engraved it — changing it slightly — for publication.

encouraged the coverage of war, murder, and, as Robert Taft, author of a history of American photography, put it, "morbid and gruesome events."[15] But most important, it sold newspapers. Henry R. Luce, founder of *Time* and *Life* magazines, wrote in 1937, "The photograph is . . . the most important instrument of journalism which has been developed since the printing press."[16] Color printing wasn't too far behind, adding visual appeal to the pages of the paper. In 1896 William Randolph Hearst issued the first comic supplement in color. He proudly called it "eight pages of iridescent polychromous effulgence that makes the rainbow look like a lead pipe."[17] In the 1920s George Gallup conducted a survey of what people read in the newspapers, and found that many of the most-read pages had pictures on them: 85 percent read the "picture page," 70 percent the comics, and 40 to 45 percent the editorial cartoons.

People saw reproduced images not just in the newspapers, but at home and on the streets, too. Andrew Jackson Downing advised in 1850 that "nothing gives an air of greater refinement to a cottage than good prints or engravings hung upon its parlor walls. In selecting these, avoid the trashy, colored show-prints of the ordinary kind, and choose engravings or lithographs, after pictures of celebrity by ancient or modern masters."[18] But the "trashy, colored show-print" — the chromolithograph — was becoming ever more popular. Chromolithography has been called "the democratic art,"[19] and it was indeed everywhere in America.

Lithography, a form of printing that uses a greasy ink applied to a special stone, was invented by Alois Senefelder in Germany in 1796. Chromolithography, which uses many stones — up to twenty, each for a different color — was developed over the course of the next forty years. The first American chromolithograph was printed in 1840, in Boston, by an English immigrant, William Sharp. Before long, calendars, advertisements, and sheet music covers were chromolithographed. The 1849 Report of the Commissioner of Patents paid the new art honor: "In chromo lithography, automaton artists rival the finest touches of old masters, and shortly will multiply by millions, their most esteemed productions."[20]

Chromolithographs were inexpensive, some costing as little as fifty cents, some up to ten dollars. Over the course of the last half of the nineteenth century, millions of chromolithographs were produced. Catharine Beecher and Harriet Beecher Stowe, in *The American Woman's Home* (1869), recommended chromos for the parlor to "give the charm of color which belongs to expensive painting. . . . The educating influence of these works of art can hardly be overestimated. Surrounded by such suggestions of the beautiful, and such reminders of art and history, children are constantly trained to correctness of taste and refinement of thought."[21] Frederick Douglass, writing about a chromolithograph of Hiram R. Revels, the first black U.S. senator, expressed widely held beliefs about the place and power of pictures: "Heretofore, colored Americans have thought little of adorning their parlors with pictures. . . . Pictures come not with slavery and oppression and destitution, but with liberty, fair play, leisure, and refinement. These conditions are now possible to colored American citizens, and I think the walls of their houses will soon begin to bear evidence of their altered relations to the people about them."[22]

In their catalogs, chromolithographers indicated what rooms the pictures should be placed in. Pastoral American landscapes, famous European sights, portraits of famous men, and religious chromos were appropriate for the living room and parlor (the most popular were reproductions of Italian Renaissance Madonnas), still lifes of food and game for the dining room, fruit and flower pieces for the dining room or parlor. One chromo of tomatoes was advertised as appropriate for "dining-rooms, for restaurants, for vegetable and provisions dealers, for seed-stores and others."[23]

Chromos were popular art. D. J. Kenny wrote in 1875 that "it is almost impossible to estimate too highly the value of the work done by lithography in popularizing art among the people. . . . Nine tenths of the illustrations we see placarded in railway waiting rooms, hotels, and other places of public resort are the product of lithography."[24] Mark Twain put it even better, in his novel *A Connecticut Yankee in King Arthur's Court*. The Yankee finds that one of the things he misses most is the chromolithograph. "I had been used to chromos for years, and I saw now that, without my suspecting it, a passion for art had got worked into the fabric of my being, and was become part of me." He continues: "In our house in East Hartford, all unpretending as it was, you couldn't go into a room but you would find an insurance-chromo, or at least a three-colour God-Bless-Our-Home over the door; and in the parlour we had nine."[25]

Some intellectuals, worried about the erosion of their prestige as gate-keepers of Culture, denounced chromolithography. Edwin Lawrence Godkin, editor of the *Nation,* wrote in 1874 that chromos "diffused in the community a kind of smattering of all sorts of knowledge, a taste for 'art' — that is, a desire to see and own pictures — which, taken together, pass with a large body of slen-derly-equipped persons as 'culture,' and give them an unprecedented self-confi-dence in dealing with all the problems of life, and raise them in their own minds to a plane on which they see nothing higher, greater, or better than themselves." He went on to deprecate America as "a chromo civilization." Charles Congdon, in the *North American Review* in 1884, called his an age of "over-illustration," and worried about "the intellectual indolence that a habit of indulgence in mere picture-gazing" would bring.[26]

Others worried about the spread of illustrated books, increasingly com-mon around the turn of the century. The ease of reproducing photographs in books meant that the author had less control; they feared that the illustrator would sway the reader more than the author, that illustrations forced people to form certain images in their mind. One letter to the editor asked, "Are they try-

Advertisements were everywhere in the nineteenth-century city. Giant multipart chromolithographs made these advertisements brighter than ever.

ing to pauperize our imagination, or do they think the public hasn't any?"[27] Another complained that illustrations made a book or magazine into "a mere picture album," that they subverted books from an intellectual exercise into a commodity whose main purpose was to look pretty.[28] A 1911 editorial in *Harper's Weekly* complained: "We can't see the ideas for the illustrations. Our world is simply flooded with them. They lurk in almost every form of printed matter." Illustrations, the editorial feared, had become a "mental drug. . . . A young mind, overfed pictorially, will scarcely be likely to do any original thinking."[29] The *Nation* criticized those who thought that "the growing aversion to reading, and the increasing fondness for labor-saving and the thought-saving graphic representation" was a sign of progress — not, as the *Nation* thought, a "distinct reversion to barbarism."[30]

PICTURES EVERYWHERE

Pictures were everywhere, in books, magazines, newspapers, on the inside walls in houses and the outside walls of buildings. The 1880s and 1890s were, as the historian Neil Harris puts it, "a visual age."[31] Not only pictures but also electric lighting brought a new visual excitement to cities, and a new invention, the movies, provided another dimension to pictorialism. (See MOVIES.) People had learned to use images, and came to enjoy and expect them.

In the last decades of the nineteenth century and the first decades of the twentieth, pictures of all sorts found new uses in politics and government, in business, and in science and technology. And most important, they found new personal uses. Technology that made it easier to take pictures emerged quickly in the last half of the nineteenth century. Dry plates, invented in 1853, and handier to use than the earlier wet plate process, were the first step. In 1871 Richard Leach Maddox invented the gelatin dry plate, which, with improvements over the next few years, made photography much simpler.

One of the first Kodak box cameras, introduced in 1888. The Kodak was the first cheap, easy-to-use camera. Kodak's motto was "You press the button, we do the rest."

In the last twenty years of the nineteenth century, photography truly became a popular activity, a form of mass entertainment. Men and women alike were taken with the new hobby. Historians speak of the democratization of photography: in 1872 some 50 million photographs were made. Factory-prepared film — after 1887 long strips of celluloid replaced glass plates — made it easy for amateurs to take photographs. The great breakthrough was George Eastman's Kodak camera, introduced in 1888. "You press the button, we do the rest" was the

The composite photograph, a fad at the turn of the century, was a way of using photography to statistically "average" groups of people — physiological types, classes, residents of particular cities, or members of political groups — to capture what was thought to be their essential visual qualities. The photographs of members of a group were superimposed one on top of the other; photography itself became an information-processing machine. Lewis Hines took this composite picture of girls employed in a cotton mill in 1913.

An extensive system of images controlled Philadelphia's Baldwin Locomotive Works in the late nineteenth century. It included:

- the order, in the Specification Book;
- a preliminary elevation of the engine, in two-inch scale, called an Erecting Drawing;
- a collection of Card Books, which included sets of all drawings for each component of a locomotive, from which the draftsmen copied details (one of the cards is shown here);
- the Law Books that told the draftsmen general guidelines on drawing new cards, general rules for materials strength, and details about what each machine on the floor could do: maximum sizes, accuracy, and so forth;
- lists of cards needed, which were sent to each foreman, so he would know what plans and cards to requisition.

In addition, there were printed rules and regulations, for example, "Instructions to Foremen" and "Time-keeping and Pay Regulations," and physical images like foundry patterns and gauges. A dozen kinds of images provided control over workers and work.

Kodak marketing slogan, and it was pretty close to true. Each camera came pre-loaded with film for one hundred pictures, after which the owner sent it back to the factory for developing. Kodak had sales of $2.3 million in 1899, and $9.7 million in 1909.

The rise of the picture postcard in the 1890s contributed to the increased personal use of photographs. Though some decried the picture postcard as "vulgar pictorialism," because people sent postcards or snapshots instead of writing letters, they were incredibly popular. Starting in 1906, Kodak would develop pictures directly into postcards for only a few cents. In 1903 some 800 million postcards were mailed in the United States. Three years later, at the height of the postcard craze, over 1.2 billion were sent.

Cameras seemed to be everywhere, even where they weren't wanted. In the 1890s photographs of actors, actresses, and the socially prominent started to show up in gossip columns. Before long, celebrities complained. The *New York Times* wrote disapprovingly in 1902 about "Kodakers" lying in wait to snap pictures.

Photography and printed photographs played a key role in social reform. Jacob Riis's *How the Other Half Lives: Studies among the Tenements in New York*, a classic of reform literature published in 1890, was the first American book to use a large number of halftones. Riis intended his pictures to convince his audiences of the need for change; they were a means of communication. It was a Progressive movement belief that to see is to know, and to know is to act. Sarah Greenough, a historian of photography, writes:

> Riis is typical of the many turn-of-the-century crusaders who used photography as a tool to provide visual proof for their ideas. . . . For them photography was an empirical tool, and they used it as they would have used any other mechanical aid, to provide data to augment their spoken and written words, their charts and statistics. Photography became a way for these men and women to organize, classify, symbolize, and perhaps most important, understand issues such as urban growth, ethnic diversity, cultural change, and industrialization, which otherwise were unknown, fearsome, and seemingly out of control.[32]

Riis's images, and those of other social reformers, were widely published. Photographs, or rather their halftone reproductions, made the foul conditions of sweatshop and tenement come to life. They demanded change.

Images played a major role in propaganda. Photography was the key to modern advertising, starting in the early twentieth century. Advertising photographers went to work making posters during World War I, creating a war of posters which exhorted patriotism, made graphic the enemy's atrocities, and sold bonds. The persuasive power of images continued after the war, both in advertising and in the posters that managers hung in factories to suggest good work practices and proper behavior. During the Great Depression, the U.S. government found the power of photography particularly valuable in demonstrating the need for federal programs, and their successes. The Farm Security Administration and the Federal Arts Project built on the legacy of Riis, and a long line of documentary photographers followed them. Governments used the power of photography for organization and classification. In France, Alphonse Bertillon photographed 100,000 criminals and arranged their images in a complex filing system. Fingerprint files, another way of capturing people's images, were started in several countries.

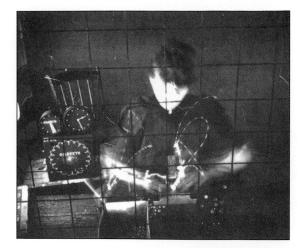

One of the most interesting uses of photography for business purposes is illustrated by the pictures taken by Frank Gilbreth, one of the founders of the field of scientific management. Gilbreth took thousands of stereo pictures in his attempt to find "the one best way" to do a job. He thought that by using pictures he could determine scientifically the exact nature and order of the movements the worker should make to work as efficiently as possible.

Gilbreth made this stereo image (1917) by attaching lights to the worker's hands; when photographed in near dark, her hand motions show up as streaks. He put a grid in front of her and clocks next to her to make it easier for him to analyze her motions. From these pictures, and from models he built using them, Gilbreth came up with new ways to do the job.

Businesses, too, found pictures useful. Like governments, businesses used photography and other images to help run their operations. They also quickly discovered ways to use the "truth" of photography and the public's quick recognition of images as trademarks in their advertising. The use of pictures in businesses was especially important in manufacturing enterprises. Technology is hard to describe in words; pictures are necessary. Technical drawings have a long history dating back to a Renaissance tradition of "machine books" that demonstrated the technical prowess of engineers and "manuals" that captured the skills of miners, dyers, and builders. Starting in the Enlightenment, pictures of technology and industry were featured in encyclopedias. Pictures in manuals and instruction books were a key element in teaching about new machines.

Engineers made extensive use of images in their work. Mechanical drawing not too different from that used today began in the late eighteenth century. By 1835 Charles Babbage, a British scientist, could write that "the power of making mechanical drawings [is] essentially requisite" for an engineer.[33] Drawings served as a first step in design. As the engineer Ferdinand Redtenbacher put it in 1852: "A machine that has been drawn is like an ideal realization of it, but in a material that costs little and is easier to handle than iron or steel. [It can be] conveniently submitted to the severest criticism."[34]

Drawings also served to control the process of production. By means of drawings, writes Peter Jeffrey Booker, a historian of engineering drawing, "the measurements and proportions of all the parts can be so sharply and definitely determined from the beginning that when it comes to manufacture it is only necessary to imitate in the materials used for construction exactly what is shown in the drawing."[35] Historian Eugene Ferguson suggests that drawings "changed radically the balance of power between managers and workers," shifting the locus of decision-making from the shop floor to the drafting room.[36] Blueprints let managers break the work down into separate pieces for separate workers. This made possible an increase in speed, scale and economy of production, and all the other advantages Adam Smith outlined in his analysis of the division of labor. It also made possible the planning of projects that are simply too big and complex for a single craftsperson to make alone.

It was outside the factory, in advertising, that pictures found their greatest business use. "When the history of advertising is written the present will be known as the 'picture period'," wrote one advertiser in 1896.[37] One sort of image found especially wide use: the trademark. Trademarks were a condensation of an image, a shorthand way of advertising, an icon that people could remember. Textile manufacturers had long wrapped their cloth in labels with pictures, but now manufacturers of all sorts of products began to create brand names and images, and to put them not just on their products, but in their advertisements, on their stationery, and on their delivery wagons and trucks. Trademark law came of age at the end of the nineteenth century as many companies sued to protect the symbols that represented them. Supreme Court Justice Felix Frankfurter summed up the legal view of the value of trademarks in a 1941 decision: "The protection of trade-marks is the law's recognition of the psychological function of symbols. If it is true that we live by symbols, it is no less true that we purchase goods by them."[38]

Advertising agencies began to build large art departments. In 1894 only about 30 percent of advertisements contained illustrations. By 1919 some 90 percent did. The aim of modern commercial art, according to a 1928 book, *Packages That Sell*, "is to convey the idea intended as quickly as possible."[39] It was the art of information, or at least the art of persuasion.

The middle years of the twentieth century saw continuous technological advances in photography and printing. Film gained greater sensitivity, less graininess, and better color accuracy. (The first commercial color film was introduced in 1907, the first color roll film in 1942.) Cameras improved, too. Better lenses allowed shorter exposures. A typical lens in 1908 was f6.8; just thirty years later a good camera had an f2.8 lens. Average exposures went from $\frac{1}{25}$ of a second to as short as $\frac{1}{500}$ of a second.

Flash powder, for night and indoor shots, had been introduced in the 1880s; the electric flashbulb was introduced in 1929, making night photography and high-speed photography much more convenient. The first commercially successful 35-mm camera, the Leica, was produced in 1924. The photoelectric exposure meter was introduced in 1932. The Polaroid instant camera, invented by Edwin Land, was first marketed in 1946. Electronics found their way into cameras, just as they found their way into other tools. The first microprocessor-controlled automatic exposure system was introduced by Canon in 1976. Automatic electronic focusing, invented by Honeywell, was introduced by Konica in 1978.

These improvements in photography were accompanied by advances in printing. New printing tech-

The first businesses to use photographs on ID badges were the railroads, starting in 1861. Employee numbering schemes came later.

Trademarks are instantly recognizable, the condensation of a firm's reputation and products into a single simple image. Quaker Oats was one of the first companies to advertise a brand name directly to the consumer. The company had figured out how to make oatmeal cereal in enormous quantity by machine, but no one wanted to buy it. (People thought oats were for horses!) So Henry P. Crowell, the company president, invented a trademark — the Quaker — and made it a household image. He also added many of the gimmicks of the modern advertiser, including prizes and box-top premiums. Quaker Oats advertisements and the box it came in featured the trademark image.

niques produced photographs of better quality, and exposed new graphic forms to popular acclaim. Photojournalism found an outlet in magazines such as *Life*. Newspapers, too, used more and more pictures, and more color. *Superman,* the first real comic book, was published in 1938 (previous comic books were compilations of comic strips from newspapers); by 1943 sales of comic books had hit 18 million copies a month. The visual excitement of the times was also found in moving pictures and on TV. (See MOVIES and TELEVISION.)

ELECTRONIC PICTURES

The next revolution in picture making came when images started to go electronic. People demanded pictures with their news, but it took at least twenty-four hours to send photographs across the country by airplane. Why not send them over the telephone wires, like the stories they accompanied? One newspaper put the problem this way in 1898:

> Editors and publishers are fully conscious of the public craving for illustrations, but it is difficult to meet it because the methods of producing them are too slow to compete with the word-pictures, which can be flashed over the telegraph wires . . . and printed long before an artist has made a sketch to illustrate the same fact. But suppose it were possible to transmit the picture over the wires with the same facility as we now transmit the words. . . . What a revolution it would effect in the methods of giving news to the public.[40]

As far back as 1843 people had tried sending pictures over telegraph wires. None were technically and commercially successful, able to provide the quality people had come to expect from news photos. American Telephone and Telegraph established its Telephoto service in 1924, but abandoned it in 1933 after spending almost $3 million. The first successful combination of images and electronics came in the 1930s, when the Associated Press established its Wire-

Ivan Sutherland developed one of the first computer-aided design programs at MIT's Lincoln Labs. An engineer used the program to make preliminary drawings and the computer would complete the drawing, eliminating many intermediate drawing steps.

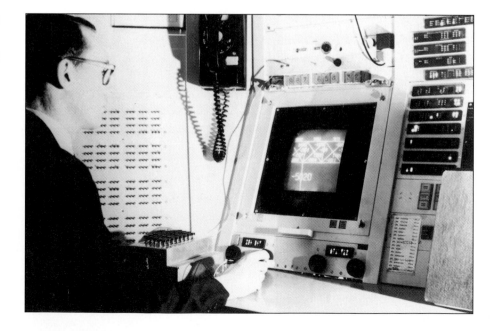

photo network. The AP, building on new work from Bell Labs and overcoming considerable opposition from those who felt that the multimillion-dollar investment was too high for an experiment, transmitted news pictures starting in 1935. It was an immediate success. (See BEYOND TELEPHONES.)

The ability to convert pictures to electrical signals was just the first step. Starting in the 1950s, computers ushered in new ways of constructing, manipulating, and using images. Engineering drawing left the drawing board for the computer screen. Photographs made digital could be manipulated as never before. They could be transmitted over phone lines as easily as voices; they could be taken by satellites circling Mars and seen immediately on Earth. Images became a part of the great digital revolution.

The first computers used teletypes for output, and so were forced to communicate in words. But EDSAC, at Cambridge University, and Whirlwind, at MIT, added graphic displays, and transmitting pictures became possible. In 1951, not long after it began operation, programmers used the Whirlwind to display missile trajectories and to calculate, in real time, the trajectory of a bouncing ball. One of Whirlwind's main purposes was to track incoming airplanes, which were shown on a cathode-ray tube map, with a blip indicating each airplane and with letters identifying it. A light pen, invented by Robert Everett, an engineer on the project, allowed a user to touch a dot indicating an airplane to get more information. Touching a dot and typing the letter *T* would designate it as a target. SAGE, the air defense computer modeled on Whirlwind, also had interactive graphics. So did the TX-2, at MIT's Lincoln Laboratory, in the early 1960s. These graphics were used, among other things, for mapping land use data. (See COMPUTERS.)

The Whirlwind and SAGE graphics were computer generated. In the late 1950s and early 1960s computer scientists at several institutions came up with ways to use the computer as a drawing machine. Ivan Sutherland, using MIT's Lincoln Laboratory TX-2, was the first to produce pictures with a computer drawing program. His 1962 Sketchpad program could draw lines and circles, and could treat groups of lines as objects, keeping them together, and using them to create new objects. Many computer scientists were inspired by a film that Sutherland made of Sketchpad in operation. Among them was a group at the ITEK Corporation, which purchased the second PDP-1 that Digital Equipment Corporation built as the basis for its Electronic Drafting Machine.

In 1959 a joint General Motors/IBM group headed by Robert Cortney started to work on a computer system for automotive engineers. They unveiled DAC-1, for Design Augmentation by Computers, in 1964. This program could rotate on the computer screen 3-D images that were described by formulas or read by a digitizing camera. The first computer-designed automobile part was the trunk lid for the 1965 Cadillac. In 1966 the *Wall Street Journal* quoted an expert: "Computer graphics will permit the designer to create the shape of an automobile body, a ship's hull, an airplane fuselage, or a tobacco pipe with consummate ease. The computer will behave like a skilled, sympathetic and experienced pattern-maker . . . or like a super-sculptor, working from meager information furnished by the designer at the computer console."[41] It would be many years before this dream would come true. (See COMPUTERS.)

These early computer graphics technologies were very expensive and

One way to create computer images that look real is by ray tracing, a technique invented in the early 1980s. Ray tracing is just what it sounds like: the computer traces thousands of rays of light as they interact with imaginary objects and come to the "eye" of the computer screen. (Actually, the rays are traced backward, starting from the eye. That way, only the ones that end up in a particular place actually need be traced.) This takes an enormous amount of calculating. To show a simple sphere, for example, takes about 100 million calculations. In 1985, it took an hour on a large computer. Today, on a fast workstation, it can be done in "real time," allowing images to be calculated as they are moved about on the screen.

slow, but improvements came quickly. Throughout the 1960s more powerful computers, including specialized graphics hardware, and new software brought breakthroughs in computer graphics. Cheaper memory helped make possible higher resolution and color.

Once computer graphics got to be reasonably priced, it found new uses everywhere. Computers were used to create computer art and computer movies. Graphic presentations of statistical, geographical, and scientific data proved to be more useful than numerical presentation. And computers were used to manipulate photographic images. Graphics became the new frontier of computers. Artists used the computer as a new tool. They used computers to create "realistic" images — that is, to re-create within the computer what goes on in the real world of light and objects — and as a sketchpad, a high-tech easel. Scientists found that pictures created by the computer were often the best way to visualize their data.

Not only could the computer present data in graphic form; it could also manipulate the data, an application called computer-aided engineering. A bridge truss could be drawn on the screen and "tested" by applying a weight; the mathematical calculations of the stresses on the structures could be shown by changing colors. Airplanes could be "flown" on the screen to test their aerodynamics.

Engineers and architects use computers to compose and test their designs on the screen before they are actually built. Left and center, two- and three-dimensional architectural plans. Right, a color diagram that shows stress on a mechanical part.

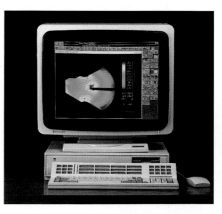

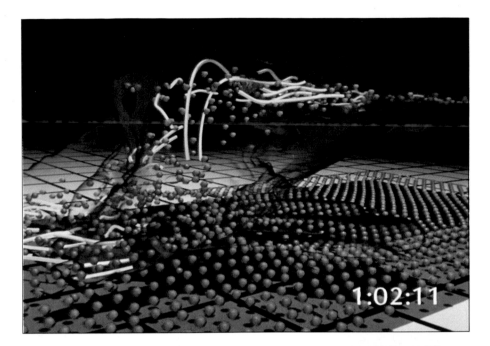

"Visualization," taking reams of data and converting them into a picture that allows a scientist to see the unseeable, is the latest trend in science. Shown here are is a computer model of a severe storm. Orange dots show rising air, blue dots falling air; yellow streamers trace the path of a few of the particles. Below is a "map" of the distribution of galaxies and clusters of galaxies in one region of the universe.

(The calculations required to determine and graphically display fluid dynamics data pushed the limits of supercomputers until the late 1970s, when the Cray-1 was able to solve some of these problems.) Programs can represent data in graphic images, making them easier to understand. The first use was the most obvious one: statistics. Computers could plot charts faster and more accurately than any person. Next came computerized maps: it made sense

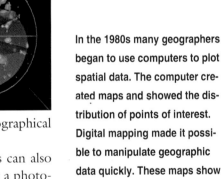

for the computer to plot maps from data, and to represent data in geographical form — what came to be called Geographic Information Systems.

In addition to creating and manipulating images, computers can also modify images. Digital photography starts with a digital image, either a photograph scanned to convert it into a pattern of numbers that represents the color of each of thousands or millions of points, or a photograph taken by a digital camera, like a still video camera. An all-electronic camera — the MAVICA — was introduced by Sony in 1982. Versions of these cameras introduced in the

In the 1980s many geographers began to use computers to plot spatial data. The computer created maps and showed the distribution of points of interest. Digital mapping made it possible to manipulate geographic data quickly. These maps show the predicted spread of gypsy moths, taking into account distance from earlier infestations and temperature.

early 1980s had some 280,000 pixel elements — not enough to compete with the high resolution of a film camera. A decade later improved versions began to find use among newspaper and wire service photographers, who needed to transmit their photography quickly over phone lines.

It's easy for a computer to change the colors of the image, replacing each with a different shade, for example, for color correction. Or images can be sharpened by comparing each point with the points around it, calculating where the changes are sharpest, and altering the colors to highlight the differences. The scale of colors can be stretched, using a technique called gray scale transformation, which remaps a limit-

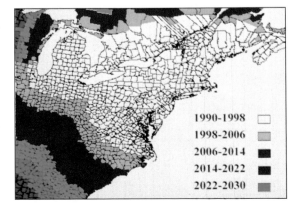

1990-1998
1998-2006
2006-2014
2014-2022
2022-2030

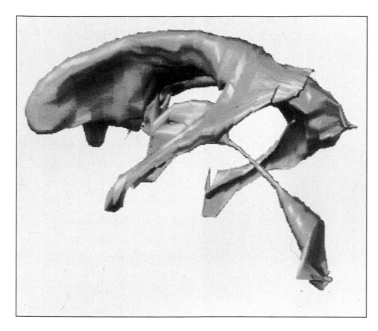

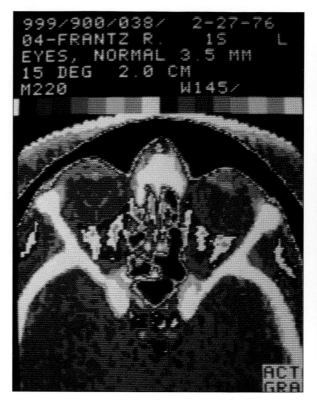

This image shows a three-dimensional representation of the ventricular system of the human brain. A medical artist used a computer to construct this model from a series of frontal sections of a brain.

BIT-MAPPED
GRAPHIC

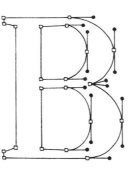

VECTOR
GRAPHIC

Computer painting programs manipulate dots on the screen. These programs use bit-mapped images; the artist indicates the place for the dots and their pattern. The computer helps by providing tools that remember patterns or act on the existing dots on the screen.

"Drawing" programs are different from painting programs. They represent objects on the screen as vectors, lines represented by mathematical formulas. A common system uses Bezier functions to represent curves by beginning and end points and by control points along the way. These control points exert influence on the line, pulling it in their direction. This makes it easy to manipulate the shape by moving the control points, and it also means that the shape is independent of the resolution of the screen. If the design is to be printed out on a very high resolution printer, for example, the computer can calculate the exact location of the curve to whatever level of detail is necessary.

ed range of grays to a range that stretches all the way from black to white, making it easier to distinguish details of the image. (This technique is commonly used on satellite pictures.) Computers make possible photographic manipulation by treating the image as digital data. But just as computer manipulation of photographs can make them clearer and more useful, it can also be used to falsify them.

The technology developed for NASA and the movies has begun to find its way into the home. There were 250 million cameras in the United States in 1991, used to take billions of photographs a year. Most of those photographs are printed using silver-based chemistry not too different from that invented a century and a half ago. But soon much photography will be digitized. Digital cameras will find wider use. So too will the PhotoCD, a compact disk that holds one hundred photos, and can also store sound, graphics, and text. The PhotoCD was introduced by Kodak in 1992 in an attempt to keep photography from going completely digital, eliminating the film market. A PhotoCD is taken with a regular camera. Instead of (or in addition to) being printed, the image is scanned, digitized, and stored at high resolution on a PhotoCD using the same technology a regular CD uses to store digitized music. (See RECORDED SOUND.) The pictures can be viewed on a television screen or computer monitor, manipulated like any digital data, sent over phone lines, and printed when needed.

When images become digital data, they merge into the vast digital sea, capable of infinite transformation. This means, sometimes, that they should be mistrusted; it's easier and easier to alter digitized images. But they are also easier to use: sometimes graphics can make information much simpler to grasp than can words. Pictures are everywhere in our world, and have been everywhere for at least a century. In 1911 a magazine editor complained, "Our world is flooded with them."[42] It still is, more than ever.

A cross section of the brain, produced in 1974 by Dr. Robert S. Ledley of Georgetown University on the first full-body computer tomography scanner. Computerized medical imaging is one of the most important uses of computer technology in medicine. The computer takes the information from many x-ray images that record the density of the brain from many directions, calculates the density at each point, and displays it as a cross section or as a three-dimensional image.

FOR FURTHER READING

A good recent summary of the history of photography is Sarah Greenough et al., *On the Art of Fixing a Shadow: One Hundred and Fifty Years of Photography* (1989). Thoughtful suggestions about the meaning of photography can be found in Jonathan Crary, *Techniques of the Observer: On Vision and Modernity in the Nineteenth Century* (1990); and Alan Trachtenberg, *Reading American Photographs: Images as History from Mathew Brady to Walker Evans* (1989).

A helpful source for understanding the changing uses of pictures in America is a classic, Robert Taft, *Photography and the American Scene: A Social History, 1839–1889* (1938; reprint 1964). See also Richard Rudisill, *Mirror Image: The Influence of the Daguerreotype on American Society* (1971); Elizabeth Lindquist-Cock, *Influence of Photography on American Landscape Painting* (1977); and Neil Harris, "Pictorial Perils: The Rise of American Illustration," and "Iconography and Intellectual History: The Halftone Effect," both in his *Cultural Excursions: Marketing Appetites and Tastes in Modern America* (1990). On pictures in journalism, see Michael L. Carlebach, *The Origins of Photojournalism in America* (1992).

The history of chromolithography is covered in Peter C. Marzio, *The Democratic Art: Pictures for a Nineteenth-Century America: Chromolithography, 1840–1900* (1979).

There is no good history of computer graphics. A good introduction to the techniques and a brief history can be found in *Computer Images,* part of Time-Life Books' *Understanding Computers* series (1986); and George H. Stalker and John Simon,

"Some Matters at the Heart of Computer Graphics: Why They Are So and Some of the Implications of Their Being So," in *From Sand to Circuits and Other Inquiries,* ed. John J. Simon, Jr. (1986). A more technical introduction is Jim Clark, "Roots and Branches of 3-D," *BYTE* (May 1992): 153–164; see also the other articles on computer graphics in that same issue.

The history of images in technology is found in a beautiful book by Ken Baynes and Francis Pugh, *Art of the Engineer* (1981); and in Ralph Greenhill, *Engineer's Witness* (1985). For more detail, see Peter Jeffrey Booker, *A History of Engineering Drawing* (1963); and Eugene S. Ferguson, *Engineering and the Mind's Eye* (1992). For images in science, see the essays in Michael Lynch and Steve Woolgar, eds., *Representation in Scientific Practice* (1990). For the use of computer imagery in science, see Richard Mark Friedhoff, *Visualization: The Second Computer Revolution* (1991).

For interesting thoughts on digital photography and the digital manipulation of images, see William J. Mitchell, *The Reconfigured Eye: Visual Truth in the Post-Photographic Era* (1992).

NOTES

1. Quoted in Robert Taft, *Photography and the American Scene: A Social History, 1839–1889* (1938; reprint 1964), p. 3.

2. Quoted in Richard Rudisill, *Mirror Image: The Influence of the Daguerreotype on American Society* (1971), p. 54.

3. Rudisill, *Mirror Image*, p. 240.

4. T. S. Arthur, "American Characteristics: The Daguerreotypist," *Godey's Lady's Book* (May 1849): 352; quoted in Rudisill, *Mirror Image*, p. 70.

5. Rudolph Arnheim, *Art and Visual Perception* (1974), p. 284.

6. John Armes, *On Video* (1988), p. 16.

7. John Berger, *Ways of Seeing* (1972), p. 48.

8. Taft, *Photography and the American Scene*, p. 68.

9. Hermann von Helmholtz, *Handbook of Physiological Optics*, vol. 3, trans. George T. Ladd (1962), p. 303; quoted in Jonathan Crary, *Techniques of the Observer: On Vision and Modernity in the Nineteenth Century* (1990), p. 124.

10. Quoted in Sarah Greenough et al., *On the Art of Fixing a Shadow: One Hundred and Fifty Years of Photography* (1989), p. 27.

11. Quoted in Elizabeth Lindquist-Cock, *The Influence of Photography on American Landscape Painting, 1839–1880* (1977), p. 27.

12. Lindquist-Cock, *Influence of Photography*, p. 45.

13. Quoted in Heinrich Schwartz, *Art and Photography: Forerunners and Influences* (1985), p. 111.

14. Neil Harris, "Iconography and Intellectual History: The Halftone Effect," in *Cultural Excursions: Marketing Appetites and Cultural Tastes in Modern America* (1990), p. 307.

15. Taft, *Photography and the American Scene*, p. 449.

16. Quoted in Taft, *Photography and the American Scene*, p. 449.

17. Quoted in Daniel Boorstin, *The Image or What Happened to the American Dream* (1962), p. 125.

18. Quoted in Edgar de Noailles Mayhew and Minor Myers, Jr., *A Documentary History of American Interiors from the Colonial Era to 1915* (1980), p. 188.

19. Peter C. Marzio, *The Democratic Art: An Exhibition on the History of Chromolithography in America, 1840–1900* (1979).

20. Quoted in Marzio, *The Democratic Art: An Exhibition*, p. 25.

21. Catharine Beecher and Harriet Beecher Stowe, *The American Woman's Home* (1869), pp. 93–94.

22. Quoted in Marzio, *The Democratic Art: An Exhibition*, pp. 53–54.

23. Quoted in Marzio, *The Democratic Art: An Exhibition*, p. 65.

24. D. J. Kenny, *Illustrated Cincinnati: A Pictorial Handbook of the Queen City* (1875), p. 147; quoted in Peter C. Marzio, *The Democratic Art: Chromolithography, 1840–1900 — Pictures for a Nineteenth-Century America* (1979), p. 131.

25. Mark Twain, *A Connecticut Yankee in King Arthur's Court* (1889; reprint 1986), p. 79.

26. Edwin Lawrence Godkin, *Nation*, September 24, 1874; quoted in Marzio, *The Democratic Art: Chromolithography 1840–1900*, p. 1. Congdon quoted in Neil Harris, *The Land of Contrasts, 1880–1901* (1970), p. 8.

27. Katherine Gordon Hyle to the editor, *New York Times*, November 5, 1904; quoted in Neil Harris, "Pictorial Perils: The Rise of American Illustration," in *Cultural Excursions*, p. 340.

28. "The Contributors' Club," *Atlantic Monthly* (January 1904): 137; quoted in Harris, "Pictorial Perils," p. 341.

29. "Over-Illustration," *Harper's Weekly*, July 29, 1911, p. 6; quoted in Harris, "Iconography and Intellectual History," p. 313.

30. [Rollo Ogden,] "Knowledge on Sight," *Nation*, July 20, 1893: 306–307; quoted in Harris, "Iconography and Intellectual History," p. 342.

31. Harris, *Land of Contrasts*, p. 7.

32. Greenough et al., *On the Art of Fixing a Shadow*, p. 137.

33. Charles Babbage, *On the Economy of Machinery and Manufactures* (1835); quoted in Ken Baynes and Francis Pugh, *Art of the Engineer* (1981), p. 13.

34. Ferdinand Redtenbacher, *Prinzipien der Mechanik und des Maschinenbaues* (1852); quoted (and translated) in Peter Jeffrey Booker, *A History of Engineering Drawing* (1963), pp. 187–188.

35. Booker, *History of Engineering Drawing*, p. 188.

36. Eugene S. Ferguson, *Engineering and the Mind's Eye* (1992), p. 101.

37. Quoted in Harris, *Land of Contrasts*, p. 8.

38. Quoted in Arthur J. Pulos, *The American Design Adventure, 1940–1975* (1990), p. 271.

39. Richard B. Franken, *Packages That Sell* (1928), p. 12.

40. *Penrose's Pictorial Annual* (1898); quoted in Peter C. Marzio, *Men and Machines of American Journalism* (1973), p. 114.

41. Steven Coons, quoted in "Electronic Sketching: Engineers Focus Light on Screen to Design Visually via Computer," *Wall Street Journal*, October 24, 1966; quoted in H. Chasen, "Historical Highlights of Interactive Computer Graphics," *Mechanical Engineering* (November 1981): 32–41.

42. "Over-Illustration," *Harper's Weekly*, July 29, 1911, p. 6; quoted in Harris, "Iconography and Intellectual History," p. 313.

THE TELEGRAPH.

AL STATION.

Electrical communications originated with the telegraph. Invented by Samuel F. B. Morse in the 1830s, within a few decades telegraph lines crisscrossed the continents and reached around the world. The telegraph laid the technological, business, and cultural foundations for the wonders of communications to follow.

COMMUNICATION
TELEGRAPH

IN 1837 THE U.S. SENATE CALLED FOR PROPOSALS to establish a nationwide telegraph system. What the senators had in mind was a visual telegraph, a gigantic semaphore system that used a series of giant towers holding huge wooden indicators. The towers were built within sight of one another. To relay a message, the operator in each tower read the position of the indicators on the previous tower and changed the indicators on his tower to match. This procedure was repeated down the line.

This sort of visual telegraph had been conveying messages across France since the 1790s. By the 1840s there were over 3,000 miles of visual telegraph lines in France, and over 500 towers. A message could be sent eighty miles in under three minutes. The system was expensive and had a limited capacity, but its success showed that there was a demand for high-speed communications. That demand increased as commerce increased, and as military and political activity heated up. (One of the main users of the French system was the national lottery, which used it to send winning numbers across the country.) At the time the Senate issued its call, there were several small visual telegraph systems in the United States, used to send word of ships' arrivals from ports to downtown merchants who were eager for news of incoming cargo, and willing to pay for that information.

Samuel Morse submitted a proposal to the Senate. But his proposal was not for a visual telegraph. Rather, he proposed to build a telegraph system that used electricity to relay messages — something new and different. After a good deal of lobbying, Morse won the government's support. His electromagnetic telegraph would be the basis for the development of modern communications technology.

INVENTING THE TELEGRAPH

Electricity began to look like a solution to the communications conundrum in the second half of the eighteenth century, almost as soon as scientists began to experiment with it. They realized that electricity moved through wires very quickly, almost instantaneously. If you could encode your message in the electricity fed into one end of a wire, and then retrieve it at the other end, you

Joseph Henry published this drawing of his electromagnetic signaling system in *Silliman's Journal* in 1831. It was connected through more than a mile of wire to cable. When the current was turned on, the magnet would pull the bar toward it, ringing the bell.

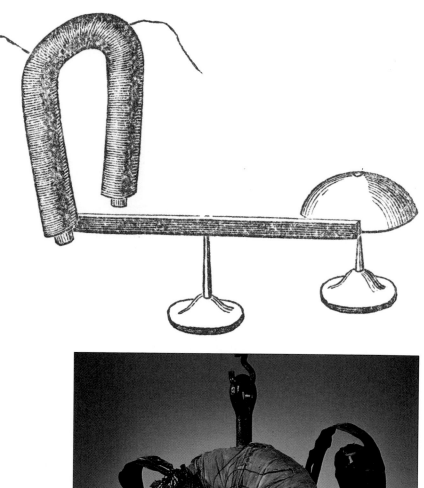

Henry experimented with increasing the power of electromagnets in order to better understand electromagnetism. His most powerful magnet could lift 2,300 pounds.

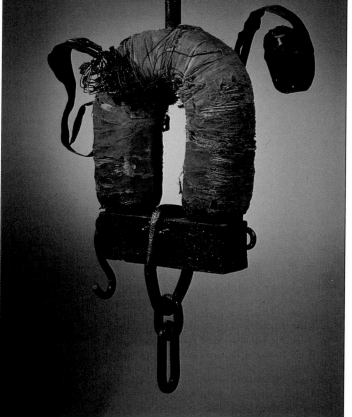

had an electrical communications system. The idea was easy. But to make it work in a practical way was to take many years.

A form of electrical telegraph was a common feature of many popular science demonstrations in the second half of the eighteenth century. The earliest ones — suggested as early as 1753 — used static electricity, which could produce sparks or move pith balls at a distance. Tiberius Cavallo, one of many scientists who undertook electrical experiments, noted that "by sending a number of sparks at different intervals of time according to a settled plan, any sort of intelligence might be conveyed instantaneously."[1] Others followed with improved static electric systems — one of them, at a Long Island, New York, race track, sent messages over several miles of wire — but these electrical message systems never became more than a toy, a parlor game. This was in part because of the intrinsic limitations of static electricity, and in part because most scientists were more interested in understanding the phenomenon and demonstrating it to the public than in applying it commercially.

To make a practical system required improvements on both the sending and receiving ends. Improvements in batteries helped make the sending side of the telegraph possible. Scientists needed better batteries for their own experiments, and so they experimented with new materials and arrangements, attempting to increase battery power and life span. In 1800 Alessandro Volta, of Pavia University in Italy, invented the "voltaic pile," or chemical battery. It used a row of disks of zinc and silver, separated by felt disks soaked in brine, to produce a continuous source of electricity. In 1836 John Frederic Daniell was able to demonstrate an improvement he called a constant battery, one that would put out a good amount of power continuously and would last more than a few hours. This and other improved batteries were a key technology in the development of the telegraph.

Meanwhile, advances in understanding electromagnetism led to improvements on the receiving end. In 1819, in Denmark, Hans Christian Oersted discovered that electricity running through a wire would deflect a nearby compass needle, and deduced that electricity created a magnetic field. Other scientists found ways to make the field stronger. In 1825 William Sturgeon, in England, discovered that a piece of iron bent into a horseshoe shape and wrapped with the wire conducting electricity would form a powerful magnet. Joseph Henry, an American scientist, found that he could increase the power of this electromagnet by insulating the conducting wire, and by using many small coils rather than a single coil that covered the entire horseshoe. Henry noted in a paper announcing his discoveries that they would be useful in making a telegraph. He even set up a demonstration, building a device that used an electromagnet to ring a bell separated from the battery by over a mile of wire. But his interests were scientific, not practical, and he was content to show his invention to his classes at the Albany Academy. He didn't pursue practical applications.

Electric telegraph systems were a staple at the well-attended scientific lectures of the day. People who kept up-to-date in science knew that an electrical telegraph was possible, but they realized that there were many practical and financial problems. It's a long way from scientific demonstration to money-making proposition. (Not everyone thought an electromagnetic telegraph would work. In 1825 Peter Barlow, of the Royal Military Academy in England, published the wrong answer to the question of how quickly the electricity flowing through a wire lost power, "proving" to his satisfaction that an electrical telegraph of more than a few hundred feet was impossible.)

Samuel Morse, in New York City, was one of the many inventors who played with electrical telegraphy. Morse, born in 1791, had attended Yale University, where he studied liberal arts and the sciences, and enjoyed lectures on electricity. Toward the end of his college days he took up painting. Upon graduating, Morse went to Europe to study with Washington Allston and Benjamin West, the most famous American painters of the day. He returned to the United States in 1815, hoping to find fame and fortune as an artist. But his specialty was historical paintings, which were going out of fashion, and he was unable to make a living selling them. Instead, he became an itinerant portrait painter and salesman for a fire engine pump he and his brother had invented. Over the course of the next twenty years, Morse tried to make his living as a painter. In 1835 he was appointed professor of "the literature of the arts of design" at New York University. But he despaired of ever earning much by his painting and teaching.

Morse turned instead to inventing. Inventing a telegraph, he thought, would earn him enough money so that he would be able to return to painting, and to paint what he wanted. This was not a practical scheme, but Morse was not a practical man. He was one of the best artists in the country but not particularly skilled as an inventor or a scientist. Neither was he a talented mechanic or an accomplished commercializer. His principal qualification was that he combined some of all of these talents, and was able to bring together the right people to work for him. He was also able to use his personal and political connections to gain first government and then commercial support for his work. He had no qualms about claiming more credit than was his due. Like many others of his day, he believed in the idea of the great inventor and began to see himself as one. (The telegraph would indeed make Morse wealthy, but he never returned to painting.)

Morse visualized the basic elements of an electric telegraph in 1832, on his return from Europe aboard the *Sully*. The subject of the French physicist André Marie Ampère's experiments came up one day at lunch. On being told that electricity flows instantly through wire, Morse remarked (so he later recalled), "If this be so and the presence of electricity can be made visible in any desired part of the circuit, I see no reason why intelligence might not be instantaneously transmitted by electricity to any distance."[2] He was not the first to have the idea, or even to put it in those terms: remember Cavallo's almost identical comment many years earlier. But Morse knew nothing about earlier attempts to build electric telegraphs, which may have been an advantage. He had lots of time on board the *Sully*, and he spent much of it filling a notebook with sketches of telegraphic ideas.

Morse put aside his *Sully* notebooks until early 1837, when, after hearing that a French inventor had built a telegraph (Morse didn't know that it was an improved visual telegraph), he began to try to build his own. Morse based his telegraph on a small amount of theoretical knowledge and on a simple trial-and-error experimentalism. His theory was simple, based on popularizations of recent scientific work on electricity. For advice he turned to Dr. Leonard Gale, a professor of geology and mineralogy at New York University. In exchange for his scientific advice, Gale became a partner in Morse's invention, receiving a

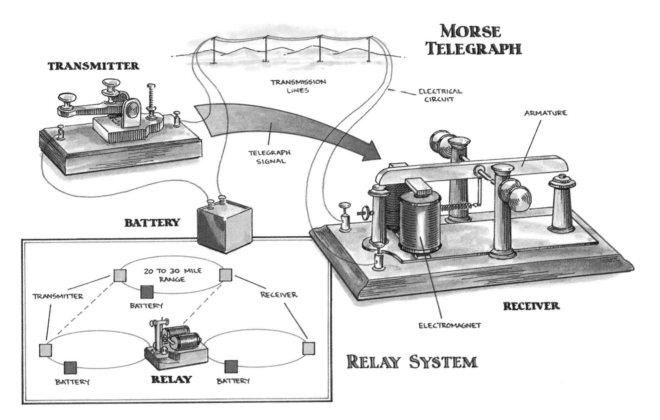

MORSE TELEGRAPH

TRANSMITTER

TRANSMISSION LINES

ELECTRICAL CIRCUIT

ARMATURE

TELEGRAPH SIGNAL

BATTERY

20 TO 30 MILE RANGE

TRANSMITTER

BATTERY

RECEIVER

BATTERY

RELAY

BATTERY

ELECTROMAGNET

RECEIVER

RELAY SYSTEM

Attach a battery to one end of a loop of wire and a bell to the other, put a switch or key between them, and you have a simple telegraph. The telegraph key is an on-off switch; holding it down completes the circuit, and the bell or buzzer at the other end sounds (or a mark is made on a strip of paper). Move the key according to a prearranged code — short and long bursts called "dots" and "dashes" — and you can send messages. (To save wire, many telegraph systems ran wires only one way; electricity flowing through the ground provided the complete circuit.)

A simple telegraph like this only works over a few miles because the signal loses power as it travels down the wire. So a "relay" is essential. The relay is like a receiver except that instead of making a noise, it closes another circuit, retransmitting the original message.

share of the patent and profits. Perhaps the most important thing Gale did for Morse was to tell him about Joseph Henry's work and introduce him to Henry, who was then teaching at Princeton. Morse visited Henry several times for help with the telegraph. Henry found Morse to "have very little knowledge of the general principles of electricity, magnetism, or electro-magnetism,"[3] but he thought that Morse's ideas were better than what he had seen on his recent trip to Europe, and helped him out. Henry, who believed (with good reason) that his own work on electromagnets was the basis of the telegraph, at first thought of protesting Morse's patent. But he felt that scientists should not receive patents, and so he changed his mind and instead supported Morse's application — a decision he later regretted.

Morse's telegraph was based on the principle of electromagnetism. When electricity passes through a coil of wire, it produces a magnetic field. You can turn this magnetic field on and off by opening and closing a switch, disrupting the flow of current from the battery; you can see when the field is on or off by setting a piece of metal near the magnet. The switch can be in one place, with wires running to a magnet in another, and so the principle can be used to send messages.

The tricky parts are the practical details of how to open and close the circuit, and how to indicate the state of the magnet. Morse's first transmitter (in foreground) used type slugs, each one encoded with a number. The numbers represented words. When the handle was turned, the slugs moved from left to right. The right side of the lever followed the pattern on the slugs, up and down, and so the left end moved down and up, making and breaking the electrical contacts as the pair of wires at

far left dipped into and out of cups filled with mercury. (This turned out to be more complicated than necessary; a simple spring-loaded key operated by hand would have done the job.)

Morse's receiver (in background) was also more complicated than it might have been. It was made of an artist's canvas-stretcher to which was attached a pendulum holding a pencil, an electromagnet to move the pendulum, a clockworks, and two pulleys with paper tape stretched between them. The clockworks moved the tape at a steady rate. When a signal was sent — when the circuit was closed — the electromagnet pulled the pendulum to mark the tape with the pencil.

Morse's experimentation was even cruder than his theory. He was not a good mechanic. Lacking money and technical skills, he used what was readily available to build his telegraph, whatever mechanisms and devices he could put his hands on. For the frame of his receiver Morse used an artist's canvas stretcher — something he would have had around his shop. He used the works from a clock to move the paper tape. Morse derived some elements of his telegraph from things he had seen in his brother's print shop. His transmitter resembled the composing stick a printer used to assemble letters, his coded lead slugs, printer's type. Like most inventors Morse borrowed from previous inventions and from the things around him. He made use not only of preexisting technologies — the clock, the electromagnet — but also of preexisting ways of thinking about information.

The device worked, sort of. But he clearly needed mechanical assistance to make it practical, just as he had needed Gale's scientific assistance to make it work in the first place. He hired Alfred Vail to build an improved device. Vail had been a student at New York University, and had worked in his father's ironworks, where he had become a proficient mechanic. In exchange for a one-quarter interest in the patent, Vail agreed to invest his time and his father's money in the new invention. He signed a contract agreeing to construct a telegraph and put it into operation, at his own expense and on his own time, and to pay the costs of obtaining the patent. Furthermore, any inventions Vail made would belong three fourths to Morse and one fourth to Vail.

The second Morse telegraph, the one redesigned and constructed by Vail (Morse apparently had little to do with it), was very different from Morse's first machine. It was much better built and more reliable. There was a new code, perhaps Vail's work (at least, Vail's son claimed it was), in which dots and dashes stood for individual letters, not for numbers that in turn stood for words.

The invention of a code was a key element in inventing the telegraph, almost as important a breakthrough as the machinery. Pre-Morse telegraphs tended to use codes that were not really codes at all. Some inventors assumed that a telegraph should have one wire for each letter. Others tried to invent machines that would send the shape of the letter, so that the code for an *E*, say, looked like an *E*.

Morse's first telegraph used a simple cipher to send messages. The sender and receiver each had a dictionary in which every word was assigned a number. To send a word over the wire, the sender simply tapped out the number, separating digits of the same number with short spaces, and separating the numbers from one another with longer spaces. So, to send the message "Successful experiment," Morse would look in his dictionary and find that the code for "successful" was "215," and the code for "experiment" was "36." He would then tap out the message (or, in the first telegraph, insert the encoded type slugs):

```
 ••     •     •••••      •••      ••••••
 2      1       5          3          6
```

and at the other end of the line, the telegrapher would look it up in his dictionary: "215," "36" — "Successful," "experiment."

This cipher system had its problems. The major one was that it required either memorizing lots of arbitrary numbers or looking up every word. And so, when in 1837 Alfred Vail rebuilt Morse's telegraph, he came up with a new code. Instead of sending only one type of signal over the line, Vail decided to use two, a long and a short, or a dash and a dot, to represent not words but the letters of the alphabet. This meant that the code was far more flexible, and much quicker. (Notice that more common letters have shorter codes, which increased speed considerably.) This new code is similar to modern Morse code. To send the same message, the code would look like this:

```
•••  ••−   •••  ••• •   •••  •••   •−•  ••−   •−
 S    U     C     C   E   S    S    F    U    L
```

```
 •    •−••  •••••  •   •••  ••   −−   •   −•   −
 E     X      P    E    R    I    M   E    N   T
```

This code required more signals to be sent, but fewer codes to be memorized, so it didn't require a code book. It was easy to learn the forty or so symbols needed to send any message. Before long, telegraphers could send and receive Morse code at what seemed an incredible speed, up to thirty words per minute.

The new telegraph was demonstrated several times in early 1838, to widespread amazement and acclaim. The *Morristown* (N.J.) *Jerseyman* described the scene at one public demonstration:

The telegraph instruments used on the Baltimore-Washington line in 1844 were much better built and more reliable than those Morse had demonstrated a few years earlier. Vail's mechanical abilities are apparent in their design and construction. The receiver (right) is a replica.

PROFESSOR MORSE'S ELECTROMAGNETIC TELEGRAPH

It is with some degree of pride, we confess, that it falls to our lot first to announce the complete success of this wonderful piece of mechanism, and that hundreds of our citizens were the first to witness its surprising results. . . . Others may have suggested the possibility of conveying intelligence by electricity, but this is the first instance of its actual transmission and permanent record.[4]

Morse finally obtained his patent in 1840, a patent with obvious practical potential. But before the telegraph could be put to use, inventors had to devise better technology and investors had to build telegraph networks. Invention was just the first step in a much more complicated story.

Morse assumed that the federal government should support his telegraph, just as he had earlier assumed that the federal government should support his artistic endeavors. He wanted the government to buy his patent and operate the telegraph for the public good. After all, it was in response to a call for plans for a visual telegraph that Morse had originally started work. And it seemed reasonable. Carrying mail was assumed to be the government's job. Why not carrying messages by telegraph, too?

One of the most ardent supporters of the telegraph in Congress was Maine Congressman F. O. J. Smith, chairman of the Committee on Commerce. (Some measure of his character can be gained from his nickname, "Fog.") In a report on telegraphy Smith outlined his almost religious belief in the power of communications technology in the sort of language that would become commonplace in such descriptions: "The influence of this invention over the political, commercial, and social relations of the people of this widely-

WHEATSTONE TELEGRAPH

While Morse and Vail were inventing their telegraph, other inventors were working on similar systems. In 1837 William Fothergill Cooke and Charles Wheatstone patented and demonstrated in England a needle telegraph. Wheatstone was a scientist, familiar with the needle galvanometer, in which current in a coil causes a magnetized needle to twist. The Cooke-Wheatstone telegraph used this principle to communicate information. They began with a five-needle, five-wire device that indicated each letter of a message directly. By 1841 they had simplified their telegraph receiver to a single-needle device that used a two-element code. The American telegraph built by Morse and Vail made use of the lessons learned in this British system.

extended country . . . will . . . of itself amount to a revolution unsurpassed in moral grandeur by any discovery that has been made in the arts and sciences. . . . Space will be, to all practical purposes of information, completely annihilated between the States of the Union, as also between the individual citizens thereof."[5] Smith had good reason to write so glowing a blessing for the telegraph, for he had secretly become a partner with Morse (and Gale and Vail) in the telegraph project. Morse had the original idea and the leadership, spirit, and diligence needed to keep the enterprise alive. Gale knew the science. Vail provided the technical know-how, and actually built a practicable machine. Smith, who now owned one fourth of the patent, was to provide the political clout necessary to get government aid. He lobbied hard, both on and off the House floor, for government support for the telegraph.

Morse left for Europe in 1838 to apply for patents for the telegraph there, without much success. In December 1842 he returned to Washington to lobby once more for a government subsidy for a trial telegraph line. He set up a telegraph system connecting two committee rooms in the Capitol to demonstrate the device. Smith worked behind the scenes. Finally, in March 1843, Congress voted to allocate $30,000 to build a telegraph line between Washington, D.C., and Baltimore. The congressional vote was on economic lines. Senators from states with commercial interests, which traditionally supported internal improvements such as roads and canals, supported the telegraph.

The process of building a practical system uncovered all the defects in the early versions of the telegraph. Morse, Gale, and Vail were put on the government payroll to build the line, and hired Smith to do the construction. Smith in turn hired Ezra Cornell (a mechanic turned plow salesman, he later founded Cornell University with the fortune he gained from telegraphy) to actually do the work. There were many difficulties. By the time the first long-distance line

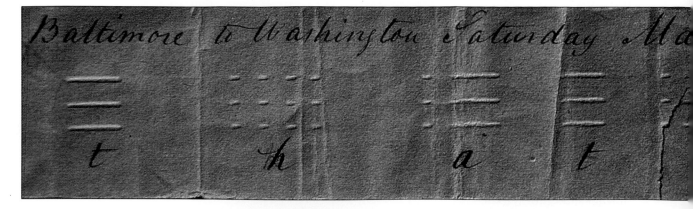

"What hath God wrought" — the first intercity telegraph message.

was operational, in 1844, Vail had replaced the port rule transmitter with the key — a simple spring-loaded switch — that would become the standard telegraph transmitter. A new receiver used a stylus to record the message, and was much more reliable than the earlier version. Underground wiring proved unreliable, and Vail and Cornell, desperately reading everything they could about English telegraphs, discovered that Wheatstone and Cooke's telegraph used poles, and invented a way of attaching the wires to poles.

The line was completed in 1844. The first official message was "What hath God wrought." One of the first uses of Morse's telegraph line was to relay news of the presidential ticket selected at the Whig convention in Baltimore from Annapolis Junction (the furthest point the line then reached) to Washington. The crowd at the Washington station was skeptical, until the train brought the news an hour later.

After a flurry of activity relaying news from the Whig and Democratic presidential nominating conventions held that year in Baltimore, no one showed much interest in the telegraph. Few customers paid to send messages. People didn't know, right away, what sort of message was worth paying a high price to send instantly. Businesses weren't set up for dealing with telegraph messages. For a new technology to be successful, customers have to be told that they need it, and shown how to use it, and how to reorganize their operations around it. They have to convince themselves of its value.

Morse hoped that the government would continue to build telegraph lines. In private hands — in the hands of "a company of speculators," as he put it — the telegraph would be a monopoly, a "means of enriching the corporation at the expense of the bankruptcy of thousands." He wanted the federal government to buy the patent from him and then to sell the rights for private use, and regulate that use. He argued that not only was the telegraph a grand invention, giving man almost godlike powers, but that it was also an essentially democratic technology. Morse claimed that it deserved to be known as the "American telegraph" not merely because it was invented here but also because it was "more in consonance with the political institutions under which we live, and is fitted . . . to diffuse its benefits alike to the Government and to the people at large."[6]

But Morse's rhetoric failed to persuade the government to continue subsidizing the line. After lengthy debate and continued losses, the government gave it up. Each of the part owners of the telegraph patent began to look for a buyer for his share, and in 1845 the first of many telegraph companies was formed. The

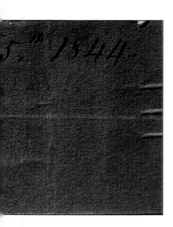

patentees received shares in the companies in exchange for the right to use the telegraph patent. Future development of telegraphy in America was left to private enterprise. (The government did occasionally subsidize lines that seemed especially useful or expensive, including the first transcontinental line in 1860.)

Slowly at first, but then more quickly, the Magnetic Telegraph Company found business. By 1846 telegraph lines extended from Washington, D.C., to Portland, Maine, and west as far as Milwaukee, altogether some 1,200 miles. When the Mexican War broke out in 1846, there was an enormous demand for news from Texas, seven days away by railroad, horse, and boat. Newspaper publishers and readers wanted the news more quickly, and called for the rapid extension of telegraph lines, which were completed before the end of the war. James Gordon Bennett, publisher of the *New York Herald,* boasted of having spent $12,381 for 79,000 words of telegraphic news in the first week of 1848 alone. (See WORDS.*)*

Lottery runners and brokers soon joined the journalists. By 1850 the telegraph was more than just accepted; it was the rage. Bankers and businessmen realized that they could profit from immediate knowledge of stock prices and other crucial data. Railroad managers found they could use the telegraph to control their far-flung empires. By 1847 lines reached from New York to New Orleans, and in 1854 there were over 30,000 miles of telegraph lines in the United States.

THE TELEGRAPH AND THE AMERICAN EMPIRE

Newspapermen hailed the telegraph as "unquestionably the greatest invention of the age," as the *Utica* (N.Y.) *Daily Gazette* put it in 1844.[7] The new technology of communications evoked hyperbole about the strengthening of the American republic, and indeed uniting the world. Samuel Bowles, editor of the *Springfield* (Mass.) *Republican,* wrote in 1851: "The increase of facilities for the transmission of news brought in a new era. The railroad car, the steamboat, and the magnetic telegraph, have made neighborhood among widely disseevered States. . . . These active and almost miraculous agencies have brought the whole civilized world in contact."[8]

The telegraph arrived on the scene at a difficult moment in American

history. The United States was expanding across the continent. It was faced with threats of Southern secession. Regionalism was on the rise. Many Americans hailed the telegraph as the tool that would bind the country together. James Gordon Bennett, editor of the *New York Herald,* predicted that the telegraph would "blend into one homogeneous mass . . . the whole population of the republic. . . . [It could] do more to guard against disunion . . . than all the most experienced, the most sagacious, and the most patriotic government, could accomplish."[9] Senator Lewis Cass of Michigan believed that "the telegraph has come with its wonderful process to bind still closer the portions of this empire."[10]

Some thought even bigger. The telegraph might bind together not just the United States but the whole world. The first step was to connect Europe and the United States, a technological challenge of the highest order.

A transatlantic telegraph cable was first proposed in 1852. The cable would run from New York to Newfoundland (where it could serve, temporarily, as a relay for news brought via steamer from Europe), and then to Labrador, across the coast of Greenland and Iceland to the Orkney Islands, and then to Scotland. The cable would connect the telegraph networks of Great Britain and Europe to those of Canada and the United States. It would run some 2,500 miles, 1,500 miles of it under water, at an estimated cost of £500,000. Cyrus Field, a retired New York businessman, was taken with the idea, finding it, a historian wrote a few years later, "the sublimest work of the age."[11] He asked Morse if it could be done, and Morse said yes. And so in 1854 Field established the New York, Newfoundland & London Telegraph Company.

The Atlantic cable was hailed as the eighth wonder of the world and as a symbol of Anglo-American unity (left). The Chamber of Commerce of New York City awarded gold medals to all those involved.

Why an Atlantic cable? Profit was clearly an important motive for Field, the promoter who led the project, and the wealthy individuals, mostly British, who put up the money. The telegraph system in the United States had proved its usefulness, and had already made many of the men who invested in it wealthy. But this new venture was a risky way to make money, speculative at best. No one knew how much demand there would be for a transatlantic cable, or even if it was possible. It meant pushing the technological limits. And that was part of its charm: many Americans were taken with technological challenges. There were less sublime reasons, too. It would later become clear that the investors' goal was as much to capture the Eastern telegraph market and control foreign news entering the country as it was to actually build an Atlantic cable.

After much difficulty and many financial shenanigans, the best route connecting the continents was chosen. Plans were made, money was raised, and in August 1857 the grand Atlantic cable expedition began. Just four days into laying the cable from Ireland, though, the cable snapped. A second expedition was organized, and after a great deal of difficulty, on August 4, 1858, the first transatlantic telegraph cable was a reality.

It never worked very well — it took twenty-six hours to get the first message across — and failed completely within a few weeks. Only a few messages were sent, including formal messages exchanged between President Buchanan and Queen Victoria. Some news traveled under the oceans, though problems with the cable limited what could be sent. The telegrapher in Newfoundland wired his European counterpart, "Please give some news for New York; they are mad for news."

In the brief period between the time of the first message and the cable's failure, the American people celebrated widely. One newspaper wrote: "Their language has all the extravagance of incipient delirium. [The cable] is pronounced next only in importance for mankind to the 'Crucifixion.' "[12] On September 1, over 15,000 New Yorkers turned out for an enormous parade of celebration, the biggest parade New York City had ever seen. Why did people celebrate? Very few had immediate financial interest in the cable or expected to earn anything from the information that would flow over it. They celebrated it on more general principles, as a national victory, as a great technological accomplishment, and as a triumph of the new Age of Information.

In the popular reaction to this technological adventure, we can see what would become a common American response to progress, or hopes for progress, in information technology. In the expectations of its promoters and the public, in the reasons for attempting it, and most of all in the celebration that accompanied its early success, we capture something of the meaning of the telegraph for those who saw its first achievements. Their views reflected a more general enthusiasm that many Americans felt for new technology. America was in the midst of the most rapid period of industrialization the world had ever known. From its origin as an agricultural colony, the United States had become one of the world's preeminent industrial powers, and almost everyone thought that technology was the reason why. Americans celebrated the "ingenious Yankee," praised his cleverness at machines, and admired his ability to "get things done." That a project was technologically challenging was in itself a reason to do it — or so many people believed in the booming, vibrant America of the 1850s. Many Americans loved technological challenges. That something might be impossible seemed almost enough reason to try it. In the parade celebrating the cable, marchers accompanied floats bearing examples of the latest technology, not just the telegraph but also the sewing machine and the printing press.

Furthermore, there was a profound belief that communications technology was a special sort of technology, that easier exchange of information would, by itself, draw America and England together. Communications, and by extension communications technology, was thought an unmitigated good. An article in the *Liverpool Journal* put it thus: "A quarrel between the two great Anglo-Saxon nations can only arise in misconception; and if there is a desire not to misapprehend, misconception cannot exist where communication is free and instant."[13] "The Anglo-Saxon race," wired the mayor of Savannah, Georgia, to the mayor of New York, "has made of the lightning of Heaven the swift messenger of peace."[14] Ralph Waldo Emerson wrote of the telegraph line that connected England and France: "Every message it transmits makes stronger by one thread the band which war will have to cut."[15] (It's no coincidence that this desperate hope that communications would solve problems manifested itself on the verge of the Civil War and the failure of endless debate to solve the problems that would tear the country apart.)

Related to the belief in the value of technology was a worldview which held that nature was something to be conquered, to be overcome. Americans were conquering the West, both by force of arms, driving the Native Americans out, and technologically, with railroads and telegraphs and agricultural machinery. The cable would conquer the Atlantic in the same way. It would, as a popular saying of the period had it, "annihilate time and space." For those to whom time was money and space an obstacle, annihilating time and space was the highest goal.

And it was not just the physical world that had to be conquered. Other peoples, too, were to be converted, or civilized, if not annihilated. Many Americans, like many Europeans, believed that it was important to spread Western civilization. Convinced that technology was the greatest triumph of mankind, they believed that it was their duty — almost a religious duty — to spread that technology around the world. New communications links were a key means of disseminating Western culture and technology. Underlying the rhetoric of the importance of "civilizing" the world through technology — the so-called white man's burden — were racial notions about the importance of the Atlantic cable in uniting the "Anglo-Saxon race." The upper classes of both England and the United States were sure not only that Western culture was superior to the culture of the rest of the world — prowess in technology "proved" that, after all — but that the culture of England and its former colonies was the best of all. The Atlantic cable, by joining the two countries, would serve to promote their interests, which were the interests of "progress."

But in addition to these cultural predilections, there were more specific economic reasons that helped spur the Atlantic cable project. The New York and London merchants who backed it lived in a world of information. Their profits depended on their ability to discover information before their competitors, and to use that information more quickly and with greater cleverness than anyone else.

In the years before the Atlantic cable, journalists and businessmen had eagerly adopted each new technology that came along to speed their reception of news from Europe. In 1838 it took thirteen days for steamships to cross the ocean to America. To cut off the last few hours, they would send fast boats out to meet the steamships and bring back the news a few minutes before anyone else could get it. Starting in 1848, a group of New York newspapers shared the cost of chartering a fast steamer from Boston to meet ships from Europe at Halifax, Nova Scotia. When the steamer returned to Boston, the news was telegraphed to New York. It was expensive but worth it. Fresh news was valuable, stale news worthless.

For merchants fresh news meant the difference between profit and loss. A merchant who heard first that, say, rainy weather in Egypt might mean a bad cotton crop, and stocked up on cotton, or invested in the stock of a cotton mill that had a large inventory, would stand to make a nice profit. News that war might break out in India could affect everything from the price of stock in New England textile mills to, literally, the price of rice in China. Information was the key, and more and fresher information was better. These merchants lived in an Information Age. Their hopes and fears and expectations and beliefs about the new information technology were, in some ways, not too far removed from ours.

The immediate consequences of the first transatlantic telegraph cable were small. Few messages moved under the ocean on the wire in the few weeks before it failed. No great fortunes were made or lost on news or price information that arrived electrically, in minutes, rather than by boat, in weeks. But the pressures, economic and cultural, that had led to this first cable remained, and not long after the failure of the cable, many of the same investors, entrepreneurs, and engineers tried again. The second cable was based on improved technology,

The Civil War demonstrated the value of the telegraph for military communications and control. Military officers found the telegraph an effective tool for coordinating movements of troops and supplies and monitoring distant battles from central command points. The telegraph also offered new opportunities for espionage. Soldiers could use a handy pocket telegraph to listen in on enemy wires. Cutting telegraph lines became a new tactic for disrupting enemy communications.

TELEGRAPH OPERATOR TAPPING REBEL TELEGRAPH LINE NEAR EGYPT, ON THE MISSISSIPPI CENTRAL RAILROAD.—FROM A SKETCH BY MR. KORIZ.

especially better insulation, and took into account lessons learned in the first attempt. In 1866 the Eastern and Western hemispheres were tied together — forever — by an information conduit.

Reception speed on the 1866 cable was at first about eight words per minute, increasing later to about fifteen words per minute. At this speed the cable found users. Newspapers in the United States headlined news from Europe "from telegraphic reports." The increased speed with which information flowed meant that prices throughout much of the world began to move in sync. The price of wheat in Odessa would affect the price in Chicago, or a run on a bank in Boston could have immediate implications in Glasgow. The world moved closer to becoming a single market. Transatlantic telegraphic communications brought closer cultural contacts, too. A German immigrant in Texas could wire directly back to his brother in Berlin, if he could afford it. The success of a show in London would set plans afoot in New York. Fashions and ideas flowed more easily and more quickly from continent to continent.

These are specific consequences of the Atlantic cable, and they might be multiplied endlessly. For the United States was entering the Information Age, and the effects of increased ease of access to information, the faster flow of information, and just plain *more* information showed up everywhere. But the consequences of this vast flow of information did not always approach the desires of its supporters. After all, just because people had the ability to talk to one another didn't mean that they had anything worth saying. Henry David Thoreau questioned the power of technology to change people when he wrote in *Walden* in 1854: "We are in great haste to construct a magnetic telegraph from Maine to Texas; but Maine and Texas, it may be, have nothing important to communicate. . . . We are eager to tunnel under the Atlantic and bring the Old World some weeks nearer to the New; but perchance the first news that will leak through into the broad, flapping American ear will be that Princess Adelaide has the whooping cough."[16]

Telegraphic messages from one side of the Atlantic to the other did not mean the end of quarrels between England and the United States. Stringing telegraph cables around the world did not signal the beginning of a new age of wisdom or of peace. Just as the increased communications that came with the widening American telegraph network did nothing to prevent the Civil War, so worldwide telegraph networks did not bring world peace and understanding. Indeed, the Civil War brought about a large increase in the American telegraph network, and the telegraph was to play a key role in military strategy. The messages that passed through these far-flung communications links were messages not of peace and unity but of unprecedented technological warfare.

THE TELEGRAPH AT WORK

Railroads were among the first businesses to take advantage of the telegraph. Charles Minot, superintendent of the Erie Railroad, was one of the first railroaders to realize how valuable the telegraph might be. In 1849 he used the telegraph to relay ahead information about a train's cargo so that enough space was allotted for it on the barges to which it was to be transferred. A more important application came in 1851, when Minot used the telegraph to signal ahead to a stationmaster to hold a late eastbound train so that the westbound train could move rather than having to wait for the delayed train. (The engineer refused to obey the unusual orders, not trusting his job and his train to the newfangled telegraph. Minot had to run the train himself.)

For the next few years the telegraph was used only in exceptional situations. The managerial system of the railroad was set, and it took a while for the telegraph to be accepted. But by the middle of the decade the telegraph saw greater use. In 1854 a newspaper declared, "The electro-magnetic telegraph is beginning to be applied . . . to facilitating the operations of railways; securing greater safety by obviating the danger of collision, accidents and so forth."[17]

The Erie was also the first railroad to use the telegraph as an everyday management tool. Daniel McCallum, Minot's successor as superintendent, was delighted with the telegraph. He wrote in 1856: "It would occupy too much space to allude to all the practical purposes to which the telegraph is applied in working the road; and it may suffice to say, that without it, the business could not be conducted with anything like the same degree of economy, safety, regularity, or dispatch."[18] McCallum established managerial procedures that included hourly telegraphic reports on the position of all trains on the line, as well as special reports on any train more than ten minutes late. All of this information was transmitted to headquarters, where a dispatcher kept track of the position of every train on the track. If there were any delays or other problems, decisions were made at the division level by men who specialized in decision-making. Instructions were sent back to the men in the field. This was the beginning of the "timetable and train order" system that survives to the present day. Business historian Alfred Chandler wrote in his review of railroad management, "What impressed other railroad managers was that McCallum saw at once that the telegraph was more than merely a means to make train movements safe, but also a device to improve better coordination and better administration."[19]

Other businesses also began to use the telegraph. Though for most companies it was too expensive, at first, for everyday use, companies with perishable products that needed to be shipped over long distances found it worthwhile. The Swift and Armour meat packing firms, for example, spent some $200,000 a year on telegraph messages in the 1880s. The telegraph changed the relationship of distant factory owners and the men who managed the factories. Financial institutions made especially heavy use of the telegraph. The stock ticker, which relayed prices from the floor of the exchange to brokers and customers throughout the country, became a technological symbol of wealth. Newspapers came to depend on telegraphed news; between 50,000 and 70,000 words a day passed over the telegraph wires for the Associated Press in 1877. (See WORDS.)

The telegraph was the first of many information machines that would shorten the time for decision-making and increase the pace and stress of the business day. The business historian JoAnne Yates has outlined the ways in which the telegraph changed business. In some industries — those that dealt in commodities that were standardized, easily described, and with many potential buyers, such as coal or wheat — increased communications encouraged the growth of markets, and changed the nature of those markets. The main activity of the merchant and broker of the early nineteenth century was arbitrage — taking advantage of the differences in price of a commodity at different places. The telegraph tended to equalize prices across the country, and so shifted speculation from arbitrage to futures, that is, from trading commodities between places to trading them between times. In other industries — those with time-dependent products, such as perishable foods, or those with specialized sales and support needs, such as machinery — the telegraph and the railroad helped bring about increased managerial control.

By the last third of the nineteenth century the telegraph had become a fixture of American life. *Harper's Magazine* waxed rhapsodic in an 1873 article titled "The Telegraph":

> Every phase of the mental activity of the country is more or less represented in this great system. The fluctuations in the markets; the price of stocks; the premium on gold; the starting of railroad trains; the sailing of ships; the arrival of passengers; orders for merchandise and manufacturers of every kind; bargains offered and bargains closed; sermons, lectures, and political speeches; fires; sickness and death; weather reports; the approach of the grasshopper and the weevil; the transmission of money; the congratulations of friends — everything, from the announcement of a new planet down to an inquiry for a lost carpet-bag, has its turn passing the wires.

The size of the telegraph network was beyond belief: "The mind is almost bewildered with the thought of such an immense labyrinth, such complex organi-

zation . . . a web spun of two hundred thousand miles of wire spread over the face of the country like a cobweb on the grass." The president of Western Union called it "the nervous system of the commercial system."[20] The 1880 Census counted over 32 million messages traveling between more than 12,000 telegraph offices connected by 291,000 miles of wire.

The expanding network was based on a flowering of technological innovation. Telegraphy was the "high tech" of the nineteenth century, and many people with an interest in electricity and a desire to make a fast profit tried their hand at improving it. They devised ways to send many messages over one wire, to speed up transmission, to print and store messages, and to send messages over longer distances — as well as ways to get around Morse's patents. There were improved printing telegraphs, which printed the message on a paper tape, as well as new "sounders," which a trained telegrapher could listen to and decode the message, as well as new switching systems and new systems for local telegraphy.

As the demand for telegraph transmission grew, telegraph companies looked to new technology to allow them to send more information over the lines. The most important inventions were the multiplex telegraph, which allowed several messages to be sent over the same line, and machines that encoded messages and sent them more quickly than human operators could.

Telegraph companies looked to the multiplex telegraph to save them the enormous cost of building new lines. Within a few years of the invention of the telegraph, every telegraph company was trying to invent a way to send more messages over one wire. The first step was sending two messages in opposite directions on one wire, or a "duplex" telegraph. J. B. Stearns of Boston was the first to come up with a good practical system, introduced in 1873. Then in 1874 Thomas Edison built a successful "quadruplex" telegraph, which could send two

Telegraph companies charged senders by the word, so senders invented a new form of condensed, elliptical language known as "telegraphese" to reduce their bills. Cutting the number of words in half cut the bill in half. By the 1880s many businessmen used telegraphic codes. Some companies used codes for secrecy, others to make operators pay closer attention to the words. Codes also served to standardize communications; salesmen could only use phrases found in the official code book. Most important, businessmen used codes to save money.

There were many published codes. The *ABC Telegraphic Code* listed 25,000 business phrases that could be sent with a one-word code. *Jacob's Friend-to-Friend Cable Code* encoded vacationer's greetings. A cotton purchaser using *Shepperson's Cotton Trade Cipher Code* could send one word to describe the kind and quality of cotton he bought. The American Code Company even sold a book of "401,000,000 pronounceable words," so that customers could make their own codes. If the first letter of a code word was mistransmitted, you could still find it in the *Terminal Index,* "invaluable for quickly correcting mutilated code words." And if, even with codes, telegraph costs were too high, you could use *Pieron's Code Condenser,* which reduced two code words to one.

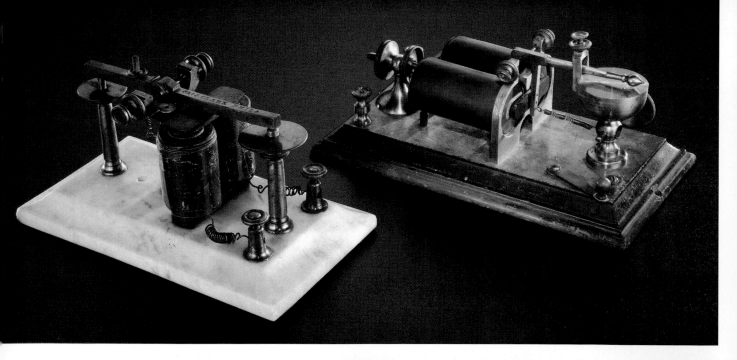

Early telegraph receivers printed the incoming messages. But around 1850 operators realized they could tell the difference between dots and dashes by the noise of the instrument. As a result, a new type of receiver which made a louder noise was developed. "Sounders," like those shown here, were simple and easy to repair and thus suitable for small and isolated stations. In the United States there were many small stations, and teaching operators Morse code made better economic sense than purchasing expensive printing equipment.

American businesses with private lines tended to use printers for financial reporting and sending information between offices. Thomas Edison (who had his start as a telegraph operator and made his reputation and first fortune with improvements to the telegraph) invented this receiver to print out gold and stock prices in 1873.

messages from each end of the line; Western Union bought the patent from him for $30,000.

In 1876 Alexander Graham Bell and Elisha Gray both invented "harmonic telegraphs," which used what would come to be called frequency division multiplexing — sending each message at a different frequency. They designed receiving instruments that would respond to only one frequency to sort the messages out at the far end. (See TELEPHONE.) By the early twentieth century as many as seventeen telegraph signals could be transmitted on one wire, often in addition to one telephone signal; each message was sent on a different frequency.

Another system used time-division multiplexing. These systems, starting in the 1860s, used a clockwork mechanism at each end of the telegraph line to spin a rotor that would connect one instrument to the line at a time. The two mechanisms were synchronized, and spun at high speed; each circuit was connected often enough so that it seemed to have the whole line to itself. This was an astonishing feat of electromechanics! But it was hard to synchronize the line, and this method was generally thought to be impractical. Émile Baudot, in France, realized in 1874 that it was possible to combine time-division multiplexing with automated sending and receiving equipment and get the advantages of both. He invented an entirely new sort of telegraph system that developed into what came to be the Teletype, a typewriter to replace the telegraph key.

Solutions to business problems were as important as technological solutions. There were dozens of telegraph companies, often with incompatible technology. They sometimes refused to relay messages to one another, or to car-

Alongside the telephone and telegraph systems was a lesser-known, special purpose communications system that used Teletypes to send messages. Teletypes, developed after World War I, used a typewriter keyboard to send from, and a typewriter mechanism to print out the message at the far side. In 1937, when this picture of a teletype room at a large corporation was taken, the TWX system (AT&T's teletype service) served 11,000 stations; by 1962 there were 60,000 TWX stations in the United States. Teletype systems were among the first communications systems to be computerized. In the early 1960s International Telephone and Telegraph bought large numbers of Digital Equipment Corporation's first model of computer, the PDP-1, to store and forward teletype messages and replace the people who had done it before. The Teletype almost disappeared in the 1980s, the victim of fax machines, electronic funds transfer, and electronic mail.

Telegraph operators called themselves "knights of the key." Skilled Morse code operators were much in demand in the early days of the telegraph. They felt a sense of power in their role as a vital link in the new telegraph system — a power the Telegraphers' Protective League used to organize the United States's first nationwide strike, against Western Union, in 1870.

In the early days of the system, many telegraphers were skilled in the technology and were responsible for many improvements in the field. Many inventors who started out working on the telegraph would contribute to the telephone, the radio, and the other electrical technologies that were built on the base of telegraphy. Some of them went on to a rewarding career in telegraphy or elsewhere — Western Union promoted almost all of its managers from the ranks of telegraphers.

But for the telegraphers who started after 1880, and for women telegraphers (in 1900, about 12 percent of operators were women) it was a dead-end occupation. Telegraphers were among the first of a new kind of semiskilled white-collar workers, early members of a new lower middle class. In 1910, when this picture was taken, about 600 telegraphers were employed in this main operating room of Western Union in New York City.

One corner of Western Union's telegraph switching office in New York City, circa 1910. How did a telegraph message get to the right place — from, say, John Smith in Philadelphia to Jane Smith in Frederick, Maryland? John would go to his local telegraph office and deliver the message. The telegrapher there would pick the line that ran in the right direction, say, the Philadelphia-Washington line, and key the message in, with a note at the beginning that it should be relayed by the Baltimore office. At every intermediate stop between Philadelphia and Washington, the message would click out on the receiver, but the telegraphers at most of those offices would ignore it because the message wasn't addressed to them. At the Baltimore office, though, a telegrapher would pay attention. He'd copy it down on paper, then retransmit the message on the line that ran west from Baltimore to, say, Pittsburgh, this time with a note at the top that the Frederick office should pay attention. At the Frederick office, the operator would write out the message and hand it to a telegraph messenger for delivery.

Boston had the first American telegraphic fire alarm system, installed by William Channing and Moses Farmer in 1852. This box dates from that year. Activating the alarm sent a coded signal indicating the location of the box to a central office. Telegraphic fire alarms became the nerve center of fire stations, and they became increasingly complex, connecting many alarm boxes to a central fire station.

ry messages for newspapers with whose politics they disagreed. One historian of the industry has called the first decades of the telegraph industry an "era of methodless enthusiasm."[21] There were clear advantages to cooperation, and the American Telegraph Confederation, organized in 1853, was the first step in this direction. There were even further advantages to consolidation, and the mid-1850s saw a shakeout in the industry. Hiram Sibley's New York and Mississippi Valley Printing Telegraph Company was the most aggressive, buying up dozens of lines. When it was reincorporated as the Western Union Telegraph Company in 1856, it controlled most of the West. In 1866 it purchased the United States Telegraph Company and the American Telegraph Company. With over 37,000 miles of line and 2,250 telegraph offices, it won a near-monopoly over the entire country.

In addition to the interurban market, which Western Union pretty much monopolized, there was a growing intraurban telegraph market. Starting in the 1870s, small firms provided specialized services over private lines, using small, inexpensive printing telegraphs that didn't require a skilled operator. Stock tickers were the first, adopted in 1867 by the New York Gold Exchange. Soon they were joined by district telegraph systems, invented in 1871 by Edward

Calahan, which allowed customers to call for a messenger, doctor, or carriage, or for police or fire service, by pushing a button. The button set off a clockwork mechanism that sent a message to the central station indicating the box number and what service was needed. The systems became especially useful for night-watch and fire and police services. By the mid-1870s seventy-nine cities in the United States and Canada had municipal systems; by 1900 over 600 cities used these systems.

But by 1900 the telegraph was also beginning to see a new competitor. The telephone, invented in 1876, was spinning its own web of wires. (See TELE-PHONE.) The telegraph system still continued to grow. Messages of commerce and friendship, news and information were called into the telegraph office, typed onto transmitters, and relayed around the world. At its peak in 1945 the tele-graph system carried some 236 million messages. But it could not compete with improving long-distance telephone service, or, in the 1980s, computer mail sys-tems and fax machines. By 1990, some 150 years after its invention, the tele-graph system would all but disappear.

FOR FURTHER READING

The story of the invention of the telegraph is told best in Carleton Mabee's biography *The American Leonardo: A Life of Samuel F. B. Morse* (1943). Almost everyone in-volved with the invention had supporters who wrote giving their side of the story. For Joseph Henry's, see the *Annual Report of the Board of Regents of the Smithson-*

Prior to World War I, telegraphs were used almost exclusively for business. Wealthy individuals might have a stock-ticker in their homes, and call boxes connected some homes to central tele-graph offices; turning a handle on the call box identified the caller and summoned a mes-senger. But most people only sent telegraphs when their speed made up for their ex-pense. Notices of births or deaths or emergencies of one kind or another went by tele-graph.

After the War, telegraph companies began to encour-age wider use. Western Union established a new rate struc-ture designed to attract social correspondence. There were special rates for birthday, Christmas, and Easter greet-ings, and even a "Tourate" for messages sent by tourists to friends and family back home. Vacationers could say "Having a good time, wish you were here" by telegraph rather than postcard. For those who couldn't think of what to say, the telegraph company would send a fixed-text message, a conventional greeting from ex-positions or tourist attractions. The telegraph company provid-ed special preprinted telegrams for every occasion.

25¢ FOR ANY OF THE PREPARED TELEGRAMS SHOWN BELOW **20¢** LOCALLY **15 WORDS OF YOUR OWN** COMPOSITION *(See reverse side)* **35¢**

TO ANY WESTERN UNION POINT IN THE UNITED STATES

VALENTINE GREETING by Western Union

Send the following telegram, subject to the terms of the Western Union Telegraph Company, which are hereby agreed to

CHECK THE MESSAGE YOU SELECT. IT WILL BE DELIVERED ON AN ATTRACTIVE BLANK IN AN APPROPRIATE ENVELOPE.

206 ☐ If you were seven and I were nine, I'd say "Please be my Valentine."
217 ☐ This is sent in your direction with all my love and my affection.
219 ☐ Please save my heart from being wrecked. Send Cupid's answer to me collect.
222 ☐ To the sweetest girl in the world, hoping that she will be my Valentine.
223 ☐ You're lovely and sweet, a treasure divine. You're all I want for my Valentine.
224 ☐ Give me just a little sign that you will be my Valentine.
225 ☐ I know I'm lucky because you're mine; you'll always be my Valentine.

227 ☐ Valentine greetings to the finest partner in the world.
228 ☐ To the one who is still my sweetheart after all these years.
230 ☐ All the love of all my heart for you, today and all these years.
232 ☐ Valentine greetings to the sweetest person in the world on the world's sweetest day.
240 ☐ Roses are red . . violets are blue . . sugar you're sweet . . Via WU WU WU.
241 ☐ Be my Valentine, be my honey. We'll live on love and Daddy's money.
247 ☐ You're my sweetheart, you're my beau. You're the sweetest Valentine I know.

248 ☐ Greetings and all my love on Valentine's Day.
249 ☐ All my love to the one who will always be my sweetheart.
250 ☐ I send ten thousand kisses to the sweetest of all Mrs.
251 ☐ Although we are far apart, I send you all my love, sweetheart.

(Additional texts on reverse side)

SAVE TIME . . . Telephone Western Union from home, office or coin box. Merely give name, address, signa-ture and text number selected.

Western Union will purchase anything anywhere for you and deliver it.

SING-O-GRAMS—Telegrams deliv-ered in song for many occasions. (At full rates)

If you prefer to compose your own telegram, check here and write it on the reverse side of this blank. Cost 35¢ for first 15 words.

(Signed)

Sender's Name_____
752

ian Institution . . . for the Year 1857 (1858): 85–117. For Alfred Vail's side, see A. Vail, *Electro-Magnetic Telegraph* (1845); and J. Cummings Vail, *Early History of the Electro-Magnetic Telegraph from Letters and Journals of Alfred Vail* (1914). An attempt to sort out these stories, but with a bias toward Henry, is William B. Taylor, "Henry and the Telegraph," in *Annual Report of the Board of Regents of the Smithsonian Institution . . . for the Year 1878* (1879): 262–360.

The technical development of the telegraph is described in W. James King, "The Development of Electrical Technology in the Nineteenth Century: 1. The Electrochemical Cell and the Electromagnet," and "The Development of Electrical Technology in the Nineteenth Century: 2. The Telegraph and the Telephone," in *Bulletin 228: Contributions from the Museum of History and Technology* (1963). Other sources include Alvin F. Harlow, *Old Wires and New Waves: The History of the Telegraph, Telephone, and Wireless* (1936). The changing business contexts of telegraph invention are described in Paul Israel, *From Machine Shop to Laboratory: Telegraphy and the Changing Context of American Invention, 1830–1920* (1992).

The story of the development of the telegraph industry is told in James D. Reid, *The Telegraph in America, Its Founders, Promoters, and Noted Men* (1879); and, exhaustively, in Robert Luther Thompson, *Wiring a Continent: The History of the Telegraph Industry in the United States, 1832–1866* (1947). For a more theoretical approach, and also for information on European telegraphy, see Gerald W. Brock, *The Telecommunications Industry: The Dynamics of Market Structure* (1981).

The story of the Atlantic cable is told in Vary T. Coates and Bernard Finn, *A Retrospective Technology Assessment: Submarine Telegraphy: The Transatlantic Cable of 1866* (1979); Henry M. Field, *The Story of the Atlantic Telegraph* (1893; reprint 1972); and in no end of contemporary descriptions. On its popular reception, see chapter 1 of Daniel J. Czitrom, *Media and the American Mind: From Morse to McLuhan* (1982).

For an excellent analysis of the way the telegraph changed people's thinking about communications, see the final essay in James W. Carey, *Communication as Culture: Essays on Media and Society* (1988). On telegraphers, see Edwin Gabler, *The American Telegrapher: A Social History, 1860–1900* (1988). On the use of the telegraph in business, see JoAnne Yates, *Control through Communication: The Rise of System in American Management* (1989), and Alfred Chandler, *The Visible Hand: The Management Revolution in American Business* (1977).

NOTES

1. Quoted in William B. Taylor, "Henry and the Telegraph," *Smithsonian Institution Annual Report* (1878), p. 265.

2. Quoted in Carlton Mabee, *The American Leonardo: A Life of Samuel F. B. Morse* (1943), p. 149.

3. "Deposition of Joseph Henry, in the Case of Morse vs. O'Reilly," in *Annual Report of the Board of Regents of the Smithsonian Institution . . . for the Year 1857* (1858): 114.

4. Quoted in Mabee, *The American Leonardo*, p. 199.

5. House Report 753, 25th Congress, 2d session; quoted in Richard John, "A Failure of Vision? Samuel F. B. Morse and the Idea of a Post Office Telegraph, 1844–47," unpublished paper, p. 20.

6. Samuel Morse to C. G. Ferris, December 6, 1842; quoted in John, "A Failure of Vision?" p. 25.

7. Quoted in Peter Marzio, *Men and Machines of American Journalism* (1973), p. 56.

8. Quoted in Marzio, *Men and Machines of American Journalism*, p. 53.

9. James Gordon Bennett, *New York Herald*, May 3 and June 6, 1844; quoted in

Thomas R. Hietala, *Manifest Design: Anxious Aggrandizement in Late Jacksonian America* (1985), p. 196.

10. Quoted in Hietala, *Manifest Design*, p. 197.

11. James D. Reid, *The Telegraph in America: Its Founders, Promoters, and Noted Men* (1879), p. 400.

12. *Daily Picayune*, August 19, 1858.

13. *Liverpool Journal*, August 7, 1858; quoted in *Daily Picayune*, August 27, 1858.

14. Read to the congregation at New York's Trinity Church during service before the benediction, September 1, 1858, from *Frank Leslie's*, September 18, 1858.

15. Ralph Waldo Emerson, *English Traits* (1856; reprint 1950), p. 609.

16. Henry David Thoreau, *Walden* (1854; reprint 1951), p. 67; quoted in Mitchell Stephens, *A History of News: From the Drum to the Satellite* (1988), p. 273.

17. Quoted in Robert Luther Thompson, *Wiring a Continent: The History of the Telegraph Industry in the United States, 1832–1866* (1947), p. 210.

18. Daniel C. McCallum, "Superintendent's Report," March 25, 1856, in *Annual Report of the New York and Erie Railroad Company for 1855* (1856); reprinted in Alfred Chandler, ed., *The Railroads: The Nation's First Big Business* (1965), p. 104.

19. Alfred Chandler, "The Railroads: Pioneers in Modern Corporate Management," *Business History Review*, no. 1 (1965): 30.

20. "The Telegraph," *Harper's New Monthly Magazine* (1873): 334.

21. Thompson, *Wiring a Continent*, p. 203.

GENERAL VIEW, WIRELESS STATION
ARLINGTON, VA.   JULY, 2-12

Wireless telegraphy —
sending telegraph mes-
sages without wires — was
one of the first applications
of science to communica-
tions. It found its first use
at sea, especially in emergencies. The technology of
wireless telegraphy would
help make radio possible.

COMMUNICATION
WIRELESS TELEGRAPHY

B Y THE END OF THE NINETEENTH CENTURY THE telegraph and telephone, along with the electric light and power industry, were proof that electricity was the wonder of the age. Physicists and "electricians" — what we would today call electrical engineers — had begun to have a good idea of how electricity worked. Universities had established departments of electrical engineering. Large companies such as Bell Telephone and General Electric had established research departments to find technical answers to practical problems. The public looked forward to the next electrical miracle.

That miracle was wireless telegraphy — "wireless" for short. Telegraph without wires was followed before too long by telephone without wires. William Crookes, the British scientist and visionary, suggested the possibilities of a "new and astonishing" world of wireless in an 1892 article, "Some Possibilities of Electricity." Reviewing recent work in the physics of electromagnetism, he declared, "Here then is revealed the bewildering possibility of telegraphy without wires." He suggested the form this might take, extrapolating from the model already established by the telegraph. "Any two friends," he wrote, "having first decided on their special wavelength and attuned their respective instruments to mutual receptivity could thus communicate as long and as often as they pleased by timing the impulses to produce long and short intervals in the ordinary Morse code."[1]

But no one knew how to make money from radio. Crookes defined wireless narrowly, based on the precedents set by the telegraph. His article was widely read, and his notion that wireless was nothing more than telegraph without wires served, in some ways, to restrict the development of the new technology. For the next twenty years inventors and entrepreneurs would struggle to make money from wireless against fierce competition from cable, telegraph, and telephone — and one another. Not many customers were willing to pay for the expensive, unreliable communications provided by early wireless companies. Not many people needed to communicate beyond reach of the cables that had stretched across the country and around the world. Because of this, wireless technology would be characterized by a relentless search for markets, fierce competition, and rapid technological innovation. Not until the 1910s did a new generation of wireless pioneers begin to think of broadcasting as a goal. Only when the market was thus redefined did wireless really take off.

EARLY EXPERIMENTS

The physics Crookes referred to in his article dated back only about thirty years, to the theoretical work of James Clerk Maxwell. Maxwell, perhaps the greatest English physicist since Newton, was the first to propose a successful theory of electromagnetism. He showed that light was only one type of electromagnetic radiation, and made a series of predictions. Electrical circuits, he suggested, could resonate and produce electromagnetic fields. Furthermore, a second circuit with a similar resonant frequency would register these fields. Maxwell's work set the course for modern physics. And with his suggestions about electromagnetic fields, he also set the course for early radio.

Maxwell was not an experimentalist, but experimentalists read what he wrote. Some tried to prove his theories, others to disprove them. Heinrich Hertz, a professor of experimental physics at the Technical High School in Karlsruhe, Germany, was in the latter group. Hertz's experiments seem simple in retrospect. He would generate electromagnetic waves of a known frequency and measure their wavelength. Multiplying the wavelength by the frequency gave the speed, which was not infinite, as the doubters had forecast, and as Hertz had believed. Rather, it was identical to the speed of light — just as Maxwell had predicted. Hertz's apparatus suggested that electromagnetic radiation — that is, radio waves — could be used for communications, just like light. His experiments, and Maxwell's theories, would lay the groundwork for radio.

Hertz's apparatus was easy to make, and so many other physicists repeated his experiments. Oliver Lodge, a professor of physics from Liverpool, England, had been working along the same lines as Hertz, and, after reading Hertz's results, expanded upon his experiments. In 1894 Lodge built a wireless system using a spark gap as a transmitter, and a coherer — which detects radio signals by using the tendency of some materials to stick together when a radio wave passes through — as a receiver. He discovered that he could use the resonant properties of electrical circuits both to produce waves of a certain frequency and to detect them. The principle was similar to the resonances of two tuning forks of the same pitch; the vibrations of one would set off the other.

Lodge's discoveries, along with Hertz's, lay the groundwork for wireless telegraphy. But laying the foundation was not the same as erecting the building. Hertz and Lodge were physicists, not entrepreneurs. Looking back some years later, Lodge wrote that the idea of wireless telegraphy was obvious, but at the time he didn't see the point to it. (He was constrained by Crooke's definition of wireless.) Why bother "thus with difficulty [to] telegraph . . . across space instead of with ease by the highly developed and simple telegraphic and telephonic methods rendered possible by the use of a connecting wire"?[2] He believed, too, that commercialization was not a proper activity for a scientist.

Others weren't so constrained. Lodge's science inspired men who thought they could find fame and fortune by improving and commercializing the wireless. One of these men was Guglielmo Marconi. When he read of Hertz's

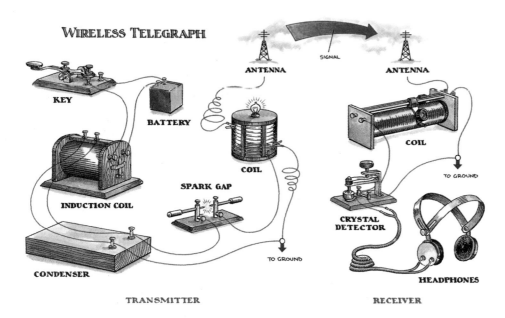

Whenever there is a change in electric current, as when a spark jumps across a gap, electromagnetic waves are emitted. When these waves, which flow through space at the speed of light, hit another wire, they cause a current to flow in that wire at the same frequency as in the first wire. Wireless telegraphy encodes Morse code messages by turning the transmitter on and off. The message is deciphered from the changing current in the receiver.

Early transmitters were simply spark gaps which put out electromagnetic waves of many frequencies. Later transmitters — which used "tuned" circuits, rotary devices, or vacuum tubes — sent out only a narrow range of frequencies, which meant that more than one station could broadcast at a time.

At the receiver, the signal was sensed by the use of a diode, a device that allows the current to flow in only one direction, converting it into direct current, which is easy to detect.

experiments in 1894 he was twenty years old and trying to decide what to do with himself. Marconi was not a scientist. He thought of himself as an inventor and a businessman. Where Lodge saw some interesting science in Hertz's work, Marconi saw money. He thought that there would be profit in wireless transmission, and he devoted himself to making a practical wireless system. He would be the first of many attracted to the wireless in the hope of striking it rich.

With the support of his father, a wealthy Italian merchant, Marconi repeated Hertz's experiments, at ever longer distances. But Marconi found little interest in wireless in Italy, and so he decided to move to England. In England there was considerable enthusiasm for a technology that could communicate with ships at sea: the British empire depended on its navy, and British commercial might depended on shipping. Moreover, in England he could get support from his mother's family, wealthy whiskey merchants. Marconi arrived in England in 1896, and applied for a patent on his wireless receiver the same year.

Lodge and other scientists, including A. S. Popov in Russia, and E. Branly in France, devised a variety of types of coherers to detect radio signals. In the Lodge coherer (the three devices in the foreground) the filings in the tube stick together when radio waves pass through. In Branly's design coherence occurs between the lower ends of the steel points and the polished steel plate. When coherence occurred, the contacts would conduct electricity. Some coherers included a "decoherer," or "trembler," a little hammer to tap them automatically after each signal.

Marconi had vision, drive, a flair for publicity, and good family connections. He impressed William Preece, chief engineer of the British Post Office, who became one of his supporters. Preece was charged with finding a way to communicate with ships and lighthouses. To this end he had experimented with inductive telegraphy, a system that used two long wires parallel to each other. One served as a transmitter, the other a receiver; a current in the first induced a current in the second. This worked, but it had one major drawback: the wires had to be about as long as the distance between them, a serious problem in communicating with ships at sea! Preece had just about given up on inductive telegraphy when Marconi arrived in England. Preece looked over Marconi's ideas, thought them promising, and urged that the Post Office undertake some tests. He wrote of Marconi's wireless that "enough has been done to prove its value and to show that for shipping and lighthouse purposes it will be a great and valuable acquisition."[3]

But Marconi's demonstrations were inconclusive — it was clear that the wireless needed more work — and Preece was unable to persuade the British government to support further development. Marconi instead turned to private funding. He organized the Wireless Telegraph and Signal Company in July 1897, mostly with money raised by his English relatives. The company's initial objective was to provide radiotelegraphy for lighthouses and lightships around the British Isles, but its first sales were to the British War Office for equipment to use in the Boer War. Marconi was a fine publicist for his equipment. He got a lot of attention when he radioed yacht race reports to newspaper reporters on shore, both in England and in the United States. And he graciously installed a wireless system for Queen Victoria so she might communicate with the Prince of Wales on board the royal yacht. The newspapers loved it!

In 1900 Marconi formed a new company, the Marconi International Marine Communications Company, to sell wireless for maritime use. To get around British laws nationalizing the telegraph and telephone system, the company decided not to sell equipment. Instead, customers would lease it, along with the operator, and had to agree to communicate only with other Marconi stations. This was an ideal way of enforcing a monopoly. In 1901 Marconi signed an agreement with Lloyds of London to relay shipping information, and his company started to prosper.

The possibilities of ship-to-shore communications were a driving force in the invention and rapid improvement of wireless. Marconi's report on the International Yacht Races in 1899 brought the invention its first American publicity. One of the main uses of the wireless was to send daily news reports to luxury liners, and to allow passengers on board the ships to keep in touch with their stockbrokers or wire ahead for hotel reservations. Contact with shore and other ships was extremely important in emergencies, of course. Wireless proved its value soon after its invention when, in 1900, a Russian ship was able to rescue a

Marconi and his transmitting and receiving apparatus, about 1900.

stranded fishing boat after receiving a wireless message. But the most significant early maritime use of the new wireless technology was in navigation. The Greenwich Observatory broadcast radio time signals that navigators could use to correct their clocks. Correct time was essential to calculating location at sea. Getting the correct time was an age-old problem in navigation, one that had worried navigators and inspired clockmakers for centuries. Radio solved it at last.

IMPROVING THE WIRELESS

Marconi's achievement was met with awe and wonder. His companies dominated the field by means of their technology, their clever leasing agreements, and their purchase of most of the important wireless patents, and because of Marconi's endless promotion. Marconi continued to improve his system. He focused on increasing the distance the signals could travel — that was the most easily measured indicator of success, and he was eager to prove himself — and ignored other issues, especially tuning.

Marconi took on the Atlantic Ocean as a challenge. In 1901 he succeeded in transmitting the letter *S* — three dots — from a transmitter at Poldhu in Cornwall to a receiver in Newfoundland. The Poldhu transmitter was huge. Its antenna was supported by twenty wooden masts, each 200 feet high, arranged in a circle. The antenna in Newfoundland was a 400-foot wire supported by a huge kite. Marconi listened for a transmission at prearranged times, and on December 12 claimed to hear the message. He couldn't prove it; it wasn't strong enough to drive a printer, and there was no independent observer present. But the press, already much taken with Marconi, played up the story. The publicity stunt worked. But that's all it was; there wasn't much of a market for transatlantic wireless telegraphy because transatlantic cables could do the job better. (At the turn of the century, there were twelve telegraph cables operating across the Atlantic, carrying more than 25 million words a year at about twenty-five cents a word.)

In the last few years of the nineteenth century many inventors tried to improve on Marconi's system. The problem with his early spark transmitters was that they could not be tuned. They were "dirty," putting out a signal that covered a large part of the spectrum, which meant that every receiver picked up the messages from every transmitter. Oliver Lodge was the first to realize the importance of "syntony" in radio, in 1897. Syntonic circuits had a particular resonant frequency at which they vibrated. This meant that they wasted much less power and broadcast a narrower signal. Lodge patented this idea. Marconi then improved on it by finding ways to vary the resonances to tune his circuits, and by hooking the antenna to the transmitter inductively rather than directly, which afforded increased power. This meant that he could transmit at a given frequency, with high power. Marconi received a patent in 1900, and after extensive court battles eventually purchased Lodge's patent, too.

Syntonic circuits were followed by another transmitter breakthrough: continuous waves. This new technology, developed in the early years of the twentieth century, would eventually make possible tuned transmissions, longer-

Marconi's transmitting station at Poldhu, Cornwall, from which he sent the first transatlantic signal in 1901. At left are transformers; in the wooden racks are capacitors; at far right is the spark gap, which actually sent the signal.

distance transmission, and, most important, transmission not of just the dots and dashes of Morse code but of the human voice. Many inventors took on the challenge of continuous-wave transmission and reception.

There were three ways to improve existing transmitter technology. One was to use very high spark frequencies (about 5,000 times a second), enough to transmit the frequencies of the human voice. A second technique was to use oscillating arcs, and a third to use alternators, high-frequency alternating current generators, which would produce continuous waves. Reginald Fessenden, a Canadian who had worked for Edison and had been in charge of wireless development for the U.S. Weather Service, was convinced that he could design a continuous-wave transmitter that would be capable of transmitting speech. He established the National Electric Signaling Company in 1902 and began experiments. With his new transmitter, built by General Electric, Fessenden could transmit good audio, and he eagerly did so. On Christmas Eve 1906 Fessenden broadcast recorded music, and then played the violin for his astonished listeners, Marconi wireless operators who had never before heard anything but dots and dashes on their headphones.

New transmitters were matched with a new receiver. The coherer was slow and balky; there was a clear need for a better device. In search of a better receiver, inventors investigated the effects of radio waves on a wide range of materials. In 1902 and 1903 Lee de Forest and Reginald Fessenden independently invented electrolytic detectors that made use of platinum wires in an acid solution to detect radio waves. In 1902 Marconi invented a magnetic detector based on the effects of radio waves on a changing magnetic field. Several inventors experimented with the effects of radio waves on minerals. They found that silicon, galena, and carborundum, among others, if just barely touched by a small piece of wire — called a cat's whisker — would rectify the radio waves, turning

Fessenden's broadcast station with its Alexanderson transmitter, about 1905.

Cyril Elwell, an electrical engineering student at Stanford University, raised funds from his professors to develop an improved arc transmitter. By decreasing the size of the arc he increased the distance it could transmit. He also was able to control frequency much better, so that transmitters interfered with each other less. He demonstrated the system for the navy in 1912, transmitting from Arlington, Virginia, to Honolulu, a new distance record. Over the next five years, Elwell's Federal Company built a worldwide wireless system for the navy, including this station in Arlington.

their alternating current into easily detected direct current. These crystal detectors were cheap, and were quickly adopted.

John Ambrose Fleming's 1904 invention of the vacuum tube would soon make all of these clever but complicated and quirky receivers and transmitters obsolete. Fleming, a professor of electrical engineering at the University of London, and Marconi's scientific adviser, had formerly worked for the English Edison Company. There he had done some experiments with the "Edison effect," the tendency of electric current to flow from the filament of a light bulb to a positively charged plate sealed in the bulb. It represented a problem for light bulb manufacturers because electrons would flow

from the filament to the glass bulb, darkening the glass. But Fleming showed that the effect could be very useful for wireless receivers. He applied the radio signal to the plate in the tube. The signal drew electrons from the filament during the positive half of the cycle. These electrons would re-create the "envelope" of the radio signal, the original audio information. With appropriate circuits, this signal could be applied to a pair of headphones.

Other inventors were also working on vacuum tube receivers. Lee De Forest was one. De Forest, born in Iowa in 1873, received his Ph.D. from Yale's Sheffield Scientific School in 1899. He was fascinated by radio, and even more by the chance to make money by improving it. Indeed, he was so interested in radio that he ignored the work he was assigned at Western Electric, where he found employment after graduation, in order to tinker with wireless receivers. He then went to work for the American Wireless Telegraph Company, but was fired after refusing to reveal his improvements to their system. De Forest had his eye on the prize. He wrote: "I will not let it go into the hands of any company until that company is my own. . . . If I fail it will not be for grit, nor because I was afraid to try."[4]

De Forest devoted himself to the wireless, reading scientific journals in the public library and working in his home laboratory. Between 1900 and 1906 he received more than thirty patents, none of great importance. One was for an electrolytic detector not too different from Fessenden's, a patent that would become the subject of the first of De Forest's many patent suits. He took Marconi as his role model, and invited the press to countless public demonstrations of his equipment. (These demonstrations included one yacht race where both he and Marconi tried to demonstrate the superiority of their equipment, and ended up jamming each other's signals.) And he set up one company after another, many of them of dubious legality, to sell his inventions and make his fortune. "Soon, we believe, the suckers will bite," he wrote in his diary.[5] De Forest spent more time out hustling to sell his patents and stock in his companies than he spent in the laboratory. His De Forest Wireless Telegraph Company included a glass-walled laboratory where investors could see him at work, so he could hustle and invent at the same time!

In 1906 G. W. Pickard and H. H. C. Dunwoody discovered independently that certain crystals touching each other or touching a metal point can detect radio waves. (Radio waves cause an electric current to flow in one direction across the junction.) This reliable, inexpensive arrangement, popularly called a "cat's whisker," was quickly adopted by thousands of radio hobbyists.

While experimenting with his newly invented electric light in 1881, Edison noticed a "phantom shadow." The shadow was caused because the filament blocked the electrons from hitting the glass and darkening it. The migration of electrons within the tube became known as the Edison effect. Edison made no further use of it, but others built on this discovery to create the vacuum tube.

The three-element tube invented by Lee De Forest in 1906 was first used to detect radio waves. Others experimented with modifications of the tube and found it could both amplify signals and produce radio waves. A relatively inexpensive item, it quickly became popular with radio amateurs. De Forest called his tubes audions; three-element tubes were later known as triodes.

De Forest continued his investigations, receiving patents for detectors that used the effect of radio waves on flames. These flame detectors led to his 1906 breakthrough invention, the three-element vacuum tube, or Audion. The Audion consisted of a filament, which was the source of electrons; a plate, to receive the electrons; and in between them a grid which would control the flow of electrons between the filament and the plate. It's uncertain if De Forest knew of

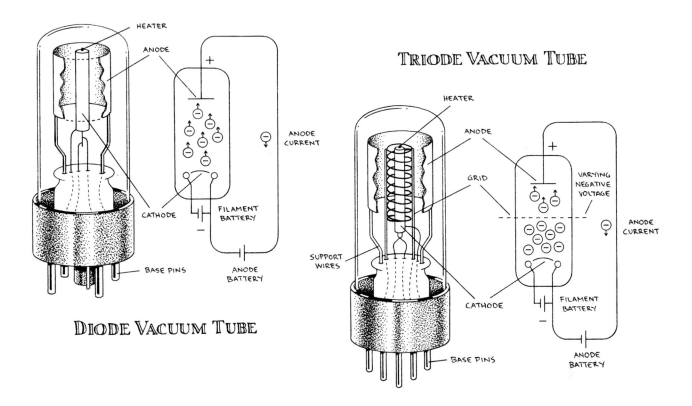

DIODE VACUUM TUBE

TRIODE VACUUM TUBE

Inside a vacuum tube electrons flow from the elements with a higher potential to the elements with a lower potential. A two-element tube (called a diode) has a cathode and an anode. A heater allows electrons to flow from the cathode (emitter) to the anode (collector) when a positive charge (which attracts electrons) is applied to the anode (as shown). However, if a negative charge (which repels electrons) is applied, no current will flow. Thus the tube serves as a one-way valve, or rectifier. Because it only lets electricity flow one way, it converts alternating current into direct current. This kind of tube can also serve as a radio receiver.

If a third element is added, the tube is called a triode. In addition to the cathode and anode, a triode has a grid. A very small negative voltage in the grid can control a much larger amount flowing between the cathode and the anode. A vacuum tube set up in this way acts as an amplifier.

Fleming's tube. He denied having heard of it, but his denial is hard to believe. We know that De Forest kept up with the scientific literature, and it seems unlikely that he would have missed notice of Fleming's invention. Furthermore, De Forest was the sort of person who hated to give anyone else credit. But even if he had heard of it, the two inventions were fundamentally different, though superficially similar. The Audion could do more than detect signals; it could also amplify them, which would make a dramatic difference to radio.

The Audion was a major breakthrough, and De Forest's 1908 patent was to be one of the most valuable ever issued. It allowed greatly improved wire-

Wireless telegraphy caught the public eye when the *Titanic,* the world's largest luxury liner, struck an iceberg on April 14, 1912. The ship's wireless telegraph operators flashed the international distress signal, CQD, and the message "We are in collision with berg. Sinking head down; 41.46N, 50.14W. Come soon as possible." But on the closest ship, which could have reached the *Titanic* before it sank, no one was listening. Other ships did not arrive until after the *Titanic* had gone down. The *Carpathia,* the *Titanic* rescue ship, sent news of the disaster by wireless to shore. Not long after the *Titanic* disaster, the United States Government required that all American ships install wireless equipment. Shown here is the wireless room of the S.S. *America.*

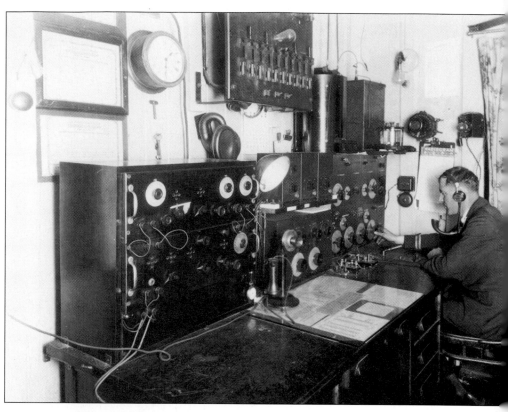

less communication and led to the development of a family of vacuum tubes that would make it possible, over the next few years, to broadcast radio. But De Forest and his competitors were still thinking along the lines that Crookes had suggested years before. They were exploring a narrow market niche for their technology, wireless telegraphy or at best wireless telephony.

PUTTING WIRELESS TO WORK

Marconi, De Forest, Fessenden, and Armstrong turned an interesting scientific principle into a useful and practical form of communication — useful and practical, but with a very limited field of applications. Wireless had a hard time competing with wired telegraphs, which by 1900 had reached almost every town in America and extended to Europe, Asia, and around the world. Telegraphs provided cheap and reliable communication. Telephones, too, were competition. It's no wonder that wireless pioneers had such a hard time selling their invention. They were limited to niche markets, customers with special communications needs and the ability to pay dearly for them. (See TELEGRAPH and TELEPHONE.)

As Marconi realized, the most obvious use for wireless was for ships at sea. Wireless was clearly valuable in case of emergency, and it had advantages in the day-to-day running of the ship. It made navigation easier since time signals broadcast by wireless meant it was easier for ships to know exactly where they were. It was also used by passengers, who could keep in touch with friends and business associates on shore. Only the largest ships installed wireless in the early

years. But when the quick thinking of the wireless operator on the *Republic* during a 1909 collision led to the rescue of hundreds of passengers, a law was passed requiring all large ships to carry wireless equipment. The sinking of the *Titanic* three years later was to lead to new, stronger regulations.

Further improvements in radio location finding during World War I completely changed the way navigators at sea did their job. Not long after broadcasting started, engineers realized that by using a loop antenna they could locate the source of the signal. Radio beacons along the coast allowed navigators on board ships and airplanes to determine their longitude and latitude. Before the invention of the radio beacon, the navigator had to make detailed astronomical observations and then undertake complicated mathematical calculations to figure out where he was. Radio changed all that.

Before World War I, the navy was generally unenthusiastic about wireless telegraphy. Ships' captains were given extraordinary authority, for they were out of the reach of direct command most of the time. They weren't pleased to see the navy adopt a new technology that would, as they saw it, keep them under the thumb of shore-based officers. And since the navy was run by captains and former captains, it was slow to adopt radio. Even after it did, the navy used the equipment little and maintained it poorly. Not until the navy's radio system was reorganized in the early 1910s and supporters of the new technology gained some power was radio put to use. And not until the First World War demonstrated the value of radio did the navy adopt it wholeheartedly. Wireless also played a role in field communications in the war, but its unreliability and ease of interception reduced it to an auxiliary to the extensive wired communications systems.

An American army wireless operator. Wireless telegraphy was used by both sides in World War I, but problems with the technology meant that whenever possible, wires were run.

Hundreds of thousands of boys and men, and a smaller number of girls and women, played with wireless sets for the thrill of communicating with other amateur radio operators across the country.

Some amateurs made their stations from parts, others purchased their equipment or assembled kits like this one from the Electro-Importing Company. The Electro-Importing Company was run by Hugo Gernsback, who established *Modern Electrics* magazine to promote his store. Gernsback would go on to establish some of the most important early science fact and science fiction magazines, promoting a whole host of new technologies.

Specialized business customers also found wireless valuable. One of de Forest's most important customers was the United Fruit Company, which grew and exported bananas from South and Central America to the United States and around the world. United Fruit established a wireless service that connected its offices in a half dozen Latin American countries to its ships. This replaced an earlier system that had depended on cable service to Panama, land cables to Nicaragua and Costa Rica, and then canoe trips of up to sixty hours to the outlying offices.

By far the largest group to adapt wireless was amateur tinkerers, or "hams." Most amateurs were young men who built their own equipment be-

A ham radio operator, 1992. Amateur radio didn't disappear when broadcasting went commercial — far from it. In the United States in 1992 over one-half million licensed amateurs continued to talk to one another and to other amateurs around the world, both communications for its own sake and to serve as an emergency communications system. Ham radio operators explored new high-frequency areas of the spectrum, opening up new territory for commercial broadcasters.

cause they liked to play with the latest technology, or because they enjoyed the experience of communicating with distant places. With simple equipment anyone could talk in Morse code to people miles away. It was a thrilling prospect, even if they didn't have much to say. Most of the time the subject of conversation was the distance the signal reached, or the technology used. Before long there were thousands of hams in the United States. They formed clubs, read hobbyist magazines, and exchanged cards verifying their radio contacts. On many occasions they passed along information during emergencies when other systems failed. A popular magazine described the amateurs in 1910: "In the past two years another wireless system has been gradually developing, a system that has far outstripped all the others in size and popularity. . . . Hundreds of schoolboys in every part of the country have taken to this most popular scientific fad, and, by copying the instruments used at the regular stations and constructing apparatus out of all kinds of electrical junk, have built wireless equipments that in some cases approach the naval stations in efficiency."[6]

As wireless proved its value, especially in maritime disasters, it became more professional. The U.S. government decided to regulate it, and there were battles between amateurs and professionals over the new laws. The tragedy of the *Titanic*'s unanswered distress call prompted an international outcry and spurred governments around the world to regulate wireless communications. Congress responded to pressure from American radio users (especially the navy, which warned of "etheric bedlam") by passing legislation in 1912 that regulat-ed wireless by licensing all broadcasters. Subsequent laws established the Feder-al Radio Commission in 1927 to allocate frequencies and license operators. The FRC (and its successor, the Federal Communications Commission, formed in 1934) would not only assign radio frequencies but would play a major role in shaping the technology and uses of radio and television by determining standards and promulgating and overseeing broadcast rules.

These standards and assignments were the result of extensive lobbying on behalf of broadcasters and manufacturers. Amateur radio operators lost out in these battles. The navy, which used wireless to keep in touch with its ships, was angry about interference from amateurs' transmitters and occasional malicious pranks. In emergencies such as the *Titanic*'s sinking, the hubbub of radio signals impeded communications. Amateurs were forbidden to broadcast during World War I, except under special conditions. New allocation rules moved amateurs to the shortwave area of the spectrum, which was generally thought to be useless.

But short waves proved to be more useful than anyone had thought. Amateurs discovered in 1921 that they could be received over long distances, and soon commercial operations began to use them. The knowledge gained by amateurs about shortwave transmitting and receiving turned out to be very valu-able. Hams were at the forefront of the extension of wireless from sending cod-ed signals over the air to sending voices over the air. Amateurs' increased knowl-edge about the properties of radio waves helped improve techniques of sending and receiving. From their ranks came a new generation of electronics engineers.

The narrow market niche for wireless resulted as much from cultural ex-pectations as from technology. Almost everyone thought that wireless's lack of secrecy and privacy were major drawbacks. No one wanted to send messages to everyone, or so the promoters of wireless thought. Their assumptions were shaped by their background in the telegraph and telephone business, and by the early marine markets for wireless. These expectations for the technology limited its use as much as its technical limitations did.

Only slowly did people begin to realize that wireless's lack of privacy could be an advantage, not a disadvantage. Reginald Fessenden, whose 1906 Christmas Eve concert is generally considered the first radio broadcast, was one of the first to understand that wireless's ability to be received by many might be a selling point. In part this came about because of his successes in transmitting voice; there was a much wider market for voice than for Morse code. De Forest, too, realized that there might be a market for broadcasting. He was a great opera fan, and was sure that many people would pay to have opera transmitted into their homes.

David Sarnoff, manager of the Marconi Company in the United States, also shared this vision. Sarnoff would have a chance to test his ideas when the Radio Corporation of America was created in October 1919 and he became commercial manager. The end of the war had brought confusion to the wireless field. The navy, which had obtained a monopoly over most broadcasting during the war, tried to keep that control afterward. Amateur operators, eager to get back to their transmitters, prevented that. The Marconi Company's monopoly was abhorrent to Americans who feared foreign influence, and there was con-siderable pressure to rationalize a complex patent situation under American control. The patents needed to make receivers and transmitters — some 2,000 patents altogether — were in the hands of competing firms. It made sense, these large firms argued, to establish a patent pool, so that they could be shared. General Electric bought a controlling interest in American Marconi and established the Radio Corporation of America to take over Marconi's business in the United States. The agreement that established RCA made that firm sales agent for GE and Westinghouse, which would manufacture radio receivers. AT&T — American Telephone & Telegraph — would have the sole rights to sell broadcast transmitters.

This solution to the patent and competition problem was too complex to work for long, and it fell apart when wireless telegraphy and telephony evolved into radio broadcasting. By 1920 wireless had a new name. Starting as early as 1906, wireless telegraphy began to be called radiotelegraphy; by 1920 the prefix alone carried the meaning. *Radio* came from the word *radiate*, appropriate to the new use of the technology, for it radiated in all directions. Wireless was about to turn into radio. (See RADIO.)

FOR FURTHER READING

The best technical histories of wireless telegraphy are two books by Hugh G. J. Aitkin, *Syntony and Spark: The Origins of Radio* (1976), and *The Continuous Wave: Technology and American Radio, 1900–1932* (1985). These are complemented by Susan J. Douglas, *Inventing American Broadcasting, 1899–1922* (1987), which fills in the cultural and social side of the story. For more on the military use of the radio, see Douglas's essay "The Navy Adopts the Radio, 1899–1919," in *Military Enterprise and Technological Change,* ed. Merritt Roe Smith (1987).

Overall histories of radio include George G. Blake, *History of Radio Telegraphy and Telephony* (1974); Stanley Leinwoll, *From Spark to Satellite: A History of Radio Communication* (1979); and, for the personal side of the story, Tom Lewis, *Empire of the Air: The Men Who Made Radio* (1991).

NOTES

1. William Crookes, "Some Possibilities of Electricity," *Fortnightly Review*, February 1, 1892; quoted in Hugh G. J. Aitkin, *Syntony and Spark: The Origins of Radio* (1976), p. 112.

2. Oliver Lodge, *Signalling without Wires* (1902); quoted in Aitken, *Syntony and Spark*, p. 116.

3. W. H. Preece, "Signaling through Space without Wires," *The Electrician*, June 11, 1897, pp. 216–218; quoted in Aitken, *Syntony and Spark*, p. 181.

4. From Lee de Forest's journal; quoted in Tom Lewis, *Empire of the Air: The Men Who Made Radio* (1991), p. 39.

5. From de Forest's journal; quoted in Lewis, *Empire of the Air*, p. 42.

6. Robert A. Morton, "The Amateur Wireless Operator," *Outlook*, January 15, 1910, p. 131; quoted in Susan J. Douglas, *Inventing American Broadcasting, 1899–1922* (1987), p. 195.

By the middle of the twentieth century the telephone, invented in 1876, had become our connection to the world. The telephone found its first use as a business tool, but its ease of use gave it universal appeal. Inventors and system-builders soon discovered ways to make it possible for almost everyone to have one. The telephone brings us together for business and pleasure. It links individuals and builds communities. And more and more, it ties us to the world of computers. The telephone system would become the backbone of the America's information infrastructure.

COMMUNICATION
TELEPHONE

SHORTLY AFTER ALEXANDER GRAHAM BELL MADE his first working telephone, in 1876, he wrote: "The telephone reminds me of a child only it grows much more rapidly. What is before it in the future, no man can tell — but I see new possibilities before it — and new uses."[1] Not everyone saw these uses. The first reaction of many telegraph experts to the telephone was that it might be used to allow telegraph operators to talk to one another. No one imagined the possibilities of person-to-person communications without a trained operator to send the message.

The telephone required a new way of thinking about communications, but it wasn't long before the telephone's uses were clear to everyone. Telephone companies responded to its astonishing utility with an enormous program of innovation and system building. Just ten years after the telephone was first demonstrated in 1876, there were some 167,000 phones in the United States. By the turn of the century there were almost 1 million, each used, on average, to make five calls a day. By the 1920s the phone had become a common item in almost every home and business.

And by the 1990s the telephone system had become a link to the rest of the world and the gateway to the world of computers and information. Thousands of technological innovations in telephone switching; new transmission systems such as microwaves, satellites, and fiber optics; and, most important, the joining of information processing systems with the phone system brought dramatic new uses for the telephone network. Bell would have been astonished at the possibilities that came to pass.

INVENTING THE TELEPHONE

Technically, many of the elements of the telephone were available with the invention of the telegraph. Both transmitted electrical signals over wires. Both used electromagnets to produce sound. But it took time, work, and unusual insight to realize that the voice could be changed into electrical signals that could be transmitted over long distances and used to reproduce the original. Before the telephone there were no microphones, no speakers, no real under-

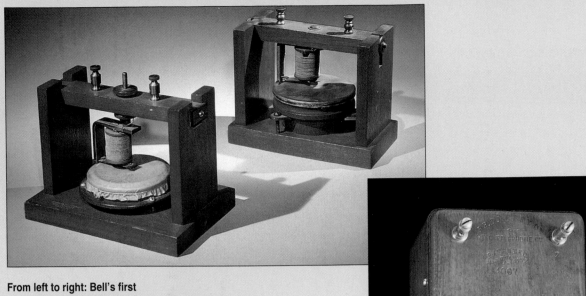

From left to right: Bell's first telephone with a membrane diaphragm, 1875, which transmitted sounds, but not words. One of Bell's first commercial telephones. Bell's 1876 liquid transmitter telephone, on which he told Mr. Watson to "come here." The telephones that Bell showed at the 1876 Centennial.

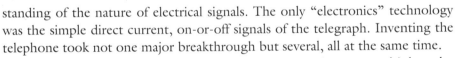

standing of the nature of electrical signals. The only "electronics" technology was the simple direct current, on-or-off signals of the telegraph. Inventing the telephone took not one major breakthrough but several, all at the same time.

The origins of the telephone lay in attempts to invent a multiplex telegraph — a telegraph that could send more than one message over a single wire simultaneously. The need for this was obvious: it would cut the telegraph company's spending on copper wire, a major expense. It would also help to clear up the astonishing clutter of wiring that was beginning to blight American cities. (See TELEGRAPH.)

In the 1870s many inventors were at work on multiplex telegraphs. Elisha Gray and Alexander Graham Bell each independently invented the harmonic telegraph, a form of multiplex telegraph that used several tuned reeds in the transmitter and receiver to send multiple independent messages. Both Bell and Gray realized that a similar device might transmit voice signals. After all, it wasn't that much of a leap from the vibrations of the reeds to sound vibrations. On February 14, 1876, Gray, a professional telegraph inventor, filed a patent caveat on a telephone system. (The caveat meant that he had an idea for a patent and would file papers soon.) On the same date, though, and a few hours earlier, Alexander Graham Bell had filed for a patent on his own telephone system.

Bell, a teacher of the deaf and a professor at the School of Oratory at Boston University, had started experimenting with electricity in 1872. His first invention was "an instrument for transmitting vibrations" to help lip-readers distinguish between the letters *P* and *B*. From this it was a short step to the harmonic telegraph. For the next five years Bell would spend his every spare hour working on the telegraph and the telephone.

Bell realized that it would be possible to transmit several signals, each at a different frequency, on one wire. A series of receivers, each tuned to one of the frequencies, would sort out the different messages. His next step was a receiver that vibrated freely in response to the complex frequencies of the human voice. After working with this new experimental setup, he reformulated the problem. His assistant Thomas Watson later recalled that Bell had explained the project thus: "If I can get a mechanism which will make a current of electricity vary in its intensity, as the air varies in density when a sound is passing through it, I can telegraph any sound, even the sound of speech."[2] This insight was the key to the telephone.

Bell soon realized that he needed help, both financial and technological. In October 1874 he agreed to give Thomas Sanders, a prosperous Haverhill, Massachusetts, leather merchant, and Gardiner Hubbard, a Boston lawyer and financier, each one third of any future patents in exchange for their financial support. With that support, Bell hired Watson, an employee of a Boston scientific instrument shop, who had made some of his earlier instruments.

Bell and Watson focused first on the multiple telegraph, which was what their financial backers thought would make money. But, as Bell later recalled, "In spite of my efforts to concentrate my thoughts upon multiple telegraphy, my mind was full of [the electrical transmission of speech]."[3] In June 1875 Bell noticed that a vibrating reed could send a signal over a wire that would make a similar reed vibrate at the other end. Not only that: the receiving reed vibrated loudly enough to be heard. In July an improved system using a membrane transmitter and receiver carried vocal sounds — not audible speech, but close. Close enough to file a patent, which arrived at the Patent Office on the same day as Gray's caveat.

To contest Bell's priority in the invention, Gray would have had to file his own patent immediately, or forgo his claim. But, though his caveat might well have been inspired by rumors of Bell's work, the telephone seemed unimportant compared to continuing his telegraph work. He wrote his patent attorney: "The talking telegraph is a beautiful thing in a scientific point of view. . . . But if you look at it in a business light it is of no importance. We can do more . . . with a wire now than with that method. . . . This is the verdict of practical telegraph men."[4] Gray decided not to contest the patent. (He would later regret this decision, and after the telephone proved its value, he would wage a long legal battle with Bell.) On March 7, 1876, Bell received a patent for "Improvement in Telegraphy," which included both a tuned-reed harmonic telegraph and a magneto-electric telephone.

Bell had halted his telephone experiments in June, but returned to them at about the time he received the patent. A discussion with the patent examiner had suggested the nature of Gray's work, and Bell decided to try a transmitter of the sort that Gray had considered, using a diaphragm that changed the resistance of the line by dipping a needle into a dish of slightly acid water. Just three days later, on March 10, 1876, Bell was successful. He wrote in his notebook: "I then shouted into [the mouthpiece] the following sentence: 'Mr. Watson — come here — I want to see you.' To my delight he came and declared that he had heard and understood what I had said. I asked him to repeat the words. He answered 'You said — Mr. Watson — come here — I want to see you.' "[5]

Bell continued to experiment with transmitters and receivers, soon replacing the liquid variable-resistance transmitter with an electromagnetic transmitter that used the sound waves themselves to induce current in the line. The same device also served as a receiver. This worked well enough so that Bell began to give public demonstrations of the telephone. The most important one was at the Centennial Exposition in Philadelphia. Bell demonstrated three induction telephones to a select jury that included Sir William Thomson, perhaps the best-known British electrical scientist, and Dom Pedro, emperor of Brazil. It made an enormous hit: Dom Pedro expressed everyone's astonishment with the new machine by exclaiming (so legend has it), "My God, it talks!" Elisha Gray, who was at the fair showing off his successful multiplex telegraph, also saw the demonstration and heard the machine talk. He went home and built his own telephone, but before long returned to his telegraph work.

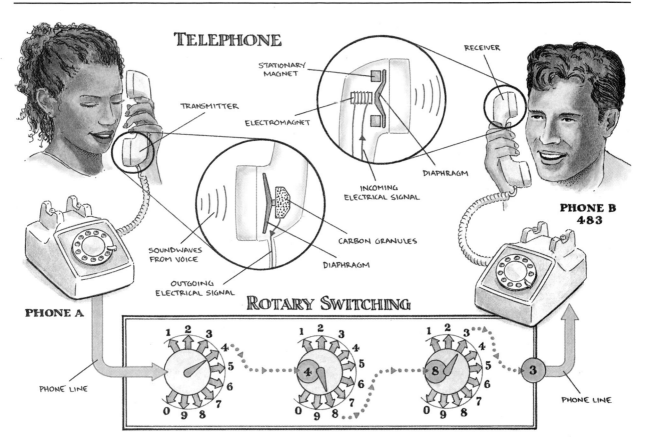

The telegraph sends simple on or off signals over a wire. The telephone sends much more complex signals whose current reflects exactly the air pressures of the original sounds.

The sending telephone uses a microphone to convert the changing air pressure of the voice into a changing electrical current. The most successful early microphone was Edison's carbon microphone, which worked by allowing more current to pass through when it was compressed by louder sounds. At the receiving telephone the modulated current drives an electromagnet, which makes a speaker vibrate. The vibrations of the speaker move the air nearby, and thus reproduce the original sounds.

The complicated part is the wiring between the two phones. It's too expensive to run a direct wire between every pair of phones, so instead each phone is connected to a central switching station. At the switching station the pulses generated by the dial (or the tones generated by the push buttons) select which lines to connect the call to. In the picture, the caller dials the number 483. The first switch connects the call to switch number 4 out of ten possibilities; the second to switch number 8 of ten; and the final to switch number 3 of ten. A three-digit number can reach up to 1,000 phones; the seven-digit local numbers we're used to can reach up to 10,000,000 phones.

INVENTING THE PHONE SYSTEM

It was a long way from a demonstration of a piece of experimental apparatus to a practical phone system, which required not just improving the telephone itself but also inventing switching systems and developing the business and legal side of the enterprise. Bell and his partners established the Bell Telephone Company and introduced commercial service in 1877. By 1880 they had installed some 50,000 phones. But they still had much work to do. They needed to make the phone easier to use. They needed to find a use that the general public would pay for. And they needed a way to tie all of the subscribers together. The men who solved these problems, the inventors of the business organization that created the telephone system, played as important a role as the inventors of the technology.

Gardiner Hubbard, who became head of the company, was a great promoter but not the most realistic businessman. He sold rights to establish telephone companies to entrepreneurs all across the country, and decided — a key decision, in retrospect — that telephones would only be rented, not sold. This allowed the company to maintain control over the technology, prevent unauthorized parties from building telephones, and, most important, make universal interconnection possible. Any phone could "talk" to any other. In the short run this decision almost bankrupted the company because its only income was from rental fees and patent royalties. In the long run the policy was responsible for the extraordinary growth of the company. The trick was surviving for the long run.

The Bell Company was based on a patent monopoly. It was as much a legal triumph as a technological one. To succeed the firm first had to fight off legal attacks from Western Union, which immediately challenged its patents and did its best to circumvent them. Western Union, the largest American telegraph company, bought the rights to the patents of Gray, Edison, and others, and established the American Speaking Telephone Company in December 1877. The lawsuits that followed raged for two years. They were finally settled in November 1879, when Western Union agreed to get out of the phone business and transfer its patents to the Bell Company in exchange for 20 percent of telephone rental receipts over the next seventeen years. But the lawsuits didn't end. The Bell Telephone Company went on the attack, bringing hundreds of infringement suits against its competitors in its first few years. One of its lawyers observed, "The Bell company has had a monopoly more profitable and more controlling — and more generally hated — than any ever given by any patent."[6]

The Bell Company's success depended on the Bell patents, and so competitors brought forward dozens of inventors to claim that they had invented the telephone first, thus invalidating the patents. One inventor who had come close was Philipp Reis, in Germany, who had constructed a variable-resistance transmitter in 1860 for use in demonstrations of the nature of sound. In his transmitter a membrane with a platinum contact point in its center vibrated against a metal plate, transmitting the rhythm and pitch of speech but not degree of loudness. The result was a speechlike buzzing, not speech. Reis did not fully understand his transmitter or his receiver (which worked by induction), and failed to see their value as a potential telephone. Antonio Meucci, an Italian immigrant who lived on Long Island, also claimed to have invented the telephone, based on a caveat he had filed in 1871. His telephone, though, was an acoustic one, a tin-can telephone, and the promoter who tried to use this caveat to break Bell's patent failed.

The Bell patent, under attack in all of these suits, was upheld in the end. But Bell's technology had many flaws, and the Bell Company realized that improvements were vital. Early phones produced weak signals that were understandable only over short distances. It took effort to learn how to use the device. One of the first advertisements for the telephone gave this advice: "Conversation can easily be carried on after slight practice and with occasional repetition of a word or sentence. On first listening to the Telephone, though the sound is perfectly audible, the articulation seems to be indistinct; but after a few trials the ear becomes accustomed to the peculiar sound."[7] Many inventors made improvements — better transmitters, amplifying receivers, ways to reduce distortion over long lines or to amplify the signal — in attempts to overcome these problems.

The first technical hurdles involved the instruments themselves. New transmitters came first. In Bell's commercial transmitter, the voice itself induced a fluctuating electric current in the line. There was no amplification. Both Bell and Gray had experimented with variable-resistance liquid transmitters that also acted as amplifiers. Although these instruments had not been effective, other inventors working on variable-resistance transmitters had better results with other materials.

The most important of these was Thomas Edison's variable-resistance carbon transmitter, invented in 1877. Edison had invented in 1873 a rheostat that used changing pressure on fine particles of graphite to vary electrical resistance. When Western Union came to Edison to invent a telephone not covered by Bell's patents — Western Union would spend millions attempting to break into the phone business — Edison realized that this principle could serve as a telephone transmitter. The changing pressure of sound waves would change the resistance in the circuit, converting the variations of the voice into variations in the electric current. (Bell's original transmitter had *produced* a varying current; Edison's transmitter varied an *existing* current, creating a clearer and louder sound.) Graphite didn't work well enough, so he tried — in classic Edison inventive style — a variety of other materials, finally settling on a button of lampblack in February 1878. This worked well, and Edison patented it. To get around this patent, the Bell Company first contested it, pointing to a similar patent received a few days earlier by Emile Berliner, and then, when it lost that case, unearthing another transmitter patented by Francis Blake.

Inventors also developed new and better receivers, again in part to circumvent Bell's patents. Amplifying receivers, in which a small incoming current controls a larger current from a battery, allowed a better-quality signal to be heard over a longer distance. Edison was successful here, too, inventing a "loud speaking" receiver in 1877 that forced a compromise between the Bell and Edison interests. Eventually all of the inventions designed to break the AT&T monopoly were subsumed by the giant telephone company and used to improve its service.

As the phone system increased in size, a new problem needed a solution. How should the phones be tied together? Connecting each phone to every other phone to create a network was a problem that got bigger as the phone system

The earliest switchboards, called crossbar switchboards, consisted of a grid of criss-crossing metal strips. A vertical bar was assigned to each subscriber. Perpendicular to these bars ran a series of horizontal bars. When a call came in, an operator would answer it, get the name of the party being called, and establish the connection by inserting plugs that would connect the parties' vertical bars with the same horizontal bar. This switchboard was used in Richmond, Virginia, in the late 1880s.

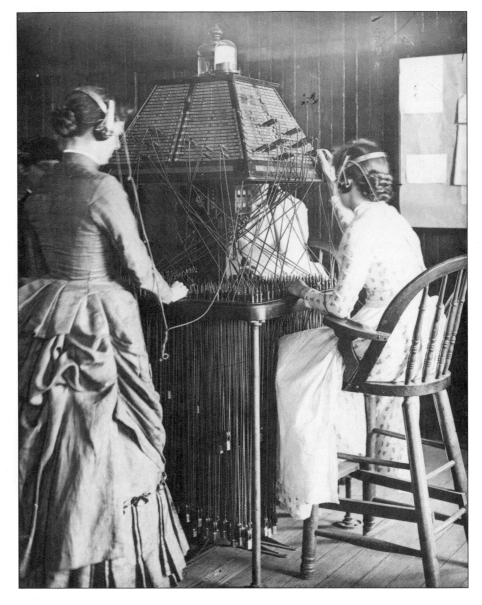

got bigger. When only a few people had phones, they could be connected directly to one another via private lines. As more people acquired phones, the local companies needed to set up central offices where an operator would connect callers to one another.

The first commercial switchboard was opened in New Haven, Connecticut, in 1878, and in the 1880s switchboards were established everywhere. These early switchboards were based on the "crossbar" system. The first operators were young boys, often telegraph messengers. One visitor to a telephone exchange described the scene: "The racket is almost deafening. Boys are rushing madly hither and thither, while others are putting in or taking out pegs from a central framework as if they were lunatics engaged in a game of fox and geese."[8] Before long the male operators, hard to keep in line, were replaced by supposedly more docile young women. For the next century women operators would run the switchboards for the telephone system.

As more and more people subscribed, the solution was the "multiple switchboard," a system that allowed each operator to connect any of the hundred or so subscribers for whom he or she was responsible to the operator responsible for the party being called, and thus to any of the thousands of subscribers in the exchange. This system was improved over the years with new methods of signaling operators. But as the phone system grew, it became obvious that the number of operators would get out of hand. The phone company's calculations suggested that before long, more operators would be needed than there were young girls suitable for the job!

The ultimate answer was automatic switching: make the caller do the work of the operator. The first automatic exchange was invented in 1889 by Almon B. Strowger, a Kansas City undertaker. Strowger had a good practical reason for inventing the automatic switchboard. Legend has it that his telephone operator was the wife of a business rival, and he was sure that she was diverting business from him to her husband. And so he devised what he called a "girl-less, cuss-less" telephone exchange. Each telephone subscriber was assigned a number; first push buttons, then dials, were added to the phones. As each number was pushed or dialed, a series of switches was closed; the final number made the final connection. The first automatic switchboard was installed in La Porte, Indiana, in 1892. Initially there were objections to the automatic switching system — customers didn't want to do what they thought of as the telephone company's job! Not until the 1930s did automatic switching become widespread.

Bell's basic patents on the telephone expired in 1893 and 1894, seventeen years after they were granted. Although AT&T made a valiant effort to continue to purchase patents to keep the system at the technological cutting edge, and greatly expanded its engineering department to find ways to apply these patents, the fundamental patent monopoly that was its base was gone. And the Bell System had grown lazy under the protection of its monopoly. The quality of service had declined, and its rates had increased.

Independent telephone companies sprang up, some 6,000 of them by 1900. In addition, there were thousands of rural systems, run by their users, each connecting up to a few dozen farm families, and usually not tied into any larger company. By 1907 almost half of the 6 million telephones in the country were not owned by AT&T. In many cities customers had to pay bills to several phone companies; otherwise they could not place calls or receive calls from subscribers to a different system. The phone system was a mess.

In 1907 AT&T was taken over by a group of New York bankers led by J. P. Morgan, who reorganized and refinanced the firm. Theodore Vail, who had resigned in 1887 because of disagreements over his policy of universal service, returned as president. He put the company back on its feet, and reiterated and reinforced his original goal: "One system with a common policy, common purpose and common action; comprehensive, universal, interdependent, intercommunicating like the highway system of the country, extending from every door to every other door, affording electrical communication of every kind, from every one at every place to every one at every other place."[9]

The reinvigorated AT&T returned to its aggressively monopolistic style, refusing to interconnect independent telephone companies and then buying them when they were close to failing — a new monopoly based not on patents but on financial and political clout. AT&T even purchased its old nemesis, the Western Union Company, and seemed on its way to becoming a nationwide telecommunications monopoly. In 1910 there were some 7 million telephones in the United States, almost all of them in the AT&T system.

There was considerable anger about the new monopoly, and AT&T felt pressed to show its advantages. Long-distance service was one of the main potential benefits of a nationwide phone system, and so the first major technical problem the newly reorganized monopoly addressed was long-distance telephony. Soon after AT&T was reorganized in 1907, the firm dramatically announced that it would provide coast-to-coast service by the opening of the 1914 Panama Pacific Exposition.

But solving the problem of long-distance telephony required a fundamentally different approach to invention than the company had used previously. Inventors such as Alexander Graham Bell, working alone, had made the first telephone inventions. The next set of inventions had come from outside inventors, most of whom worked by themselves or for small firms, and from Thomas Edison, working in what he called his "invention factory." (Edison would receive more than forty telephone-related patents.) Bell Telephone bought hundreds of inventions from outside inventors. As the problems grew more complex, though, scientific knowledge, not just inventive skill, became increasingly necessary. The phone company set up its own research and development organization to apply science to the problems of telephony.

In the 1880s the Bell Company had established an electrical department and a mechanical department, and hired several Ph.D.'s in physics to take on long-range research. In 1887 the director of the mechanical department wrote that his goal was to deal with the "many problems daily arising in the broad subject of telephony which require solution but are not studied as they will not lead to direct advantage to ourselves." By 1902 the combined electrical and mechanical departments employed some 200 researchers, including several theoretical physicists. By 1914 the laboratory was one of the most impressive research institutions in the country. Some 550 engineers and scientists worked there, researchers the president of the company described as "former professors and instructors of our universities, postgraduate students and other graduates holding various engineering and scientific degrees."[10] This laboratory, renamed Bell Telephone Laboratories in 1925, was the beginning of the corporate support for technological innovation that would be so crucial to the development of the Information Age.

The problems of long-distance telephony were tackled by these physicists. Over long distances the electrical property called capacitance — the ability of the wire to store an electrical charge — distorts telephone signals, since different frequencies of the signal travel through the wire at different speeds. Scientific theory suggested that coils of wire properly located in the circuit would solve this problem. In 1894 Michael Pupin, a professor of electromechanics at Columbia University, invented the "loading coil," and in 1900 he sold his patent to AT&T for $185,000 plus $15,000 for each year the patent stayed in effect. George Campbell, a physicist at AT&T, had received a similar patent, but AT&T decided that the idea was sufficiently valuable that it should buy up all the patents — a good thing, too, since Campbell lost an interference suit with Pupin in

1903. Campbell and his associates at Bell Labs did figure out mathematically the most efficient spacing for the coils. This innovation greatly improved the quality of telephone transmission. It also saved AT&T perhaps $100 million that would otherwise have been spent on heavy copper lines.

The final element essential for long-distance service was the repeater. The distance from New York to Denver was about the limit telephone lines could reach without amplifiers to strengthen the signal, but the management of AT&T had promised a New York-to-San Francisco line. Vacuum tubes, invented for radio by Lee De Forest and modified by a team of AT&T researchers working under Harold D. Arnold, proved ideal for amplifying telephone signals. (See WIRELESS TELEGRAPHY.) AT&T purchased the patent rights to de Forest's vacuum tube. Western Electric physicists worked day and night to improve the tubes and design an amplifier that would make the cross-country line possible. Luckily, the Exposition opened late, in 1915, by which time cross-country wire was ready, strung on 130,000 telephone poles and with seven amplifiers. Alexander Bell was stationed in New York, Thomas Watson in San Francisco, and Bell repeated his famous first telephonic words: "Mr. Watson, come here."

Completing the first transcontinental line, 1914.

Improved amplifiers proved the key to solving another problem, too. Telephone wire was expensive — the first coast-to-coast line required 1,200 tons of copper — and so AT&T tried to find ways to put many signals on one line. As early as 1918 "carrier," or frequency-division multiplexing, techniques were used on telephone lines. The carrier was an electrical signal of higher frequency than the voice signal, on which the voice signal was superimposed. But early amplifiers created distortion, making it difficult to keep the signals separate. Harold Black's 1927 invention of the negative-feedback amplifier was the breakthrough that made multiplexed telephone lines practical. In the 1930s AT&T introduced lines carrying twelve channels each, using the frequency range from 12 to 60 kHz. After a slow start owing to the depression, this system was remarkably successful. For years it formed the backbone of AT&T's low-volume circuits.

But while AT&T was showing its technological prowess, it was losing on the political front. The early twentieth century was an era of strong feeling against monopolies. In 1913 the first of what would be a long series of Justice Department antitrust investigations of AT&T was initiated. Many people thought that the phone company should be taken over by the U.S. Post Office and be run by the government, as telephone companies were in many other countries. But in December of that year, AT&T and the attorney general agreed to a settlement that would give the company a unique place in American telecommunications. In exchange for divesting itself of Western Union, agreeing not to buy any more independent companies, and allowing independent telephone firms to interconnect to the Bell System, AT&T secured government acceptance of its dominant position in the telephone market, and a virtual monopoly on long-distance communications. In exchange, the firm agreed to accept public regulation: state public service commissions would set fees to balance a "fair rate of return" to the phone company and equitable costs for consumers. Vail called this friendly regulation "independent, intelligent, considerate, thorough, and just."[11] AT&T would retain this favored position for over half a century. It remained prosperous.

By 1930 there were over 20 million phones installed in the United States, about one for every six people. Improved transmitters and receivers, along with new technology suggested by better scientific understanding of the characteristics of long lines — repeaters and amplifiers — allowed people to talk from one coast of the United States to the other. New switchframes made it possible to connect calls between any two phones. Not least important, people had learned to use the telephone. They didn't give a second thought to picking up the phone and calling across the street, or across the city. And they had come to believe that there were occasions when the expense of a long-distance call was worthwhile. The telephone had become a part of everyday life.

PUTTING THE INVENTION TO USE

In addition to the technology and the system, the success of the telephone required people to think about communications in a new way. The telephone was at first considered a scientific curiosity, without obvious business use. Businessmen depended on written records, whether letters or the printing telegraph. The Western Union Telegraph Company, the obvious purchaser of Bell's patent, had turned down the chance to buy the rights to the invention for $100,000. After all, telegraph messages could be sent as quickly as people could speak; what would be the point of replacing reliable, proven telegraph keys and receivers with telephones? Why would telegraph operators want to talk to one another? The telegraph company simply imagined fitting the new technology into the preexisting system, and saw no great advantage to it.

But the telephone was different from the telegraph. It was in people's homes, not their workplaces. It needed no special skill to operate. Since they could make a direct connection, it was more personal. And they weren't charged by the word. The telephone opened up an unimagined freedom of communication. It required new social and cultural rules about how it should be used.

Bell, trying to sell the new technology, offered an innovative vision that someday "a telephone in every house would be considered indispensable," and suggested that the nation would soon be bound together by telephone conversations. Some writers shared this vision, seeing the bright side of the new communication-rich future. A *Scientific American* article in 1880 predicted "nothing less than a new organization of society — a state of things in which every individual, however secluded, will have at call every other individual in the community, to the saving of no end of social and business complications, of needless goings to and fro, of disappointments, delays, and a countless host of those great

Businessmen quickly adopted the telephone for their work. Before long, having a secretary to answer your phone was a sign of status. The second phone on this desk was used by a stenographer to take notes on the call.

and little evils and annoyances which go so far under present conditions to make life laborious and unsatisfactory."[12]

Others predicted a different sort of future for the telephone. The vice president of AT&T hinted in 1890 at "a scheme which we now have on foot, which looks to providing music on tap at certain times every day, especially at meal times. The scheme is to have a fine band perform the choicest music, gather up the sound waves, and distribute them to any number of subscribers."[13] But before such predictions could come true, more than just improved technology was necessary. As with any new technology, the proper way in which the telephone should fit into cultural traditions needed to be negotiated. What sort of conversations were appropriate to the phone? Which ones required the intimacy of face-to-face discussions? How should people talk to one another over the phone? How could traditional standards of courtesy, of class and gender relations, be maintained? How could the wall between home and business, between private and public, be left intact? How to ensure that the telephone would not break down traditional social, personal, and legal relationships? How would these relationships change to adapt to the new technology, and how would the new technology change to adapt to traditional relationships?

In the early days telephones were mostly used for signaling — orders, alarms, business communiqués, and calls for services — and not for two-way discussion. Most people used the phone as if it were a telegraph, and that's what the phone company thought it should be used for. After all, most early telephone executives came from telegraph companies, and they promoted the telephone as if it were a new type of telegraph — a business device to make work more efficient.

Many businesses used it to centralize operations, a process already started by the telegraph and by other trends in American management. Salesmen were required to report in every day and get instructions. The telephone, *Telephony* magazine opined in 1906, "has curtailed the functions and responsibilities of a district manager as the cable has those of an ambassador."[14] The phone made it easier to separate manufacturing plants from the offices where the company sales and management staff worked, helping to create downtown office districts. (Phone calls were still followed by written memoranda or correspondence: businessmen wanted a written record for the files.) The telephone allowed better coordination between the people and machines of modern commerce and industry. It fit well with a managerial style that called for increased centralized control of labor, suppliers, and markets. The business hierarchy circumscribed the effects of the telephone; for the most part new communications devices, like new information processing technologies, fit into the culture of command and control rather than changed it.

Some businesses were completely transformed by the telephone. Police departments were among the first organizations to make extensive use of phones. In 1880 the Chicago police invented the call box. By the early twentieth century, police departments had come up with an entirely new way of policing, based on telephony. Policemen in Detroit in 1917 were told to park their cars near call boxes and wait for calls instead of patrolling the neighborhood. This innovation changed police work enormously. Instead of putting policemen on the streets, where they could prevent crime, police departments put them in cars, ready to respond only after crimes had been committed — a change that removed police from the community, and centralized the departments.

Although the first users of the phone were businesses, it wasn't long before some people started to use it for social purposes. Telephone companies initially discouraged subscribers from using the phone for "frivolous" and "unnecessary" social chatting. In part, the insistence on business use reflected common gender biases. Engineering journals often contrasted the frivolous personal conversations of women with the serious business conversations of men. The experts thought that women's conversations were unimportant and didn't make proper use of the special value of the telephone. Experts made fun of "unsophisticated" telephone users, and defined the technology as a male mode of communication: serious, businesslike, to the point.

As late as 1909 the phone company believed that "the public had to be educated . . . to the necessity and advantage of the telephone."[15] (Some, like the editor of a Philadelphia newspaper, still thought that you could contract contagious diseases by talking over the phone with an ill person.) Fewer than 5 percent of American homes had telephones in 1900. Not until the 1920s, when more than a third of American homes had telephone services, did the phone company encourage the use of the phone for social calls.

The classic 1929 sociological study *Middletown* suggests how the phone found its way into everyday life in one small city. In 1890 there were only 71 subscribers. Not until the turn of the century, said one woman of the "business class," did "'phones become common enough so that you thought of feeling apologetic at not having one." But even in 1924 only half of the homes in "Middletown" had a phone. Housewives who had them used them to order "everything from groceries to a spool of thread." Young people used the phone to ask for dates: a "semi-private, depersonalized means of approach to a person of the other sex," as the sociologists put it. Sometimes, the phone replaced visiting in person. "Radios and telephones make people farther apart," said one resident. "Instead of going to see a person as folks used to, you just telephone nowadays."[16] But generally, it served to open new communications. Women

The Telephone Way to a Happier Day

Try it today when the dishes are done, beds made, clothes in the washer. You've earned a break.

So relax a little and pick up the telephone. Enjoy a cheerful visit with a friend or loved one.

It's so easy to do, whatever the miles may be. For no one is ever far away by telephone.

It helps to make any day a happier day at both ends of the line.

"It's fun to phone"

BELL TELEPHONE SYSTEM

WILLING WORKER

ALERT, efficient household servant to run errands, order supplies, deliver messages to a large and growing list of people.

OTHER DUTIES: Stand guard for an emergency. Be ready to summon doctor, police, fire department. Make it possible for many other people to keep in touch with you.

FAST, completely trustworthy and willing to serve twenty-four hours a day, 365 days a year. No vacations. No time off. Pay — less than a cent an hour.

Who Could This Wonder Worker Be?

Why, the telephone, of course. Night and day this alert, efficient servant is always ready to serve you. And the cost is small. Even though increases in telephone rates are still needed to catch up with past increases in costs, your telephone will continue to be a big bargain. Few things in all this world give you so much for so little as the telephone.

BELL TELEPHONE SYSTEM

AT&T started a major advertising campaign in the early 1950s, at a time when the government was threatening to break up the company on antitrust grounds. AT&T advertised the value of the service it provided and tried to persuade people to use the telephone more often. It stressed new low rates on long distance — "You can bring them home often . . . by long distance" — and the power of phone conversation to set friendships aright — "If he'd only call her up everything would be all right. Just one little telephone call can save so much time and worry."

Some of the advertising was for new types of phones. In the late 1950s, AT&T introduced the Princess phone, intended to appeal to women and teenagers, and the first color phones, intended to fit better in a domestic setting. The phone company was trying to be friendly. In 1963, AT&T introduced the Touch-Tone phone, which marked the beginning of a transition to a new, more powerful, and more sophisticated telephone system. Originally marketed as a convenience, before too many years went by the Touch-Tone phone would become the key to access into computerized switchboards and information services.

found the telephone particularly useful. Especially for women at home with children, it served as a tool for keeping in touch, for maintaining family and community connections.

By World War II the telephone was a fact of life. Almost everyone had one, or had access to one. Long-distance calls, still reserved for special occasions, were becoming more common. In 1900 there had been about 1.3 million telephones in the United States, one for every fifty-seven people. By the 1950s there was one telephone for every three people, a total of some 50 million phones.

The hit of the **AT&T** pavilion at the 1964 New York World's Fair was the Picturephone. The first phone to transmit pictures as well as sound was demonstrated in 1927, but not until the 1960s was the technology available to make the system seem commercially feasible. At the Fair, visitors who tried the phone liked it; 60 percent said that it was "very important" or "important" to see the person they were talking to. **AT&T** spent over $500 million on development in the 1960s and 1970s, but sold only a few hundred of the devices.

The Picturephone failed because it transmitted a terrible picture and cost too much. But most important, it seemed that no one really wanted to see the person they were talking to. They didn't want to have to pay attention to the person on the other end of the line, or to be seen not paying attention. There wasn't much usable information gained through the use of video, at least not the sort of information people were willing to pay for. Pictures didn't add enough to make up for the inconveniences.

The idea of the Picturephone has survived for a long time, its name now changed to the more modern-sounding "videophone" (upper right). Technological advances in video and data compression have made it cheaper and improved its quality. But it still doesn't sell. Not every technological innovation can be turned into a profitable product. Consumers have to need it, or be convinced that they need it.

More and more the country was interconnected. Private service became the rule as the number of party-line phones peaked at 16 million and began to decline. Radiotelephone service to Europe started in 1927, the beginning of a worldwide network. By 1937 more than sixty countries could be reached. About 86 million calls were made in the United States every day. And prices were coming down, too. A three-minute call from New York City to San Francisco cost over $20 in 1915, half that in 1930, and only $2.50 in 1945. A call from New York to London, $75 in 1927, was only $12 in 1945. Bell's dream that someday everyone would be able to talk to anyone else in the world, Vail's dream of universal service, was coming true.

NEW TECHNOLOGY

The telephone system boomed after World War II, changing dramatically as the advances in electronics that the war had brought were applied to the system. (See RADIO.) There were new switching systems, several generations of them. There were new transmission media, and, starting in the 1960s, a whole new way of dealing with information: digitally. The postwar electronics revolution transformed the telephone network. It wasn't long before the line between computers and communications was beginning to get fuzzy, before the telephone would be the cutting edge of the new age of computers.

As the telephone system grew larger, the problems of interconnection grew ever more complicated. In the beginning telephone operators had switched calls manually, connecting the caller with the number he or she desired by moving a plug. Early panel switching frames had automated that process, starting in the 1890s, and had been improved by crossbar switching systems, first installed in 1938. This equipment increased the network's capacity because it could establish a call, and then go on to switch other calls while the first one continued. It also could find alternative routes to make a connection, if necessary. This and other new technologies allowed improvements such as long-distance dialing, introduced in 1951. By 1956 many customers could dial many of the telephones in the country, and 89 percent of phones had dial access for local service.

Transistors, invented at Bell Laboratories by scientists interested in improving AT&T's switching, found wide use in the telephone system in the late 1950s. (For more on the transistor, see RADIO.) They replaced vacuum tubes, making possible better amplifiers, which allowed more phone calls to be carried on each wire, as well as, after some preliminary problems, better reliability. In the 1960s transistors were used in a new kind of telephone switch, based on stored-program control; essentially, the switching system became a computer. The first electronic switching system was installed in commercial service in 1965, the result of some thirty years and $500 million of development. This allowed not only greater reliability — a downtime of two hours in forty years was the desideratum — but also a wide range of custom services. As early as 1966 descriptions of the network compared it to a computer:

> The telephone system is itself a computer. Its components are dispersed across the continent but they work as one. Equipped with more than 90 million input-output stations, this enormous computer can be commanded to provide any one of the 3 million billion "answers" it takes to connect any one of its stations — telephones — with any other and do it in a matter of seconds. Indeed, [the newest telephone] systems, like computers, are internally programmed and are endowed with the same kind of quasi-human memory ascribed to commercial computers.[17]

The first computerized switchboard, the No. 4 Electronic Switching System, first saw commercial service in 1976. This device was a true computer, driven by several million lines of software. It cost some $400 million to develop, and some 2,500 person-years of work, much more time and money than anyone had thought it would. It could handle 500,000 calls per hour, and made possible a wide range of new services, including toll-free 800 numbers, call forwarding, and sophisticated call routing. Because the phone system was controlled by comput-

A microwave tower in
Cartersville, Georgia, 1958. By
the mid-1960s, microwave towers were a common element of
the American landscape.

ers, it was flexible and reprogrammable. By 1982 half of all calls were switched
electronically.

At the same time that electronics were finding their way into telephone
switching, the telephone system itself began carrying more and more data, in addition to ever more telephone conversations. In the 1920s AT&T had begun to
carry broadcast radio and signals between stations. In the 1950s television signals and computer data joined the information flowing over the lines. To meet
this demand, engineers turned to new transmission media.

The first step was coaxial cable, installed on intercity lines starting in
1940. Coaxial cable is wire in which one conductor surrounds the other. This
drastically reduces interference, and allows a much wider frequency range. Within a few years, coaxial cables were capable of transmitting 600 voice circuits, in
addition to a television signal; a new system installed in the 1970s could carry up
to 132,000 conversations. The country was criss-crossed by coaxial cables. They
were the backbone not only of the telephone system but also of the radio and
television networks.

Microwaves, very high frequency radio, began to supplement these cables starting in 1950, and connected the coasts in 1951. Microwave technology
came of age during World War II as part of the crash program to develop radar.

Echo I, launched in 1960, was the first experimental communications satellite. It was a sphere 100 feet in diameter with a metallic surface to reflect radio signals.

Bell Labs took the work its researchers and others had done for the war effort and applied it to communications. (Other firms that had participated in the wartime radar effort also wanted to get into this business but were prevented from doing so when the FCC enforced the Bell monopoly on telephony.) The first systems could carry 2,400 voice circuits (or one television program). By 1973, 1,500-circuit channels were common, and by 1980 these microwave channels could carry almost 20,000 telephone conversations. Microwave towers became a part of the landscape, connecting almost every city.

At the same time, satellites became another alternative. The use of communications satellites had been suggested in 1945 by Arthur C. Clarke, in a science-fiction magazine. Nine years later John Pierce, of Bell Labs, independently had the same idea, and followed through on it. *Echo*, a passive repeater — a big balloon with a metallic surface that would reflect radio signals — was launched in 1960. It was an experimental success, and suggested that communications satellites might work. The first satellite to carry regular telephone conversations was *Telstar*, designed by Bell Labs and launched in 1962. It could carry several hundred conversations. Intelsat, an international communications consortium, launched a series of communications satellites starting with *Early Bird* in 1965. *Early Bird* could handle 250 phone calls at once. By the mid-1970s there were dozens of satellites carrying telephone and television. The more advanced ones, such as AT&T and GTE's *Comstar*, launched in 1976, could carry 30,000 calls at once. Satellites allowed the number of transatlantic telephone calls to increase by a factor of ten in one year, from 1974 to 1975.

The new switching systems and transmission media were joined, in 1962, by a revolutionary new digital way of transmitting data. In the traditional analog system the electrical signals in the wire look like the sound waves in the air; that was Bell's big breakthrough. But in a digital telephone system *information* about the sound wave — not a representation of it — is sent over the wire. Information about the amplitude of the speech wave is sampled thousands of times a second, so that it can be reconstructed at the other end.

INFORMATION THEORY

Even before digital transmission was a practical possibility, mathematicians had already begun to explore the possibilities of information encoding and decoding. The first important paper was written in 1928 by R. V. L. Hartley. Claude Shannon at Bell Labs read this, and in 1948 wrote his *Mathematical Theory of Communication*. This book established a philosophy of information from the point of view of communications, and, as important, a mathematical measure of information and of the information capacity of a communications channel. It provided a new way of thinking about information and communications. Shannon's key breakthrough was his notion of information not as meaningful data, but rather as "the resolution of uncertainty." To measure information, he said, the question to answer is: How much do we need to know to resolve uncertainty? That is, one way to measure information is the minimum number of yes/no questions required on the average to arrive at the given data.

Shannon's information theory led to an outpouring of research on the mathematics of information, and, after a while, vast practical application. Perhaps the most important results were new ways to compress information. The typical data sent over phone lines or computer channels has an enormous amount of predictability. The letter *q*, for example, is almost always followed by the letter *u*. In a fax, a blank spot on a page is most often followed by another blank spot. Voice, too, is predictable. Assigning codes to letters, colors, or sounds that take predictability into account means that the size of messages can be much reduced, often by astonishingly large factors; computers can reconstruct the data at the other end. This means that much more data can be sent over a given channel.

This represented a fundamental change from the analog system, and it opened a new horizon in communications. Digital information was in many ways easier to deal with than analog information. A signal was either a one or a zero, either on or off, and so small changes in the signal, small distortions, didn't matter. The original could be reconstructed exactly, without error. Moreover, digital information could be coded and compressed, to increase the throughput. Most important of all, digital information was the language of computers. When digital communications techniques met digital computer techniques, there was an information explosion.

The first digital transmission over regular cables was achieved by Bell labs in 1956. Illinois Bell installed the first commercial digital system, called the T1 system, into service in Chicago in 1962. The T1 system carried twenty-four voice signals — 1.5 megabits — on a pair of wires. Maximum distance on these early digital lines was about fifty miles. Intercity digital cables followed, as did digital microwave, but improvements in analog systems meant that long-haul digital systems were not commercially competitive. Not until the 1980s would digital transmission come into its own. By 1982 there were more than 130 million miles of digital transmission lines.

Digital transmission proved synergistic with another new technology: fiber optics. Fiber-optic cables use laser light traveling through glass, rather than electrons traveling through copper, to carry information. Laser light can be modulated at enormous rates, making possible very high rates of digital transmission. Corning Glass Works produced the first commercial fiber-optic cable in 1970. By 1980 there were 3,700 miles of fiber-optic cable installed in the United States, and much more in the planning stage. The technology improved at a tremendous rate. Between 1970 and 1990 there were five generations of fiber-optic systems; every telephone firm wrote off billions of dollars of investment in microwave towers and copper cable, and earlier fiber optics, as obsolete. By the late 1980s fiber was used everywhere, on almost every intercity route, and on many local runs.

The new, broader channels of telecommunications meant that the telephone system was in an ideal position to be put to an entirely new use. First the military, and then universities and businesses, began to link computers into networks, making it possible to access information from anywhere in the country and to share information between computers. New uses for communications continually pressed the capacity of the information highways, and new capacity brought forth new uses. (For more on the uses of the digital phone system, see BEYOND TELEPHONES.)

The telephone as bearer of bad news, from *If a Man Answers,* 1962. Telephones were the villain in several popular films in the 1960s.

THE END OF THE BELL SYSTEM

But at the same time that AT&T was installing sophisticated new technology, it faced criticism on a number of fronts. The 1960s and 1970s were hard times for the phone company, and in 1982 the Justice Department would succeed in its attempt to break up AT&T.

In the 1960s many people felt that the telephone was getting out of control, that it was inescapable. Technology, it seemed, was running our lives. Some believed (falsely) that the telephone company had changed the ring on phones so people would jump to answer the phone when it rang, what one writer called the "Anxious Ring." Others complained that they couldn't turn off their phone — that was official Bell Telephone policy — that there was no privacy, no way to get away from the rest of the world. The phone would always ring at the most inopportune time. Another common complaint was that service had reached an all-time low. The number of obscene phone calls skyrocketed in the mid-1960s, with some 375,000 complaints in 1966. In 1969 one third of the pay phones in New York City were vandalized each month.

In the 1960s several movies featured the telephone company, playing with people's fears of its pervasiveness, its ubiquity. The wrong number was one plot device that found wide use. In *I Saw What You Did* (1965), a group of teenage girls call numbers at random and say, "I saw what you did and I know who you are," to anyone who answers. One of the people they reach is so provoked by the call that he murders his wife. He's called again, provoking another murder, and finally, after the teenagers visit, almost murders them. That's what you'd have to call an "Anxious Ring"! Even more anxiety-producing was a 1967 comedy, *The President's Analyst*. The president's psychiatrist is kidnapped by "the Telephone Company," which, angry because of constant complaints about bad service, plots to take over the country. It's apparently foiled by the CIA and the KGB, working together against a force stronger than either of them. But in the last scene Telephone Company robots are plotting their revenge.

Perhaps the most widespread demonstration of the new fear of depersonalization was the fight against the all-number telephone number, introduced in the 1960s. Especially in cities, many people wanted to keep the two-letter exchange rather than trade it for a number. They wanted to be able to give their telephone number as MOhawk 4-3664, rather than 664-3664. AT&T backed off slightly, and let it be known that they had installed special equipment that would automatically translate the "MO" the customer dialed into its numerical equivalent!

Some users, instead of longing for the old ways, went into the future faster than the phone company could have imagined. The early 1970s saw the rise of "phone hackers," people who used simple electronic signaling devices, called blue boxes, to fool the phone company's switching system into letting them make long-distance calls without paying for them. The blue boxes generated the tones that the phone company used for switching. When the long-distance switching system had been designed in the 1950s, the equipment to generate these tones was large and expensive. By the 1970s transistors and integrated circuits made it easy and cheap for anyone with a bit of electronics skill to build these devices.

People used blue boxes for a variety of reasons. Many were designed and used by engineering students, who took pleasure in fooling the phone company. These "phone phreaks" delighted in telephone-switching sports, such as routing a call around the world only to ring at a nearby phone, or routing a call via satellite and cable back and forth across the ocean. Some early users were blind people, who took pleasure in the sense of power the blue box gave them despite their lack of vision. Others were members of the "counterculture," who saw phone hacking as a way to thumb their noses at the "establishment." "Captain Crunch," one of the most famous phone phreaks, explained his hobby to *Esquire*: "I do it for one reason and one reason only. I'm learning about a system. The phone company is a System. A computer is a System. Do you understand? If I do what I do, it is only to explore a System. Computers. Systems. That's my bag. The phone company is nothing but a computer. . . . Ma Bell is a system I want to explore."[18]

Before long, blue boxes were being sold to anyone who wanted to save money on long-distance calls, and didn't mind committing what seemed to them a very minor criminal offense. The telephone company had lots of money, after all. In fact, some $20 million of free calls were made each year in the early 1970s, before the phone company changed the way that long-distance calls were signaled and put an end to the fad. Phone hackers subsequently found new ways to steal phone service — using stolen credit cards and exploiting bugs in private branch exchanges and voice mail systems — and in 1992, estimates of phone fraud were as high as $4 billion.

While blue box hacking and fraud were a minor inconvenience, the phone company faced a much more serious threat on a different front. Since 1913 AT&T had been a monopoly subject to strict government supervision, and its corporate culture had come to focus on providing reliable, universal basic service. Many businesspeople and consumers felt that the company was slow in responding to the new opportunities that the increasing convergence of computers and communications offered. Backed up by government regulation, it would not allow users to attach devices to their phone that would connect two-way radios or computers into the phone system, except in carefully regulated ways. It did its best to prohibit long-distance competition. But new technologies such as computers and microwaves offered opportunities for competitors, and small telecommunications firms began to chip away at the AT&T monopoly.

The first sign of change came in 1968, when the Federal Communications Commission ruled in favor of the Carter Electronics Corporation, which sold a device (called the Carterfone) that allowed customers to connect a radiotelephone into the main phone network. (The Carterfone had no electrical connections to the phone system — it was merely a cradle in which the handset of the phone sat — but that was more connection to the phone system than the existing rules allowed.) The long-distance regulations began to change when, in 1969, MCI Communications was allowed to sell long-distance service over its own microwave phone links, and then connect into the AT&T network, skimming off one of the most profitable parts of the business. The potential of new technology was starting to fray the edges of the phone system.

AT&T had a hard time dealing with some of the new competition. In part, that was because of the corporate culture of the company, which had long been a protected monopoly. In part, it was a result of a 1956 consent decree that AT&T had signed with the government to settle an antitrust suit. That decree had allowed AT&T to continue its monopoly over the telephone manufacturing business in exchange for agreeing not to enter the computer business. (At the time, very few saw the synergy of computers and communications. That came about only after new computer switching systems and digital lines had become common.) In many ways, signing the decree handicapped the company.

Everything was back up in the air again when, in 1974, the Justice Department filed a new antitrust suit against AT&T. The Justice Department wanted to force AT&T to allow interconnects to the system, intercity competition, and, most important, the purchase of telephone equipment on the open market, not solely from its subsidiary, Western Electric. When, after ten years and hundreds of millions of dollars of legal expenses, the case was settled, AT&T talked the Justice Department into allowing it to keep Western Electric, and instead to divest itself of all the local operating companies. The government had wanted to chop off AT&T's head; instead, the company persuaded the government to chop off its arms and legs.

On January 1, 1984, AT&T got out of the local phone business, spinning off seven separate operating companies. AT&T kept its long-distance operations and its manufacturing and research branches, and began to move into nonregulated businesses, especially the computer business. The seven "Baby Bells" expanded into all sorts of information-related businesses, from telephone directory publishing to cellular phones to computer sales — everything except over-the-phone information services, phone equipment manufacturing, and long-distance telephone service. (In the 1990s Congress would back off, allowing the Baby Bells entry into some aspects of the manufacturing business and letting them provide some information services.) Perhaps most important of all, anyone could go into the phone business. New long-distance companies sprang up, and many large firms began to run their own local exchanges, tying their phones directly into long-distance carriers.

AT&T's choice had hinged on beliefs about the future of the telephone. Charles L. Brown, president of AT&T, was an engineer, and he was willing to bet that the future lay with new technologies of information, not with the local exchanges. He wanted to get into the computer business, to try to ride the synergy of a communications-computer mix. Regulation of the industry, he said, had become "a fence with a one-way hole," letting competitors in but not letting AT&T out. He summarized his hopes for what he called the "new order in the telephone industry" at a press conference announcing the breakup. After first assuring the public that the break would "encourage competition, and it will do so without sacrificing the American consumer's need for economical, dependable, and readily available telephone service," he went on to describe the advantages he saw for the company, and eventually, the consumer: "No one contemplated twenty-five years ago that a revolution in modern technology would largely erase the difference between computers and communications. As a consequence, the Bell System has been effectively prohibited from using the fruits of its own technology. And this new decree will wipe out those restrictions completely."[19]

The Reagan administration was split on the political implications of divestiture, but the assistant attorney general in charge of antitrust was a free-market ideologue who believed in competition and thought that breaking up the phone company would increase choice and lower prices. Competitors were after equal access to the system; they thought that they could best AT&T on technological grounds. The Justice Department decided to let them try.

Judge Harold Greene, who would oversee the consent decree for many years, summarized his hopes for the settlement in an interview in 1985. It would mean more competition, he said, and "competition will give this country the most advanced, best, cheapest telephone network."[20] Most advanced, best, cheapest — it sounded good, but the three desiderata weren't always possible, and were sometimes pulling in different directions. And so the settlement was, according to historian Steve Coll, a mystery to the public, "a great, impenetrable muddle . . . too complex, too fractured, and, above all, too boring."[21] Boring it may have been, but it was important, for it was to change the phone system forever. In the short term it would bring confusion. In the long term, though, it promised an increased pace of technological change and a new world of telecommunications.

The results of divestiture were complex, and are still being played out. In the short run the new deregulated system made life more complicated for most people who dealt with the phone company. Perhaps the overwhelming reaction was confusion. In the early days of the breakup no one knew which company was responsible for which services. Lawyers profited, of course: the telecommunications law division of the Washington, D.C., Bar Association doubled in size every year for several years after divestiture. Divestiture meant higher costs for local calls, which had been subsidized by long-distance fees. The quality of service went down, too, and the cost of installing and repairing telephone equipment rose. Before the breakup, 80 percent of the public said that they were happy with their service. In 1985, 64 percent of Americans thought divestiture was a bad idea, and many called for the reunification of AT&T.

But divestiture did have the intended effect of increasing competition on long-distance lines and on other information services, as well as increasing the rate of technological innovation. In the mid-1980s the number of local telephone calls grew by only 3 to 5 percent a year, but as long-distance rates fell, the number of long-distance calls jumped by 14 percent a year, the amount of data transmission by 25 to 30 percent a year. In 1984 Americans spent a total of about 150 billion minutes on the phone. The record for the most long-distance calls made in one day was 177 million, set in 1992, when cheap air fares were announced.

Divestiture also brought about a vast range of new services. These innovations included automation of telephone credit cards; expanded use of 800 numbers, which allowed the receiver, not the caller, to pay for calls; pay-per-call 900 numbers, which found their first use in the mid-1980s for "telephone sex" operations (by 1990 this was a $2.4 billion-a-year business); and new options for phone service from call forwarding, voice mail, and Caller ID to the cellular mobile phone. All of these services were made possible by the integration of communications and computers. The telephone switching system had been computerized since the 1960s — in the most general senses it *was* a computer — but it was always thought of as a single-purpose computer, a machine to connect one phone to another. Now the phone companies began to use the switching system in new and different ways.

Each of the new services brought with it all of the social and political issues that accompany most communications innovations. Caller ID, for example, raised questions of privacy; lots of telephone callers would prefer not to be identified when they make calls. Many people found sexually oriented 900 numbers offensive, and Congress passed laws to limit them. Voice mail, while often very useful, seemed impersonal and unpleasant, another level of remoteness, of dealing with machines rather than with real people. (A 1992 poll found that 80 percent of callers found voice mail irritating.) Cellular phones, while an enormous time saver to salespeople and others who need or want to keep in touch at all times, has meant for some people that they can never be out of touch, even when they'd rather be. There can be such a thing as too much communications.

But communications innovation continues, and people find new ways to communicate. The phone system continued to grow in size and complexity. In the United States in 1982 there were more than 1 billion miles of phone lines and over 22,000 switching centers. Over 750 million calls were made each day from some 175 million phones. The system had cost, over the years, about $170 billion. The information infrastructure of the telephone network was put to uses that its inventors and builders could not have imagined. That story is told in BEYOND TELEPHONES.

FOR FURTHER READING

There are several general histories of the telephone, most of them dating from the centenary of its invention. Most accessible is John Brooks, *Telephone: The First Hundred Years* (1976). Gerald W. Brock, *The Telecommunications Industry: The Dynamics of Market Structure* (1981), contains a good summary of the American telephone industry, especially for the period after World War II.

The best early history of the telephone is Robert V. Bruce's biography: *Bell: Alexander Graham Bell and the Conquest of Solitude* (1973). For details on Bell's competitor, see David Hounshell, "Elisha Gray and the Telephone: On the Disadvantages of Being an Expert," *Technology and Culture* (April 1975). For the details of early improvements, see W. James King, "The Development of Electrical Technology in the Nineteenth Century: 2. The Telegraph and the Telephone," in *Bulletin 228: Contributions from the Museum of History and Technology* (1963). Later technologies are covered in detail in Robert J. Chapuis, *One Hundred Years of Telephone Switching (1878–1978)*, 2 vols. (1982–1992). Milton Mueller, "The Switchboard Problem: Scale, Signaling, and Organization in Manual Telephone Switching, 1877–1897," *Technology and Culture* (July 1989), discusses managerial solutions to the switchboard problem.

AT&T's archives are superb, and a number of scholarly studies have examined the business strategy of the company. These include Robert W. Garnet, *The Telephone Enterprise: The Evolution of the Bell System's Horizontal Structure, 1876–1909* (1985); George David Smith, *The Anatomy of a Business Strategy: Bell, Western Electric, and the Origins of the American Telephone Industry* (1985); and Neil H. Wasserman, *From Invention to Innovation: Long-Distance Telephone Transmission at the Turn of the Century* (1985).

Bell Laboratories and its predecessors were responsible for much of the improvement in telephony. As part of AT&T's defense against the breakup of the telephone system in the 1970s and 1980s, it published a multivolume technical history of invention at Bell Labs, M. D. Fagan, ed., *A History of Engineering and Science in the Bell System* (1975). For a very readable overall history of Bell Labs, see Jeremy Bernstein, *Three Degrees above Zero: Bell Labs in the Information Age* (1984). On recent technological changes to the telephone network, see C. David Chaffee, *The Rewiring of America: The Fiber Optics Revolution* (1988); and the chapter titled "The Telecommunications Explosion," in Tom Forrester, *High-Tech Society: The Story of the Information Technology Revolution* (1987).

The breakup of AT&T, a major event in recent business history, has inspired several good books. Most accessible is Steve Coll, *The Deal of the Century: The Breakup of AT&T* (1986). For economic and business details, see Peter Temin, *The Fall of the Bell System: A Study in Prices and Politics* (1987).

The telephone is more than a business or technical phenomenon, of course. For its effects on American social history, see Claude S. Fischer, *America Calling: A Social History of the Telephone to 1940* (1992); and Lana F. Rakow, *Gender on the Line: Women, the Telephone, and Community Life* (1992). For its uses in business, see JoAnne Yates, *Control through Communication: The Rise of System in American Management* (1989). For its effects on culture, see Carolyn Marvin, *When Old Technologies Were New: Thinking about Electric Communication in the Late Nineteenth Century*

(1988); and, a very difficult but fascinating book, Avital Ronell, *The Telephone Book: Technology — Schizophrenia — Electric Speech* (1989). For a warning about some of the possible problems of advanced telecommunications, see John Wicklein, *Electronic Nightmare: The New Communications and Freedom* (1981).

NOTES

1. Quoted in Robert V. Bruce, *Bell: Alexander Graham Bell and the Conquest of Solitude* (1973), p. 205.

2. Thomas A. Watson, *Exploring Life* (1926), p. 62; quoted in Bruce, *Bell*, p. 144.

3. Alexander Graham Bell, court testimony; quoted in Bruce, *Bell*, p. 144.

4. Elisha Gray to A. L. Hayes, November 2, 1876; quoted in David A. Hounshell, "Elisha Gray and the Telephone: On the Disadvantages of Being an Expert," *Technology and Culture* (April 1975): 157.

5. Alexander Graham Bell, "Notebook: Experiments Made by A. Graham Bell," vol. 1, entry for March 10, 1976; quoted in Bruce, *Bell*, p. 181.

6. Quoted in Thomas Hughes, *American Genesis: A Century of Invention and Technological Enthusiasm, 1870–1970* (1989), p. 151.

7. Quoted in Robert W. Lucky, *Silicon Dreams: Information, Man, and Machine* (1989), p. 202.

8. Quoted in John Brooks, *Telephone: The First Hundred Years* (1976), p. 66.

9. Quoted in Stewart Brand, *Inventing the Future at MIT* (1987), p. 32.

10. Quoted in Jeremy Bernstein, *Three Degrees above Zero: Bell Labs in the Information Age* (1984), pp. 5–7.

11. *AT&T Annual Report* (1907); quoted in Brooks, *Telephone*, p. 132.

12. Quoted in Carolyn Marvin, *When Old Technologies Were New: Thinking about Electric Communication in the Late Nineteenth Century* (1988), p. 65.

13. Quoted in Marvin, *When Old Technologies Were New*, p. 80.

14. Quoted in Ithiel de Sola Pool, *Technologies without Boundaries: On Telecommunications in a Global Age* (1990), p. 68.

15. Marvin, *When Old Technologies Were New*, p. 81.

16. Robert Staughton Lynd and Helen Merrell Lynd, *Middletown: A Study in Contemporary American Culture* (1929), pp. 140, 173, and 275.

17. Rommnes, "Managing the Information Revolution," *Business Automation* (August 1966): 31; quoted in Arthur R. Miller, *The Assault on Privacy: Computers, Data Banks, and Dossiers* (1971), p. 18.

18. Quoted in Ron Rosenbaum, "The First Computer Freaks," *Esquire* (June 1983): 384.

19. Quoted in Steve Coll, *The Deal of the Century: The Breakup of AT&T* (1986), p. 332.

20. Quoted in Coll, *The Deal of the Century*, p. 358.

21. Coll, *The Deal of the Century*, p. 193.

Not just people but computers, too, could talk over the telephone network. By the late 1960s, the system designed for voices was carrying more radio, television, and computer data than conversations. The telephone network became a key part of the nation's information infrastructure, carrying everything from electronic mail to checking account balances for automatic teller machines.

COMMUNICATION
BEYOND TELEPHONES

I N 1989, WHEN STANLEY PONS AND MARTIN FLEISCH-
mann at the University of Utah claimed to have discovered "cold
fusion" — a way to release the power of the atom in a test tube, with no
radioactive waste or danger, and at almost no cost — the scientific community was abuzz. Could it be true?

Scientists everywhere wanted to know the details, and wanted to know
what other scientists found when they tried to re-create the experiments. Some
turned to the telephone or the mail to spread the information. But many more
turned to new telecommunications technology, especially the fax machine and
electronic mail. Experimental results, theoretical explanations, and arguments
and refutations spread around the world much faster than any traditional sort of
publication would have allowed, and reached a much larger audience than simple phone calls would have made possible. It was, wrote Frank Close, historian
of the cold fusion story, "a new genre in scientific communication. . . . You
logged in at any time and read the latest gossip or hard news and sent in any in-
sights you had gathered yourself." Information "flashed around the world like
an electronic chain letter."[1] Cold fusion didn't survive the rapid spread of information about it. Detailed communication permitted scientists to debunk the
theory.

Information flowed faster, in greater quantities than ever before, as the
communications infrastructure of the United States and the world grew in capacity, and as new technologies allowed computers to communicate across the
wires. Banks depended on two digital communications networks to move some
$1.7 trillion a day in payments in 1991. In 1992 an estimated 20 million people
with access to electronic mail could send messages to others on the system at the
touch of a key. Computers traded information on inventory, orders, credit ratings, and more. There seemed to be no end of uses for instantaneous communication between computers and their users. And so, in the 1980s and 1990s,
the telephone system was rebuilt around computer technology with fiber-optic
cables carrying digital signals at rates unimaginable just a few years earlier.

Electronic newspapers, delivered to the home not by the paperboy but over wires, radio, or television, have seemed obvious for years. In the 1930s, the radio fax newspaper saw some success — at night you would tune your radio-fax to a particular station, and it would receive and print out a newspaper for you through the course of the night.

In the 1970s the radio newspaper was reconceived as "video-text," a way to turn the television into a means of getting at textual information stored in a computer. Ceefax, launched by the British Broadcasting Company in 1976, used the blank space in the TV signal to transmit data. AT&T tried a similar service in 1979, which also provided information from telephone directories. Newspaper publishers, upset with the competition, sued and forced AT&T to shut down these experiments. Several newspapers tried their own experimental systems that allowed households to get news, view a community bulletin board, and do shopping, but these systems never took off.

Only when news was combined with interactive communications did this form of news delivery prove successful. Dow Jones provides financial news and access to financial data bases over its system, and CompuServe offers news and talk to a larger audience. Prodigy, a service paid for in part by on-line advertising, reached the largest audience of all — some 1.75 million members in 1992. Its largest competitor, CompuServe, has more than a million subscribers.

DIGITAL CONVERSATIONS

The astonishing improvements in the capacity of the telephone system that occurred after World War II were driven by increased demand. More people than ever before had telephones, and as rates fell, they made more calls, and over longer distances. Radio and television networks, based on telephone interconnections, also grew enormously in size and in the number of programs they transmitted. AT&T, the nation's long-distance phone monopoly, invested heavily in increasing the capacity of its network (see TELEPHONE). This capacity found a startling new use in the 1950s. Suddenly computers were talking on the phone. By the 1960s communication between computers was a driving force in both telephony and computer design.

The first major attempt to combine computers and telecommunications — to let computers talk on the telephone — came in the 1950s, when the U.S. Air Force contracted with IBM to expand the technology of the pioneer Whirlwind computer into the SAGE (Semi-Automatic Ground Environment) system. SAGE tracked incoming aircraft and directed defending aircraft to intercept them. A network of twenty-three SAGE Direction Centers was built across the continental United States in the 1950s and 1960s to defend the United States against Russian bombers. Some 1.5 million miles of dedicated phone lines interconnected the Direction Centers. Over these phone lines computers talked to one another, received data from radar stations, sent information to missile bases, and allowed use of the computers from a distance. (For more on SAGE, see COMPUTERS.)

To translate digital computer code into a form that could be sent across telephone lines, SAGE engineers developed "modems" (modulators/demodulators), which took in the digital language of the computer and translated it (modulated it) into analog signals that the phones could handle. At the other end the

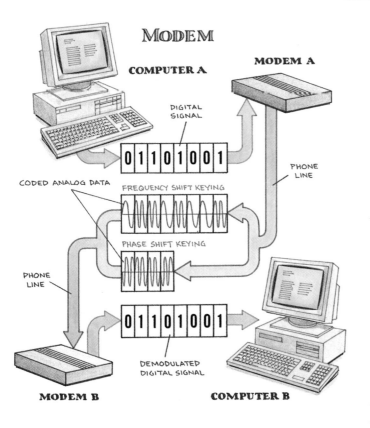

MODEM

COMPUTER A

MODEM A

DIGITAL SIGNAL

01101001

CODED ANALOG DATA

FREQUENCY SHIFT KEYING

PHASE SHIFT KEYING

PHONE LINE

PHONE LINE

01101001

DEMODULATED DIGITAL SIGNAL

MODEM B

COMPUTER B

A modem converts the binary information of the computer into an analog signal, or sound, that can be sent over the phone lines. That is, it "modulates" it from a digital to an analog signal at one end of the line, transmits the analog signal, and then "demodulates" it — turns it back into digital — on the other end.

Early commercial modems sent data at a rate of only about 300 bits per second. As the speed of data transmission increased — as the zeros and one of the digital data got closer together — the echo on phone lines made them blend together. Engineers developed clever techniques to increase the speed of transmission. By 1990, 9,600 bit-per-second modems were commonplace, and much faster modems were available.

Low-speed modems use frequency-shift keying (FSK). The modem sends a high-frequency tone to indicate a one and a lower frequency tone to indicate a zero. Each zero or one lasts 1/300 or 1/1,200 of a second, and so the modem can send 300 or 1,200 bits per second. Information can be sent both ways on the same line by using two other tones in the opposite direction. At the other end of the line, the second modem listens for the tones and converts them back to zeros or ones.

Higher-speed modems encode not one bit at a time, but two or more bits. One method is by shifting the phase of the carrier signal (phase shift keying, or PSK). Every 1/1,200 second, the phase of the signal is shifted. In a 4,800-baud modem, a shift of 0°, for example, might represent 00; of 90°, 01; of 180°, 11; and of 270°, 10.

Modems don't just send the bits representing data. They also send error-correcting and timing information to ensure the accuracy of the message. Modern modems incorporate a variety of compression schemes, too, to allow even higher rates to be transmitted.

demodulator translated the signal back into binary code. These modems were not the first devices that allowed computers to talk over phone lines — teletypewriters had been used earlier — but they were the first that could send digital information at high speed. Modems would become indispensable tools for building information networks.

The rise of time-sharing — the use of many terminals connected to one computer — brought a new demand for modems, and by the early 1970s they were becoming common. "Service bureaus" rented out time to many businesses. Each had a terminal and a modem, and would dial up over the telephone when they wanted to use the machine. A few firms began to provide access to computer databases for anyone with a computer and a modem. Dialog Information Services, for example, put on-line the text of many major newspapers and magazines (a service called Nexis), and almost all court decisions (a service called Lexis), and hundreds of others similar databases. By 1986 Dialog was the largest on-line service, with more than 3.8 billion words in its Nexis database. CompuServe and The Source, both founded in 1979, were the first large consumer dial-up services; they not only made "bulletin board" information available but also allowed users to talk to one another, the beginning of commercial electronic mail. CompuServe had some 90,000 subscribers by 1983, and almost half a million by 1988. In 1992 the leading American commercial networks had about 3.3 million customers. The largest system in the world was the Minitel system, in France. Its most common services are weather reports, directory assistance, stock quotes, and, most popular of all, dating services. "More than half the traffic," reported the *Times* of London in 1986, "consists of calls from people who are interested in sex."[2] In 1991 some 6 million users of the Minitel system logged an average of 5 million calls a day.

Computers could talk to other computers over the phone, too. Businesspeople wanted their computers to be able to talk to one another, to exchange data. Many firms needed small, on-site computers connected over the telephone line to their big computer, to take some of the load off the main computer. The small machine could store data-entry information, for example, and then upload it to the big computer at night, when telephone rates were lower. (See COMPUTERS.)

Computer networks began to show up in public places. The first automatic teller machines (ATMs) appeared in the early 1970s, and by 1981 there were more than 26,000 of them in the United States. These devices included microprocessors to control access and regulate the disbursement of money, and also a phone link to a central computer that kept track of account balances. Related to these were the credit card checking devices, called transaction phones, which appeared in the mid-1970s. These devices would automatically call a central database to make sure that the card was legitimate, and that the user had sufficient credit for the purchase. In 1983 American Express approved 250,000 credit card transactions a day from its computer center.

Computer links appeared everywhere. Retail stores of all sorts tied their inventory control into central computers, and even into the computers of their suppliers, a telephone link from the laser bar-code reader that identified the item being purchased to the store's central inventory computer, and from there to the manufacturer's scheduling computer and order delivery system. Electronic Data Interchange (EDI) standards allow firms to exchange information so that their computers can relay information directly, without the necessity of continually rekeying it. Some large firms would deal only with suppliers who used EDI, and by 1992 almost 40,000 American companies did. (The use of Electronic Data Interchange raises many legal problems: how to guarantee reliability and accuracy; whether a contract without a signature is legally enforceable; and so on.)

Electronic links were joined by another new use of the phone system: the facsimile, or fax machine. The fax machine had been around for many years — the first patent for facsimile transmission had been granted to an English clock-

To use this 1941 fax machine, you'd wrap the page you wanted to send on the cylinder, which would spin rapidly while the page was scanned. It took five minutes to send a page.

maker, Alexander Bain, in 1843, and the first commercial system was established in France in 1865 — but it was used in only a few specialized applications. Newspapers used faxes for transmitting photographs; the military, shipping lines, and airlines used them for transmitting weather maps; railroads for transmitting train orders. In the late 1930s several newspapers developed a scheme of distributing a page or two of news, overnight, by radio facsimile; none lasted very long. Western Union used facsimile machines in the 1950s, but only so that business could send and receive messages to and from central telegraph offices. The first general-purpose business facsimile was the Xerox Telecopier I in 1966. These machines required four to six minutes to send a page of text. They were expensive, too, and only about 5,000 were sold each year. Improved models by competitors brought the price down and the speed up, and sales rose. But they were still too expensive and too slow for widespread use. In the 1970s and 1980s, several firms (and the United States Post Office) went into the business of transmitting faxes from city to city for a fee.

But the market would change completely in the 1980s. In 1980 a new international standard for digital fax machines, based on research at Nippon Telephone & Telegraph, was adopted. (The Japanese found facsimile transmission especially useful because their language was difficult to transmit using telegraph or telex.) The new standard, along with new technologies, allowed an increase in the speed of fax transmission, from minutes per page to pages per minute. Ever lower prices for microprocessors and new scanning and printing technologies changed the fax machine from an expensive, special-purpose device to an inexpensive, easy-to-use office machine. The fax market took off. Numbers skyrocketed from 100,000 sold in 1983 to 200,000 in 1986 to 2 million in

A fax machine uses a photocell to scan a document. It encodes the patterns of light and dark into digital signals and sends those signals over the phone lines using a built-in modem. At the receiving end, the signals are converted back into digital signals, decoded, and used to drive the printer to produce a facsimile of the original page. Most fax machines use a hot element to print on thermosensitive paper. More expensive fax machines use a device much like a laser printer.

Until the 1980s faxes were slow and complicated, taking five minutes or more to send a page. Digital technology allowed much higher speeds by making possible the compression of the signal. For example, instead of sending information about each pixel of a long white space, a single signal telling its length can be transmitted.

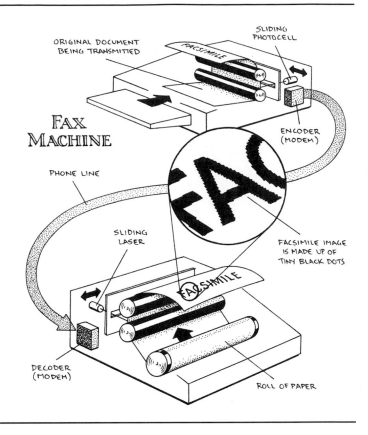

FAX MACHINE

ORIGINAL DOCUMENT BEING TRANSMITTED
FACSIMILE
SLIDING PHOTOCELL
ENCODER (MODEM)
PHONE LINE
FACSIMILE IMAGE IS MADE UP OF TINY BLACK DOTS
SLIDING LASER
FACSIMILE
DECODER (MODEM)
ROLL OF PAPER

1991. In that year some 17 billion pages were transmitted by some 6 million fax machines and 1.1 million computer fax modems.

Suddenly every business needed a fax machine, and that put more pressure on everyone else to get one, too. You could fax your lunch order to the corner deli, or wait until the last minute to finish a report and fax it in. Faxes replaced mail in many uses; a two- or three-page fax cost less to send across the country than a one-ounce first-class letter. The faxed newspaper reappeared; every minute seemed vital to those who depended on up-to-date news. Faxes found special use in overseas business as a way of dealing with different time zones and different languages. (In 1990 the majority of telecommunications between Japan and the United States consisted of fax machines talking to one another.) And of course, junk fax was not far behind, along with fax art and obscene fax calls.

One of the most commented-on effects of the telecommunications revolution was the reinvention of home work — what futurist Alvin Toffler called the "electronic cottage." White-collar workers who were interacting more with their computers than with their fellow workers began to wonder why they should have to come into work at all. Why not just stay at home, dialing up the computer to download data and upload finished reports, and rely on the fax and telephone for contact with their coworkers? These arguments were strengthened by periodic energy crises and by traffic congestion. In the late 1970s some futurists predicted that as much as two thirds of the work force would soon be working at home. But the advantages of increased flexibility were offset by decreased human contact — the interaction one got at the water cooler never made it onto the computer net — and the feeling that home-workers, out of sight, would be passed over for promotion. In the late 1980s researchers put the number of "telecommuters" at fewer than 100,000. (A larger number, several million workers, use computers in home businesses.) Tom Forester, reviewing the evidence in 1989, concluded that "the electronic cottage is largely a myth."[3]

Some firms began to extend the idea of telecommuting to overseas workers. Cheap international phone rates meant that low-paid workers in the Philippines or Hong Kong could be hired to do data entry for American firms. Programmers in India or Russia could be hired at a fraction of the price of American programmers, their work transmitted over fiber-optic lines or via satellite to their employers.

While it has been the white-collar worker who has received the most publicity, the jobs that proved most amenable to home work were in fact data-entry jobs. Working at home provided a much-desired flexibility, especially for parents taking care of children, but could fall prey to the traditional ills of long hours and lack of health and safety regulations protecting working conditions. In 1983 the AFL-CIO called for a complete ban on "electronic homework." "If history is any guide," said a spokesman, "we can say with certainty that abuse of electronic homeworkers is inevitable."[4] It would be hard to unionize home-workers, or to protect their rights. Home work never quite took off as futurists predicted.

COMPUTER NETWORKS

In the 1980s computer networks of all sorts stretched across the country. The fax machine was everywhere. It seemed that almost everyone had to have a modem hooked to his or her computer to call data services, bulletin boards, or computer networks, and a fax machine, the latest instantaneous way of sending mail. Cellular phones meant that you were never out of reach. So many computers and fax machines and cellular phones were hooked to telephone lines that many locations began to run out of telephone numbers and needed new area codes.

The better and faster the communications technology, the more demand there was for information. The market for communications seemed endless. One way to deal with it was with new technologies of transmission: new kinds of cables or radio signals, new ways to encode data digitally, new ways to reduce the amount of data sent by compressing it. More and more the telephone switching system became a computer, and the data sent over the system was computer data — even if it originated as speech. The telephone would become a key part of a new system of computers and communication. Indeed, starting in the 1980s it would be hard to draw the line between the two.

The first nationwide computer network was ARPANET, sponsored by the Defense Department's Advanced Research Projects Agency (DARPA), which opened in 1969, connecting four universities. DARPA realized that there was much to be gained from better communication among researchers. That way they could share new tools instead of reinventing them, and share resources, get-

Packet switching works by taking a digital message and chopping it into small pieces. To each piece of data — each "packet" — is added information about the order of that packet in the message and the destination for the message. Each packet includes:

1. Preamble: identifies starting point of packet, lets other senders know not to send out a packet.
2. Address: every node reads this, but ignores the rest of the message if it's not for them.
3. Sender address: where the packet is from.
4. Data: the information being sent.
5. Checking information and sequence number: the receiving computer looks at this to make sure the packet was received properly.

At each node (or packet switch) in the network, a computer reads the information about the destination and forwards the packet in the right direction. At the destination, the pieces are reassembled.

Packet switching is used not only to connect computers together across the country, but also to tie together computers in local-area networks. Packet-switched networks, like Ethernet, allowed computers in offices to trade electronic mail, or computer-controlled machines in factories to share information to direct, control, and monitor production.

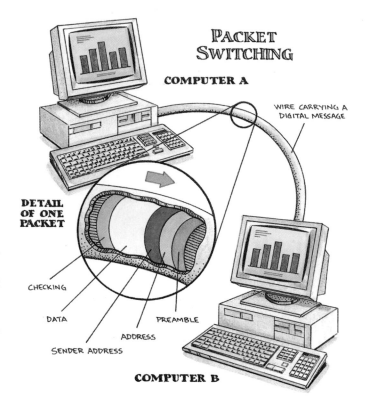

PACKET SWITCHING

COMPUTER A

WIRE CARRYING A DIGITAL MESSAGE

DETAIL OF ONE PACKET

CHECKING

DATA

SENDER ADDRESS

ADDRESS

PREAMBLE

COMPUTER B

ting more use out of expensive computers. ARPANET tied together computers so that users could remotely access other computers on the network, transfer files between computers, send electronic mail, and share information on computer "news groups." ARPANET and its successors allowed big scientific projects or supercomputers to be used "over the phone," with researchers around the world submitting data and programs and getting back results — all from the privacy and convenience of their own terminals. By 1980 ARPANET spanned the country, connecting over four hundred host computers at university, government, and military sites. More than 10,000 people had access. ARPANET had an enormous impact on the practice of computer science, as well as other fields of science, and then began to reach into politics and culture.

The success of ARPANET spurred the creation of a great variety of networks based on packet-switching principles. Some were commercial, including Telenet, started in 1972, and Tymnet, originally a time-sharing firm that expanded into a common-carrier packet-switching firm a few years later. These networks were available to anyone who paid for them; they allowed local-call access to computer databases such as Nexis and Lexis, or to national bulletin boards such as CompuServe and Prodigy. Other networks, such as FidoNet, were set up by computer hobbyists. They were free, or at least very cheap, taking advantage

of low nighttime phone rates to transfer information around the network, or even making clever use of many free local telephone calls to hopscotch information across the country. In 1987 there were 4,000 "bulletin boards" linked by these hobbyist networks; in 1992 there were 44,000. In that same year, it was estimated, some 20 million Americans used computer networks regularly. Government agencies and large business firms set up their own bulletin boards linked by their electronic mail networks.

The next step was hooking together all of these networks. The Internet, as the network of networks came to be called, in 1992 linked more than 17,000 networks in thirty-three countries, all together more than 500,000 computers, and was growing at a rate of 15 percent a month. More than 1 million people used the Internet every day. Among its uses were remote log-in (allowing a user on any computer to log onto any other computer on the network), file transfer (millions of files — hundreds of gigabits of data — were on-line in 1992, available for the asking), electronic mail, electronic journals, and thousands of electronic bulletin boards. Many university library catalogs were on-line, as well as increasing amounts of textual information, everything from song lyrics to oral history transcripts. The Internet connects almost all of the electronic mailboxes in the world, an estimated 20 million in 1992.

The main control room of EDS-NET, Electronic Data System's network, which connects EDS's information processing centers and its customers. Large firms established their own worldwide, privately owned digital communications networks.

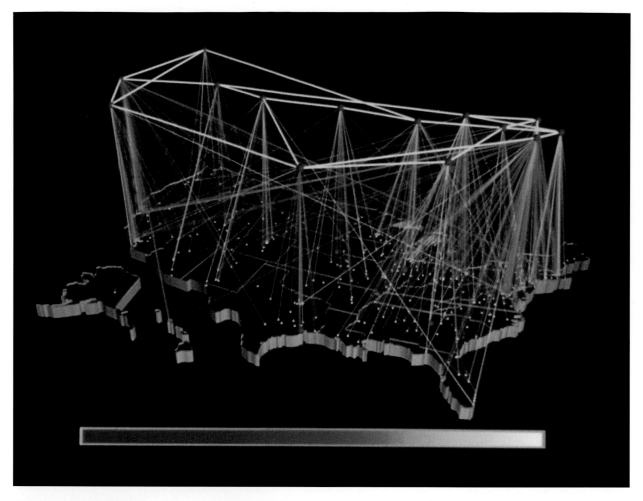

This computer-generated map shows Internet traffic for the month of September 1991. White lines represent 100 billion bytes of data; purple lines represent zero bytes.

Computer networks served to define scientific communities and to speed the process of scientific inquiry. They became a key part of science, allowing scientists all over the world to use supercomputers, log into remote resources such as radio telescopes or expensive experimental apparatus, or to trade data. They also became important to engineers, making possible collaboration with colleagues around the world. Ideas and even engineering designs could be sent over the network, instantaneously.

Businesses were the largest user of electronic mail, or E-mail. Computer firms have taken the lead, some of them with tens of thousands of electronic mailboxes. In all there were at Fortune 2000 firms in 1992 some 12 million corporate employees with E-mail addresses. Tandem Computer's 11,000 employees sent about 60 million messages in 1991. Electronic mail enabled people around the world to work together on projects, and allowed requests for information to reach the right person right away. As one believer in E-mail put it: "A person . . . on electronic mail can say 'Help' to 10,000 people. . . . The next morning he may have 15 answers to the problem, of which 13 are wrong. But he has answers."[5]

Electronic mail also became an enormously popular means of everyday correspondence. As more and more people had E-mailboxes, it became a social medium. Thousands of "electronic bulletin boards" and "conferences" covering everything from jokes to orchid-growing information were available for exchanging information and ideas.

As electronic networks stretched around the world, they had unforeseen political uses. Amnesty International has made good use of computer networks to spread word of political prisoners more quickly than it could by letters, and more cheaply than phone calls. "Alternative" networks exist, including PeaceNet and EcoNet in the United States, GreenNet in England, and AlterNex in Brazil, which sponsor conferences on topics ranging from socially responsible investing to ecology. GlasNet and Relcom, Russian electronic networks, carried news about the 1991 Soviet coup before it appeared on the television networks. And the networks were a major source of information about the coup in Russia. One message relayed over the Internet during the coup read: "Moscow is full of tanks and military machines, I hate them. They try to close all mass media, they shutted up CNN an hour ago, Soviet TV transmits opera and old movies. But, thanks heaven, they don't consider Relcom [E-mail] mass media or they simply forgot about it. Now we transmit information enough to put us in prison for the rest of our life :–)."[6] Information about the popular support for Boris Yeltsin came in via E-mail, and was posted for wider distribution. Afterward, some participants declared that the news smuggled in from outside was critical to the success of the resistance to the coup.

Electronic mail presents interesting challenges. Everything moves more quickly, and the possibility of instant response can make it hard to stop and consider things as fully as with a slower, more reflective form of correspondence. It's often hard to bring E-mail discussions to an end; it's so easy for discussions to continue, no one participant can guide the discussion toward closure. And it's difficult to express the nuance that inflection or body language allows in normal conversation. (One answer is the "smileys," or "emoticons," that are included in messages: the ":–)" in the message about the Soviet coup, read sideways to suggest a smiling face, indicates a statement intended to be ironic or humorous, or at least not to be taken too seriously.) Still, the advantages seem worth the new risks of getting loaded down with junk E-mail, or of being overwhelmed by the amount of information available.

NEW INFORMATION INFRASTRUCTURES

In the 1980s data networks became a key piece of the nation's infrastructure, seemingly as critical to the national economy as the highway system or the pipes that bring water to cities. Infrastructure is the domain of politicians, and the design of the nation's information infrastructure has become a political issue. There is a debate about the role of the government in building computer networks, and even more about how the wires that already go to almost every house — the phone and, to a lesser extent, the cable TV system — should be used.

Some politicians saw computer networks as a key to national competitiveness in science and technology. In 1992 the Senate passed a new national program to design and build the National Research and Education Network (NREN), a high-speed data highway. Vice President Albert Gore, Jr., then a senator from Tennessee, wrote, "If we do not break the communications gridlock, our foreign competitors could once again reap the benefits of U.S. technology while we remain mired in the past." The bill authorizing the program uses the language of international competition and scientific progress to explain the need for the new network. Gore, like other supporters of NREN, urged that hundreds of millions of dollars be spent to build the network, a gigabits-per-second optical "backbone" that would tie together all of the computer networks, and would be the "infrastructure for the global village."[7]

But the politics of the information infrastructure, like the politics of roads and water mains, is a complex business. Should the new data highway be designed for high-speed traffic, for the few hundred scientists who need access to supercomputers, or for the tens of millions of schoolchildren who would like to dial into local libraries? (Or should the money just be spent on allowing those libraries to buy more books, or stay open longer?) Should its structure be centralized, with government- or corporate-run switching centers at its heart, or decentralized and flexible, even if that turns out to be more expensive? Indeed, what should the role of the government be in creating and paying for the new infrastructure?

The political battle over the local information networks was much more ferocious. Not many people care about how supercomputers are connected, or who uses them. But everyone cares about their local phone and cable TV service, about how much information and entertainment is available to them, and how much it costs.

The "local loop" — the telephone connection to the home and office — is still, in most places, a few thin copper wires, as it has been for some one hundred years. Cable TV wiring is a coaxial cable, designed to carry a few dozen channels of television. But there's ever greater demand for transmitting data to the home and office, for computers, fax machines, more television, and a whole array of future possibilities. There are several technologies that will widen the electronic pathways — all of them expensive, and all of them potentially enormously profitable.

The phone companies looked to new technologies to use their old lines: digital service, fiber optics, and signal compression. The links between phone offices used fiber optics carrying digital signals. But the local loop was analog; computer communications, for example, had to be converted to an analog signal for use on the phone line. But that technology seemed increasingly backward. Why not make the entire connection digital? Why not extend the digitalization of the telephone system right to the phone on the desk?

That promise goes by the name of ISDN — Integrated Service Digital Network, a completely digital system that promises no end of possibilities. ISDN is a fully digital telephone system. Instead of converting computer data to analog signals, as is done at present, it converts voice signals to digital signals right at the telephone. About half of the telephones in the United States should have access to ISDN by 1994. Digital phone lines can carry any kind of information. Nicholas Negroponte, director of MIT's Media Laboratory, sees an all-digital future: "I can see no reason for anyone to work in the analog domain anymore — sound, film, video," he said in the late 1980s. "*All* transmission will be digital."[8]

Accompanying ISDN, in many places, may be the rewiring of the phone system with fiber-optic cable. The main trunks of the phone system were rewired with fiber optic in the 1980s (see TELEPHONE), and in the early 1990s plans were being made to replace the entire system of copper wire with fiber-optic cable. New Jersey Bell, for example, plans to replace the state's 56.3 million miles of copper with fiber by 2010. This is not cheap, though: it's estimated that to connect every residence and business in the United States to a fiber-optic network would cost more than $100 billion. Estimates for the entire new system range up to $325 billion. Before public utility commissions allow that cost to be added to telephone customers' monthly bills, they'll have to be convinced that the customers are getting their money's worth. And that might be hard to do. It was originally thought that ISDN would require optical fiber. But rapid improvements in data-compression technology, based on ever faster, ever cheaper computer processing power, means that it may well be possible to use the existing copper wire to send much more data than anyone ever imagined. Perhaps ISDN-like service, with several voice and data channels, could be sent over the existing network, without the expense of switching to an all-digital system.

The local Bell phone companies, hoping for permission to use their networks to provide profitable new information and entertainment services — something that they were banned from doing by the court order that led to the breakup of AT&T — promised no end of new features with their new, high-capacity lines. Services might include customized news, sports, and weather reports, or expanded directory assistance, or interactive classified ads. Why should everyone get a copy of the entire classified advertising section when only a few people want it, and those few would be better served by some sort of classified ad database they could search by computer? Indeed, why print the newspaper at all, when you could have a computer edit an individual newspaper for each reader, focusing on his or her needs and interests, and provide it instantly over the telephone wires? Why not send movies, on demand, over phone lines, and eliminate cable TV or the drive to the video store? New capacity would allow computer and voice signals to flow over one line. It might make local-area computer networks obsolete; the phone lines will have sufficient capacity to carry the information. But all of these uses remain in the future. Early users of digital telephone systems find themselves paying more for services not too different from those provided by the present phone system.

Another possibility for a new information infrastructure is to abandon the local loop altogether and replace it with a radio link. From their start in the early 1980s, cellular phones boomed from almost 1 million in 1987 to 4 million in 1990 and 9 million in 1992. The cellular phone system used computers as a way of reducing the amount of radio spectrum it required. By using many low-powered receiver-transmitter stations, cellular phone systems could reuse the same frequencies many times. Where once radiotelephones were very hard to get, because each needed to be assigned one of the few available frequencies, cellular phones have potentially unlimited numbers. And as the phones become more widespread, they've gotten cheaper both to buy and to use. New systems, to be installed in the near future, will make smaller, lighter, and cheaper cellular phones even more accessible.

Cellular phones and fiber-optic ISDN face a competitor from the skies. It's possible to provide worldwide portable telecommunications services from satellites. Future Public Landmobile Telecommunications System, or FPLMT, will be a worldwide network that acts just like the current cellular telephone

There isn't enough space on the radio spectrum for each cellular phone owner to have his or her own frequency. The problem is solved by several clever engineering tricks. Rather than assigning a single frequency to each cellular phone, the system designers assign a group of frequencies to be shared by the entire cellular phone system. When a connection is desired, the phone system picks an open frequency for the call. Cellular phone engineers took another step. They divided the area to be covered into a number of cells. This allows frequencies to be reused even more often, since each cell of the system can reuse frequencies of nearby cells. As the car moves from one cell to another, the frequencies on which it broadcasts and receives change. Computers handle the changes so smoothly that the people talking on the phone usually can't tell that it's happening.

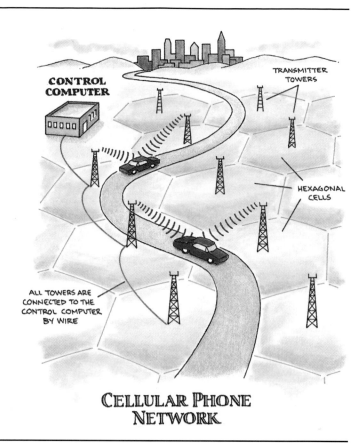

CELLULAR PHONE
NETWORK

system, except with a greater bandwidth, and reaching anywhere in the world. Several firms are looking for investments of billions of dollars to launch up to sixty-six satellites to reach what they predict will be a market of 1.8 million customers by 2002.

Existing information providers, especially newspapers and cable television interests, fear the new competition, and worry that telephone companies will use their regulated basic telephone business to subsidize their new ventures, providing unfair competition. For the first time, they argue, the Bell companies would not be neutral carriers but would be competing with those who have no choice but to use their lines. TV providers fear the competition of a second set of television programs, maybe on-demand TV, coming over the phone cables, using digital signal processing and data compression technology to ship VCR-quality video over copper wires that were once thought to be usable only for voice (the cleverly named "video dial tone"). Cable TV firms suggest that their cables might serve as a second, competitive phone system — a technology already in use in some European countries — or the two systems might somehow be joined, hooking up the cable TV's high-bandwidth coaxial cable to the digital switching system of the telephone. It's only a matter of time, it seems, until we see some fusion of computer networks, television systems, and the telephone network — what's come to be called "digital convergence." (See BEYOND TELEVISION.)

The political battles are fierce. All of the industries with an interest in providing pathways for information into the home — newspapers, cable TV companies, and television stations — have much to gain, or to lose, and so all sides have turned to heavy lobbying in Washington. The National Cable Television Association spent $14 million on lobbying and $10 million on advertising in 1990. The phone companies spent about $20 million on their lobbying efforts. Everyone involved makes grand claims for the services they might provide, if only they were allowed to compete.

While it might seem that opening wider pathways for information is an unmitigated good, enormous technological and political battles rage over the ongoing attempts to remake the information infrastructure. New technology — and a new way of thinking about how we find, sort, and use data — will be needed for a nationwide network linking millions of users to hundreds of thousands of computers and tens of thousands of databases. We'll need new ways of gathering information on networks. The library must be reinvented. How to find the information? How to copy it so that it's still usable? How to pay the owners of the copyright? Indeed, how to enforce copyright law at all when it's so easy to make copies? There's a saying in the computer community: "Information wants to be free." The hardware of the computer information infrastructure is just the first step.

Visionaries suggest all sorts of possible uses for these new information channels. Michael L. Dertouzos of MIT suggests that the first set of services might include "directories — electronic white and yellow pages — of users and services . . . and richer, universally shared resources as well: government tax codes and regulations, census data, the paintings in the National Gallery and the 15 million books in the Library of Congress."[9] Beyond that, the sky's the limit, especially when the predictions are made by the firms looking for investment and government permission to enter the market. There could be high-quality picture phone service, on-demand cable TV — an hour of video could be sent in a few seconds over fiber optics — and truly interactive television. (Holographic — three-dimensional — video seems a more distant prospect.) There could be ultra-high-speed color fax machines. Futurist George Gilder suggests that the result might be a new system where every TV set can broadcast — or rather, narrowcast — to any other, where the hierarchical networks of both the telephone and television systems are replaced by a peer-to-peer system of individual video terminals. (See BEYOND TELEVISION.)

Even broader bandwidth, sometime in the future, presents wilder possibilities: a big enough bandwidth will eventually allow shared "virtual realities," transmitting enough data to allow people to interact "physically" with one another, or with computer data, over the phone lines. Ted Nelson, a software philosopher, calls this technology "Teledildonics." A new information infrastructure with sufficiently large capacity opens up new vistas in information use.

Difficult though it might be to take even the first step, some writers have begun to imagine the last step. The information networks of the future have become one of the key locales of recent science fiction. Bruce Sterling describes what might happen in *Islands in the Net*: "The Net had been growing more expansive and seamless. Computers did it. Computers melted other machines, fusing them together. Television-telephone-telex. Tape recorder — VCR — laser disk. Broadcast tower linked to microwave dish linked to satellite. Phone line, cable TV, fiber-optic cords hissing out words and pictures in torrents of pure light. All netted together in a web over the world, a global nervous system, an octopus of data."[10] William Gibson, the premier "cyberpunk" science-fiction writer, imagines the ultimate future for the network — for "cyberspace" — as "an abstract representation of the relationships between data systems . . . the colorless nonspace of the simulation matrix, the electronic consensus-hallucination that facilitates the handling and exchange of massive quantities of data . . . mankind's extended electric nervous system, rustling data and credit in the crowded matrix, monochrome nonspace where the only stars are dense concentrations of information."[11]

FOR FURTHER READING

The history of computer communications over phone lines is outlined in Lawrence G. Roberts, "The ARPANET and Computer Networks," in *A History of Personal Workstations,* ed. Adele Goldberg (1988); and in Time-Life Books, *Understanding Computers: Communications* (1986). For a more general introduction, see Arno Penzias, *Ideas and Information* (1989); and Robert W. Lucky, *Silicon Dreams: Information, Man, and Machine* (1989), the best nontechnical book on coding and information theory.

Computer networks are a topic of ever broader interest as more and more people get E-mailboxes. The best overview is the special report on E-mail in *IEEE Spectrum* (October 1992). For some of the ways it changes work, see Lee Sproull and Sara Kiesler, *Connections: New Ways of Working in the Networked Organization* (1991). On fax machines, see Jonathan Coopersmith, "Facsimile's False Starts," *IEEE Spectrum* (February 1993): 46–49.

Economists, sociologists, and technologists, as well as science-fiction writers, have all written about the technology and meaning of the changing information infrastructure. A good overview is found in a special issue of *Scientific American* (September 1991), "Communications, Computers, and Networks." See especially the articles by Al Gore, "Infrastructure for the Global Village"; Michael L. Dertouzos, "Communications, Computers, and Networks"; and Nicholas P. Negroponte, "Products and Services for Computer Networks." For details of the effect on various parts of the economy, see Mark Hepworth, *Geography of the Information Economy* (1990); Vincent Mosco, *The Pay-Per Society: Computers and Communication in the Information Age* (1989); and Frederick Williams, *The New Telecommunications: Infrastructure for the Information Age* (1991).

More speculative works include Howard Rheingold, *Virtual Reality: The Revolutionary Technology of Computer-Generated Artificial Worlds — and How It Promises and Threatens to Transform Business and Society* (1991); and Stewart Brand, *The Media Lab: Inventing the Future at MIT* (1987). Science fiction writers have pushed the speculation farthest: see any of the "cyberpunk" writers, for example Bruce Sterling, especially his *Islands in the Net* (1988); and William Gibson, especially *Neuromancer* (1984).

NOTES

1. Frank Close, *Too Hot to Handle: The Race for Cold Fusion* (1991); quoted in Tekla S. Perry, "E-Mail at Work," *Spectrum* (October 1992): 26.

2. Quoted in Stewart Brand, *The Media Lab: Inventing the Future at MIT* (1987), p. 25.

3. Tom Forester, "The Myth of the Electronic Cottage," in *Computers in the Human Context: Information Technology, Productivity, and People* (1989), p. 224.

4. "AFL-CIO: Ban on Electronic Homework," *Profiles* (May 1985): 37; quoted in Rudi Volti, *Society and Technological Change,* 2d ed. (1992), p. 148.

5. James Treybig, quoted in Perry, "E-Mail at Work," pp. 24–25.

6. Quoted in Tekla S. Perry, "Forces for Social Change," *Spectrum* (October 1992): 31.

7. Al Gore, "Infrastructure for the Global Village," *Scientific American* (September 1991): 150.

8. Quoted in Brand, *The Media Lab,* p. 19.

9. Michael L. Dertouzos, "Communications, Computers, and Networks," *Scientific American* (September 1991): 66.

10. Bruce Sterling, *Islands in the Net* (1988), p. 17.

11. William Gibson, *Burning Chrome* (1985), p. 178.

Entertainment has been a driving force of the Information Age. Newspapers or wireless telegraphy provided useful information, but the information industry really boomed when millions of people turned to radio and television for amusement and entertainment. The changing technologies of movies, radio, and television, and whatever may come after TV, are driven by the money we're willing to spend to amuse ourselves.

The new technologies of entertainment altered our ideas of art and

ENTERTAINMENT

leisure. Jazz music changed so that it would fit onto early records. The sound of rock 'n' roll was defined by the new technology of the electric guitar. First movies, then radio and television, and even the computer created whole new categories of entertainment. Today, the entertainment industry is merging with the electronics industry as firms search for the synergies that can come from the combination of the "hardware" and "software" of Information Age technology.

Today we are surrounded by recorded sound. Music is reproduced by machines — a manifestation of the Information Age so common we hardly stop to think about it. From the invention of the phonograph in 1877 to the compact disk player in the 1980s, we've grown accustomed to a new kind of sound. Even in 1916, when this picture was taken, machine-made sound seemed to be everywhere.

E N T E R T A I N M E N T
R E C O R D E D   S O U N D

E VER THE PROMOTER, THOMAS EDISON WROTE
the press release for the phonograph even before he invented it.
"Mr. Edison the Electrician has not only succeeded in producing
a perfect articulating telephone, far superior and much more ingenious than the telephone of Bell, but has gone into a new and entirely unexplored field of acoustics which is nothing less than an attempt to
record automatically the speech of a very rapid speaker upon paper from which
he reproduces the same speech immediately or years afterward."[1] Edison wrote
this on September 7, 1877, after he had proved to his own satisfaction that sound
waves could be recorded on paper. There was no doubt in his mind that he could
fill in the details of actually making a device and making it work without too
much more effort.

INVENTING THE PHONOGRAPH

Edison was very busy that fall of 1877. He had three lines of invention
going at once, all of which would coalesce in the phonograph. First, he was trying to make a speaker for the telephone. Western Union had hired him to get
around Bell's patents, and he had already created a better microphone than
Bell's; the speaker was next. He was also trying to figure out what to do with the
device he called an electromotograph, which he had invented the previous year.
The electromotograph had a rotating, paper-wrapped cylinder on which a stylus
rested. Edison noticed that changing an electric current running through the stylus produced changes in the amount of friction between the stylus and the cylinder. He thought that the device might be useful for making a copying machine,
or perhaps for transmitting handwriting over a telegraph wire. And finally, he
was trying to figure out how Western Union might make use of the telephone.
What was needed, he thought, was a device to record voices, just as printing
telegraphs recorded Morse code. Edison had invented a machine that recorded
Morse code by embossing the dots and dashes on revolving disks of paper, and
it seemed that perhaps he could do the same with the telephone.

The first attempts at recording sound came about in a failed test of the

An early Edison phonograph, circa 1877.

electromotograph. Edison tried paraffined paper in it, to test paraffin for the friction effect. It didn't work. But when the stylus was accidentally passed over the paraffined paper a second time, Edison noticed some vibration and a slight sound. The next day Edison tried it again — not over a telegraph line, this time, but rather by speaking — yelling — directly into the diaphragm. He then ran the strip of paper back through the machine. "Batchelor [Edison's assistant] and I listened breathlessly," he later recalled. "We heard a distinct sound, which a strong imagination might have translated into the original Halloo."[2]

There was a great deal to be done before the phonograph worked, and much more before it could become a product for Edison to sell. But his mind raced ahead, dreaming up possible uses. He thought of toys first, in a flood of ideas that gives a notion of how Edison's mind worked:

> I propose to apply the phonograph principle to make Dolls speak sing cry & make various sounds also apply it to all kinds of Toys such as Dogs animals fowls reptiles human figures to cause them make various sounds to Steam Toy Engines exhausts & whistles = to reproduce from sheets music both orchestral instrumental & vocal the idea being to use a plate machine with perfect registration & stamp the music out in a press from a die or punch previously prepared. . . . A family may have one machine & 1000 sheets of the music thus giving endless amusement I also propose to make toy music boxes & toy talking boxes playing several tunes also to clocks and watches for calling out the time of day or waking a person for advertisements.[3]

Later that fall Edison substituted tinfoil for the paper, and wrapped the foil around a cylinder. He produced a working phonograph on December 3, and submitted a patent application a few weeks later.

Edison's device was indeed new, and deserved a patent. But it had a respectable pedigree. Many scientists had studied sound, and knew what sound waves looked like. In 1856 Leon Scott, a Frenchman, invented what he called a phonoautograph, a device that traced sound waves so they could be seen. You talked into the large end of a cone; the sound made a diaphragm vibrate; a rod attached to the diaphragm traced the sound waves on a piece of smoked glass.

Alexander Graham Bell tried to come up with a way to reproduce sounds from the tracings made by the phonoautograph, but his scheme was impractical. Others, too, were thinking along similar lines, especially after the invention of the telephone drew the attention of many inventors to sound. The Frenchman Charles Cros was one; he used the term "phonograph," and had similar ideas, though he never built a machine. But Edison's patent, issued February 19, 1878, made no references to earlier devices, and it was never seriously challenged. Edison was indeed the father of the phonograph.

He was a proud father. Edison had a knack for publicity, and the phonograph was a sure-fire hit. The machine even announced itself: "The Speaking Phonograph has the honor of presenting itself to the Academy of Sciences," it said; several people in the audience fainted on hearing words coming from a machine. Newspaper and magazine articles were full of wonder. *Harper's Weekly* suggested that the machine would bring about "a revolution in all departments of public singing and speaking."[4] Edison kept coming up with new ideas for his invention. In 1878 he published a long list of uses in the *North American Review*, everything from preserving languages and teaching elocution to recording phonographic books for the blind and reproducing music.

In April 1878 Edison and a group of investors (including some of the same men who were supporting the Bell telephone) established the Edison Speaking Phonograph Company. Edison received $10,000 and a 20 percent royalty, and promised to make improvements. But he lost interest, and put off work on the phonograph for other projects, especially the electric light. The phonograph fad faded within a year. There didn't seem to be any way to make money from the invention.

Edison (seated, center) and his assistants during the summer of 1888, with the new, improved phonograph.

But at about the time Edison stopped working on the phonograph, Alexander Graham Bell became interested. Bell had invented the telephone in 1876, and he was trying to make improvements in it. But he was taken with the phonograph, perhaps even more than with the telephone. He wished that he had invented it. When he heard about Edison's invention, he was jealous. He wrote a friend: "It is a most astonishing thing to me that I could possibly have let this invention slip through my fingers when I consider how my thoughts have been directed to this subject for so many years past."[5] Bell first came up with a scheme to use the phonograph as part of a talking fire alarm. Next, he thought a phonographic top might be a great Christmas gift: you'd spin the top, touch a pencil to the grooves, and it would say amusing things. Bell called it a "Swearing Top," but the idea never went anywhere.

Bell, too, stopped working on the phonograph before long, and turned his attention to the "photophone" — a way of sending phone conversations over a beam of light. That proved possible but not profitable. And so Bell decided, as he wrote in 1881, to devote his time to something that would pay. That something was, once again, the phonograph. Bell and his assistants — his cousin Chichester Bell and Charles Sumner Tainter, a mechanic skilled in the manufacture of electrical instruments — looked first at an electromagnetic system, something like a tape recorder, but that proved unworkable. They then considered a number of minor changes to Edison's machine. They came up with a new needle, and systems that used no needle at all but rather compressed air. They experimented with different shapes for records. They tried dozens of new materials, even maple syrup on paper.

Bell patented several exotic phonograph mechanisms, including magnetic and air-jet pickups, but eventually returned to fairly small improvements on Edison's basic idea. The tinfoil Edison had used was replaced with wax, and the stylus was improved so that it floated more easily over the cylinder. This was apparently mostly Tainter's invention, and his patent for it, issued in 1886, was to be the key phonograph patent. The Bell-Tainter patents and Edison's earlier patents overlapped. It seemed reasonable to Bell to join forces with Edison, who had once again become interested in the phonograph, and who had bought back control of the Edison Phonograph Company which he had established earlier. But negotiations between the two men failed. Edison believed that the Bell-Tainter patents took credit for inventions he had already made, and indeed had already patented in England. The Bell interests eventually established the Volta Graphophone Company, which soon became part of the American Graphophone Company.

Edison devoted all of the resources of his laboratory to surpassing the Bell graphophone. In the summer of 1888 he had over one hundred men at work on some sixty experiments: new materials, new motors, better diaphragms. He was spending $3,000 a month on perfecting the machine. Between 1888 and 1890 he would receive seventy-five patents on phonograph improvements. Edison now thought of the phonograph as a business machine, to take telephone messages and dictation, and even thought that cylinders might be sent through the mail, instead of letters. (For this Edison invented a collapsing cylinder.) He was opposed to the use of the machine for amusement purposes. "It is not a toy," he wrote, apparently forgetting his earlier enthusiasm.[6] The

The phonograph achieved its first success as a jukebox. This phonograph parlor was photographed in the 1880s.

An Edison talking doll. Edison established the Talking Doll Company in 1889, but the phonograph was too fragile for use in toys, and that company failed before long.

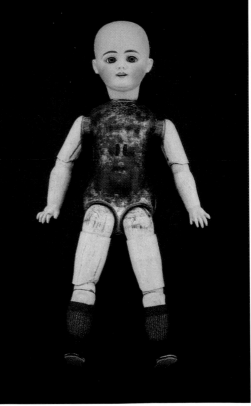

phonograph was one of his favorite inventions, and he did his best to keep it under his control, and to improve it continually. He established the Edison Phonograph Works to make the machines, investing over $1 million in manufacturing equipment.

Edison's new machine still had many problems. One of the foremost manufacturers described the phonograph as sounding "like a partially educated parrot with a sore throat and a cold in the head."[7] The batteries didn't last very long. It was hard to operate, with no easy way to stop or start: as the *Atlantic Monthly* put it, it was far too complicated for "the office boy or typewriter girl."[8] Furthermore, stenographers opposed the device as threatening their jobs. Edison was not as good at manufacturing and marketing as he was at inventing, and within a few years he sold an interest in the company to Jesse Lippincott, a Pittsburgh millionaire. Lippincott was able to buy patent rights from the Volta Company, too, and established the North American Phonograph Company.

This company, like the earlier firms, thought of the phonograph as a tool for businessmen. Its subsidiaries, set up in each state, rented out phonographs for $40 a month, and by 1891 had some 2,000 machines in use in offices. Then one of the subsidiaries found a new use: entertainment. Phonographs were equipped with a coin slot and placed in hotel lobbies and arcades. By 1891 there were almost 1,000 arcade machines — jukeboxes, we'd call them today, but with only one record per machine. The entertainment machines had their problems, mostly having to do with quality control of the records, but they were enough of a novelty to make some profit.

The phonograph continued to be the center of corporate intrigue, patent disputes, and lawsuits throughout the 1890s. But all this time it was getting better. The Columbia Phonograph Company and the Edison Phonograph Company (later the National), the two firms that survived the consolidation of the industry in the 1890s, found new materials for the cylinders; invented new needles, diaphragms, and horns for reproducing sound; increased recording time to three minutes; and, most important, found ways to reproduce the cylinders cheaply. An improved spring motor and simplified controls made the machine easier to use. Prices dropped rapidly, from $100 in 1896 to $20 in 1897 to $10 for a stripped-down machine in 1899. By 1901, when Edison perfected automatic duplicating equipment, he could make a cylinder for seven cents and sell it for fifty cents. In 1903 National was producing 25,000 cylinders a day. By the turn of the century the home market was well established. The phonograph was a commercial success, a fixture in most middle-class homes, and (as the dictaphone) in many offices.

It soon became clear that there was money to be made in selling records, not just in selling recording machines. Early records included classical performances (chopped down to fit into a two-minute recording), but more popular were sentimental songs, country songs, songs of the old country, comedy monologues in Irish brogue, country bumpkin stories, and what were called "coon" songs — white singers singing in stereotypical black accents. The first hit single, the first to "go gold" (though that phrase wasn't invented until 1942), was Enrico Caruso's recording of *Pagliacci* in 1902, which sold over 1 million records. In 1904 there were more than 800,000 phonographs in home use in the United States. About one home in twenty had one.

While Columbia and National were improving the cylinder phonograph, others were at work on more dramatic changes. In 1897 A. C. Ferguson, in New York, developed a disk that used a photographic process to record sound; it was developed like a photograph, photoengraved onto a metal plate, and played back with a stylus. More successful was Emile Berliner, who was at work on an innovation that would change the looks of the record and record player, the way recordings were made, and even the way people used them.

Berliner, a clerk in a store in Washington, D.C., liked to play with electrical inventions. In 1877 he had come up with a microphone for the telephone which used carbon granules to vary the electrical current with the voice. (Edison had invented this slightly earlier, and after twenty-five years of litigation proved his priority.) In 1887 Berliner turned to phonographs, trying to improve Edison's and Bell's work. He focused on systems that would allow easier copying. His successful phonograph (which he called a gramophone) used a needle to trace the sound pattern in a thin layer of wax on a glass or metal disk; the pattern was then made permanent by dipping the disk into an acid bath, etching the needle tracks in the disk. These disks could be copied onto a master stamper, and multiple copies made. Using a disk instead of a cylinder was not a completely new idea — both Edison and Bell had tried it — but Berliner made it work. Unlike Edison's system, where the needle vibrated up and down (called hill-and-dale recording), Berliner's phonograph used a needle that vibrated from side to side. In 1896 the Berliner Gramophone Company introduced a disk player for $25.

The Berliner Gramophone could play records louder than the cylinder

machines, and so it was more appropriate for playing music, and for family listening. (Since most
cylinder machines were used for dictation, using
ear tubes, they didn't need to be loud.) Even more
important, Berliner's records were much easier to
duplicate. Only a few cylinder records — no more
than about two dozen — could be recorded at one
time; musicians would have to perform over and
over again, standing in front of a bank of machines,
to make cylinder recordings. But from one master
disk, a large number of records could be made. The
disks were easier to store and ship, too, and were
much cheaper. But they were of poorer quality
than the cylinders, at least at first. They had more
surface noise and muddier reproduction. A cylinder ran at a constant speed, while the speed of the
disk changed as the needle approached the center.
The overall speed of the cylinder was higher, too,
which provided higher quality. Eldridge Johnson,
a Berliner associate, improved the quality with the
invention of a new way of making the master
recording and a new spring-driven motor.

Johnson established the Victor Talking Machine Company in 1901. It achieved its greatest
success when it introduced the Victrola in 1906.
The Victrola, its horn folded inside the cabinet,
looked like a piece of furniture or a musical instru-
ment rather than a machine. It was a breakthrough in design, not in technology, but it redefined the phonograph market. The Victor Company sold almost
95,000 of the expensive machines in 1910. One of its secrets was advertising:
Victor spent some $1.5 million in advertising in 1912 to convince people that a
Victrola was an essential cultural accouterment, a necessity for every middle-class
family. One 1912 advertisement read:

A Columbia Graphophone from
about 1900.

> Every home should have a Victor-Victrola:
> . . . because this instrument satisfies the love of music that is born in every-
> one of us; touches the heart strings and develops the emotional part of our
> nature; freshens the tired mind and lightens the cares and worries of every-
> day life.
> . . . because it places at your command the services of the greatest opera
> stars.
> . . . because it . . . occupies a place of honor in homes of wealth and culture
> everywhere, and has awakened millions to a proper appreciation of music.[9]

Not everyone approved of the phonograph, which replaced singing and
piano playing in many homes. John Philip Sousa predicted it would bring about
"a marked deterioration in American music and musical taste" as amateur musicians decided they would rather listen to professionals. Phonographs, he declared, were transforming musical expression into "a mathematical system of
megaphones, wheels, cogs, disks, cylinders, and all manner of revolving things,"
not "real art."[10] Peter Henry Emerson, a British photographer, dismissed all me-

Instruments were modified for recording. This Stroh violin, invented in 1901, has a horn attached so it could be heard alongside louder instruments. By the 1930s, electrical amplification began to be used, especially on guitars. The rhythms of electric guitars and electric basses would soon dominate popular music.

chanically aided art. "Art is personal," he wrote. "Photographs are machine-made goods, useful, as is machine-made furniture, machine-made fabrics, and perhaps — for the slums — machine-made music."[11] But people liked listening to records, and the phonograph became big business. In 1909 over 26 million records were sold.

Edison responded to the Victrola with a number of improvements. First, he introduced his own machine with an enclosed horn, the Amberola. Then he introduced his Blue Amberol cylinders, the highest-quality cylinder recordings ever. These had 200 grooves per inch and could play for four minutes, twice as long as his old cylinders. They were more fragile, though, and more easily hurt in the playing. But when it became clear that the disk was the wave of the future, Edison abandoned his oft-proclaimed belief in the superiority of cylinders and, in 1912, introduced his own disk phonograph. It was a completely new system, based on $2 to $3 million in investment, thousands of experiments, dozens of patents, and years of work. Oliver Read and Walter Welch, historians of the phonograph, suggest that Edison's new disk system was one of the most extraordinary breakthroughs in recorded sound. They point to "the exhaustive research and minute detail lavished upon every component of the new disc phonograph."[12] The disks used new materials, a diamond stylus, and, most important, hill-and-dale recording. Edison was convinced that he had attained the perfect reproduction of the human voice.

But just as the acoustical phonograph was reaching toward excellent reproduction, it began to lose favor. In the 1920s phonographs were finding new competition from the player piano and the radio, and sales were down. Phonograph sales fell from $105 million in 1920 to $46 million in 1930.

The player piano represented a halfway step between the record player and live music, the piano in the parlor. It had its heyday in the early 1920s, when some 2 million were manufactured in two years. (Half of all pianos made in the United States in 1923 were player pianos.) The player piano was classier than the record player, for it allowed the owner with a modicum of skill to change the music slightly as it was played, adjusting speed and the character of the sound. You didn't just "play" a player piano; you "performed" on it. As one "Defense of the Player Piano" put it, you could translate "the most delicate shades of [your] own feelings into tones."[13] In the 1920s Irving Berlin's "Say It with Music" sold 375,000 printed copies, 100,000 piano rolls, and over 1 million records.

More important was the competition from radio. One way phonograph manufacturers dealt with the problem was by refusing permission to play records on the radio, and by forbidding their recording stars to perform before radio microphones. They were convinced that they could put the upstart competitor out of business. (See RADIO.) But they also turned to the new technology of the radio to remake the record player, with the invention of electrical recording and electronic amplification.

Western Electric, a branch of American Telephone & Telegraph, made the key breakthroughs for electrical recording. Engineers at Western Electric were among the most knowledgeable anywhere when it came to the electrical transmission of the human voice. They had gained enormous skill with electronics, especially vacuum tube amplifiers, and had been working on sound recording since 1912, mostly as a way of measuring static and noise on telephone lines. Joseph P. Maxfield and Henry C. Harrison, among others there, began to experiment with electrical recording in 1917, the same year that a Bell researcher, E. C. Wente, invented the condenser microphone, which was much more accurate than earlier carbon microphones. The title of Maxfield and Harrison's 1926 paper explains it all: "Methods of High Quality Recording and Reproducing of Music and Speech Based on Telephone Research."

The Regina Hexaphone was introduced in 1908. For a nickel, the patron could hear one of the six four-minute cylinders.

The first electrical phonograph on the market was the Brunswick Panatrope, introduced in 1926, and by 1930 electrical machines had driven most acoustic phonograph makers out of business. Electrical systems had many advantages, including better high-frequency response and louder volume. But electrical recording had disadvantages, too. It was scorned by audiophiles, who claimed the new technology was "unnatural." Compton Mackenzie, the foremost record critic of the day, wrote that his wife "found this new noise quite unbearable, though it was the latest thing and first-rate of its kind. . . . I do not believe that any audience could sit still and listen nowadays to hours of electrical recording and remain sane."[14] Another critic, complaining that "mellowness and reality have given place to screaming," said that the recordings had a "peculiar and unpleasant twang" and "atrocious and squeaky tone."[15]

But electrical recording's rapid adoption was only in part based on its ability to re-create music accurately. Reactions to it were also based on changing standards of taste in music, and on changing ideas about what music reproduction should be. These changes had come about because of the radio, because of new kinds of music, because the phonograph had changed music, and, perhaps most important, because the

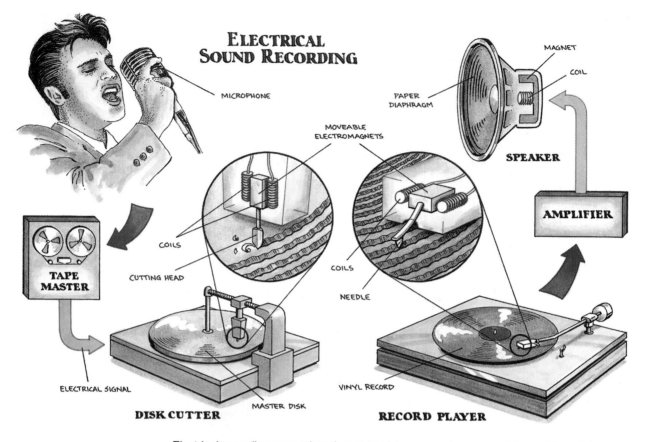

ELECTRICAL SOUND RECORDING

MICROPHONE

MAGNET

COIL

PAPER DIAPHRAGM

SPEAKER

MOVEABLE ELECTROMAGNETS

TAPE MASTER

AMPLIFIER

COILS

CUTTING HEAD

COILS

NEEDLE

ELECTRICAL SIGNAL

MASTER DISK

VINYL RECORD

DISK CUTTER

RECORD PLAYER

Electrical recording uses microphones to pick up sound waves and convert them into electrical signals. These electrical signals (usually recorded onto a master tape) power electromagnets, which in turn drive the cutting head of a disk cutter to cut a track in the record — a track that reflects the original sound waves.

When the record is played, the needle vibrates in the grooves. Its vibrations move a magnet between two wire coils, generating a tiny current. This is amplified and sent to speakers, where the current powers electromagnets that move the speakers' diaphragm.

increasing predominance of recording had changed the place of music in people's lives. Young folks, an increasingly large market, wanted to dance to the music from their record players, not listen to every word. This new generation of customers wanted loud music; they were less worried about "accuracy" of reproduction. Radio and electrical recording could pick up reflected sound, bringing the ambience of a jazz club or orchestra hall into the home. Edison's acoustic recording captured only direct sound — more accurate, perhaps, but best for unaccompanied singers. And electrical amplification, whether on radio or record, could produce a lot of bass — perfect for the heavy rhythms of jazz and the popular music of the 1920s.

Edison never understood this. He cared more about perfect reproduction and "good music" than selling records, and he thought that the record manufacturer's job was to educate the user about music rather than to sell the records the customer wanted. He refused to record jazz because he didn't like it, and was convinced that his favorite song, "I'll Take You Home Again, Kathleen," was the most popular recording. Edison responded to electrical recording with heroic improvements in acoustic recording, including a long-playing record that could play for twenty minutes on each side. But it was a failure: it was incompatible with earlier machines; there was no demand for twenty-minute records from a public used to three-minute records; and it didn't project enough volume for listeners who were used to radios, and who wanted to dance to the music.

The market had passed him by. The Edison phonograph sounded old-fashioned. Indeed, all recorded music seemed old-fashioned, compared to the radio. In 1924 radio sales boomed, while record sales fell from over 100 million in 1927 to only 6 million in 1932. Production of record players almost ceased during the depression. Sales would not rise again until the industry began seeing radio as an ally rather than a foe.

MUSIC FOR SALE

With the invention of the phonograph, music had changed. It had become a commodity, something to be bought and sold. And music had become an "industry." True, music had been marketed before the gramophone became a household object. The idea of the public concert was itself an invention in the seventeenth century. Sheet music had sold in enormous volume starting in the mid-nineteenth century, when the piano had become a fixture in every middle-class home. (It continued to sell well even in the heyday of the phonograph: the sheet music for "A Bird in a Gilded Cage," for example, sold 2 million copies in 1900, "Meet Me Tonight in Dream Land" 5 million copies in 1909.) But sheet music required an instrument, skill, and, most important, active participation. The phonograph was different. Not only was it cheap, but you didn't need special skills to use it. Evan Eisenberg, philosopher of the phonograph, notes that music became "an object that could be owned by the individual and used at his own convenience. . . . [You were free], once the cathedral of culture had been wrecked, to take home the bits you like and arrange them as you pleased. Once again mechanical invention had met capitalism's need to recreate all of life in its image. The cathedral of culture was now a supermarket."[16]

Recorded music, it seemed, could replace the original. And for most listeners, it did. How else to interpret the "tone tests" that Edison staged throughout the country to prove that there was no difference between the original singer and the Edison disk phonograph? Most listeners couldn't tell the difference between the phonograph — as scratchy and hollow as we know it must have sounded — and the singer, hidden behind a curtain. One newspaper critic wrote: "The most sensitive ear could not detect the slightest difference between the tone of the singer and the tone of the mechanical device."[17] People wanted to believe that the phonograph was as good as the real thing. (One trick was that the singers learned to mimic the phonograph!)

The phonograph began to change the way people thought about music. Claude Debussy wrote in 1913: "In a time like ours, when the genius of engineers has reached such undreamed of proportion, one can hear famous pieces

of music as easily as one can buy a glass of beer. . . . Should we not fear this do-
mestication of sound, this magic preserved in a disk that anyone can awaken at
will? Will it not mean a diminution of the secret forces of art, which until now
have been considered indestructible?"[18] And indeed, the music captured on a
phonograph record can never be exactly the same as that heard in the concert
hall. Recording is never value-free. The producer is always making decisions
about what the record should sound like. One of the most fundamental decisions that needs to be made — and it's a philosophical as much as a technical decision — is whether or not to capture the "ambience" of the hall. Should the
record sound like a concert held in an auditorium, or should it sound as though
the performers are performing for you, in your living room? There are always decisions about balance, about emphasis. Gunther Schuller, musician and one-time
record producer, put it this way: "When you record, you first disassemble the
musical subject into all kinds of components — acoustical, cyclical, directional,
instrumental, geographic — and then synthetically put it all together again. And
this is done according to someone's personal taste — it may be yours, the producer's, the composer's if he's present, the conductor's, or the union committee that says, 'I want to hear more French horns.' "[19]

Most early record producers believed that a record should be "flat,"
recording just the sounds made by the performer. Fred Gaisberg, who ran a
Philadelphia recording studio, was perhaps the first real record producer. He
recorded many of the popular stars of the day on disk for Berliner. Gaisberg traveled the United States and Europe looking for "talent," recording popular
singers and opera stars, and most were eager to record for him. He believed that
his job was to take a "sound photograph" of the artist, to get the "true" sound.
The producer's job, Gaisberg thought, was to worry about the technical details.
Walter Legge, another producer, wrote of him, "He believed that his job was to
get the best artists into the studio and get onto wax the best sound pictures of
what those artists habitually did in public."[20]

Edison was also of this school. He, too, thought that records should be
"flat," and so his records sounded good when played back in concert halls but
not so good when played in the home. Edison was also convinced that you
should be able to hear each instrument in a recording, and went to extraordinary
lengths to make this possible, even building a horn 200 feet long to record orchestras the way he thought they ought to sound. (Edison was partially deaf: to
listen to his recordings, and to make sure that each instrument was sufficiently
prominent, he would bite the side of the phonograph player!)

The second generation of record producers, starting in the 1920s,
thought differently. Electrical recording allowed a great deal more manipulation
of the sound, and producers began to take advantage of the possibilities. Legge
wrote: "I decided that recording must be a collaboration between artists and what
are now called 'producers.' I wanted better results than are normally possible in
public performance: I was determined to put onto disk the best that artists could
do under the best possible conditions." And so Legge shaped the final product
by making recommendations to the artists and by piecing "takes" together. Victor de Sabata, one of the premier conductors of the day, saw him as a fellow artist.
After recording *Tosca,* de Sabata told Legge: "My work is finished. We are both
artists. I give you this casket of uncut jewels and leave it entirely to you to make

35147

Rosario Bourdon conducts the Victor Salon orchestra. The performers had to cluster around the horn of the acoustic recorder.

a crown worthy of Puccini and my work."[21] Legge aimed at a perfect performance. Not everyone approved of this — some called it a fraud — but before long it was the rule.

As the recording studio became as much a part of an artist's life as the concert hall, music itself began to change. Because early microphones could not control the volume of individual performers, louder performers would drown out quieter ones. Singers adapted by developing a style that became known as "crooning" in the 1930s. Crooning, which started on the radio, was a soft and sentimental singing style, using a quiet, even murmuring tone of voice. Crooning swept popular music as radio and recording became more important than live performances — and live performances changed to sound more like what people were used to hearing on the radio or record player. The change disgusted traditionalists, who thought that a wider volume range was appropriate. One critic dismissed crooning as "saccharine, lugubrious, callow, maudlin, musically slovenly, lacking in vocal virility and incisiveness, short of range."[22] Oliver Read and Walter Welch expressed typical dismay: "The insinuating sotto voce, over-amplified sounds made by 'Whispering' Jack Smith and Little Jack Little represented only the more obvious misuses of the microphonic technics eventually to be foisted on the public. Rudy Vallee was to popularize the term 'crooner' and open the doors of the recording studios to a flood of trick stylists from radio." Before long, they continued, "most persons had but the slightest conception,

At a time when many radio stations refused to broadcast African-American music, blues and jazz were easy to find on record. "Race records" became popular in the 1920s. Bessie Smith was the most successful black recording artist, selling some 6 million records in the 1920s. A survey of rural Southern black residences in 1939 found that while only 3 percent had telephones, 13 percent had electricity, and 17 percent had radios, 28 percent of black families owned phonograph players. Records, writes historian Burton Peritti, "were the black sharecroppers' main contact with the larger world and their richest cultural resource." African Americans bought some five million records in 1925.

between radio and records, of what the singers or instrumentalists of either media really sounded like."[23] Especially with the early electrical systems, people liked to play with the tonal balance of the music, pumping up the bass. The music re-created in the home, whether from records or radio, became a different sort of music from that in the concert hall, which had to change to keep up.[24]

Some music, such as rural blues, gained definition when recorded. "The ten-inch, 78 r.p.m. record gave birth to the classic blues," writes Evan Eisenberg.[25] Many blues musicians learned the blues from records, and so recordings spread performance styles and songs. The music historian Robert Palmer notes: "The rise of the recording industry in the Twenties accelerated musical syntheses. For the first time white guitar players from Kentucky were able to listen carefully to black bluesmen from Texas, and rural medicine-show entertainers could hear the latest cabaret hits from New York. Early recordings documented musical changes rather than determining them, but by the mid-Thirties records were the primary source of inspiration for many musicians.[26]

The blues were, as Eisenberg describes it, a mechanically mediated oral tradition — much as jazz would be. Jazz was first recorded in 1917, by the Original Dixieland Jazz Band. Recording allowed the music to spread beyond a small black audience. Most jazz had never been written down on paper. Indeed, recording in some ways created jazz. The three-minute duration of early records helped determine the length of jazz standards, and even their structure. Music was often composed just before a recording session, since record companies didn't want to pay royalties on music that had been previously written or recorded. Recorded jazz helped make improvisation a bigger part of the jazz tradition. It also helped bring new sounds to jazz. The guitar, for example, was too quiet to compete with the other instruments in a jazz band until it had its own microphone.

Classical music began to change, too. A few composers wrote pieces expressly for recording. Igor Stravinsky, who had earlier written a piano piece that could be played only by a player piano, wrote his Serenade in A Major for record-ing. Edgard Varèse, one of the advocates of "new music," wrote in 1915, "What I am looking for is new mechanical mediums which will lend themselves to every expression of thought and keep up with thought."[27] He began to experiment in the next decades with electronic instruments, and with music produced by varying the speed of the record player turntable, and later with splicing togeth-er bits of tape.

But the classical musician who did the most with recording in the first half of the twentieth century was also one of the most popular: Leopold Stokowski. He was interested in sound, and in improving recording. He was very concerned about the quality of his recorded work, realizing that it was on records that most people would hear him, and on records that his legacy would be pre-served. The true twentieth-century concert hall, he said, was "in your living room or your automobile — perhaps even a secluded spot in the woods some-where."[28] Of 450 sides Stokowski recorded in 1917, he approved only sixty-six for release.

Stokowski insisted on close control over the details of recording and even recording technology. In 1929, when he began broadcasting, he found out about the mixer, the technician who controlled the audio mix that went out over the air. "You're paying the wrong man," he said. "He's the conductor and I'm not. I don't want this to be broadcast under my name if I'm not controlling the pianissimo, the mezzo forte, and the fortissimo."[29] Stokowski tried working the dials himself while conducting, but then settled for cueing the engineer, as if he were another instrumentalist. When he recorded, he would occasionally run the controls. He also visited Bell Telephone Laboratories, where he found himself fascinated by the new technology. Over the next few years he collaborated with the scientists there, guiding their work with his keen sense of what music should sound like. He wrote in 1932 of the importance of better recording:

> There is a very mysterious thing about music. It is psychic suggestion. That is, to my mind, the most important part of the reaction of the music lover or of anyone listening to music. The suggestive power which can carry us into the most remote spheres and realms of feeling and thought, and things that are higher than feeling — that is the important thing about music. And in order to be able to do that we must have this greater range . . . of fre-quency, of volume, and elimination of foreign noises, needle scratch, static and all those noises we hear in radio.[30]

Stokowski aimed for more than just accuracy. In 1931 he wrote, "I be-lieve the composer of the future will create his harmonies directly in tone by means of electrical-musical instruments which will record his idea exactly." Fail-ing that, he thought that electrical recording and transmission could, and should, change musical performance. He envisioned a new kind of opera, where the singers would be present only electrically, by recording or telephone; the ac-tors onstage would be chosen for their acting ability. One of his producers re-called that Stokowski "sat down at the [mixing] board with all of those knobs and dials, and started doing the most *incredible* things in terms of balances. He was practically recomposing [the] piece."[31] (Prokofiev, too, thought that the control room was the place to be. When his music was being recorded, he pre-ferred overseeing the recording to conducting.)

Not everyone thought that this technological emphasis was a good idea. One curmudgeon complained, "The image of Stokowski overshadows the ideal of Beethoven."[32] A pianist wrote after a recording session that recording "meant quickly cutting, patching and improvising . . . thinking of certain notes that had to be stronger or weaker in order to please this devilish machine; not letting oneself go for fear of inaccuracies and being conscious the whole time that every note was going to be there for eternity; how can there be any question of inspiration, freedom, . . . or poetry[?]"[33] Walter Benjamin, in an essay titled "The Work of Art in the Age of Mechanical Reproduction," suggested that mechanical reproduction destroys the ritual value of a work of art, its "aura." But when art became a commodity — as the recording came to overshadow the performance — the record came to have its own aura. To many people, "music" meant recorded music as much as it meant live performance. The phonograph had changed the nature of the musical experience.

The phonograph saw hard times during the depression but began to recover in the late 1930s. In 1939 some 33 million records were sold, over five times 1932's sales. Jukeboxes (over 400,000 in 1942) blared out the latest hits. Radio introduced new popular recordings, though much of what was heard on the radio never became popular, and one of the top songs of the war era, Spike Jones's "Der Fuhrer's Face," was considered too indecent for radio. In 1941 pop music accounted for 85 percent of record sales, classical music 15 percent. Better-quality — and, more important, cheaper — records meant more sales: some 127 million disks in 1941. But the war brought a shellac shortage, which slowed the pressing of new records, and also a strike by the American Federation of Musicians. The AFM saw the new technology of jukeboxes and recorded music stealing the jobs of musicians; they feared technological unemployment. For thirteen months no new music was recorded, and for almost two years Columbia and RCA refused to agree to the union demands of a fund for unemployed musicians.

The combination of the end of the musicians' strike and the end of the war meant a resurgence of the recording business. In 1947 over 400 million records were sold, and some 3.5 million radio-phonographs. Boom times were back, but bigger changes than most people realized were in store. After World War II new technologies began to change recorded music, and music in performance as well. Decca's "full frequency range reproduction," the result of sonar work during the war, was introduced in 1944. But even more important was the new technology of the tape recorder, perfected during the war in Germany. It would change the nature of recording, increasing the quality, quantity, and diversity of recorded music.

Alexander Graham Bell was one of the first to suggest the possibility of magnetic recording, although what he had in mind was some sort of electro-mechanical system. Oberlin Smith, an American mechanical engineer, described its advantages, and how it might work, in an article in 1888. But Valdemar Poulsen, of Denmark, was the first to demonstrate that sound could be stored on wire by a changing magnetic field. His 1898 telegraphophone found some use as a dictaphone, but could not play loudly enough for home use. In 1929 Dr. Fritz Pfleumer, in Germany, found ways to make magnetic recording on a paper tape coated with iron oxide. The first commercial tape recorder, called the Magnetophone, was produced in Germany in 1935. It, too, was used as a dic-

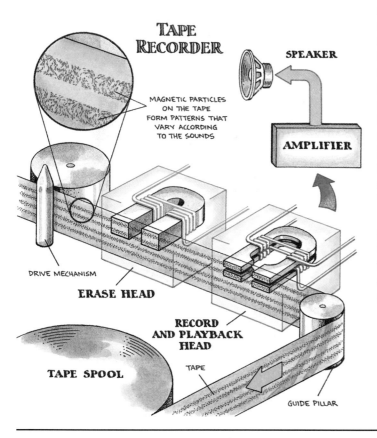

TAPE RECORDER

MAGNETIC PARTICLES ON THE TAPE FORM PATTERNS THAT VARY ACCORDING TO THE SOUNDS

SPEAKER

AMPLIFIER

DRIVE MECHANISM

ERASE HEAD

RECORD AND PLAYBACK HEAD

TAPE SPOOL

TAPE

GUIDE PILLAR

A tape recorder records electrical signals (produced by a microphone) by using an electromagnet to magnetize small particles on the recording tape. The signal is passed to a recording head containing an electromagnet. As the tape passes over the head at several inches per second, the magnetic emulsion on the tape aligns itself with the magnetism of the head, encoding the original sound signal in the pattern of magnetism over the length of the tape. A stereo tape recorder has two tracks, as shown. Altogether there are four tracks on the tape, two on the "A" side and two on the "B" side.

To replay the sound, the tape passes under the playback head (in most tape recorders, the same head is used for both recording and playback), and the magnetic signals in the tape create a magnetic change and consequently a current flow. That current is amplified and heard through a speaker.

tating machine. During the war the Germans improved the tape recorder enormously and put it to use in radio stations, recording and rebroadcasting propaganda. (Hitler insisted that all radio programs be recorded so that nothing unauthorized could be broadcast.)

The German designs for the tape recorder were large and bulky, but after the war, engineers at several American manufacturers improved the device and adapted it to commercial and home use. The tape recorder first found wide use in radio, where it was an obvious improvement over transcription disks. It first appeared in American recording studios in 1949, and within a year was considered an essential piece of equipment. (See RADIO.)

Good, cheap tape recorders made it easier to enter the music business. In 1939 Columbia and its subsidiaries and partners were responsible for the vast majority of record sales. In 1949 there were eleven record producers; by 1954 there were two hundred. Before long there were thousands. Although a few companies sold most of the records, no longer could they control the entire market for music. Record producers sprang up all over the country, producing a wider variety of records with more types of music than ever before. Local and regional producers specialized in jazz, folk, country and western, or rhythm and blues. The tape recorder made it easy for small musical groups to record demo tapes, and to get their music heard by record producers. (In many cases, the tape recorders came *after* the small firms started to make it big: many small recording studios used secondhand equipment, and rock 'n' roll didn't require the lat-

The 45-rpm record player, introduced in 1949, was RCA's answer to CBS's long-playing records.

est in full-frequency sound reproduction.) It even looked as though tape recorders might replace record players in the home, as sales grew from 255,000 units in 1954 to 700,000 units in 1959.

Phonograph manufacturers fought back with new technology. In 1948 CBS introduced the long-playing phonograph record (LP), which could store up to twenty-three minutes of music on each side, a vast improvement over prewar records. The records were made of a new material, Vinylite, which allowed more grooves, as many as three hundred per inch, up from eighty-five or so. The LP that CBS introduced, masterminded by Peter Goldmark at CBS Laboratories, represented an entirely new system of recording: a new material, a new cutting technique, and a redesigned, lightweight pick-up arm. The LP's longer playing time meant that it was well suited for classical music, musical shows, and collected works. Columbia licensed its LP record technology to any company that wanted to use it. This meant that record stores quickly filled up with LP records. Within six months of the LP's introduction, Columbia had sold 1.25 million records.

Archrival RCA Victor considered adopting Columbia's new standard, but instead responded with a new standard of its own: the 45-rpm record. The "45," introduced in 1949, also reproduced sound well but could store only a few minutes of music. RCA tried to get around this problem by introducing the "world's fastest record changer" and promoting the compact size of the records. RCA spent over $5 million to promote the 45, and CBS spent almost as much pushing the LP. The LP would find favor with classical music aficionados, the 45 was a convenient medium for popular music. It was a hit with teenagers and radio "disk jockeys." Within a few years both companies were issuing both types of records, and the "battle of the speeds" was over.

Rock 'n' roll helped make sales of 45s skyrocket: in 1959 some $200 million worth of rock 'n' roll records were sold. The new formats, along with the introduction of the tape recorder, brought new classical music to the market, too. Between 1950 and 1954 some 10,000 new recordings of classical music were put on sale, including much that had never been recorded before.

On the heels of the LP and the 45 came stereo. Experiments with stereo had been tried for many years. Early systems cut the playing time of a record in half. In the 1930s researchers at Bell Laboratories and EMI in England discovered a way to record both channels of stereo in a single track of record, and stereo began to take off. Lots of people were unhappy about the need to buy new equipment, especially those who had just purchased a record player for LPs or 45s. One enthusiast wrote a letter to *Stereophile* magazine insisting that "stereo is a first-class fake, the biggest fraud ever put out by American manufacturers."[34] But most people liked the way it made music sound — fuller and richer — and within a few years, stereo sales soared.

A new technology that allowed improved sound quality, stereo, and longer play time; new trends in music; and more disposable income all caused sales of hi-fi equipment and records to soar in the 1950s. Indeed, the term "high

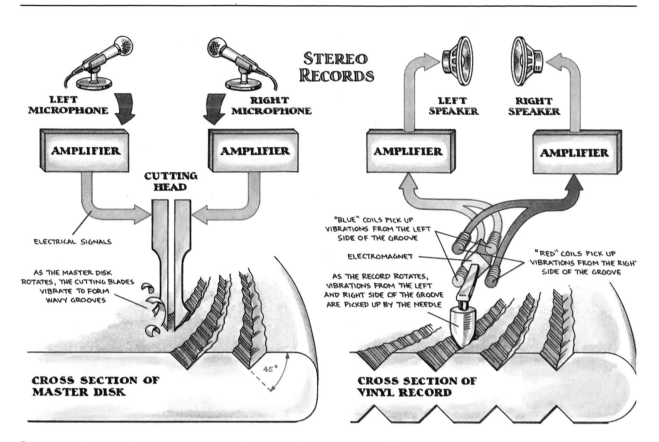

STEREO RECORDS

LEFT MICROPHONE

RIGHT MICROPHONE

LEFT SPEAKER

RIGHT SPEAKER

AMPLIFIER

AMPLIFIER

AMPLIFIER

AMPLIFIER

CUTTING HEAD

ELECTRICAL SIGNALS

AS THE MASTER DISK ROTATES, THE CUTTING BLADES VIBRATE TO FORM WAVY GROOVES

"BLUE" COILS PICK UP VIBRATIONS FROM THE LEFT SIDE OF THE GROOVE

ELECTROMAGNET

"RED" COILS PICK UP VIBRATIONS FROM THE RIGHT SIDE OF THE GROOVE

AS THE RECORD ROTATES, VIBRATIONS FROM THE LEFT AND RIGHT SIDE OF THE GROOVE ARE PICKED UP BY THE NEEDLE

45°

CROSS SECTION OF MASTER DISK

CROSS SECTION OF VINYL RECORD

Stereo records record two separate signals from two microphones so that they can be played back at the same time on two speakers a small distance apart. This gives the illusion of spatiality, apparently reproducing the locations in space of the performers.

A few stereophonic records were made in the 1910s using two separate tracks, one for each channel, but this cut the recording time in half. The trick to stereo reproduction on records was to double the information in the record groove. The first way to do this, invented in 1931 by Alan Dover Blumlein in England, was to record two signals in the track, one using the "hill and dale" technique of the early Edison recordings, the other the "lateral" technique of Berliner. Engineers at Bell Laboratories improved this a few years later with a system called "45/45," which tilted the Blumlein system by 45°. Each signal was cut 45° to the surface of the record, but still at 90° to each other.

When a stereo record is played, the needle vibrates in one direction in response to one channel, and in a perpendicular direction in response to the other. A separate coil picks up the motion for each channel, and sends it to separate amplifiers and then to separate speakers.

fidelity," invented in the 1930s, now became a catchphrase among a certain crowd, and the quest for the best record-playing equipment became a mania. Amateur electronics buffs bought components and assembled hi-fi systems. To many, the equipment became more important than the music. In the "Song of Reproduction," from the Michael Flanders and Donald Swann revue, *At the Drop of a Hat* (1959), the hi-fi addict was parodied:

> With a tone control at a single touch
> I can make Caruso sound like Hutch,
> I never did care for music much —
> It's the high fidelity![35]

Not everyone was an audiophile, but almost everyone had a record player. Most people bought complete systems, "home entertainment centers" that held radios, television sets, and record players, all in one stylish piece of furniture. In 1957 Americans spent almost $3 billion on radio, television, and phonographs — and almost $600 million on radio and television repair. Record sales reached $460 million, almost twice the amount sold in 1955.

Record sales had increased only in part because of the vast improvements in the technology of records and record players. Changes in radio and television, and in popular songs, made a difference, too. Improved transmission technology and increased demand for popular music meant an increase in the number of radio stations. Better AM transmitters and the introduction of FM improved sound quality for radio broadcasts. Indirectly the spread of television helped, too: dramatic shows moved to TV, leaving radio the preserve of recorded music. The introduction of rock 'n' roll music on TV also helped promote recordings. "American Bandstand" started in Philadelphia in 1956. It went nationwide the following year to an audience of 8 million teenagers, who sent in 45,000 letters a week.

Recorded music provided cheap material for radio, and more radio stations played more popular music. Radio disk jockeys all but determined which songs became popular, a situation that led to the great "payola" scandals of the 1950s. In the 1950s and 1960s a d.j. would receive several thousand records a week, and so record companies would help him decide what to play by means of bribes. Congressmen, already convinced that rock 'n' roll was a major cause of juvenile delinquency, made payola into a major scandal, complete with congressional hearings in 1959. But the close connection of radio and recording continued. "What sells records is radio" is how one executive of Capitol Records put it.[36] (See RADIO.)

The music that people heard on their hi-fis and stereos was designed to be heard at home. American record producers of the 1950s made use of the tape recorder and the new technology of the recording studio to alter the recorded sound. It became easy to patch together the best pieces from many takes, to add echo, to erase noises, to play with the treble and bass. They started with "overdubbing," recording the orchestra or band first, and then the soloist, singing or playing along to the recording. Even "live" performances could be manipulated, as microphones showed up in concert halls to "correct" the sound, that is, to make it sound more like the recordings people were used to. Some prewar record producers would select the best takes and paste them together, but the postwar generation of producers went even further. They believed that a record

producer should translate a live performance to vinyl in much the same way that a movie producer translated a stage play to film. This approach appalled some critics, but it found widespread acceptance in the United States in the 1940s and later, especially in popular music. Record producers played with the sound, mixing the microphones, adding echo, changing frequency responses, all aimed at getting the best recording, or the recording they thought would sound best on the typical home record player: sound with less bass so that the needle would stay in the groove, and with more treble to make up for the weak treble in most home speakers.

Multiple microphones became common in the mid-1960s. The idea had its start in radio dramas, and then in the movie business, where several microphones were needed to pick up the sound as it occurred. That equipment found favor first in classical music recording, which used sixteen or more microphones, carefully placed about the auditorium or recording studio, to accent, emphasize, or focus on individual instruments. Each microphone was recorded on a different channel of a multitrack tape recorder and then "mixed" to get just the right effect. By the 1970s some mixers had as many as forty-eight inputs and twenty-four outputs, and the engineer could control not just signal level but also equalization, or the number of different frequencies in the sound, as well as reverberation, or echo, and the spatial placement of the signal in the stereo field. The

The control room, where the decision about what gets put on tape is made, is the key to modern recording. The mixer, in the foreground, controls the input from each of the several microphones in the sound studio. Even the musicians listen to the music on headphones.

engineer at the mixer could define the sound. The final result could be pieced together, the producer picking and choosing from among various tracks and various takes until it sounded just right. "It is at this juncture," writes C. A. Schicke, a recording executive, "that the producer can, in a sense, play god."[37]

And especially in popular music, the producer was God. Sam Phillips, who recorded many Nashville musicians in the 1950s, did his best to pull certain sounds out of people. He shaped Elvis Presley's music, for example, deciding what sound would sell, and producing that sound. The same was true at Motown Records, where Berry Gordy made every group he recorded sound like "Motown sound." Even in classical music, producers couldn't resist the opportunity to play with the sound. The record became a distinct new art form, separate from live performance. And, as amplification became a key part of the performance, it was hard to tell the reality from the recording. Gunther Schuller writes:

> The producers of these kinds of recordings take what they call a "creative" approach. What I would more accurately call it is a "synthetic" approach, where the producers determine in advance the precise acoustical properties and musical relationships which they're trying to achieve in the recordings . . . . [In rock music the sound is] synthesized and modified by the producers in order to achieve a certain sound that is new or fashionable or current. In the best of these endeavors, the electronics are part of the creative effort.[38]

In a 1959 article titled "How No-Talent Singers Get 'Talent'," the *New York Times* feared that popular musicians were using technology to hide their flaws:

> Recording techniques have become so ingenious that almost anyone can seem to be a singer. A small, flat voice can be souped up by emphasizing the low frequencies and piping the result through an echo chamber. A slight speeding up of the recording tape can bring a brighter, happier sound to a naturally drab singer or clean the weariness out of a tired voice. Wrong notes can be snipped out of the tape and replaced by notes taken from other parts of the tape. . . . Almost every pop recording made today, even by well established talent, carries some evidence of the use of echo chambers, tape reverberation, over-dubbing or splicing.[39]

Where the *Times* saw fraud, certain musical groups saw opportunity. Some insisted on control of the mixer. In the late 1950s Buddy Holly mixed his own music, overdubbing tracks to create new sounds. The Beatles' *Sergeant Pepper* album, released in May 1967, was the first major work of popular music to take full advantage of multitrack recording and mixing; the group spent 700 hours in the studio, creating sounds that could exist only on a recording. For many groups the record was primary, the concert secondary. The disco music of the 1970s represented the apotheosis of the producer. The record was everything for disco; some groups didn't exist except within the recording studio. Producers were far more important than the acts they orchestrated.

Glenn Gould, one of the greatest pianists of the 1960s and 1970s, defended the recording's priority even for classical music. Indeed, he gave up concerts to focus entirely on recording. He produced his own records, meticulously, insisting on a perfection never possible in a concert. For Gould, recorded music was an independent art, "as distinct from live music as film is distinct from theater."[40] He thought that radio and television were homogenizing forces, which could be countered by the staying power of records. Records, he wrote, "breed tolerance and even eccentricity." Gould believed that only on records could he achieve perfection: "Strangely, I have always preferred working in a studio, making records or doing radio or television, and for me, the microphone is a friend, not an enemy and the lack of an audience — the total anonymity of the studio — provides the greatest incentive to satisfy my own demands upon myself without consideration for, or qualification by, the intellectual appetite, or lack of it, on the part of the audience."[41]

Others worried that the demand for perfection was affecting performances, both recorded and live. Gunther Schuller wrote that recording in "takes" made for a more relaxed atmosphere, but he feared that "something of quality has gone out of it — the spontaneity and excitement and drive and forward thrust of a performance are now often missing."[42] Some critics thought that live performances in the 1970s and 1980s were increasingly concerned with accuracy and less with emotions. Performances attempted to mimic the perfection obtained only with recordings.

Perfect or not, music was everywhere. It became a universal background noise, much to the anger of some music lovers. One social critic complained in 1961 that music wasn't listened to anymore: "Far commoner [a way for music to reach us] is the sound from the car radio as we drive along; or from the AM-FM radio while we cook a meal, wash the dishes, or work in our basement; or from the automatic-record-playing hi-fi as we play cards, read a book, or make conversation. . . . We are music-soothed and music-encompassed as we go about our business. Now the appropriate music for any occasion is that which need not be followed but can simply be inhaled."[43]

Perhaps the ultimate in all-encompassing music was Muzak. Muzak, Inc., had started in the 1920s piping music in over telephone circuits to factories to keep workers happy. In 1957 there were almost 50,000 selections in the Muzak library. Muzak played 200 million miles of tape per year, and was, for a while, the world's largest user of the telephone lines. Fifty million Americans heard it daily. It was, as a Muzak representative put it, "music to hear, not to listen to."[44] The music was designed to keep workers energetic and maintain productivity; the music at the start of the day was calm, in late morning cheery, in the afternoon more peppy and rhythmic. "Elevator music," it came to be called, and it seemed to be everywhere — though, of course, most people never noticed it.

One reason, perhaps, was that they couldn't hear it over their Walkman. Tape cassettes were introduced by Phillips in 1963, and improved by R. M. Dolby's invention of noise-reduction circuitry in 1967. Cassettes outsold open-reel and cartridge tape players for the first time in 1968, and in 1985 began to outsell records. Quadraphonic (four-channel) sound was a short-lived "improvement," starting in 1971 but pretty much disappearing by 1980, the victim of competing standards. About as short-lived was the eight-track tape, introduced in the early 1960s by William Lear, mostly for use in cars. But it was the Sony Walkman, a small portable tape player with earphones, introduced in 1980, that swept the world. It was a minor technological improvement — a smaller radio and tape recorder — but the combination of privacy, personal choice, and the possibility of having music available all the time was irresistible. In 1982, the first year they were marketed in the United States, some 5.6 million Walkmans were

In the 1980s, rap musicians began to play with the technology of the record player to create new music. Afrika Bambaataa, Kurtis Blow, and Grandmaster Flash and the Furious Five turned the turntable itself into an instrument. Grandmaster Flash (Joseph Saddler) is credited with developing some of rap's key techniques: rotating records back and forth to make a new "scratch" beat; "phasing," or manipulating turntable speeds; and "needle rocking," making an echo effect by switching back and forth between two turntables — techniques that others, like these disc jockeys in a Bronx, New York, playground, quickly copied. The d.j. created new music by using the technology of recorded music. In the late 1980s, as digital sampling became available at lower cost, some of the same techniques were accomplished with more sophisticated technology.

sold. Over the next ten years Americans would buy more than 80 million Walkmans, their competitors, and successors.

MUSIC GOES ELECTRIC, ELECTRONIC, AND DIGITAL

The music played by Muzak, or listened to on the Walkman, more often than not represented a new kind of electrified music. Some of the electronics of the recording studio found their way into the instruments themselves. Why play an organ into a microphone when you could use the electronics to create the tones in the first place? Keyboards went electronic with the invention of the electronic organ by Laurens Hammond in 1929. His Hammond Instrument

Company sold its first electric organ in 1935, and 3,000 within two years. Although the Hammond organ and the Rhodes electric piano were originally derided for their "nonmusical" sound, before long this sound came to be desired by musicians and audiences.

Another way to make electric instruments was to build the microphone into the instrument. Electric guitars work this way. Guitars had been electrified since the 1930s, but not until the late 1950s did the electric guitar gain its characteristic sound in rock 'n' roll. The electric sound came to symbolize rock music. Chuck Berry's "Johnny B. Goode" becomes a star by playing an electric guitar. It's the electric guitar that triumphs over classical music in "Roll Over Beethoven." In the early 1960s Dick Dale, one of the originators of surfing music, worked with Leo Fender, manufacturer of the solid-body guitar, to improve the amplifier and develop the reverb technology that gave his music its "surfing" sound. The key was feedback, pushing the amplifier beyond its usual limits to produce new sounds. Jimi Hendrix revolutionized the blues by pushing the electric guitar even further, using the wah-wah pedal and fuzz box to shape the music. The electronics were as much the instrument as the guitar itself.

The synthesizer, invented by Harry Olson and Herbert Belar at RCA in 1955, pushed the limits of the electric organ by allowing infinitely more variation in the shape of the notes. Early synthesizers were programmed like computers, with punched paper tape. Robert A. Moog, a doctoral student at Cornell University, improved the synthesizer, making it programmable in real time. His 1964 commercial version was the first that musicians found practical. The synthesizer first received public acclaim in 1968, when Walter Carlos's "Switched-On Bach" sold more copies than any classical recording before it.

By the 1980s, rock 'n' roll music required electronics engineers as much as it required musicians. Bands traveled with dozens of speakers, computers, electronic instruments, and complex mixing boards to re-create in concert the sound they created in the recording studio. When Pink Floyd toured the United States in 1980–81 to promote their album *The Wall,* they carried with them 45 tons of equipment, including a 45,000-watt PA system. In the picture: Megadeth, a heavy metal band, almost overwhelmed by their speakers.

Sequencers allow musicians to compose, perform, and record their music on the computer.

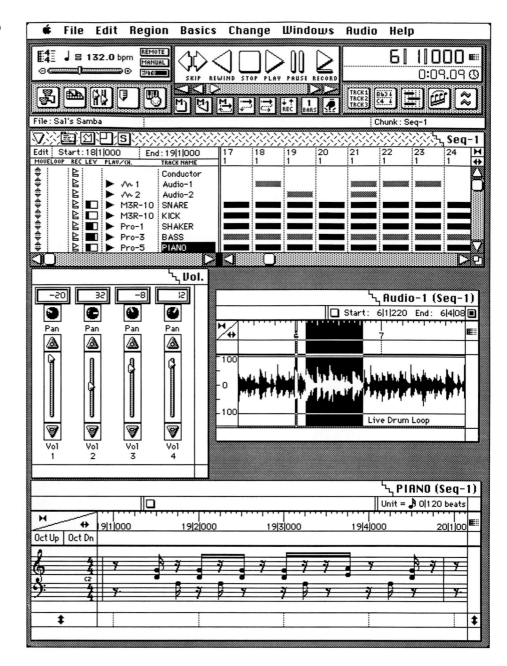

Cheaper electronics allowed the synthesizer to find wide use in rock 'n' roll. Rock musicians used the synthesizer to imitate other instruments, first the piano, and then, with the invention of the "strap-on" synthesizer, the guitar. (The technology reflected its new use; these synthesizers had a "pitch bend" wheel to copy the sound of pulling on guitar strings.) In the 1970s microprocessors were added to synthesizers to make them programmable. At first this was to make it possible to store and recall any instrumental setting at the touch of a button. The new ease of use of the synthesizer led to a "synthesizer sound" which was a big hit on MTV in the early 1980s, a sound that came to be called, appropriately enough, "synth-pop" or "techno-pop." By 1980 portable synthesizers were cheap, easy to handle, and easy to use. The guitar lost favor, and the sale of synthesizers soared. (Some rock bands held out against the new technology: Boston's 1978 *Don't Look Back* album states on the sleeve that no synthesizers or computers were used; so too do several of Queen's albums from the mid-1970s.)

The synthesizer could be more than just a piano or a guitar. With the introduction of "digital sampling" in the 1970s, the synthesizer could act like any instrument, or like a totally new instrument. Any sound could be "sampled," or digitized, processed, and recorded; then the synthesizer could modify that sound and replay it at any frequency. This became a key technique of rap musicians, who captured and manipulated snatches of previously recorded songs — a digital version of what they had previously done by mixing together bits of music taken from several records. The synthesizer became an all-purpose instrument. In the late 1960s primitive analog programming capabilities were added; called "sequencers," they could play a series of notes in sequence. Digital sequencers appeared in the 1970s; they could memorize the notes played on a keyboard and play them back. As instruments became digital, musicians wanted to connect them so that they could communicate with one another — so that one synthesizer could control another, for example. In 1981 David Smith, then president of Sequential Circuits, Inc., proposed a standard musical interface for communication between electronic keyboard instruments. An official standard called MIDI, for Musical Instrument Digital Interface, was developed in 1983, and was widely adopted by 1986.

MIDI's original purpose was to allow electronic instruments to "talk" to one another. The digital data recorded according to the MIDI standard could tell a dozen or more synthesizers what to do. Because the language was digital, it was easy to manipulate by computer, and soon computer sequencing programs appeared. A computer that understood MIDI made it possible to edit the music easily on the computer screen, and even have it printed out as sheet music! You could play a tune on a keyboard, record it, edit it, orchestrate it, manipulate it on the computer, and play it back on any number of instruments, or, with digital sampling, on one instrument that could sound like any instrument. Modern sequencers can replace conductor, band, and recording studio. Musicians had feared losing their jobs with the introduction of the record player; for many the nightmare came true with the computerization of music. One person and a computer could sound like an entire orchestra.

The new electronic music was usually heard on a new electronic medium. Digital recording represented a fundamentally new approach to recording music, the first major breakthrough since electrical recording some sixty years earlier. Instead of reproducing the shape of the sound wave on a record, it samples the sound — records its volume — some 40,000 times a second, and converts this number to a digital representation, one of about 65,000 sound levels. This digital data can be stored and manipulated. (Digital sampling was first developed for telephone transmission; see TELEPHONE.)

Digital recording began to see wide use in the 1970s, but it had its biggest effect when it was joined with a new form of digital music playback: the compact disk. The CD was announced by Phillips Industries in 1978 in a joint development effort with Sony. Its antecedents were not audio equipment but

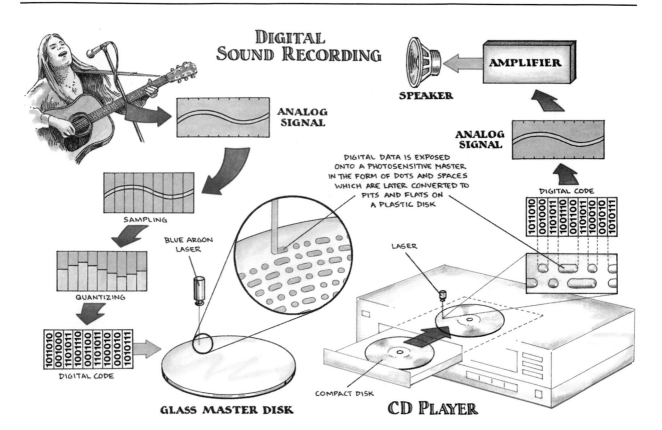

DIGITAL SOUND RECORDING

ANALOG SIGNAL

SAMPLING

QUANTIZING

DIGITAL CODE

BLUE ARGON LASER

DIGITAL DATA IS EXPOSED ONTO A PHOTOSENSITIVE MASTER IN THE FORM OF DOTS AND SPACES WHICH ARE LATER CONVERTED TO PITS AND FLATS ON A PLASTIC DISK

GLASS MASTER DISK

SPEAKER   AMPLIFIER

ANALOG SIGNAL

DIGITAL CODE

LASER

COMPACT DISK

CD PLAYER

Digital sound recording is fundamentally different from analog sound recording. Instead of the pattern of the sound waves being reproduced in the grooves of a record or the patterns of magnetism on a tape, *information* about those sound waves is stored in the form of digital signals. To do this, the sound is sampled thousands of times a second. At each sampling, the amplitude of the wave is noted and converted to a binary representation. If a wave is sampled at twice the highest frequency, it can be reconstructed exactly.

When AT&T's engineers set up its first digital lines in 1962, they decided to sample 8,000 times a second — twice the 4,000 hertz that telephone lines had traditionally transmitted. The amplitude of each sample is measured and placed into one of 256 (2^8) categories — low fidelity, but good enough for phone conversation. Digital telephone lines must transmit about 64,000 bits per second ($8,000 \times 8$), and it takes about 21,000 bits to send one spoken word on a digital telephone line.

When the compact disk came along, high fidelity was the key goal. The comparison with phone digitalization is revealing. CDs sample 44,100 times a second, enough to capture 22,050 hertz — about as high a frequency as the human ear can hear. They take a sixteen-bit sample, that is, they divide the amplitude into 2^{16}, or about 65,000 categories. Including stereo and the error-correcting information which makes it possible to correct any data missed during playback, it takes some half-million bits to encode one spoken word on a compact disk.

The data on a compact disk is recorded as a series of closely spaced pits in the surface of the disk. The pits are arranged in a spiral track whose total length is more than 3.5 miles. To play back the CD, a laser retraces the spiral track, starting at the center. When it hits a pit the light is scattered; when it hits a smooth spot it's reflected. Those reflections are detected and converted to the digital code, which in turn is converted to an analog signal and fed to the speakers.

the video disk, introduced by the same firms in 1975. (See BEYOND TELEVISION.) The Phillips-Sony CD standard was accepted as a world standard in 1982, and CD players were introduced in the United States in 1983. Although audiophiles objected to it, claiming that its sound was harsh — objections very similar to those that had greeted electrical recording a half century earlier — it quickly won public favor. It produced better sound than all but the best records played on the most expensive equipment; it did not wear out because there was no contact between the CD and the pickup; and it allowed longer recording time, about sixty-five minutes (later extended to eighty minutes).

The CD began to replace LPs, just as the LP had replaced the "78." Sixteen million CDs were sold in 1985, and almost 400 million in 1988 — more CDs than LPs. The LP began to disappear from record stores, as record companies began to distribute music only on CD and cassette. The record industry, which had been in decline since 1978 with sales of $4.13 billion, started to take off again. In 1986 sales hit almost $5 billion. Profits were up, too, because CDs sold for more than the equivalent LP. CDs couldn't be recorded at home, but their successors in the early 1990s, Sony's MiniDisk and Phillip's Digital Compact Cassette, could. The threat of perfect, easy-to-make copies set off copyright battles that delayed the machines' introduction, and resulted in copy protection to prevent serial copying and new taxes on the machines and on blank tape and disks.

With digital sampling and computer-controlled synthesizers, music came into the computer age. But music had long been mechanized. Technology has been changing the way we think about music, and the way we use it, since the very first days of the recording industry.

FOR FURTHER READING

There are several good general histories of sound recording: C. A. Schicke, *Revolution in Sound: A Biography of the Recording Industry* (1974); Roland Gelatt, *The Fabulous Phonograph: From Tin Foil to High Fidelity* (1955); and, focusing on the technology, Oliver Read and Walter L. Welch, *From Tin Foil to Stereo: Evolution of the Phonograph*, 2d ed. (1976).

On Edison and the phonograph, see Robert Conot, *A Streak of Luck* (1980); and Andre Millard, *Edison and the Business of Innovation* (1990).

For an introduction to the way technology and music interact, see H. Wiley Hitchcock, ed., *The Phonograph and Our Musical Life* (1977); Robert E. McGinn, "Stokowski and the Bell Telephone Laboratories: Collaboration in the Development of High-Fidelity Sound Reproduction," *Technology and Culture* (January 1983): 38–75; and a wonderfully imaginative book, Evan Eisenberg, *The Recording Angel: Explorations in Phonography* (1987).

On electrical and electronic instruments, the *New Grove Dictionary of Musical Instruments,* ed. Stanley Sadie (1984), is the best source. Steve Jones, *Rock Formation: Music, Technology, and Mass Communication* (1992), shows the ways technology is used in rock music. *BYTE*, 11, no. 6 (June 1986), was devoted to an overview of computers and music.

NOTES

1. Quoted in Robert Conot, *A Streak of Luck* (1980), pp. 120–121.
2. Quoted in Conot, *A Streak of Luck,* p. 119.

3. Quoted in Conot, *A Streak of Luck,* p. 124.

4. *Harper's Weekly,* March 30, 1878; quoted in Oliver Read and Walter L. Welch, *From Tin Foil to Stereo: Evolution of the Phonograph,* 2d ed. (1976), p. 24.

5. Thomas A. Watson, *Exploring Life* (1926), p. 97; quoted in Robert V. Bruce, *Bell: Alexander Graham Bell and the Conquest of Solitude* (1973), p. 252.

6. Quoted in Read and Welch, *From Tin Foil to Stereo,* p. 55.

7. Eldridge Johnson, quoted in Roland Gelatt, *The Fabulous Phonograph: From Tin Foil to High Fidelity* (1954), p. 84.

8. Quoted in Andre Millard, *Edison and the Business of Innovation* (1990), p. 80.

9. Quoted in John Harvith, *Edison, Musicians, and the Phonograph: A Century in Retrospect* (1987), p. 2.

10. John Philip Sousa, "Menace of Mechanical Music," *Appleton's Magazine* (September 1906): 208; quoted in Lawrence W. Levine, *Highbrow/Lowbrow: The Emergence of Cultural Hierarchy in America* (1988), p. 163.

11. Peter Henry Emerson, *Naturalistic Photography,* 3d ed. (1899; reprint 1973); quoted in Levine, *Highbrow/Lowbrow,* p. 162.

12. Read and Welch, *From Tin Foil to Stereo,* p. 200.

13. Ernest Newman, *The Player Piano and Its Music* (1920); quoted in Jeanne Allen, "The Industrialization of Culture: The Case of the Player Piano," in *Changing Patterns of Communications Control,* ed. Vincent Mosco and Jane Wasco (1984), p. 105.

14. Quoted in Evan Eisenberg, *The Recording Angel: Explorations in Phonography* (1987), p. 112.

15. Quoted in Gelatt, *Fabulous Phonograph,* p. 232.

16. Eisenberg, *The Recording Angel,* p. 29.

17. *London Advertiser,* quoted in Read and Welch, *From Tin Foil to Stereo,* p. 204.

18. Quoted in Eisenberg, *The Recording Angel,* p. 55.

19. Quoted in Harvith, *Edison, Musicians,* p. 402.

20. Quoted in Eisenberg, *Recording Angel,* p. 116.

21. Quoted in Eisenberg, *Recording Angel,* pp. 117 and 119.

22. Quoted in Henry Pleasants, *Great American Popular Singers* (1963), p. 27.

23. Read and Welch, *From Tin Foil to Stereo,* pp. 238–239.

24. Whitney Balliett, *American Singers* (1979), pp. 74–75.

25. Eisenberg, *Recording Angel,* p. 141.

26. Robert Palmer, "Rock Begins," in *The Rolling Stone Illustrated History of Rock & Roll,* 2d ed., ed. Jim Miller (1980), p. 7.

27. Quoted in Eisenberg, *Recording Angel,* p. 132.

28. Quoted in Eisenberg, *Recording Angel,* p. 152.

29. Quoted in Eisenberg, *Recording Angel,* p. 151.

30. Leopold Stokowski, in *Bell Laboratories Record* (January 1932); quoted in Robert E. McGinn, "Stokowski and the Bell Telephone Laboratories: Collaboration in the Development of High-Fidelity Sound Reproduction," *Technology and Culture* (January 1983): 53.

31. Quoted in Eisenberg, *Recording Angel,* pp. 151 and 153.

32. Daniel Boorstin, *The Image: Or What Happened to the American Dream* (1962), p. 172.

33. Ferruccio Busoni, *Letters to His Wife* (1938); quoted in McGinn, "Stokowski and the Bell Telephone Laboratories," p. 73.

34. Letter to the editor, *Stereophile* (1962); reprinted in *Stereophile* (February 1992): 70.

35. Michael Flanders and Donald Swann, "Song of Reproduction," in *At the Drop of a Hat* (1959).

36. David P. Szatmary, *Rockin' in Time: A Social History of Rock and Roll* (1987), p. 121.

37. C. A. Schicke, *Revolution in Sound: A Biography of the Recording Industry* (1974), p. 158.

38. Quoted in Harvith, *Edison, Musicians,* p. 398.

39. "How No-Talent Singers Get 'Talent,'" *New York Times,* June 21, 1959, sec. 6, p. 16.

40. Quoted in Eisenberg, *Recording Angel,* p. 105.

41. From Glenn Gould, *Selected Letters,* ed. and comp. John P. L. Roberts and Ghyslaine Guertin (1992); quoted in *New Yorker,* November 23, 1992: 138.

42. Quoted in Harvith, *Edison, Musicians,* p. 406.

43. Boorstin, *The Image,* pp. 174–175.

44. Quoted in Boorstin, *The Image,* p. 177.

The new technology of the movie, invented in the 1890s, changed the way people saw the world. It transformed popular entertainment, bringing a new national culture to vast new audiences. It brought drastic changes to the way people used their leisure time. In the 1950s movies found new competition from television, and in the 1980s from videocassette recorders. But movies survived, both on the big screen and as program material for more recent forms of entertainment.

ENTERTAINMENT
MOVIES

THOMAS EDISON WAS THINKING ABOUT THE phonograph when he decided to invent a moving picture machine. He was used to working by analogy with earlier inventions: the movie camera and projector would just be a phonograph for pictures. The phonograph had recorded sound vibrations on tracks around the edges of a cylinder, and Edison thought that pictures could be recorded in the same way. In his early drawings he suggested ways of putting a series of tiny photographs onto a cylinder recording: "I am experimenting upon an instrument which does for the Eye what the phonograph does for the Ear," he wrote in a patent caveat.[1]

INVENTING MOTION PICTURES

Edison wasn't the first to think about moving pictures. There were already toys that used a rapidly changing succession of pictures to create the illusion of motion — even some that projected the image. The Zoopraxiscope, invented by Eadweard Muybridge in the 1870s, for example, had a succession of drawings on the edge of a wheel. Viewed through a special device, it looked as though the clowns were dancing, or the horses running. This was a kind of animation. In 1878 and 1879 Muybridge designed a series of cameras to take pictures of people and animals in motion. Etienne-Jules Marey, in France, expanded this work, inventing a "photographic gun" that allowed him to record pictures like these around the edges of a disk; a separate device projected them onto a screen. These were the first motion pictures.

Edison and Muybridge met in 1888 to discuss the possibility of joining a Zoopraxiscope with a phonograph to produce simultaneous sound and pictures. Edison assigned an assistant, W. Laurie Dickson, to begin experimental work on the device, which came to be called the Kinetoscope. In 1889 Edison met Marey, and adopted from his experiments the idea of using a strip of film rather than separate cards with pictures. Edison's first commercial Kinetoscope could hold about 225 pictures — about fifteen seconds of action at fifteen frames per second. Edison marketed this machine in the same way he had marketed the

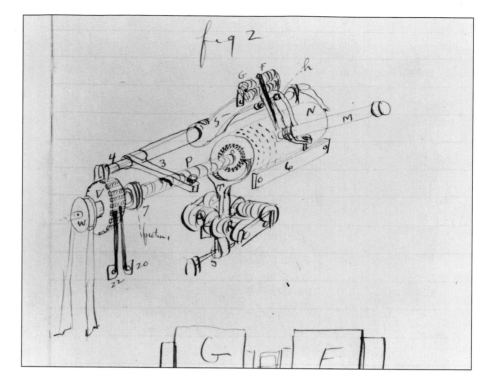

phonograph, as a coin-operated attraction in arcades. It was popular, but not particularly profitable, even when it was improved to hold films up to ninety seconds long. Most of the "movies" were of vaudeville performers — and you could see the real thing, often, right next door. Edison was not too far wrong, if a bit short-sighted, when he wrote to Muybridge in 1893: "I have constructed a little instrument which I call a kinetograph [that is, a Kinetoscope], with a nickel and slot attachment. Some twenty-five have been made, but I am doubtful there is any commercial feature in it, and fear it will not earn their cost. These zootropic [sic] devices are of too sentimental a value to get the public to invest in."[2]

Many other inventors were also hard at work on motion picture projectors in the 1890s. Dickson, who had left the Edison lab, invented the Mutoscope, which used flip cards. Thomas Armat and C. Francis Jenkins invented the Phantoscope, a movie projector, in 1895; Edison bought the rights to it and renamed it the Vitascope. In France, at about the same time, the Lumière brothers, Auguste Marie Louis Nicholas and Louis Jean, invented a machine that was both camera and projector. Their first public showing, on December 28, 1895, marks the beginning of the movie theater. By 1900 the Lumières had produced 1,299 short movies.

Movies first appeared at vaudeville palaces, often at the end of the show. Ten or twelve films, each about one minute long, would entertain an audience for the length of time a vaudeville act usually performed. These movies were a novelty, but they fit rather nicely into accepted forms of entertainment, for they were just another novelty act. Vaudeville played to a middle-class audience. Working men and women couldn't afford a quarter for a show, but they could afford a nickel, and in cities across the country entrepreneurs began to open theaters called nickelodeons. At this price the movie found its first true audience:

working-class people, most of them immigrants, who were eager for entertainment. The working class was growing not only in size but also in wealth, political strength, purchasing power, and leisure time, and they found the films the perfect entertainment.

Nickelodeons opened across the country, especially in immigrant neighborhoods in big cities. In 1907 there were an estimated 5,000 nickelodeons in the country, with 2 million admissions a day. In 1908 there were 600 in greater New York City alone, with an estimated daily attendance of 300,000 to 400,000. Kansas City's population of 250,000 bought 450,000 movie theater tickets a week. In 1910 there were some 20,000 nickelodeons in the northern cities. In some areas as many as 80 percent of schoolboys went to a movie once a week.

As would be the case with so many other new forms of mass entertainment, some Americans worried about the movies, and feared that they were destroying the American character. A 1912 Nebraska survey warned that movies "engendered idleness and cultivated careless spending" at the "expense of earnest and persistent work." Movies stirred up "primitive passion" and "daydreaming"; the author feared they would "lead children and adolescents especially away from right ideals and morality."[3] The Reverend Richard H. Edwards asked, "Why has the love of spontaneous play given way so largely to the love of

Edison's coin-operated kinetoscopes and phonographs were ready for customers at the Kinetoscope, Phonograph and Graphophone Arcade in San Francisco, circa 1900.

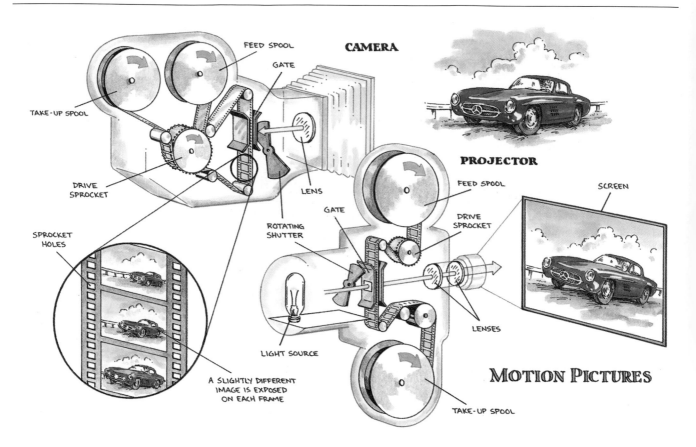

CAMERA

FEED SPOOL

GATE

TAKE-UP SPOOL

DRIVE SPROCKET

LENS

PROJECTOR

FEED SPOOL

DRIVE SPROCKET

GATE

SCREEN

ROTATING SHUTTER

SPROCKET HOLES

LIGHT SOURCE

A SLIGHTLY DIFFERENT IMAGE IS EXPOSED ON EACH FRAME

LENSES

TAKE-UP SPOOL

MOTION PICTURES

Movies work because the eye can be fooled into seeing continuous motion when it sees a rapid succession of slightly differing pictures.

To make a motion picture, a long strip of film moves rapidly through the camera, advancing and stopping, advancing and stopping, twenty-four times a second. Each time the film stops the shutter opens and then closes. The film advances to the next frame, and the shutter opens and closes again. (A clever mechanism synchronizes all these motions.) The result is a succession of images taken only a fraction of a second apart. Motion picture cameras make use of clever mechanisms to move the film in precise synchrony with the shutter. (Until the 1920s the film advanced at sixteen frames per second; that's why old movies appear jerky, the action speeded up.)

A motion picture projector works in exactly the same way as a motion picture camera, but in reverse. Instead of the light coming in and exposing the film, light is projected through the film. One frame is projected, the shutter is closed, the film is advanced, the shutter is opened, and the next frame shown. It all happens fast enough to look like continuous motion.

merely being amused?"[4] Authorities occasionally cracked down on the movies. In 1908 New York City police closed down all the theaters in the city, fearing that they would corrupt minds. Darrel O. Hibbard, a YMCA official, wrote in 1921: "From children's and divorce courts we hear of people going astray due to the movies. Therefore we need a law to step in and do for film what it did for meat and drug inspection, or the cinematographer will continue to inject into our social order an element of degrading principle."[5] The complaints these critics made would be echoed by the critics of TV fifty years later.

But there was another side to the argument. In 1908 the *Nation* called film "the first democratic art." Jane Addams wrote in the following year that for "hundreds of young people . . . going to the show is the only possible road to mystery and romance."[6] Historian Lary May suggests that many films were indeed antiauthoritarian, playing on the themes of rebellion and injustice. This was especially true for the half of all films that were imported; European films tended to "reflect values that were the antithesis of Protestant optimism."[7] From the beginning, movies represented a challenge to conventional morality. The poet Vachel Lindsay found hope in this: "Whitman brought the idea of democracy to our sophisticated literati, but did not persuade the democracy itself to read his democratic poems. Sooner or later the kinetoscope will do what he could not, bring the nobler side of the equality idea to the people who are so crassly equal."[8] Movies, Lindsay suggested, would be the first truly American cultural form.

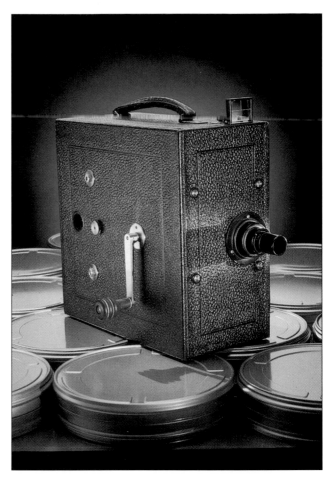

A hand-cranked 35-mm movie camera, circa 1920, used for amateur productions.

The movie business took several steps to answer the criticisms, and to consolidate the role of the movies in American society. New kinds of movies, a new kind of theater, a new image for movie makers (Hollywood!), and new technology helped make movies more respectable. "Hollywood movies," writes Michael Rogin, "imagined the ideal America that the moguls and their immigrant audience aspired to enter."[9]

Starting in the early 1900s, films became longer — lasting ten to fifteen minutes — and gained a new narrative structure. Most popular were Westerns and comedies. Feature films followed, and producers created new forms of narrative and new techniques of presentation. D. W. Griffith's 1915 movie *The Birth of a Nation,* a three-hour narrative, helped establish modern cinematic style: close-ups, tracking, cross-cutting, and many of the other techniques we've grown used to. The subject matter, too, was serious, even reactionary: the movie celebrated the Ku Klux Klan.

Another form that the public came to expect was the newsreel, photojournalism brought to life. Newsreels began in the early 1900s, and by 1910 had evolved into a standard "magazine" format that remained until they were eclipsed by TV in 1967. An early Pathé newsreel advertisement described the form: "A film issued every Tuesday made up of short scenes of great international events of unusual interest from all over the world. An illustrated magazine on a film. The news of the world in pictures."[10] (There were local newsreels, too.) The available technology — heavy, fixed cameras — often determined what was reported as news. Oftentimes, "news" was reenacted for the camera, a combination of on-the-spot reporting and re-creation.

The movies became a big business. In 1909 ten of the largest film producers established the Motion Picture Patents Company, a cartel that restricted the distribution of films to licensed exhibitors by controlling the manufacture of films and access to film stock. There were many independents, too. Altogether, some one hundred small firms produced over 2,000 films each year; another 2,000 films were imported from Europe. In 1909 the movie industry formed the National Board of Censorship of Motion Pictures to establish and enforce codes of morality for motion pictures. New theaters were impressive structures — movie palaces — and they helped make movies more mainstream. (City building codes, enacted to close down the disreputable nickelodeons, played a role, too.) The movie industry also created the idea of the movie star as celebrity, and invented Hollywood as a place where dreams came true, just like in the movies. Movies, writes communications historian Daniel Czitrom, "produced a new sort of culture, both a product and process with explicitly popular appeal."[11]

NEW TECHNOLOGIES

Newsreel crews went wherever the news was — and sometimes re-created the stories they had missed.

In the 1920s films became increasingly spectacular, to better compete with the new entertainment available in most homes on the radio. As part of their attempts to compete and attract ever larger crowds, moviemakers invested in dra-

matic new technologies. Convinced that the public wanted realism, they found ways to add color and sound to black and white silent movies.

Music had always accompanied motion pictures, produced by theater organs or orchestras or by phonographs started in synch with the movie. But the "talkies" added synchronized speech. The trick was the coordination of the visuals and the audio. Bell Labs introduced its Vitaphone system in *The Jazz Singer* in 1927. This was a crude system that used an electrical phonograph started by hand at certain points in the film. Lee de Forest and, perhaps independently, a German firm, Tri-Ergon, came up with synchronized sound systems for movies that encoded the sound as a pattern of grays on the edge of the film, where it was not seen on the screen but could be read by a photoelectric cell. RCA and Western Electric introduced commercially successful systems in 1928, and within a year, the silent film was obsolete. Almost all of the 5,000 feature films produced in the 1930s were talkies.

Sound changed the movie business. Sound movies were substantially more expensive to make than silents, and so fewer, more extravagant movies became the rule. Many smaller production companies couldn't compete and went out of business. It also changed the nature of movies. Spoken conversation, a necessity in talkies, changed the structure of films. Narrative became even more important, and character development, difficult in the silent movie, became central. Heroes and heroines were the focus of almost every movie, and all of the issues addressed in the movie were resolved by individual action. Movies moved faster, too, becoming more emotionally involving and more self-contained. The audience could be overwhelmed by sound, adding extra force to the emotional

The beginning of sound meant major changes to the way movies were shot. Movie sets had been noisy places, with directors yelling, cameras whirring, and stage crews at work; often movies were filmed outdoors. But sound required a carefully controlled environment — a "sound stage." The sound man — a technician — usually had the final say over which cut was to be used, often overruling directors and actors. Sound made movies much more expensive. Shown here, filming and recording the lion's roar for the MGM logo.

A cartoon from the American Federation of Musicians, protesting movie sound. They weren't the only ones upset. Lee De Forest, one of the inventors of radio, complained about the quality — "The present shrieking noises, at best, are only a sad burlesque of fine music, painful to endure" — and mourned the "thousands of musicians actually put out of employment by this loud speaking robot."

THE · ROBOT · ON · THE · RUN !

Oh! I went to the canned goods fair;
All the prunes and the tunes were there,
    And the tin-canny laugh
    Of a cheap phonograph
Made me want to get right up and swear.

The canned orchestra gurgled and squawked,
All the voices gummed up when they talked;
    And the only thing good
    In that whole neighborhood
Was the door, out of which we all walked.
                                        —H. B. S.

power of film. All of these trends had been apparent before sound appeared; the new technology reinforced them.

Talkies also used music in new ways. The historian Michael Rogin suggests that producers used jazz music as the key to making their movies more "American," and to show and celebrate the process of Americanization. Many of the early sound movies focus on jazz, which, Rogin writes, is presented as "a white man's music with black roots that turns immigrants into Americans."[12] In *The Jazz Singer,* for example, the Jewish hero, the son of immigrants, becomes "American" by appearing in blackface, and by becoming a jazz singer rather than a cantor, as his family wanted him to. And, as sound killed the live stage show that had once been a feature of movie theaters, it produced a new kind of movie, with chorus girls onstage, like the *Gold Diggers of Broadway* (1930). Before long, these evolved into the musical. Music became part of the movie business, and soon movie music was licensed to be played on radio and sold to the public as records. (RCA used the opportunity to become the first entertainment media conglomerate, with interests in radio, movies, recording, and vaudeville.) The combination of electronic sound and movies was the first step toward a unified entertainment and electronics industry. (See BEYOND TELEVISION.)

Sound required major changes in production, lighting, and equipment, and it seemed easy enough to add color. As with sound, movies had long used color, though not naturalistic color. Some movies, or portions of movies, were hand-tinted. Some used pretinted film to give sections overall color. (A director might tint only the key objects in movies, such as the red flag in Sergei Eisenstein's *Potemkin,* for artistic effect.) By 1920, 80 percent of the movies produced in Hollywood were being tinted in some fashion. There was also a long and tortuous history of producing movies in natural colors. The list of names of color processes gives some idea of the varieties: Cinechrone, Cinecolorgraph, Kromo-scope, Pathecolor, Biocolor. Technicolor, invented by Herbert T. Kalmus and Daniel Comstock, was the technology used in *The Toll of the Sea,* in 1921, the first successful color film.

Color got better, with Technicolor, Inc., investing millions of dollars in new research and equipment. The first full-length color film was *Becky Sharp* in 1935. But not everyone appreciated color. Producer Douglas Fairbanks complained that it destroyed "the simplicity and directness which motion pictures derived from the unobtrusive black and white," and many traditionalists opposed the new technology.[13] Still, it seemed the wave of the future. A reviewer of *Vagabond King* (1930) wrote: "The naive enthusiasts who have been denouncing color in favor of black and white as the only 'art' form of the movies must be either color-blind or simply ignorant of the art quality. . . . Color is one of the most important means of cinematic expression."[14]

But was color to be a special technique, or just a form of realism that would come to be expected? While many directors found imaginative ways to use sound to heighten emotions, only a few were able to take control of the technology of color for their own ends. Margaret Thorp raised the issue in her 1939 *America at the Movies*:

> Technicolor is still in a primitive state. Only its most earnest students are aware that it ought not to be used casually, as it is now generally used, merely to heighten reality by reproducing the tints of nature. Actually, the experts say, technicolor in regulating the emotion in a scene, in making contrasts and climaxes, has a power even greater than that of the camera, and, like music, color, if not skillfully regulated, may work contrary to the photographic effects. Certainly many of the things that are now being done with color are bad for the artistic taste of the [American moviegoer].[15]

Indeed, Thorp continues, the only truly artistic use of color was to be found in Walt Disney cartoons. Color found use mostly in musicals, with their brightly colored costumes, and because the bright lights Technicolor required made for especially glamorous effects. Color was associated with fantasy; *The Wizard of Oz* (1939) is the best example. Only about 10 percent of the feature films made in the 1940s were in color.

Movie patronage reached about 100 million each week in 1929, and then fell off. But even in 1935, 40 percent of adults went to the movies at least once a week. Attendance began to decline after World War II, even before television became popular. Many movie theaters closed in the 1950s (often to be replaced with drive-ins); many others lost money. And when TV came along, it looked as if the movie studios were in serious trouble. As the movie historian Robert Sklar writes: "With the advent of television, the history of motion-picture production appeared in an entirely new light, not so much a fulfillment of the nation's entertainment needs as a diversion, an accidental detour caused by a temporary technological inadequacy."[16]

The relationship of movies and television was complicated. Television programming built on radio programming, which had been based on vaudeville. Early movies had been based on vaudeville, too; but with the possibilities of longer running time and the demand for narrative, movies had turned more and more to the theater for source material. These different traditions had led to different sorts of entertainment, at first complementary, but increasingly in competition with one another. (See TELEVISION.)

The movie moguls' first response to television was to ignore it, just as phonograph manufacturers had at first ignored radio. They next considered various ways to take advantage of the new technology. Some suggested that perhaps people would pay to see large-screen television in theaters. Others, deciding it was easier to switch than fight, began to produce programs for TV or just bought television stations. (They also proposed, in conjunction with AT&T, a form of cable TV on telephone wires that proved to be technologically before its time.) Just as the studios had begun to produce radio shows in the 1930s, now they began to move into the television business. In 1954 movie studios began selling their old movies to TV stations. Hollywood learned that television represented an enormous market for films — as well as a competitor.

One way the movie studios competed was with technological innovations. As Cole Porter put it in the 1955 musical *Silk Stockings*:

> Today to get the public to attend the picture show,
> It's not enough to advertise a famous star they know.
> If you want to get the crowds to come around,
> You've got to have glorious Technicolor, breath-taking Cinemascope,
>   and stereophonic sound.[17]

Color experienced a resurgence as a weapon against the television networks. An improved form of Technicolor and a competing color technology from Eastman Kodak were easier to use, and produced more accurate, less gaudy images than the original Technicolor. In 1952 more than 50 percent of films were in color. This percentage fell in the late 1950s as a cost-cutting effort, but when color television became widespread, movies switched back to color again. In 1967, 75 percent of feature films were shot in color.

The first wide-screen technology was Cinerama. Based on a device developed by the military for training aerial gunners, it used three projectors which projected onto a single huge curved screen. It was introduced in 1952 and was a great novelty, giving a sense of depth that had never been experienced before. But it was too expensive to be widely adopted. CinemaScope, introduced a year later, was more successful. It used a traditional camera and projector, but with a special lens that spread the image across a wide screen. It was cheaper than Cinerama, and, with the solid support of Twentieth Century-Fox behind it, was widely adopted; more than 10,000 theaters were equipped to show CinemaScope films by 1954. Epics were particularly impressive on the wide screen, and the new technology encouraged a spate of blockbuster films. Both Cinerama and CinemaScope made use of the latest in sound reproduction.

Three-dimensional movies were another attempt to compete with television. *Bwana Devil* (1952) was the first 3-D movie, and it set the style for the fad, which failed within six months. Movie historian John Izod suggests that the reason was that studios were carried away by the technology: "The studios were so keen to exploit the system that arguably they killed it by sacrificing plot, character, and quality to cheap screenplays that arbitrarily contrived a succession of excuses for hurling objects at the audience. Add to that the discomfort some people suffered from the spectacles, and the doubling of the image where pro-

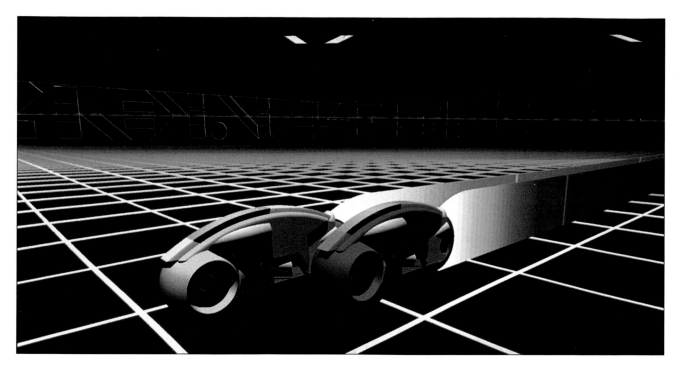

jection was imprecise, and you have the probable causes of the short life of this phenomenon."[18]

The number of theaters fell, reaching a low of 13,750 in 1970. Only 920 million admissions were sold that year, less than half the number sold just five years earlier. The number of pictures released was down to only 367.

Movies responded by surrendering the cultural center to television and going for the margins. Film in the 1970s and 1980s appealed to a young audience that wanted to get out of the house, and see things that couldn't be shown on television. The studios responded with sex and violence: they made more R-rated movies (23 percent of all movies in the late 1960s, and 56 percent in 1985, even though standards had been relaxed). "The basic ingredients of movies," wrote producer Richard Zanuck in 1988, "are action, sex, violence and stars."[19] They also continued to produce extravaganzas too expensive or technologically demanding for television, or movies that worked best on the large screen, *Star Wars*. A survey in 1985 found that only 8 percent of adults who had attended a movie in the previous month were over fifty-five; 70 percent were between eighteen and thirty-four.

The new strategy worked, at least for a while. The number of theaters increased again, reaching 23,555 in 1987. Admissions climbed, to over 1 billion in every year of the 1980s. Box office receipts climbed faster, as prices rose, to $3 billion in 1987.

Movie studios had reached an accommodation with television. Everything was up for grabs again, though, when new technology appeared on the scene. The new technology of the videocassette recorder, the home video camera, and even the video game gave the consumer of moving images a vast range of new choices — though, many have suggested, no real alternatives — and offered new possibilities for individual control. Once again, our relationship with

Hollywood discovered computer-generated graphics in the mid-1970s. *Westworld* (1973) and *Futureworld* (1976) used computer images to show a robot's-eye view of the world. Computer graphics began to compete with traditional animation in the early 1980s. *TRON* (1982) was the first movie with a substantial amount of computer animation; its action took place inside a video game. It was not a success (it was all graphics and no plot) but the techniques established for it found wide use. Ever-greater computer power allowed for increasingly realistic images. *The Last Starfighter* (1984) required between 24 and 72 billion calculations for each frame. Shown is a computer-generated image from *TRON*.

the pictures on the screen would change. That story is told in BEYOND TELE-VISION.

FOR FURTHER READING

Good general histories of the movies that include material on the changing technology include Lary May, *Screening out the Past: The Birth of Mass Culture and the Motion Picture Industry* (1980); Daniel J. Czitrom, *Media and the American Mind from Morse to McLuhan* (1982); Robert Sklar, *Movie-Made America: A Cultural History of American Movies* (1976); and John Izod, *Hollywood and the Box Office, 1895–1986* (1988). On the way that movies relate to broadcasting, see James L. Baughman, *The Republic of Mass Culture: Journalism, Filmmaking, and Broadcasting in America since 1941* (1992).

On the way in which color entered the movies, and what people thought about it, see Neil Harris, "Color and Media: Some Comparisons and Speculations," in *Cultural Excursions: Marketing Appetites and Cultural Tastes in Modern America* (1990), pp. 327–329.

NOTES

1. Thomas Alva Edison, Caveat 110, October 17, 1888; quoted in Robert Conot, *A Streak of Luck* (1980), p. 394.

2. Thomas Alva Edison to Eadweard Muybridge, February 21, 1894; quoted in Conot, *A Streak of Luck,* p. 400.

3. Joseph R. Fulk, "Effect on Education and Morals of the Motion Picture Shows," *National Educational Association Proceedings* (1912), pp. 456–461; quoted in Lary May, *Screening out the Past: The Birth of Mass Culture and the Motion Picture Industry* (1980), p. 41.

4. Richard H. Edwards, *Popular Amusements* (1915); quoted in Daniel J. Czitrom, *Media and the American Mind* (1982), p. 43.

5. Darrel O. Hibbard, "Letter," in *Outlook,* July 13, 1912; quoted in May, *Screening out the Past,* p. 43.

6. Jane Addams, *The Spirit of Youth and the City Streets* (1909); quoted in May, *Screening out the Past,* p. 38.

7. May, *Screening out the Past,* p. 37.

8. Vachel Lindsay, *The Art of the Moving Picture* (1915), p. 224; quoted in Czitrom, *Media and the American Mind,* p. 58.

9. Michael Rogin, "Making America Home: Racial Masquerade and Ethnic Assimilation in the Transition to Talking Pictures," *Journal of American History* (December 1992): 1052.

10. Quoted in Peter Marzio, *Men and Machines of Modern Journalism* (1973), p. 130.

11. Czitrom, *Media and the American Mind,* p. 37.

12. Rogin, "Making America Home," p. 1056.

13. Quoted in H. T. Kalmus, "Technicolor Adventures in Cinemaland," *Journal of the Society of Motion Picture Engineers* (December 1938); quoted in Neil Harris, "Color and Media: Some Comparisons and Speculations," in *Cultural Excursions: Marketing Appetites and Cultural Tastes in Modern America* (1990), p. 325.

14. Alexander Bakshy, "Films," *Nation,* March 19, 1930: 337; quoted in Harris, "Color and Media," p. 326.

15. Margaret Farrand Thorp, *America at the Movies* (1939), p. 257.

16. Robert Sklar, *Movie-Made America: A Cultural History of American Movies* (1976), p. 276.

17. Cole Porter, "Stereophonic Sound," from *Silk Stockings* (1955).

18. John Izod, *Hollywood and the Box Office, 1895–1986* (1988), p. 140.

19. Quoted in James L. Baughman, *The Republic of Mass Culture: Journalism, Film-making, and Broadcasting in America since 1941* (1992), p. 207.

The radio brought news
and entertainment into the
home, helping to establish
a national audience for
them. In the late 1920s,
when this picture was tak-
en, radio was a family affair. But when television replaced radio in the living
room and new electronics
technology made radios
smaller, radio became an
individual activity, and radio stations began to spe-
cialize.

ENTERTAINMENT
RADIO

D AVID SARNOFF, WHO WORKED AS CHIEF IN-spector for the Marconi Wireless Telegraph Company of America, was one of the first men with a vision of what radio might be. "I have in mind a plan of development," he wrote in a memo in 1915, "which would make radio a 'household utility' in the same sense as the piano or phonograph." Recent improvements in radio technology, he assured his superiors, meant that everyone could own a "radio music box." "The idea," he wrote, "is to bring music into the house by wireless."

Sarnoff's memo continued: "The receiver could be arranged for several different wavelengths, which should be changeable with the throwing of a single switch or pressing of a single button." It wasn't just entertainment that the radio music box promised, but also baseball games, lectures, and events of national importance. "The proposition would be especially interesting to farmers and others living in outlying districts removed from cities. By the purchase of a 'Radio Music Box' they could enjoy concerts, lectures, music, recitals, etc., which may be going on in the nearest city."[1]

Sarnoff's idea went nowhere. The Marconi Company was in the business of wireless telegraphy to ships, not broadcasting to a general audience. (See WIRELESS TELEGRAPHY.) A year after RCA was established in 1919, Sarnoff, now the firm's commercial manager, again made his proposal. The directors of the firm agreed to put up only $2,500 to explore the idea. RCA was established for radiotelegraphy, not broadcast radio.

WIRELESS BECOMES RADIO

But Sarnoff was onto something. If the dots and dashes of wireless could be sent over the air, why not voices? If wireless transmitters could send messages between individuals, why couldn't one person communicate with many? New technology that could turn wireless telegraphy into radio was available. In 1906 Reginald Fessenden had broadcast music from a wireless transmitter that used continuous waves. In the same year Lee De Forest had invented the Audion, which would make home radio receivers and higher-power transmitters possible.

MAR.1925 **RADIO** 35CENTS

BROADCAST

A GOOD FOUR TUBE RECEIVER

Choosing a B-Battery Eliminator

Who Is To Pay for Broadcasting and How

DOUBLEDAY, PAGE & COMPANY   GARDEN CITY, NEW YORK

The happy radio amateur.

These inventions, and a host of others, paved the way for commercial radio broadcasting.

Thirty years earlier the technological changes that turned the telegraph into the telephone had transformed the entire communications system in ways that telegraphers had not imagined. Telegraph companies' first response to the telephone had been to wonder why telegraph operators would need to talk to one another! In some ways it was easier to create a new technology than to imagine what to do with it — or how to make money from it. The invention of technology for sending voices over the air, rather than just Morse code, would bring equally profound changes in the way radio waves were used, and to the people who used them. The social and cultural effects would be dramatic and far-reaching.

Broadcast radio would start not with the big wireless manufacturers and users but with amateur broadcasters. In 1922 there were some 15,000 transmitting stations in the United States, almost all of them run by amateurs, and perhaps 250,000 people who listened to their broadcasts. Most amateurs looked down on people who just listened to broadcasts. Most of them believed that radio should be an active medium of communication. Amateurs, mostly young men, looked at radio as a hobby, and sometimes as a public service. But a few amateurs had a different vision. In the 1910s some of them started broadcasting news and music on irregular schedules, not expecting their listeners to talk back to them. But these were small operations, broadcasting to other amateurs. Receiving a broadcast required a good bit of skill and perseverance, a far remove from Sarnoff's "throwing of a single switch or pressing of a single button." No one had yet figured out how to make money from it.

One of these amateurs was Frank Conrad, a Westinghouse engineer who began regular broadcasts from his Pittsburgh home in 1916. Westinghouse executive Harry P. Davis noticed an advertisement for a Pittsburgh department store:

> Victrola music, played into the air over a wireless telephone, was "picked up" by listeners on the wireless receiving station which was recently installed here for patrons interested in wireless experiments. . . . The music was from a Victrola pulled up close to the transmitter of a wireless telephone in the home of Frank Conrad . . . a wireless enthusiast who "puts on" the wireless concerts periodically for the entertainment of the many people in this district who have wireless sets.
>
> Amateur Wireless Sets, made by the maker of the Set which is in operation in our store, are on sale here $10.00 up.[2]

Davis later wrote that this ad "caused the thought to come to me that the efforts that were then being made to develop radio telephony as a confidential means of communication were wrong, and that instead its field was really one of wide publicity."[3] Westinghouse, which had been a major supplier of radios to the war effort, needed a new market now that the war was over. Broadcast radio might be it.

And so, on November 2, 1920, Westinghouse established the first commercial radio station, KDKA. (The first news KDKA broadcast was the result of the presidential election — an echo of the first news carried by the telegraph three quarters of a century earlier.) The new station was a success. Westinghouse marketed its first civilian receiver, the Aeriola, Jr., in 1921, to take advantage of the audience the station provided. Before long KDKA was joined by other stations, thirty by 1922, over 500 in the next year. These early stations were operated by local stores, newspapers, appliance dealers (who, like Westinghouse, used them to sell radios), churches, and governments. In 1933 about half of all radio stations were operated by radio manufacturers, about one fifth by radio sellers.

As radio broadcasting boomed, so did the radio manufacturing industry. Early sets were based on technology developed for wireless transmission. They were often sold as kits, or even just plans, and early radio enthusiasts built their own. In 1923 there were some 5,000 radio parts manufacturers, who sold $136 million in parts and plans, as well as some 200 radio set manufacturers. One of the earliest was Frank Angelo D'Andrea, who designed, built, and marketed FADA crystal sets. They sold for $2.25, and by early 1922 he had sales of $50,000 each month.

It took several major technological breakthroughs to make radio receivers a consumer product. The key technology was de Forest's Audion, a three-element tube, invented in 1906. The first applications were to wireless receiving, where it made possible detection and some low-level application of the signal. By 1912 de Forest showed that the Audion could oscillate, or generate continuous waves. At almost the same time Edwin Armstrong, Irving Langmuir, Alexander Meissner, and Robert Goddard (later of rocket fame) discovered the same thing. (See WIRELESS TELEGRAPHY.) The ability to modulate the tube — to put a voice or music signal on the radio frequency carrier — was developed in the period 1912–1914. One of the key breakthroughs was new high-vacuum technology, developed at Bell Labs, General Electric, and other laboratories. De Forest commenced experimental broadcasting activities at Highbridge in the Bronx, New York, in 1915, and Bell Labs developed an overseas radiotelephone test from Arlington, Virginia, the same year.

New radio receiver technologies helped complete the radio broadcast system. The crystal sets developed for wireless by G. W. Pickard and H. C. Dunwoody (see WIRELESS TELEGRAPHY) were early applied to the detection of voice transmission. The heterodyne system of detection, developed by Fessenden for wireless as early as 1901, became useful for radio when Edwin Armstrong developed circuits that converted incoming signals to easily amplified intermediate frequencies, in 1917–1920. The regenerative receiver, patented by Armstrong in 1914, was a highlight for the budding radio industry: it permitted inexpensive, sensitive receivers to be easily manufactured. Other systems of audio and radio frequency amplification proliferated in the transition to broadcast radio after 1920. There were to be endless patent battles over almost all of

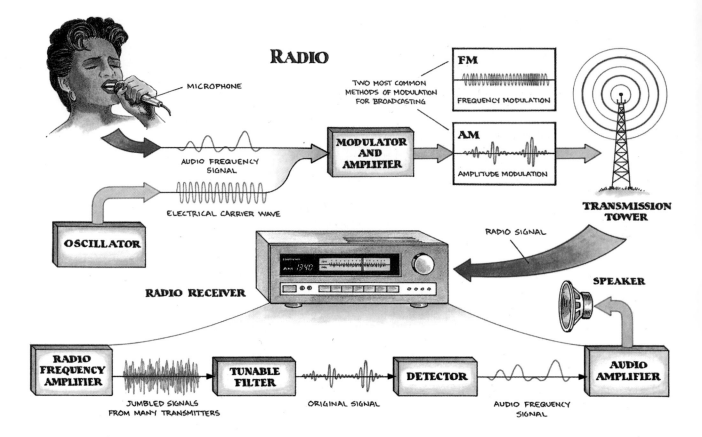

RADIO

MICROPHONE

TWO MOST COMMON
METHODS OF MODULATION
FOR BROADCASTING

FM
FREQUENCY MODULATION

AM
AMPLITUDE MODULATION

AUDIO FREQUENCY
SIGNAL

ELECTRICAL CARRIER WAVE

MODULATOR
AND
AMPLIFIER

TRANSMISSION
TOWER

OSCILLATOR

RADIO SIGNAL

SPEAKER

RADIO RECEIVER

AM 1340

RADIO
FREQUENCY
AMPLIFIER

TUNABLE
FILTER

DETECTOR

AUDIO
AMPLIFIER

JUMBLED SIGNALS
FROM MANY TRANSMITTERS

ORIGINAL SIGNAL

AUDIO FREQUENCY
SIGNAL

Radio works by first converting the sound waves produced by voice into an electrical signal that is equivalent to the sound waves. (This is done by a microphone, just as for electrical recording and the telephone.) Next, the electrical signal is used to modulate a carri-

these technologies, but together, they began to make radio into a consumer business.

In 1922, 100,000 radios were sold, at an average cost of $50. In 1929 the cost had increased to over $100 — about four weeks' wages for an average worker — but quality had improved, and the market had increased enormously, to more than 4 million radios. By 1930 more than one half of all American homes had radios. The Census for that year provided more details on radio ownership: 56 percent of native-born whites, 14 percent of African Americans, and 46 percent of immigrants owned radios; about 30 percent of rural families owned a radio, while almost four fifths of middle-class families did. Eighty percent of radio owners listened to their radio on an average day.

The radio manufacturing business grew quickly, but with enormous turnover. It was cheap to enter, and men with a bit of knowledge and not much money could design a radio, buy parts, hire workers, and put a new brand on the market. Of the firms founded between 1923 and 1932, 594 lasted only one

er, a high frequency electrical wave that is easy to transmit and receive. Either the amplitude of this high frequency wave or its frequency can be modulated.

AM radio uses amplitude modulation. The transmitter superimposes the message signal — the voice, the music, or whatever — on the *amplitude* of the much higher frequency carrier signal. (AM radios broadcast on frequencies of 535–1,705 kHz, frequencies much higher than a typical signal (voice frequency) of about 1 kHz. A kiloHertz (kHz) is 1,000 hertz, or 1,000 cycles per second.) The receiver subtracts the constant-frequency carrier, and what's left is the original message. Each radio station is limited to a band of only 10 kHz, which means they can broadcast only signals up to 5 kHz — which means low fidelity, since we can hear up to almost 20 kHz.

FM radio uses frequency modulation. Instead of changing the *amplitude* of the carrier signal as with AM, FM signals change the carrier's *frequency* to carry the information. The variation in the carrier's frequency is proportional to the amplitude of the signal. When the speech signal is at its maximum, the carrier is about 75 kHz higher than usual; when at a minimum, about 75 kHz lower. (The carrier frequencies used in FM radio are very high, about 100 MHz, so the change in frequency is less than 1/1,000 the carrier frequency.) FM radio is of higher quality than AM because it includes a wider frequency range and has less static and less interference between stations. The FM band has considerably more spectrum space than the AM band because when it was introduced in the 1930s electronics could deal with much higher frequencies than it could earlier, when AM had been introduced.

The signal, either AM or FM, is amplified and transmitted. The radio receiver works backward from the signal it receives to produce a sound wave. The radio picks up the entire frequency band, amplifies it, and then puts it through a tunable filter to pick out just the frequency of interest — the frequency produced by the original oscillator. A detector, or demodulator, removes this carrier wave, producing a signal equivalent to the original produced by the microphone. This signal is amplified and then passed to a loudspeaker, where an electromagnet makes the air vibrate, reproducing in sound waves the electrical signal — and the original voice or music.

---

year; only eleven manufacturers lasted for more than twelve years. By 1930 a few large, well-established firms, among them Atwater-Kent, Zenith, RCA-Victor, Stromberg-Carlson, and Philco, dominated the industry. They shared the market with a great many small, underfinanced firms. Most of the large firms moved into the industry from related fields: Atwater-Kent had made automobile ignition systems; Philco had been in the storage battery business. In 1933 nine firms accounted for 74 percent of radio sales, and 122 firms divided the remaining 26 percent.

Early radio manufacturers faced an untamed industry, with boom followed by bust. Fierce competition meant small profits. Industry spokesmen were pleased with the ever-swelling demand, but lamented the industry's lack of orderliness. *Electronics* magazine complained in 1930: "Every year since 1924 radio has undergone an annual overproduction. Each year manufacturers, racing for supremacy and low production costs, have swelled their totals — and ended by unloading their excessive output at bargain prices."[4] Radio manufacturing

Buying a radio, the first complex piece of electronic gear that most people ever saw, wasn't easy.

companies profited from lowering prices, not by making technological advances. (The big advances in the 1920s were the plug-in radio and the moving-coil loudspeaker.) The technological base of the radio industry in these early days was fairly simple, widely known, and easily available to manufacturers. Designs for radios were published, and it was difficult to keep secrets in an industry with a rapid turnover of employees and a product so easy to analyze. Furthermore, few manufacturers made their own tubes; most bought them from the same large manufacturers, who controlled their manufacture by means of a patent pool. In the early days of the radio industry production skill, not technological knowledge, was the key to success.

Radio manufacturers had a boom market, but the industry was crowded, and the Great Depression clearly hit hard. Sales fell 40 percent in 1930. Indeed, the overall quality of radios slid in the 1930s; the depression public wanted lower prices, not higher fidelity. In the early 1930s many manufacturers looked for niches where they could hide from the overproduction that characterized the industry.

One niche was car radios. In 1931 fewer than 1 percent of cars on the road had radios. Only about 100,000 car radios were sold in the United States, fewer than 3 percent of all radios sold. Car radios faced many obstacles. Most people thought that driving a car was dangerous enough without the added distraction of a radio. There were technical problems caused by radio static from the spark plug. And they were difficult to install — you had to rip most of the roof off the car — and expensive, often a significant fraction of the price of the automobile. These technical problems were solved by several manufacturers, and car radio sales soared. Over 700,000 were sold in 1934; by 1940 some 7.5 million cars, over one fourth of all cars on the road, had a radio in their dashboard.

Another niche was special-purpose radio. Police radio was one. Police departments had early seen the advantages of mobile radios to assist them in their work. The Detroit police force was the first to use radios successfully, in 1920 sending messages over commercial radio stations to communicate with officers. Next it set up its own station, with the call letters KOP, and in April 1928 began broadcasting to police cars. Bayonne, New Jersey, set up the first two-way network for police work in 1933. Mobile radio took off in 1936, when RCA and GE entered the field, and the Federal Communications Commission allocated permanent channels for police communications. In 1930 there were twenty "public safety service" radio stations. In 1937 there were 535. Police departments' command structure changed with the new technology. Central headquarters took advantage of their immediate communications with officers in the field to seize some of the power that had previously been exercised at the precinct level.

Radio production was a fairly simple operation. More assembly than manufacturing, it rewarded businessmen who could keep prices down and volume up. Manufacturers bought the tubes and, in many cases, preassembled components and subassemblies from specialized manufacturers. Workers, mostly women, were hired when the market was strong, and laid off when demand decreased. Most radios were sold around Christmastime, and even full-time radio assembly workers usually worked less than six months a year. Shown here are scenes from the Motorola radio factory in the 1940s.

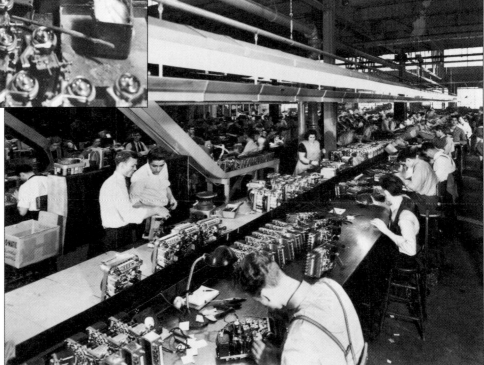

Transmitter technology was much more complicated than receiver technology, and there were many fewer competitors. The key improvements in transmitter technology were the directional antenna and, especially, higher power, which seemed to be the cure-all for reception problems of any sort. The breakthrough that made higher power possible was H. S. Brown's 1927 invention of an amplifier that used negative feedback. Brown invented negative feedback as part of his work on telephone circuits (see TELEPHONE), but it had immediate application to radio transmitters, too. Station WOR in New Jersey was the first to take advantage of the new technology, in 1935.

The agreement that had established the Radio Corporation of America in 1919 had given AT&T the exclusive rights to build radio transmitters, and in the 1920s AT&T began to sue infringers to enforce its rights. Cries of monopoly brought the government into the business of regulating broadcasting, assigning frequencies, and limiting the power of broadcasters. This would have an enormous effect on the industry. Unlike newspapers, which worked under the principle of freedom of the press, radio broadcasters were government licensed, and were obligated by law to present "fair" programming, "in the public interest, convenience, and necessity," as the Communications Act of 1934 put it. Broadcasters would have to consider the interests of their listeners, their advertisers, and the government as they decided what to broadcast.

WHAT'S ON?

Ordinary people enthusiastically embraced radio, and enjoyed hearing news and music from far away. At first many people bought radios just to see what they were like. They fiddled with the dials, counted the stations they could receive, and marveled at how far away they were. Distance seemed half the fun of radio. "There is something fascinating about hearing a concert from a long way off," wrote one early listener. These listeners looked at radio as a game of skill. One wrote in 1924: "In radio it is not the substance of communication without wires, but the fact of it that enthralls. It is a sport, in which your wits, learning and resourcefulness are matched against the endless perversity of the elements. It is not a matter, as you may suppose, of buying a set and thereafter tuning in upon what your fancy dictates. . . . Someday, perhaps, I shall take an interest in radio programs. But at my present stage they are merely the tedium between call letters."[5]

Radios were sold in radio stores, electrical stores, musical instrument stores, hardware stores, department stores, and sporting goods stores, as well as by door-to-door salesmen. In 1929 there were some 16,000 "radio and music stores" in the United States; in 1939, there were only about 3,000 such establishments.

"The Distance Fiend," a poem by A. H. Folwell published in the *New Yorker* and reprinted in *Radio Broadcast*, described another listener:

> He was a distance fiend,
> A loather of anything near.
> Though WOOF had a singer of opera fame,
> And WOW a soprano of national name,
> He passed them both up for a Kansas quartet
> A thousand miles off and hence "harder to get."
> New York was too easy to hear.
> He was a distance fiend.[6]

But by the mid-twenties the novelty of listening to the radio had worn off. Listeners became more interested in the quality of reception and the ease of tuning the set. Hundreds of radio manufacturers competed to sell radios that were designed to be easy to use, and to blend into family living rooms. In 1924 *Radio Broadcast* magazine had asked its readers to report the most distant station they could pick up. In 1927 the magazine asked what they wanted to hear.

By 1930 radios had become standard fixtures in American homes, and national networks began to reshape American culture. Radio broadcasting was in full swing. Listeners sought out favorite programs and showed more interest in Amos 'n' Andy's latest escapades than in trying to hear distant stations. ("Amos 'n' Andy" was the first national hit, attracting some 40 million listen-

The nerve center of New York City's police radiotelephone system in the 1930s. The dispatcher at the center table receives a call, picks a car to send it to, and passes the message to the radio man, at the left.

A radio operator at a county bank receives the latest market price reports and posts them for farmers.

ers.) Families that had once banished the radio to the attic or basement now welcomed into the living room radios designed for good sound, ease of operation, and stylishness.

Like all the earlier improvements in communications, radio seemed a way of tying the world together. Marconi set the tone when he wrote in 1927: "[Radio], I maintain, is the only force to which we can look with any hope for the ultimate establishment of permanent world peace."[7] Radio promoters proclaimed that the radio connected listeners to the great events of the world. They declared that it would be a "tremendous civilizer," that it would bring "mutual understanding to all sections of the country, unifying our thoughts, ideals, and purposes, making us a strong and well-knit people."[8] "I believe the radio will be a potent factor in making the twentieth century the age of the brotherhood of man," wrote James E. Freeman, Episcopal bishop of Washington, D.C., in 1926.[9] Radio held the promise that it would encourage quiet, reflective thought about politics. Listening in the privacy of their own home, citizens could consider the positions of politicians and not be distracted by the roar of the crowd. Politics would be less demagogic, more rational.

These hopes soon fell by the wayside. As the historian Neil Harris writes, "Political demagogues . . . found they could exploit the radio waves as easily as predecessors had manipulated the laws of collective imitation."[10] Woodrow Wilson, speaking in Des Moines in 1919, recognized that there might be bad news as well as good coming over the radio: "Those antennae of the wireless telegraph are symbols of our age. All the impulses of mankind are thrown out upon the air and reach to the ends of the earth; quietly upon steamships, silently under the cover of the Postal Service, with the tongue of the wireless and the tongue of the telegraph, all the suggestions of disorder are spread through the world." Radio, Wilson suggested, was disseminating the "poison of revolt, the poison of chaos."[11]

These plastic radios from the late 1930s and 1940s were up-to-date in every way — bright colors, modern styling, and newly developed materials.

Early radios, like this 1923 Radiola, were not easy to use. The listener had to turn several dials to pull in distant stations, and the batteries often leaked. One of the main areas of improvement was making radios easier to tune; another was getting rid of the batteries. After 1925, more and more radio manufacturers designed their sets to look like furniture. They moved out of the garage and into the living room, and radio listening gained a family appeal. These new sets used loudspeakers, not headphones. By the 1930s, style was as important as technology.

But most listeners tuned out these big thinkers and tuned in the news, and, best of all, the music. And the night spoke in many voices. Announcers read news from the local paper. Entertainers and musicians came to the studio to play for the invisible audience beyond the microphone. Some stations played phonograph records over the air — it was the cheapest way to fill air time — but many station managers feared that the public would not approve. A 1923 lawsuit by the American Society of Composers, Authors, and Publishers (ASCAP) meant radio stations had to pay for the right to broadcast music on the air, which raised the price. An even bigger obstacle was that most radio producers and recording artists were convinced that playing records on the radio would hurt sales. Musicians had mixed feelings about the new medium. John Philip Sousa wrote in 1928 that "through this medium the masses are becoming acquainted as never before with the best of the world's music," but insisted that it would never replace live performances. "The rapport between performer and audience is invaluable," he continued. "I have refrained from broadcasting for this very reason; I am reluctant to lose the warm personal touch with my audience."[12]

More famous voices spoke from the radio. Franklin Delano Roosevelt was the first president of the United States to communicate regularly with the American people by radio. Speaking informally, Roosevelt used his "fireside chats" to explain and promote his New Deal programs. Will Rogers became the country's most popular humorist because of his skillful use of radio. His folksy

Radio manufacturers liked to show off their radios in elegant home settings.

W.H.A. Broadcasting

Broadcasting at WHA, the University of Wisconsin radio station, 1932 — a photo from the station's scrapbook.

humor appealed to the whole family, and each listener felt that Rogers spoke directly to him or her. Some churches and evangelists sponsored early broadcasts; about 15 percent of early radio stations were owned by churches. One of the most prominent and outspoken was Aimee Semple McPherson, a Los Angeles evangelist. She wrote in her autobiography, "My soul was thrilled with the possibilities this media [*sic*] offered for the spread of the gospel."[13]

But who should pay for radio? It was not obvious, at first, and in the 1920s it was a much-debated subject. Some universities and churches and other nonprofit organizations established radio stations. Some people preferred public financing for stations. Some thought that radio manufacturers should support production — after all, they had the most to gain. Others proposed a tax on each radio sold, the proceeds to go to broadcasters. (This last system was adopted in many European countries.)

Advertising did not seem a likely possibility, at first. There was a lot of resistance to the idea of advertising on radio, with radio broadcasters and listeners alike opposed. Among the first advertisers were those who were banned from print media, such as "Doctor" J. R. Brinkley, who established his own station to sell patent medicines and his goat-gland operations, guaranteed to restore men's sexual potency. Herbert Hoover, as secretary of commerce responsible for oversight of the radio industry, suggested that it was "inconceivable that we should allow so great a possibility for service and for news and for entertainment and education, for vital commercial purposes to be drowned in advertising chatter. . . . People won't stand for that. It would kill the radio industry."[14]

Indeed, even advertisers themselves were suspicious. *Printers' Ink*, an advertising trade journal, warned that radio was a "poor advertising medium."[15] Radio station owners feared that listeners might just turn off the radio rather than listen to advertisements. It was impossible to show advertisers who was listening. Furthermore, advertisers thought of consumers as female, and knew that the radio audience was mostly male.

The networks sold radio advertising by convincing advertisers that the medium was well suited to the sort of psychological appeal that advertisers thought worked well. They emphasized that radio was at the center of the home, and advertisers of the time were convinced that the home was the best place to reach consumers. Radio, wrote advertising executive Frank Arnold, provides "American businessmen . . . with a latchkey to nearly every home in the United States." Radio was a "guest in the house." "In the midst of the family circle, in moments of relaxation, the voice of radio brings to the audience its program of entertainment or its message of advertising."[16] What more could an advertiser want? It took a while to get used to the idea. The first advertisements began to appear in 1924. By the late 1920s the answer to the question "Who is to pay for broadcasting?" was clear. Private industry paid for most broadcasts and supported programs that attracted audiences for its advertisements. By 1935 more than $100 million was spent on radio advertising.

At about the same time advertising appeared, so too did the first national broadcasting. Audiences wanted national news and sports and better musical programming. The first attempts to provide national programming were the "superpower" stations that broadcast with enough power to reach much of the country. (In 1924 David Sarnoff proposed that six superpower stations could serve the whole country.) But the solution that was settled on was hooking radio stations together with telephone lines, and transmitting programs to stations over these lines.

The reason for this kind of national network solution, radio historian Susan Smulyan has shown, was as much commercial and cultural as technological. AT&T's ownership of part of RCA and its key role in the radio patent pool, as well as the desire to avoid the appearance of monopoly by using local programs, influenced this decision. The simultaneous emergence of advertising and networks was not a coincidence. National brand products demanded national advertising. The telephone lines that tied stations together were very expensive, and only advertising seemed able to support the network system. The National Broadcasting Company, the first radio network, celebrated its founding on November 15, 1926, with a four-hour star-studded extravaganza. Twelve million listeners tuned in twenty-four stations.

Network radio allowed millions of people to hear the same news, the same music, and the same jokes, at the same time. Local radio had featured diverse programming, including ethnic, regional, or African-American music. But network programmers and advertisers believed that white middle-class men listened to radio, or at least controlled the family radio, and that if network radio didn't reflect a white, middle-class America — or a carefully controlled ethnicity, like that of the Goldbergs or Amos 'n' Andy — it would lose its audience. Early network radio was a leveler. The variety show, based on a vaudeville format, was the norm, but with more emphasis on one-line jokes. This developed into the situation comedy as characters appeared week after week. An immediate, shared experience, radio had an enormous impact on American culture, homogenizing it and shaping it in what radio broadcasters and advertisers thought of as middle-class ways.

Broadcasters changed radio to make it easier to sell. The earliest advertising was fairly subtle — musical groups named after the products playing music that represented the product. The Clicquot Club Eskimos, for example, advertised Clicquot Club ginger ale, and played "peppy musical numbers of lively tempo" to suggest the "ginger, pep, sparkle and snap" of the soft drink.[17] Broadcasters trying to appeal to women at home during the day developed programs of useful instruction about household activities and products so that women would listen closely. Radio home economists instructed women on everything from cooking and sewing to shopping and the latest labor-saving machinery. Betty Crocker promoted General Mills flour as she gave cooking instructions.

Instructional programs in the morning were followed by soap operas — dramas sponsored by detergent manufacturers — in the afternoon. Each soap opera was designed to sell a particular product. The hope was that loyalty to the soap opera would transfer to loyalty to the brand name. At least the first part was successful: one researcher, after interviewing hundreds of soap opera fans in 1941, found that "the stories have become an integral part of the lives of many listeners." They provided "a model of reality by which one is taught how to think and how to act."[18] By 1940 more than sixty soap operas filled more than 60 percent of daytime radio hours. But mostly it was music that filled the air: by 1941 music accounted for three quarters of radio airtime, and almost half of all radio stations played music exclusively. Radio had come to have an enormous effect on popular music. Classical music, too, changed with the introduction of radio. Aaron Copland suggested that radio helped bring classical music to a wider audience, and brought new music to the United States. (See RECORDED SOUND.)

In the evening came the biggest hits. Radio in the 1920s had been fairly relaxed; in the 1930s it was increasingly frenetic. It featured vaudeville performers who had left the stage and moved to the studio; they told jokes and starred in comedy shows. The performers of the early 1930s, including Jack Benny, Fred Allen, and George Jessel, would shape radio for decades to come. Quick verbal humor and unsophisticated drama interspersed with popular music would define the medium. They experimented with the possibilities, and found new forms of entertainment that exploited the technology, fit radio's economic structure, and seemed familiar enough to listeners to be appealing. Some of the best shows were those that exploited the possibilities of a medium that required listeners' imagination to fill in the impossible details — shows such as "The Shadow," or Orson Welles's "War of the Worlds." You could hear lots of different things on the radio in the 1930s and 1940s: country music, opera, symphonic music, jazz, soap operas, continuing plotted comedies, sketch comedy, news from around the world, kids' shows, dramas, and educational programs.

Radio advertising became an enormous success, with gross sales increasing from $4 million in 1927, to over $50 million in 1936, to $300 million in 1945. And advertising came to shape radio; programs merely filled in the time between commercials. "Broadcasting in America," wrote Paul F. Lazarsfeld, the premier analyst of radio, in 1940, "is done to sell merchandise; and most of the other possible effects of radio become submerged in a strange kind of social mechanism which brings the commercial effect to its strongest expression."[19]

In the 1930s newspaper publishers were scared of the new radio industry, seeing it as competition. After all, who would buy a newspaper if they'd already heard the news on the radio? Newspaper owners responded by putting pressure on wire services not to sell news to radio stations, and by trying (and failing) to get legal restrictions on broadcast news. The "Press-Radio War" came to an end with an agreement that radio stations could broadcast only two five-minute bursts of news a day, with no news story more than thirty words long. Furthermore, radio announcers were only to comment on the news rather than report it — which is why to this day radio and television newspeople are called "commentators." The agreement died after radio stations began to buy time in newspapers to advertise their program schedules, publishers started buying their own radio stations, and World War II gave radio news a new identity.

Radio news came into its own during the war. In 1938 CBS invented the "World News Roundup," which used shortwave reports from around the world. H. V. Kaltenborn's reporting of the Munich crisis of 1938, some 102 broadcasts in eighteen days, including live interviews with the men who were dividing Europe, brought world events to life for the listening public. In the next few years radio would play a key role in creating an interest in world events, and in combating American isolationism.

The attack on Pearl Harbor came on a Sunday afternoon; it was a radio exclusive. Radio reporter Edward R. Murrow electrified Americans with his reporting on the bombing of London. Other reporters accompanied troops onto battlefields, their live reports relayed by telephone across the Atlantic to listeners throughout America. In 1939 only 25 percent of the public cited radio as their principal source of news. In 1942 networks aired some two hundred news broadcasts a week, and 73 percent of Americans counted on the radio to find out what was going on in the war. Radio propaganda came into its own, too, with American shortwave radio aimed at Europe, and the Armed Forces Radio Service boosting the morale of American troops with fifty hours of radio programming every week.

THE WAR AND AFTERWARD

World War II changed radio. The radio industry geared up for the war effort, dropping almost all civilian production to take on military work. In 1941 the president of the Institute of Radio Engineers outlined the challenge: "Radio and its allied arts will have much to do . . . in the event this country goes to war. Some of these applications will be to the handling of communications. . . . But in addition electronic technicians are finding totally new employments . . . in navigation and in searching out the enemy, whether he come by sea, land or air. . . . The most intricate military control equipment, much of it based upon radio devices, will be commonplace in our services when and if war comes to us."[20]

During the war American factories turned out an astonishing amount of military hardware, and an unprecedented amount of it contained electronics made by radio manufacturers. A typical tank had $5,000 worth of electronics, a typical bomber more than $50,000. The military demand for radio and other electronic devices vastly exceeded the levels of output of the prewar industry. Employment rose from approximately 110,000 workers to 560,000 workers. Radio set manufacturers' sales went from $240 million in 1941 to $4.5 billion in 1944.

The military's demand for radio and its new offspring, radar, meant that prodigious scientific resources were brought to bear on the industry. The mobilization of scientific and engineering talent was coordinated by the National Defense Research Committee, established in June 1940. This committee, which established military research programs at universities, put a heavy emphasis on electronics. These university research centers, among them antisubmarine warfare programs at Columbia, radar at MIT, radar and radio jamming at Harvard, and electronic calculating machines at the University of Pennsylvania and elsewhere, became the focal points of electronics research both during and after the war. This was practical research, and inventions at these universities were rapidly transformed into products for manufacturing by the firms that had previously manufactured radios. These projects were hugely expensive: the nation spent some $2.5 billion, for example, on developing and producing radar.

The war transformed the radio industry into the electronics industry, and gave it its scientific foundations. It also, as the historian Paul Foreman has argued, gave electronics the military basis that would sustain it for the next four decades. The electronics industry changed, one history puts it, from "a timid, consumer-oriented radio industry into a heroic producer of rugged, reliable, military equipment, capable of withstanding the battlefield extremes of temperature, humidity, vibration, and shock."[21] When Paul Galvin, president of the Radio Manufacturers Association, addressed the Institute of Radio Engineers in 1942, he looked ahead to the future: "Work hard during the war; your fun is coming after the war is over. With all the new materials, new tubes, and new ideas developed during the war you are going to have a picnic shaping them into playthings for commercial and civilian application. There will be no *status quo ante bellum* for the radio engineer."[22]

Galvin's prediction was more accurate than he could have dreamed. In the late 1940s and 1950s, the radio industry expanded at a rate four or five times that of the U.S. economy in general. The electronics industry faced an immense

pent-up civilian demand. The public had been tantalized by the dream of FM radio and television, demonstrated but not made widely available before the war. Now they wanted to have new radios, and a television set, in their homes. Dozens of new products gave the industry a broader base than ever before. In 1930 radios accounted for 90 percent of the electronics industry's sales; in 1950 they accounted for less than 20 percent.

World War II had shown how useful two-way radio could be, and after the war the market boomed. In 1945 there were 16,000 special radio stations authorized, about half of them marine radio. Just ten years later the number of private radio stations had increased by a factor of ten, to over 157,000 stations. Public safety stations increased from 5,000 to 18,000; industrial stations from 576 to 25,000; aviation from 4,000 to 44,000; land transportation from 0 to 20,000; and marine stations from 4,500 to 50,000. Taxicabs, truckers, and eventually even bicycle messengers would have their own two-way radios. The first radiotelephones — a radio connected into the telephone system — were installed in 1940. But there simply wasn't enough space available on the spectrum for all the people who wanted one, and the telephone company was leery of allowing connections into the phone network. (See TELEPHONE.)

Two-way radio, especially portable two-way radio, brought tremendous changes to these specialized markets. Radio-dispatched cabs changed the whole structure of that industry, giving the central dispatcher greater authority, and reducing the amount of cruising a cab driver had to do. Radios in factories allowed increased coordination of production processes. The managers of Kodak's main plant in Rochester, for example, installed a system of twenty-four two-way radios in 1949 to improve communications between truck drivers, locomotive engineers, mobile crane operators, and fire crews. This system allowed managers to regain control of plants that had begun to seem too sprawling to manage.

This is America...

...where you can listen to your radio in your living room – – not in a hideout. Where you are free to hear both sides of a question and form your own opinion ★ This is your America

...Keep it Free!

The radio as a symbol of freedom, a 1942 poster.

Radio became a necessity for commercial pilots after the war. It had been used as far back as 1910 for airplane-to-ground transmission, and by 1920 most large airfields had radios, supplied by the Post Office, for airmail flights. But not until after World War II were two-way radios common in airplanes. In 1948 the government put forward an $836 million plan for "electronic airways," including the newly developed radar. In 1945 there were fewer than 4,000 aviation radio stations. In 1950 there were almost 24,000, and in 1955 over 44,000. Radio was applied to many improvements in direction finding. The radio beacons of the 1920s and 1930s were improved, and supplemented with distance-measuring equipment that allowed pilots to determine the distance from the beacon. Another clever use of radio signals made landing easier: the airplane's Instrument Landing System (ILS) allowed pilots to know their position relative to the glide path by glancing at an instrument in the cockpit. ILS, introduced after World War II, used two radio beams, one showing position above or below the glide path, the other right or left. Radar was installed in 1948 at airports in New York, Washington, and Chicago, lent to the Civil Aviation Authority by the army.

Commercial radio, too, changed with the arrival of new technology developed for the war effort. Television boomed when it was released from wartime restrictions, and the TV set soon usurped the radio's place in the living room. (See TELEVISION.) Radio had to find a new role. The content would change, the number of stations would increase, and the networks began to disappear. A 1947 survey of radio listeners showed the place of radio in Americans' lives at the end of the war. Fifty-nine percent of those surveyed said that they listened more than three hours a day. Asked to rank evening program preferences, 74 percent mentioned news broadcasts, 59 percent comedy programs; 56 percent quiz and audience participation programs. Popular music ranked fourth at 49 percent, with classical music well down the list at 30 percent. Over the next few years, as television captured news and dramatic programming, and radio broadcasters switched to recorded music and discovered the advantages of market segmentation, these answers would change dramatically.

The new technology of tape and improved technology of records opened radio to recorded music, which would become its mainstay after the war. Performers who had seen the way that Armed Forces Radio had used recorded transcriptions during the war insisted on them. Bing Crosby was one of the first. He wanted to record his programs at his convenience, in California, and then ship the recording to New York for broadcast. But it was hard to edit transcription recordings without losing sound quality, and listeners complained. So Cros-

The aviation radio beacons set up in the late 1920s used a clever scheme to help pilots find their way. They broadcast two separate signals, one transmitting a Morse code A (dot/dash), the other a Morse

code N (dash/dot). If the pilot was on the correct course he would pick up both signals equally and hear a steady note. If not, the note would change. Pilots flew from beacon to beacon across the country.

These early beacons, called Adcock ranges, broadcast on low frequency. During World War II technological developments made possible VHF frequencies (above 50 MHz) and a new set of radio beacons were built. These were called VORs,

which stood for VHF Omni-Range. This system used changes in the phase of radio signals to indicate directions; the actual bearing of the plane showed up on an instrument in the cockpit. In the 1950s a new signal was added to the VOR to indicate not only direction but also distance. In the 1980s, electronic processing of the directional signals and the distance information made it possible to fly directly from any point to any other, rather than flying from radio beacon to radio beacon.

Shown here is the instrument panel in the cockpit of an airplane with the latest in radio beacon receivers, circa 1940. When the pilot kept the crossed pointers in the instrument at the lower center of the board centered, he or she was on the correct course for descent. The vibrating reed indicator to the right shows the direction of the beacon signals; the one to the left indicates distance.

After World War II, the use of portable two-way radios greatly increased ease of communications between members of train crews. They made it possible, for instance, for the engineer to get word that "the rear end's moving" and to start accelerating more quickly. They made it possible for the dispatcher to know exactly where each train was. They also made it possible for engineers to "cheat" the signals, getting word early by radio. This means of getting around the rules could be dangerous, however, and was strictly forbidden.

by started using a new invention, the tape recorder, in 1947. Other performers soon followed.

Recorded music provided cheap material for radio, and so radio stations played more popular music. Radio disc jockeys determined what songs would become popular; they helped publicize and commercialize country and western, jazz, and blues music, bringing it to new audiences. Recorded music was the beginning of the end for the radio networks; any local station could survive and even prosper with a stack of records and a turntable. In 1945, 95 percent of all AM stations were network stations. By 1960 only one third of them were. Network advertising reached its peak about the same time. In the 1950s it was surpassed by local advertising and national spot advertising — national ads purchased by brokers at each station.

The technology of radio transmitters also benefited from wartime advances. Transmitters came down in price, and improved technology meant that more stations could operate in a limited broadcast space, without interference. The number of radio stations boomed from under a thousand at the end of the war, to 2,800 in 1950, to almost 4,000 by 1960. Every small town could have its own station.

In bigger cities, more stations meant that each one could target a specific group of listeners. They would play the music and deliver the news that their audience wanted to hear. Anyone who didn't like it could find another station. Among the first stations to target a specific audience were those aimed at African Americans. The recording industry had long been segmented, with separate companies producing records for black audiences; in the late 1940s and 1950s, radio stations aimed at African Americans sprang up. These stations found an unexpected audience among white teenagers. In part because of this, African-American music broadened its audience and came to have a large influence on rock 'n' roll and country music in the 1950s and 1960s. Radio brought an increasing diversity of music to a wider audience. Not everyone approved. The backlash against rock music in the late 1950s aroused racial fears to scare parents. One book, published by Christian Crusade Publications in 1966, warned that rock 'n' roll was a communist plot: "the jungle beat of rock 'n' roll . . . stimulating savage, animal emotions in the minds of millions of our young people."[23] A poster urged parents to "Help Save the Youth of America" by boycotting radio stations that played "negro records."

People tended to listen to these stations not in family groups, clustered around a living room radio in the evening, as they had done before the war, but in a new way. The television set had taken over the living room, while the radio had moved into the bedroom, or the car, or even the pocketbook. People listened to radios by themselves, or with groups of friends. They could take the radio with them wherever they went. And many of them were listening on a new kind of radio: a transistor radio.

The transistor was invented at Bell Laboratories in 1947. Walter Brattain and William Shockley, physicists at Bell Labs, had started to work on replacing vacuum tubes with a solid-state semiconductor device before the war, to improve telephone switching exchanges. When World War II came, they moved on to other projects. But the military was interested in the possibilities of semiconductors as radar detectors, and more than thirty laboratories had investigat-

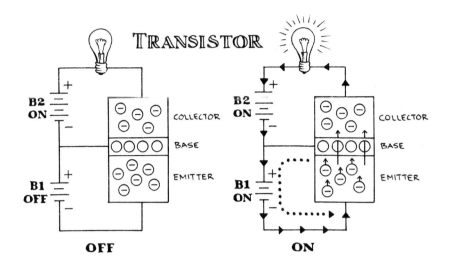

A transistor is a semiconductor device that can serve as an amplifier, an oscillator, a rectifier, or a high-speed switch, depending on how it is hooked up. It is made by joining several different kinds of semiconductor material. There are two basic types of semiconductor material. One, called an "n-type," has a surplus of electrons. (This kind of semiconductor is made by introducing phosphorus or arsenic impurities into the pure silicon or germanium semiconductor.) The other, called a "p-type," has a surplus of "holes," or areas where electrons fit. (It's made by introducing boron or indium impurities.) The presence or absence of holes and electrons determines the way that the semiconductor behaves when electricity flows through it.

In the simplest kind of semiconductor device, called a diode, an n-type semiconductor is put next to a p-type semiconductor. When a voltage is applied in one direction, electrons and "holes" cross the junction, letting current flow. Electrons can't move in the other direction, so when a voltage is applied in that direction, no current flows.

A transistor has three pieces of semiconductor, sandwiched together as shown in the drawings. One common variety has two n-type regions separated by a p-type region. When hooked up as shown, this kind of transistor (called a bipolar transistor) serves as an amplifier or a very fast on-off switch. A small current in an input circuit (lower loop, powered by battery B1) allows a much larger current to flow in the output circuit (the entire loop, powered by battery B2). In the drawing on the left, there is no current flowing from the battery B1, and so no current can flow from the emitter to the collector. But when a small current flows in the input circuit, drawing electrons toward the base-emitter junction, a much larger current can flow through the output circuit.

Transistors were a vast improvement over vacuum tubes for they were smaller, lighter, cooler, more reliable, and used less power. But when large numbers of transistors were used — in the 1950s some computers were using thousands — it became hard to wire them all together. The next step, making many transistors on one small piece of semiconductor, was the integrated circuit.

---

ed germanium and silicon during the war, learning how to purify it, and determining something of its nature. Scientists at Purdue University came close to inventing the transistor, but abandoned their work when the war ended. Bell Laboratories would take up the research after the war, and carry it to a successful conclusion.

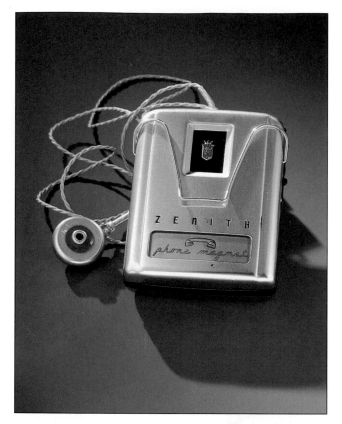

Hearing aids were the first commercial application of the transistor. This Zenith hearing aid was manufactured in 1952.

Brattain and Shockley, joined by John Bardeen, discovered the transistor effect in late 1947, filed patent applications in early 1948, and publicly announced the discovery in June 1948. Investigations continued, as researchers tried to figure out what the transistor would be good for, and how it might be used.

Engineers saw the transistor as a replacement for the vacuum tube. Transistors held out the promise of smaller devices that used less power and were more reliable. Dozens of companies went into the business after Bell Laboratories announced the invention, spread the news widely, and (because of antitrust problems) licensed it freely. In 1957 there were 850 types of transistors available from twenty-two firms, which altogether produced about 28 million transistors valued at $68 million. Just five years later, forty-one manufacturers were producing 4,500 types of transistors, some 258 million of them, valued at more than $300 million.

At first the military bought almost all of the transistors. With the cold war on, the U.S. military was quick to try out the new semiconductor technology of transistors and related components. The transistor promised to solve the problem of the unreliability of tubes, on which an increasingly high-tech military had come to depend. But early transistors were not much better, and so the military invested heavily in research and development, especially in improvements in manufacturing technologies. In 1955 the government accounted for 35 percent of the value of semiconductor sales; in 1960 it was purchasing almost one half (by value) of all semiconductors manufactured.

Transistors only slowly entered the civilian market. The first commercial product was a transistorized hearing aid. Transistor radios appeared in 1954; the first model, from Raytheon, cost $80. Transistorized car radios came soon thereafter. The use of transistors in consumer products spread surprisingly slowly; high cost, production problems, and enormously rapid change in technology held back the use of transistors in many products. In 1963, $40 million worth of transistors were used, a few in organs and hearing aids, but by far the largest part in radios.

The transistor lowered the price and decreased the size of radios. More and more, people listened not at home but in the car, or on the beach, or in the street. (By the end of the 1960s, 90 percent of cars had radios in them.) In 1960 some 25 million radios were sold. Cheaper radios and greater portability increased the already existing segmentation of the market. The first all-news station, XETRA, was established in 1961. The youth market became more important as kids got their own radios: "underground" radio stations broadcast the latest rock 'n' roll albums. Most of the new stations depended on recorded music, played by a disc jockey, to reach audiences with specific musical tastes. (This

Teenagers bought lots of transistor radios, and no beach party was complete without one. From *Where the Boys Are* (1960).

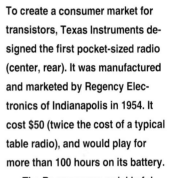

To create a consumer market for transistors, Texas Instruments designed the first pocket-sized radio (center, rear). It was manufactured and marketed by Regency Electronics of Indianapolis in 1954. It cost $50 (twice the cost of a typical table radio), and would play for more than 100 hours on its battery.

The Regency was quickly followed by other radios; left to right: Sony (1955), Philco (1959), and Emerson (1957). The inexpensive transistor radio helped open the American market to Japanese manufacturers, who were quick to use the new technology. In 1950 there were very few imported radios or televisions sold in the United States. In 1960 Americans imported 7.6 million radios, almost one third of those sold in the United States.

system was also inexpensive: one d.j. could run an entire station.) Announcers became "radio personalities." Popular music became the mainstay of radio starting in the 1950s. A 1968 survey of radio stations in large urban markets found that 40 percent had a "middle of the road" format, 15 percent played "Top 40," 13 percent "beautiful music," 11 percent country and western, and 1 percent music aimed at black audiences.

The introduction of FM, or frequency modulation broadcasting, fit well with these trends. FM had been invented in 1933 by Edwin Armstrong, the radio pioneer who had earlier made key radio inventions including the regenerative receiver, in an attempt to overcome the static and interference that plagued AM. FM was a clearly superior means of broadcasting — but one that would require broadcasters and consumers to buy new radios. Armstrong battled for years with RCA in his attempt to make FM the broadcast standard, a battle fought in the courts, at the Federal Communications Commission, and in the marketplace. In 1936 Armstrong asked the FCC to allocate spectrum space for

Candy Clark giving some last-minute instructions in the 1977 movie *Handle With Care* — the "first major motion picture," as its publicity claimed, "about the billion dollar CB phenomenon sweeping the country." The explosion of CB (citizen's band) radio use in the mid-1970s was perhaps the most extraordinary communications fad ever. CB radio was open to all: it was cheap, easy to use, and, as a "party line" form of communication, always open for business. Though the CB frequency was established in 1958, it was not much used until 1973, when the oil crisis and a truckers' strike suddenly made highway information much more valuable. In January 1977 almost one million people applied for licenses to use CB radios. Some 25 million people were using CB radios at the fad's peak. The CB radio gained its widest use as a way for motorists to warn each other about police cars. But the fad was short-lived. By 1980 CB radio was out of fashion.

FM radio. At the same time, RCA wanted spectrum space for television. RCA was not afraid of using its political clout to influence the FCC to slight FM in favor of television, and got what it wanted. A small range was allocated for experimental FM; TV got much more spectrum space. Not until another hearing, in 1940, did the FCC allocate more space for FM, forty channels in the 42–50 MHz region.

World War II stopped construction after only twenty-five FM stations had been built. During the war FM proved its value in walkie-talkies and radar, but after the war the legal battle resumed. In the late 1940s some 600 FM stations were founded. But once again, the fledgling FM industry had to compete with the new television industry, which sought the same frequency space. TV, backed by RCA's commercial and political clout, and with the support of the AM broadcasters, won. FM stations were forced to move to a new range, 88–108 MHz. All of the transmitters and receivers became obsolete overnight, and FM went into decline until the early 1960s. Advertisers wouldn't purchase time on FM stations, thinking no one listened. Not until the late 1960s would more than half of all households have an FM radio. Armstrong would never see his invention's success; he committed suicide in 1954, perhaps in despair over apparently endless court battles with RCA. Marion Armstrong, Edwin Armstrong's widow, would finally win the court battles, collecting millions in patent licensing fees, in 1967.

The revival of FM in the 1960s came about for regulatory, cultural, and technological reasons. FM had intrinsically higher quality than AM, and new recording technology, new playback technology, and better home equipment — the "hi-fi" revolution of the 1950s — meant that listeners could better appreciate FM. FM stereo broadcasting, approved in 1961, offered another quality improvement. And the 1955 approval of "store-casting," supplementary programs carried on the FM band, best known for Muzak, meant a new source of income for FM broadcasters. (See RECORDED SOUND.)

FM came into its own with classical music, public broadcasting, and "underground" music. Classical music benefited from the better sound quality that FM made possible. (Jerry Lee, a pioneer FM broadcaster in Philadelphia, suggested that the only people who owned FM stations in the early 1960s were wealthy people who used their classical music stations to impress friends at the country club, and engineers who liked its superior sound qualities but didn't know what to broadcast.) Public radio appeared on the FM dial as a result of the 1967 Public Broadcasting Act, which established National Public Radio as a production center for educational and public affairs broadcasting to a growing network of public radio stations, and which reserved space on the FM dial for new public radio stations.

But FM became best known in the 1960s for rock 'n' roll. AM radio stations that played popular music tended more and more toward Top 40 broadcasting. One early FM disc jockey described AM this way: "Top 40 AM radio aimed its message directly at the lowest common denominator. The disc jockeys have become robots performing their inanities at the direction of programmers." AM, he continued, was a "rotting corpse stinking up the airwaves."[24] "Progressive" FM stations played entire rock 'n' roll albums — at least in part, in the early years, because they had so few advertisers. As rock music became more complex, the higher-quality FM sound became even more important. Success brought changes to these stations. As advertisers realized that progressive FM could deliver more affluent young listeners, the stations became increasingly commercial.

The 1970s and 1980s saw the increasing segmentation of radio. There were more than twenty-five official categories of radio stations, some specializing in news, others in call-in shows (a return, in some ways, to radio's two-way roots), others in music of a particular era. Of the 10,000 stations on the air in 1988, slightly over one fourth had a country and western format; slightly under a fourth played "adult contemporary" music. Top 40 music was on tap at about 10 percent of stations, "nostalgia" at 7 percent, and down from there to a handful of classical music stations, jazz stations, and all-news stations.

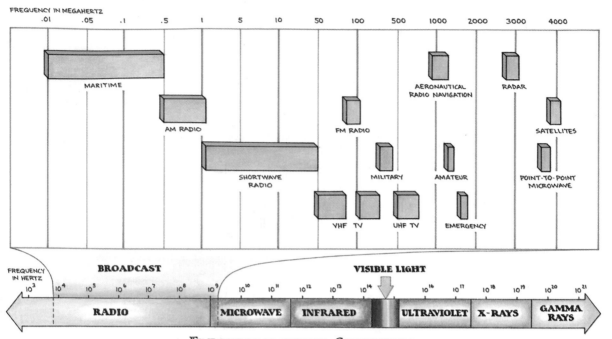

FREQUENCY IN MEGAHERTZ

.01   .05   .1   .5   1   5   10   50   100   500   1000   2000   3000   4000

MARITIME

AM RADIO

SHORTWAVE RADIO

FM RADIO

MILITARY

VHF TV   UHF TV

AMATEUR

EMERGENCY

AERONAUTICAL RADIO NAVIGATION

RADAR

SATELLITES

POINT-TO-POINT MICROWAVE

FREQUENCY IN HERTZ

BROADCAST   VISIBLE LIGHT

10^3 10^4 10^5 10^6 10^7 10^8 10^9 10^{10} 10^{11} 10^{12} 10^{13} 10^{14} 10^{16} 10^{17} 10^{18} 10^{19} 10^{20} 10^{21}

RADIO   MICROWAVE   INFRARED   ULTRAVIOLET   X-RAYS   GAMMA RAYS

ELECTROMAGNETIC SPECTRUM

The frequency of radio signals is shown by their place along the electromagnetic spectrum. The earliest radio experiments were carried out at the low end of the spectrum: Marconi's broadcasts had a frequency of about 100 Hz. As electronics technology has improved, and as the low end of the spectrum has filled up, radio increasingly has moved toward the high-frequency end of the spectrum. Higher-frequencies can carry more information than lower frequencies.

Broadcast frequencies are in great demand. In the United States, they are allocated by the Federal Communications Commission (FCC), which has to choose between competing demands for spectrum space. In the most easily used part of the spectrum, about 40 percent of the range is allocated to television, 2 percent to radio, and the rest to everything from police radio to cellular phones to paging systems. Almost every usable part of the spectrum has been allocated, and every new or expanding use has to fight for space in a complex political and technological battlefield. Only a very small portion of the thousands of allocations is shown here.

Networks returned, in a new way. In 1985 there were eighteen radio networks, most of them specializing in one kind of music, news, or talk. These new networks no longer broadcast an entire schedule of programming but rather provided hourly news, sporting events, and features. Special networks were occasionally put together for programs such as rock concerts. Satellite hookups made these networks possible, and held them together. But only 5 to 7 percent of all radio advertising was on network radio, some $328 million in 1985.

By 1990 three quarters of all listeners were tuned to FM stations. The FM audience was a generation younger, on average, than the people who tuned in to AM stations. Many AM stations lost listeners and advertisers and went out of business. In response the FCC has tried to increase the quality of AM broadcasts by "thinning" the stations to create less interference, and by opening up new room at the top of the dial and encouraging stations to migrate. AM stereo was introduced, unsuccessfully, in an attempt to compete with FM.

Both AM and FM stations have turned to satellites, computers, and robots to automate their operations, reduce costs, and ensure consistency. Some radio stations use robot CD changers to play music continuously. There's no disc jockey; the introductions to the songs, and the advertisements, are recorded digitally, on computer disk, and inserted where appropriate. Other stations make use of satellites to receive signals from a central source and simply rebroadcast them, inserting local announcements and advertisements.

The next step for radio, as for almost every other form of electronic communications, is digital. So-called CD radio, or Digital Audio Broadcasting (DAB), promises many stations CD-quality radio. There are several proposals, some of which would continue the tradition of local stations, and others, more costly, which would switch to national stations.

Perhaps the most expensive proposed new radio system would be one directly broadcast from satellites, a scheme tentatively approved by the FCC in 1992. Two satellites could cover the United States, each broadcasting one hundred stations, and the antennas to receive the data could be as small as a playing card. Skeptics wonder about the expense of the system, whether listeners would be willing to buy new radios for the new service, and whether there's any place for a national radio station when so much of the audience for radio demands local news, weather, and traffic reports. Other systems would use complex multi-frequency signals, digitally encoded, but using the same frequencies as existing FM broadcasting. The digital data would be "buried" in the analog signal, so that both systems could operate simultaneously.

It is clear that radio has not one future but many. The technology will likely segment, just as the market did. Sound quality is more important for some applications than for others: how important is high fidelity when you're listening to talk shows and traffic reports in your car? Radio has changed repeatedly over its life span, finding new markets as newer technology takes over its traditional ones. It will no doubt continue to do so.

FOR FURTHER READING

There are several excellent books on the early days of radio, when it was just emerging from wireless telegraphy. Hugh G. J. Aitken, *The Continuous Wave: Technology and American Radio, 1900–1932* (1985), is the best study of the technology of that transformation. Susan Douglas, *Inventing American Broadcasting: 1899–1922* (1987), is an excellent study of the cultural side of the transformation, as is "The Ethereal Hearth: American Radio from Wireless through Broadcasting," a chapter in Daniel Czitrom, *Media and the American Mind: From Morse to McLuhan* (1982). The personalities are brought alive in Tom Lewis, *Empire of the Air: The Men Who Made Radio* (1991).

For the history of radio programming and the radio industry, see Peter Fortanale and Joshua E. Mills, *Radio in the Television Age* (1980); and J. Fred McDonald, *Don't Touch That Dial: Radio Programming in American Life, 1920 to 1960* (1979). The commercial, technological, and cultural story of early radio is told in Susan Smulyan, *Selling Radio: The Commercialization of American Broadcasting, 1920–1934* (1994); and, more generally, in Christopher H. Sterling and John M. Kittross, *Stay Tuned: A Concise History of American Broadcasting* (1978). Radio during World War II is covered in Holly Cowan Shulman, *The Voice of America: Propaganda and Democracy, 1941–1945* (1990).

The story of the transformation of electronics after the invention of the transistor is told in Ernest Braun and Stuart Macdonald, *Revolution in Miniature: The History and Impact of Semiconductor Electronics,* 2d ed. rev. (1982). On the military basis of the electronics industry, see Paul Forman, "Behind Quantum Electronics: National Security as a Basis for Physical Research in the United States, 1940–1960," in *Historical Studies in the Physical Sciences* (1987): 149–229. On electrical engineering more generally, see A. Michal McMahon, *The Making of a Profession: A Century of Electrical Engineering in America* (1984).

NOTES

1. Quoted in Tom Lewis, *Empire of the Air: The Men Who Made Radio* (1991), p. 116.
2. *Pittsburgh Sun*, September 29, 1920; quoted in Erik Barnouw, *Tube of Plenty: The Evolution of American Television,* rev. ed. (1990), p. 30.
3. Harry P. Davis, "The History of Broadcasting in the United States," address delivered before the Harvard University Graduate School of Business Administration, April 21, 1928; quoted in Mitchell Stephens, *A History of News: From the Drum to the Satellite* (1988), p. 276.
4. Quoted in *An Age of Innovation: The World of Electronics, 1930–2000* (1981), p. 23.
5. J. H. Morecroft, "The March of Radio: Preparing for Long Distance," *Radio Broadcast* (September 1923): 361. Howard V. O'Brien, "It's Great to Be a Radio Maniac," *Collier's Weekly,* September 13, 1924: 14–15; both quoted in Daniel Czitrom, *Media and the American Mind: From Morse to McLuhan* (1982), p. 74.
6. "The Distance Fiend," *Radio Broadcast* (May 1925): 35.
7. Quoted in Clayton R. Koppes, "The Social Destiny of the Radio: Hope and Disillusionment in the 1920s," *South Atlantic Quarterly* (Summer 1969): 365.
8. Stanley Frost, "Radio Dreams That Can Come True," *Collier's,* June 10, 1922: 9; quoted in Susan Douglas, "Amateur Operators and American Broadcasting," in *Imagining Tomorrow: History, Technology, and the American Future,* ed. Joseph J. Corn (1986), p. 55.
9. Quoted in Koppes, "The Social Destiny of the Radio," p. 365.
10. Neil Harris, "Iconography and Intellectual History: The Halftone Effect," in *Cultural Excursions: Marketing Appetites and Cultural Tastes in Modern America* (1990), p. 316.
11. Quoted in Lewis, *Empire of the Air,* p. 139.
12. John Philip Sousa, *Marching Along: Recollections of Men, Women, and Music* (1928), pp. 356–357 quoted in Lawrence W. Levine, *Highbrow/Lowbrow: The Emergence of Cultural Hierarchy in America* (1988), p. 164.
13. Quoted in Gloria Ricci Lothrop, "West of Eden: Pioneer Media Evangelist Aimee Semple McPherson in Los Angeles," *Journal of the West 27,* no. 2 (1988): 57.
14. Quoted in Czitrom, *Media and the American Mind,* p. 76.
15. "Radio, an Objectionable Advertising Medium," *Printers' Ink* (February 1923): 175–176.
16. Frank Arnold, *Broadcast Advertising: The Fourth Dimension* (1933), pp. xv and 42.

17. National Broadcasting Company, *Making Pep and Sparkle Typify a Ginger Ale: Broadcast Advertising and the Clicquot Club Eskimos* (1929), pp. 4 and 6.

18. Herta Herzog, "On Borrowed Experience: An Analysis of Listening to Daytime Sketches," *Studies in Philosophy and Social Science 9* (1941): 91; quoted in Czitrom, *Media and the American Mind*, p. 85.

19. Paul F. Lazarsfeld, *Radio and the Printed Page* (1940), p. 342; quoted in Czitrom, *Media and the American Mind*, p. 131.

20. Quoted in *An Age of Innovation*, p. 45.

21. *An Age of Innovation*, p. 43.

22. Paul V. Galvin, "War Contributions of Radio Manufacturing," *Proceedings of the Institute of Radio Engineers* (October 1942): 481.

23. Reverend David A. Nobel, *Rhythm, Riots, and Revolution: An Analysis of the Communist Use of Music* (1966), p. 115.

24. Quoted in David Szatmary, *Rockin' in Time: A Social History of Rock and Roll* (1987), p. 164.

It has been only a little more than fifty years since TV was introduced. About 4 million homes had TV sets in 1950, about 45 million in 1960, about 60 million — 95 percent of all U.S. homes — by 1970. Television quickly became the primary means of receiving information and of amusement. More than that, television re-defined news and entertain-ment and brought new meaning to notions of com-munity. Television became the new family hearth and the new center of American culture.

ENTERTAINMENT
TELEVISION

N O SOONER WAS THE TELEPHONE INVENTED than people began to imagine television. And the early predictions were surprisingly accurate, at least as to what would be on: sports, news, dancing girls, education, even home shopping. The cartoonist George du Maurier showed a couple sitting in their living room watching a badminton match on a screen, in *Punch,* in 1879. In 1882 Albert Robida drew pictures showing televised coverage of an exotic war — including camels charging into battle — and a woman studying at home, watching a professor at a blackboard. Tom Swift, of course, went one better and invented color television.

It wasn't hard to predict television, or to predict what would be on. Ideas about entertainment haven't changed that much. But it would take years before the technology of the television became practical, not to mention an enormous investment in broadcasting and receiving equipment. But once it did, it fit nicely into the expectations raised by existing forms of news, communications, and entertainment — radio and movies — and so became immediately popular. Television changed our expectations, too, so much so that today, television has become the measure of our culture.

EARLY TECHNOLOGY

If sound could travel on telephone lines and through radio waves, people thought, perhaps moving pictures could, too. The trick was to convert images into electrical signals. The first to do this was Paul Nipkow, who in 1884 received a German patent on what became called a Nipkow disk. This was a rotating wheel that stood between a picture and a light sensor. The wheel had holes in it, arranged in a spiral, so that each scanned across a different horizontal stripe of the picture. A selenium sensor registered the light that fell on it, and converted the amount of light at each point into a proportional amount of current. This information was sent to a synchronized wheel, this one with a light shining through it, projecting onto a screen. The original moving picture was thus reproduced on the screen — or would have been, had the sensors been fast enough. Nipkow's system, like other mechanical systems, never worked very well.

243

In 1926 the Scottish inventor John Logie Baird, working in England, developed the first operational television system. It used a Nipkow-type disk, a photoelectric cell, vacuum tubes to amplify the signal, and a neon light bulb at the receiver. The British Broadcasting Corporation broadcast TV using Baird's system from 1929 to 1937, and some 2,000 mechanical TV sets were sold. This system produced a very crude picture, with only thirty lines of horizontal detail, compared to the 525 that would be used in electronic systems. At about the same time, C. Francis Jenkins, an independent inventor, began broadcasting images from a radio station in Washington, D.C. He, too, used a mechanical-electrical system to produce a crude but recognizable picture. These early systems provided one part of the basic solution to television. This was the idea of scanning an image one line at a time, thus converting the changes in brightness of the image into a changing electrical signal, and sending the signal to a receiver that reversed the same operations to reproduce the original.

The way to speed up both sending and receiving was to replace the mechanical parts of the system with electronics. The device that would make this possible, the cathode-ray tube, was invented by Karl Ferdinand Braun, in Germany, in 1897. The cathode-ray tube (CRT) was first developed for physics experiments, but it was soon put to use in a variety of more practical applications.

A Russian scientist, Boris Rosing, was the first to use a CRT in a televi-

Punch's notion of the television of the future, 1879.

EDISON'S TELEPHONOSCOPE (TRANSMITS LIGHT AS WELL AS SOUND)

Every evening, before going to bed, Pater- and Materfamilias set up an electric camera-obscura over their bedroom mantelpiece, and gladden their eyes with the sight of their Children at Antipodes, and converse gaily with them through the wire.

PATERFAMILIAS (*in Wilton Place*). "Beatrice come closer, I want to whisper."
BEATRICE (*from Ceylon*). "Yes, Papa dear."
PATERFAMILIAS. "Who is that charming young lady playing on Charlie's side?"
BEATRICE. "She's just come over from England, Papa. I'll introduce you to her as soon as the Game's over?"

C. Francis Jenkins's Radiovisor, his electromechanical television receiver, 1930. It used a neon bulb that blinked on and off with the signal. In front of the bulb was a Nipkow disk, and, in front of that, a magnifying glass. You'd look through the magnifying glass to see a blurry orange picture. Mechanical scanners proved too slow to transmit or receive images with sufficient definition.

sion set. His 1907 system used a mirror drum scanner (an improvement on the Nipkow disk) to produce the electrical signal, and a CRT to show the picture. A. A. Campbell-Swinton, in Scotland, suggested in 1908 that a CRT be used at both ends, transmitting and receiving. He proposed (but never built) a specially treated CRT as the camera. The image, he suggested, should be focused on the end of the CRT in such a way that when electrons hit it, as they scanned across, they would cause an electrical current proportional to the brightness of the image. This current could then be transmitted to the receiver and converted to a visual image. The idea was clever, and it turned out to be the key to the television camera. But it would take years of engineering and millions of dollars to make it work.

Philo T. Farnsworth and Vladimir Zworykin share credit for the fundamental American television patents. Farnsworth, a farm boy from Idaho, saw his first radio at age fourteen, and immediately set to work inventing television. In 1926, as a student at Brigham Young University, he interested George Everson, a California businessman, in supporting his work. With Everson's backing, Farnsworth set up a small laboratory first in Los Angeles, and then in San Francisco. The work he did there resulted in several important patents. Farnsworth's genius and enthusiasm convinced his sponsors that commercial television was just around the corner, and he received a basic patent on television in 1930.

But years of hard work lay ahead, and his California backers lacked the resources to develop and market a full-scale system. Farnsworth next persuaded the Philco Corporation, a Philadelphia radio manufacturer, to support him. By 1935 Farnsworth had spent over $1 million and developed a system supported by more than fifty patents. His system as a whole was not a commercial success, but his camera patents covered central ideas. (He was one of the few outside inventors who was ever able to collect patent royalties from RCA. Another was

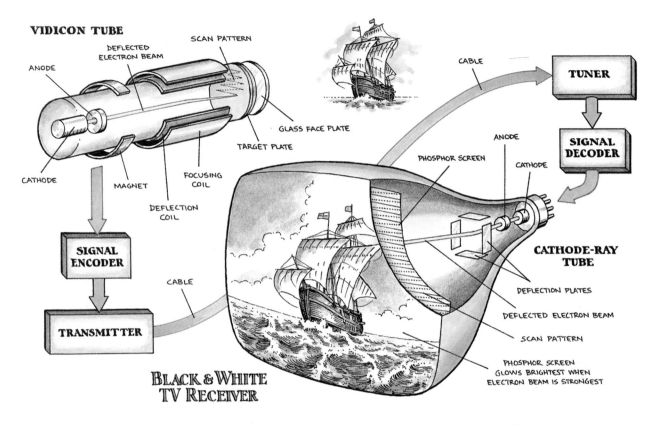

VIDICON TUBE

SCAN PATTERN

ANODE

DEFLECTED ELECTRON BEAM

CATHODE

MAGNET

FOCUSING COIL

DEFLECTION COIL

GLASS FACE PLATE

TARGET PLATE

CABLE

TUNER

SIGNAL DECODER

ANODE

PHOSPHOR SCREEN

CATHODE

SIGNAL ENCODER

CABLE

TRANSMITTER

CATHODE-RAY TUBE

DEFLECTION PLATES

DEFLECTED ELECTRON BEAM

SCAN PATTERN

PHOSPHOR SCREEN GLOWS BRIGHTEST WHEN ELECTRON BEAM IS STRONGEST

BLACK & WHITE TV RECEIVER

Many television cameras use a vidicon tube, a cathode-ray tube with a special screen onto which the image is projected. This screen changes electrical resistance when hit by light. An electron beam scans the back of this target plate left to right across the screen, then quickly back to the left and down, then left to right again — 525 sweeps per second in the American system. When hit by the beam, a brightly illuminated spot of the target plate allows a large amount of electricity to flow, a dimly lit spot only a small amount. The TV camera converts the two-dimensional image into a changing electrical voltage.

A television set has a radio receiver to capture the radio waves that transmit the television signal, circuitry to decode the signal, and a cathode-ray tube to reproduce the image.

The cathode-ray tube in the monitor is similar to the one in the camera. Just as in the camera tube, a cathode at the rear of the tube emits electrons, which are attracted toward the anode. Some of them pass through a small hole in the anode and move at high speed toward the screen at the front of the tube. On their way to the screen, the electrons pass through deflectors (in early CRTs, electrically charged plates; in later CRTs, magnetic coils) that divert them from their path. The voltage of the signal fed to these plates is varied in such a way as to sweep the electron beam from left to right across the screen, then quickly back to the left and down — in exact synchrony with the beam in the camera. The screen is coated with phosphor, so it glows wherever it's hit by electrons. It glows brighter when the beam is stronger — and the beam is stronger where the original image was brighter. So the variation in the brightness of the original image is reproduced first in the electrical signal, and then in intensity of the electron beam in the TV image.

Allen B. du Mont, an expert in radio tube manufacture, who made important breakthroughs in CRT design and manufacturing.)

Vladimir Zworykin, meanwhile, was also inventing television. Zworykin, trained as an electrical engineer in his native Russia, had worked with Boris Rosing. After emigrating to the United States in 1919, Zworykin went to work for Westinghouse. Even though Westinghouse gave him little encouragement for his television experiments, by 1928 he had developed an electronic camera tube which he called an iconoscope.

In 1930 RCA, the largest manufacturer of radios, hired Zworykin. He told David Sarnoff, president of RCA, that it would take four men and $100,000 to produce a commercial television system. In fact, RCA would invest some $13 million before it saw any profits. But Sarnoff was convinced that television would succeed, and that RCA would make a fortune selling it. As early as 1923 he had written: "I believe that television, which is the technical name for seeing as well as hearing by radio, will come to pass in due course. . . . It may be that every broadcast receiver for home use in the future will also be equipped with a television adjunct by which the instrument will make it possible for those at home to see as well as hear what is going on at the broadcast station."[1] A few years later came the first forecast of the effects that television might have. Rudolph Arnheim, a philosopher writing in 1935, was more prescient than Sarnoff: "Television is a new, hard test of our wisdom. If we succeed in mastering the new medium it will enrich us. But it can also put our mind to sleep." Arnheim warned that the time might come when television would be accepted as a substitute for life itself.[2]

NTSC STANDARD

The National Television Systems Committee, a group of 168 individuals from companies interested in TV, established the standards for television in 1941 based on careful study of human vision. The problem was to transmit enough information so that television pictures looked realistic, but as little as necessary to simplify the technology and the bandwidth of the radio signal. The committee chose to send 30 pictures each second: 24 was enough to keep the picture from looking jerky, but it was technically easier to send 30, one half of the standard frequency chosen for American alternating current. But 30 images a second produced a flickering image, and so the television standard called for each picture to be sent twice, so that the image would be refreshed 60 times a second. (This is done by sending first the odd, and then the even-numbered lines.) The number of lines on the screen (525) was chosen based on the average ability to distinguish angles. (The French chose a much higher number of lines, 819, on the grounds that French culture was more fine-grained than American.) The aspect ratio of TV (4/3 as wide as high) was based on movie standards of the day, before the invention of wide-screen movies. Horizontal detail (630 dots) was picked on the same principle as vertical, but with a bit more compromise.

As he wrote, tests of television were under way. In 1935 Sarnoff announced that RCA would invest $1 million in television tests — an announcement timed to coincide with FCC hearings on spectrum allocation. RCA began transmitting experimental TV programs in 1936. (On the RCA-Armstrong feud which helps explain Sarnoff's announcement, see RADIO.)

RCA decided to unveil TV at the 1939 New York World's Fair, where it would take its place among other astonishing new technologies that seemed on the verge of commercial introduction: robots, talking machines, the "city of the future." RCA made a test broadcast in February, a telecast of "Amos 'n' Andy," the most popular radio show. In April, President Franklin D. Roosevelt spoke at the fair's opening ceremonies, and RCA broadcast his speech and scenes of the fair to the few people with TV sets in the New York area. At the RCA pavilion visitors could watch live broadcasts and see a display of RCA TV sets. A mobile unit allowed RCA to broadcast sports events, fires, and even the scene in the theater lobby at the premiere of *Gone With the Wind*. (It couldn't broadcast big-studio movies; film companies wanted nothing to do with the new competition.)

Television sets came in sizes and shapes to fit any decor or budget.

The entry of the United States into World War II put a temporary halt to television development. The engineers who had been at work on it put their energies into radar and other war projects — work that would lead to a new flowering of electronics, and which would later be applied to television. (See RADIO.) Television was reintroduced after the war with a new national standard, more spectrum space, and, after 1950, telephone lines for national networks.

TELEVISION TAKES OFF

With its technological, business, and legal foundation solid, TV took off like a rocket. In 1946 only 8,000 homes had television sets, in 1949 almost 1 million, and by 1951 over 10 million. These families could watch some one hundred TV stations. By 1960 some 45 million households — almost 90 percent of all homes — owned a TV set. Thirteen percent owned two. There were over five hundred TV stations. Television was the prime driver of the consumer electronics industry. In 1950 sales of TV sets — almost $1.4 billion — accounted for roughly half of the electronics industry's consumer sales. In 1947 there were fourteen television set manufacturers; in 1950 there were over eighty. In 1950 a TV cost in 1950 dollars about what a radio had cost in 1930, in 1930 dollars.

But the programming on those sets came one-size-fits-all. Because commercial advertising was the main source of television revenue, programs were designed to sell audiences to sponsors. Sponsors wanted a large audience, and, just as important, the sort of audience that could buy the products they had to sell. The need to attract advertisers and show dramatic images influenced the form and content of television programming. Broadcasters filtered news and selected entertainment with an eye to what they and their sponsors thought would appeal to the families of middle America.

Early television producers experimented to discover what sorts of programming would work on television. Variety shows had moved from vaudeville to radio, and now they moved to TV. Milton Berle's "Texaco Star Theater" and

Ed Sullivan's "Toast of the Town," both premiering in 1948, were big hits. Live plays, written for television, were popular in the early 1950s, as were the staples of radio programming: crime, Western, and family shows, and soap operas, many of which came directly from radio. (Some shows appeared simultaneously on both radio and TV.) Almost all network programs were produced live.

Television news was, at first, not too different from radio news. No one knew what to show while the announcers — early on called "talking heads" — read the script. News programs sometimes ran newsreels, but these tended not to be reporting of the sort that radio had encouraged the public to expect. And so TV networks began to take their own camera crews out in the field, flying the film back to New York, or sending live reports back from studios in other cities via telephone cable.

Television soon proved it would change the nature of political discourse. The army-McCarthy hearings (1954) illustrated the potential of the medium. After ignoring Senator Joseph McCarthy's anticommunist inquisition for several years, Edward R. Murrow, the premier TV newsman of the day, took on McCarthy's smear campaign in a series of news specials. For the first time, TV news was breaking new ground. TV's real power was shown when it covered, live,

An NBC studio, 1948.

the hearings at which McCarthy accused the army of not being hard enough on suspected communists. TV exposure — a new phenomenon — helped doom McCarthy.

The first televised political campaign was the 1952 Eisenhower-Stevenson match. Dwight Eisenhower, and Richard Nixon, his running mate, ran a made-for-TV campaign, their every action designed for the best television coverage. They spent $1.5 million on TV commercials in the last two weeks of the campaign. When Nixon was accused of putting campaign funds to personal use, the Republican National Committee decided to answer with a half-hour TV ad: the famous "Checkers" speech, an enormous success. Adlai Stevenson, by contrast, was more comfortable with radio. He refused to run television commercials — refused, as he put it, to be sold "like a breakfast food."[3]

Sports proved a popular attraction, wrestling and roller derby and college baseball and football at first, and then, growing up along with television, professional sports. Game shows were an enormous hit, too. "The $64,000 Question," first seen in 1955, introduced the genre. And there were lots of imitators, each giving away more money in the attempt to attract a bigger audience.

But game show prizes were a tiny part of what television cost. TV was incredibly expensive, and all of the networks lost money in the early years. NBC Television was losing $2 million a year in the late 1940s, money that was wrung out of radio networks. Television destroyed radio in other ways, too. As early as 1954 television advertising had surpassed radio advertising. In 1955 the thirteen most popular programs on radio were daytime soap operas. Just five years later they had all been canceled, and the soaps had moved to daytime television. (See RADIO for the way that radio changed in response to television.)

Television looked as if it might destroy the movie studios, too. In the early 1950s the studios wanted nothing to do with TV, hoping that if they ignored it, it would go away. That clearly wasn't going to happen, and so in 1954 the Hollywood producers decided that if they couldn't beat television, they'd join it. Almost every studio began producing TV shows in the mid-1950s. They realized that television was a new market for their old movies, too, and in 1955 and 1956 studios began to sell their old feature films to TV stations in deals worth tens of millions of dollars. Many TV stations showed nothing but old movies.

During the Korean War no new television stations were licensed. Some cities already had stations, some did not. The difference television made to American social life became immediately obvious. In the cities with television, movie attendance dropped 20 to 40 percent. Dozens of theaters closed. Attendance at sporting events declined. Restaurants and nightclubs saw fewer patrons, libraries circulated fewer books, and radio audiences fell.

No sooner was black and white TV established than the television manufacturers started to explore the possibility of adding color. Transmitting images in color posed two major problems. It was difficult to produce clear, well-defined colors. And it was difficult to cram the additional information about color into the channels assigned to broadcasters by the Federal Communications Commission. These two problems pushed in opposite directions: fitting the color information into the allotted channel, and doing it so that existing television sets could still decode the signal, meant compromising on color quality. Proposals for color television competed with one another not just on technical grounds but on economic, political, and cultural grounds as well.

Peter Goldmark at CBS Laboratories was the first to develop a practical color television, in 1940. His system was mechanical: a camera scanned the image as a revolving color wheel spun in front of it. It then transmitted three fields — one red, one blue, one green — in sequence. (This color TV system was called *field sequential*.) At the receiver end a second color wheel, synchronized with the first, reconstructed the color image. It all happened fast enough so that the eye saw a single moving color image. The system produced beautiful color.

But Goldmark could not fit the information his system required — three times as much as black and white TV — into the standard television channel. He therefore reduced the number of times a picture was scanned (from the standard thirty per second to twenty-four) and the speed and detail of the scan (from 525 scanning lines to 405). This meant not only that the quality of the picture was worse, but also that existing black and white sets could not receive the signals. People would need a new television set even to get the picture in black and white. In 1947 CBS asked the FCC to establish color broadcast standards based on its field-sequential system.

RCA, with a huge investment in black and white television, did everything it could to block the new CBS color system. It rushed its own color system to an FCC demonstration in late 1946. The RCA system reproduced color by using three separate electron guns, one for each color. Each gun would shoot an electron beam at its own set of phosphor dots in the television tube, one set of dots for each color. (That is, when the phosphors were hit by the electrons, they would glow red, green, or blue.) This system was called *dot-sequential* TV.

RCA's color TV system was very crude, but it had potential. Because of a clever way of encoding the color information, it was compatible with existing TV; that is, black and white sets could pick up color broadcasts. And RCA had enormous influence with the FCC. It was able to convince the commission that a compatible color system was possible. In early 1947 the FCC decided to hold off on a decision about color standards, and confirmed the existing black and white standards.

Another set of hearings was held in 1949. The RCA system was still inadequate: as a *Variety* headline put it, "RCA Lays an Off-Color Egg."[4] The hearings dragged on for two years. At last, in 1951, the FCC decided in favor of CBS and the field-sequential system. But it was a hollow victory. By then there were 12 million black and white sets in American homes, which could not receive CBS signals without modification. CBS stopped its color broadcasts after only four months. In part, this was because of the small market; few people were willing to buy a new set just for the color broadcasts. It may also have been in part because color didn't add much to many shows; as one sarcastic critic put it, "It cannot be for this alone the scientific wizards of western civilization have prophesied and labored."[5] The government's decision to ban production of color sets, claiming they used materials necessary for the Korean War effort, was the final blow.

The delay gave RCA a chance to improve its system. B. D. Loughlin at the Hazeltine Corporation devised ingenious techniques to squeeze the additional color information into a standard 6-MHz channel, so that existing black and white sets could receive color signals. Engineers working under H. B. Laws at RCA, put on an eighteen-hour-a-day, unlimited budget program, designed a tube that contained three electron guns and a "shadow mask" that directed the electrons to the right phosphors. RCA would spend some $65 million to develop color television before the FCC held a second set of hearings after the war.

The investment was a success; the FCC reconsidered the issue and changed its mind. It approved RCA's dot-sequential system in December 1953, and in 1954 color television sets meeting the new standard went on sale. They had many problems. They were expensive: early 21-inch color TVs cost $900 to $1,000. (RCA wanted to start seeing a return on its investment.) They were difficult to tune: there were five knobs just for the color adjustments. The required service contract of $119 a year indicates how much maintenance they needed. And there was almost nothing broadcast in color anyway.

Color TV sales were understandably disappointing. Only 100,000 sets were sold in 1956. Prices came down that year, with color TV sets available for less than $500. And in 1958, under threat of antitrust suits, RCA made all of its color television patents (some $130 million worth of research) available to other manufacturers, royalty-free. At last sales began to take off. But not until 1964 were a million color sets a year sold, and not until 1965 were almost all of NBC's prime-time shows broadcast in color. Not until 1972 did more than half of all homes with television sets have color TVs. But, counting black and white and color together, by 1960 television was reaching into almost every American home. In 1950 the average household had the television set on about four and a half hours each day. By 1960 the average was up to six hours each day.

It's hard to generalize about programming trends over these middle years of television. All of the genres established in the 1950s continued, with some variation in popularity. The variety show and movies became less popular, the situation comedy more popular. Overall, "light entertainment" decreased, and news and public affairs increased.

But the content of these categories changed, too, in ways that are harder to define. The networks, and individual stations, worried enormously about attracting not only a large audience but also the right audience — the audience that advertisers were willing to pay for. In the late 1960s "demographics" became the industry buzzword, and programmers "aimed" shows at certain viewers. But TV programming was and is an arcane art, driven by money, advertising, an urge for respectability, and fad. Changes in situation comedies showed the meandering trend, moving, as one analyst put it, from "traditional families of the 1950s, through the upper-middle class nuclear families, the eccentric and fantasy families, and the military and rural themes of the 1960s, and then into the social sitcom of the 1970s with its single parents, working wives, controversial social issues, emancipated women, ethnic plots, sexual issues, and reaffirmation of the work ethic."[6]

Sports found a new place in American life because of television. Indeed, television changed the very nature of viewing sports. And sports coverage was often in the forefront of technological innovation: smaller cameras, close-ups, instant replays, slow motion. Instant replay, invented in 1959 and a standard technique by 1964, meant that following a baseball game required a different

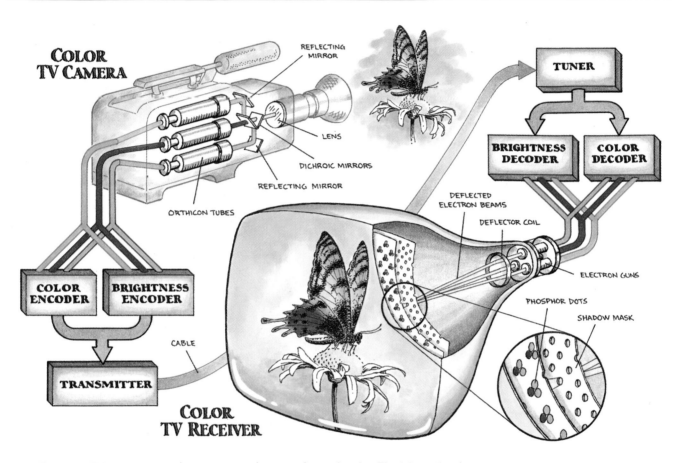

COLOR TV CAMERA

REFLECTING MIRROR

LENS

DICHROIC MIRRORS

REFLECTING MIRROR

ORTHICON TUBES

COLOR ENCODER

BRIGHTNESS ENCODER

CABLE

TRANSMITTER

COLOR TV RECEIVER

TUNER

BRIGHTNESS DECODER

COLOR DECODER

DEFLECTED ELECTRON BEAMS

DEFLECTOR COIL

ELECTRON GUNS

PHOSPHOR DOTS

SHADOW MASK

The color TV camera uses three camera tubes, one for each color. The information from these three tubes is combined to form two separate signals. One signal carries brightness information, which is what black and white sets need. A second signal carries color information. (The color signals are compressed to fit in the broadcast band, which results in less-than-perfect color.)

At the color TV set, the brightness and color signals are broken back down to three signals, representing red, blue, and green — one for each of three electron guns. Each phosphor dot of the black and white TV set is replaced by three smaller phosphor dots, one that glows in each color when hit by electrons. Between the electron guns at the back of the tube and the phosphor dots at the front is a mask with some 350,000 tiny holes in it, precisely aligned so that electrons fired from the tube controlled by the red signal hit only the red phosphor, the electrons from the tube controlled by the blue signals hit only the blue phosphor, and the electrons from the tube controlled by the green signal hit only the green phosphor.

Since color television was invented, there have been several major improvements. These include the use of vertical strips of color phosphor, which means the electron beam needs to be aligned only in the horizontal direction, and the Trinitron, invented by Sony, which uses a single electron gun to successively illuminate vertical strips.

The televised presidential debates between Democrat John F. Kennedy and Republican Richard M. Nixon were a turning point in the history of American politics. Surveys concluded that Kennedy benefited most from the four televised debates. His gains were greatest after the first debate, in which he showed himself at least a match for Nixon, who had been considered more skillful in the use of television. Ironically, many radio listeners thought Nixon won the debates.

"How will it play on television" has been a major factor in every national campaign since then. To do well, political candidates must communicate effectively as television personalities. Many of them feel they must change their personalities to fit the medium. And since television is better at portraying style than substance, strategy and personality tend to be favored over analysis of issues.

sort of attention than before. Viewers didn't need to watch the game, really; they were assured of seeing the good bits, and seeing them over and over. From 1986 until 1992, professional football used instant replays to second-guess the officials on the field. Slow motion, introduced in 1984, allowed a new level of sports analysis. Many people thought that it was more fun, and more convenient, to watch sports on TV than in person. (On video recording, see BEYOND TELEVISION.) Some predicted that television would mean the death of sports, but it had the opposite effect: the enormous payments college and professional sports received for broadcast rights revitalized them, even while changing them greatly.

Television was identified as the chief source of news for the largest segment of the population for the first time in 1963. Special news events brought out an enormous audience as TV became the town common or main street. Ninety percent of U.S. households viewed the 1960 Kennedy-Nixon debates; 92 percent watched the election returns that year; 94 percent saw the *Apollo 11* moon landing in 1969; and 96 percent saw the coverage of the Kennedy assassination. (The average family watched more than thirty-one hours of coverage at the time of the assassination.) TV had become an enormous cultural force, reshaping entertainment and the family, and establishing a new definition of American community.

People came to rely on television for their news. But television news is by its nature selective. It is committed to urgent, breaking issues because they "play" best. It's interested in what can be captured on videotape; people watch TV for pictures. For many years, at the end of each day's broadcast of "The CBS Evening News with Walter Cronkite," Cronkite would intone, "And that's the way it is." He had just finished anchoring twenty-two minutes of news selected because it was interesting, important, or amusing, because it would attract the viewers advertisers preferred, or because it could be covered effectively by the television technology of the day. It *wasn't* "the way it is" by any stretch of the imagination.

Between 1960 and 1970 the percentage of the population that claimed television rather than newspapers, radio, or magazines was the medium with the most complete news coverage increased from 19 to 41 percent. (By 1980 the figure had increased slightly more.) TV was seen as the least biased medium: more than half of the people surveyed in 1970 and 1980 thought that TV news was fair and uncolored. Viewers thought TV news was important: in 1980 three fifths of those surveyed said that TV played a significant part in their deciding whom to vote for in that year's elections, compared to only about two fifths in 1970.

But TV didn't just cover events; it changed them. "Nowadays," wrote TV critic Michael Arlen in 1968, "the television networks don't cover a political convention so much as orchestrate it."[7] Protesters outside the 1968 Democratic National Convention in Chicago chanted, "The whole world is watching," hoping that the presence of TV cameras would protect them from police nightsticks. All over the world, people knew that television would be watching them, and acted the way they thought they should because of that. The war in Vietnam was a television war not only because TV cameras brought it into the living room, but because the politicians and generals who were fighting the war acted differently on account of that. So, too, did coaches on the football field and politicians on the stump. People and institutions altered their behavior for the camera.

On television the world seemed to blend together in a hodgepodge of fiction and nonfiction, of drama, comedy, and news. TV meant information overload. From the antics of the Beverly Hillbillies to civil rights marches in the South, from the escapism of "Star Trek" to famine in Africa, from endless triumph in World War II movies to the endless war in Vietnam, television came to be our vision of the world.

Television carried an enormous quantity of information. But it filtered that information, revealing only certain aspects of the events it covered. The entertainment host and the news anchorman were the most obvious information filters, but producers, cameramen, scriptwriters, advertisers, and others also helped determine what appeared on the screen. Television coverage of the war in Vietnam, for example, reflected the political climate in the United States, and shifted as that political climate changed. Advertisers were especially important agents of selection, for without sponsorship there was, by definition, no market. Indeed, the technology itself acted as a filter, allowing coverage of some events and hiding others. The powerful sights and sounds of television seemed to draw viewers into the middle of world events. But both the choices producers make as they edit programs and the nature of television itself restrict what viewers see. TV might appear to make us all eyewitnesses to world events, but an eyewitness and someone watching television interpret events very differently — sometimes one more accurately, sometimes the other.

This new definition wasn't accepted by all. No sooner was TV a part of American life than people began to worry about it. Critical articles with titles such as "Video Slavery" appeared as early as 1955. Archibald MacLeish put it with the most feeling: "The emotionless emotions of adolescent boys are mass produced on television screens to do our feeling for us, and a woman's longing for life is twisted, by singing commercials, into a longing for a new detergent, family size, which will keep her hands as innocent as though she had never lived."[8] The best-known early criticism came in 1961 when Newton Minnow, chairman of the

FCC, characterized TV as a "vast wasteland . . . a procession of game shows, violence, audience participation shows, formula comedies about totally unbelievable families, blood and thunder, mayhem, violence, sadism, murder, western badmen, western good men, private eyes, gangsters, more violence, and cartoons. And endlessly, commercials — many screaming, cajoling, and offending."[9] Minnow's warning was eagerly taken up by newspapers and magazines, which were afraid of competition from television and eager to denounce it.

Others worried about the effect that watching TV had on children. In the 1950s and 1960s there was an enormous concern with juvenile delinquency, and it seemed to many that television was a cause. Senate hearings denounced television. In 1961 child psychologists conducted studies showing that children who watched violence on TV were more likely to be violent, even imitating the violence they saw there. (Television was a convenient scapegoat for bigger problems that were harder to deal with.) People were concerned: in a 1963 poll about one half of the people surveyed worried about the effects of television on children. For better or worse, children continued to watch TV.

Concern about commercial television was strengthened because of the obvious potential of television. A Ford Foundation study in 1961 outlined the possibilities: "Students in today's classrooms can be eyewitnesses to history in the making. . . . They can see and hear the outstanding scholars of our age. They can have access to the great museums of art, history, and nature. A whole treasure-trove of new and stimulating experiences that were beyond the reach of yesterday's students can be brought into the classroom for today's students."[10] The Carnegie Commission report that led to the establishment of the Corporation for Public Broadcasting in 1967 set its goal: "Television should enable us not only to see and hear more vividly, but to understand more deeply."[11]

By the 1960s television was the dominant mode of entertainment and communications in America. It had become central to our culture in ways that were hard to understand. Many writers tried to make sense of it, tried to grasp the meaning of television to our society. Some criticized the role of advertisers, arguing that the problem was commercial control of the central element of American culture. But the writer who became best known was Marshall McLuhan, a professor of English at the University of Toronto. His critique — more accurately, his celebration — of the electronic media sums up that era's feeling of television's importance. For McLuhan, television marked nothing less than a new stage in the evolution of human consciousness.

McLuhan wrote a series of books — *Understanding Media, The Medium Is the Message, The Gutenberg Galaxy* — on the subject. He spoke in aphorisms. On the nature of the video image, for example: "With TV, the viewer is the screen. . . . The TV Image is . . . a ceaseless forming contour of things limned by the scanning-finger. The resulting plastic contour appears by light *through,* not light *on,* and the image so formed has the quality of sculpture and icon, rather than of picture."[12]

McLuhan argued that the new electronic media meant a change in the way people viewed the world, ushering in what he called "The Age of Electronic Communication." He wrote that "the medium is the message," by which he meant that the medium is more important than its content. Television, he said, brought on a numbness or trance state. The medium is not a bridge between man and nature; it is nature. Television is a "cool" medium, and as such requires the audience to fill in the details. It is tactile and kinetic, not like reading but like touching. Television, "the new electronic interdependence," he wrote, "recreates the world in the image of a global village."[13] It is hard, often, to figure out what McLuhan meant; but his emphasis on the centrality of television struck a chord in the mid-1960s and 1970s. He exemplified his own theory: the style of his message was more important than its content.

MORE CHANNELS

By the end of the 1960s it seemed as if the television market was saturated, or close to it. Almost every family had a television set, or two or three, and many had color TV. There were portable TVs, too, made possible by the introduction of the transistor. And television broadcasters had extended their reach to every part of the country — almost 700 stations in 1970. But the 1970s and 1980s saw the beginning of a second television revolution. New technologies to bring video to the home — cable, satellites, the VCR — would bring about a second video revolution. And an expansion of video's reach would redefine the way Americans saw the world. The amount of television people watched (or at least the amount of time the set was turned on), which had held constant for many years, leaped to more than seven hours a day, on average, by 1988.

Cable television was the first way for nonbroadcast TV to enter the home. CATV — Community Access Television — was the first name for wired television, and it developed for technological reasons. Areas far from cities could not get good reception without enormous, expensive antennas to bring in the signal. It made economic sense to build a single large antenna to serve many viewers, the signals distributed by wire from the antenna to the viewers' homes. These systems started in 1948, in several small towns across the country. The first installations were built either so that individuals could get better reception or, in some places, so that stores could get good reception and sell more TVs. The 1948 FCC freeze on new television station assignments helped, too; if a town couldn't get its own station, it could use CATV to pick up a station from a town nearby. By 1965 there were 1,570 CATV systems, each serving on average about 1,000 homes.

The Federal Communications Commission imposed a freeze on new cable operations in 1966, in response to the interests of the broadcasters, who saw cable as competition. Broadcasters called cable TV operators pirates, signal thieves who picked up their signals for free and then charged customers for them. When the freeze was lifted in 1972, cable TV was ready to take on new markets. It expanded from rural areas with bad reception into urban markets. It really took off after 1975, when cable operators began to receive programming from communications satellites. The marketing ploy now was the promise not of better reception of network broadcasts but of additional channels. Cable TV subscribers would get more of everything: more sports, more movies, more special events. (The first advertising-supported cable network was the Madison Square Garden Network, which started in 1977.) They'd also get fare not available to viewers of over-the-air television, notably local government services and "adult" movies.

Cable TV had technological promise that went beyond just more of the same. Home Box Office introduced pay television in 1972. This brought first-run movies and special sporting events into the home. In 1973 the FCC mandated that all stations be bidirectional, so that the viewer could communicate back to the broadcaster. This allowed "pay-per-view" TV, programs whose signal was scrambled unless the customer paid to receive it. In 1980, 25 percent of the almost 18 million homes with cable TV also paid for special programs. Cable brought several experiments in "interactive" television, too, experiments that promised great breakthroughs but never attained much success. (In the 1990s interactivity would again be the rage: See BEYOND TELEVISION.)

Cable television brought a wider range of material into the home than the handful of channels most families could receive over the air. Local-access programming, a requirement of most cable TV franchises, opened cable studios to anyone who wanted to produce television programming. (The only catch, of course, was that almost no one watched it.) In 1979 C-SPAN — Cable Satellite Public Affairs Network — began full-time, unedited coverage of the U.S. Congress, political campaigns and other public affairs. Programs, or whole channels, were braodcast in a variety of languages, and for a variety of special interests.

Cable TV took off in the late 1970s and early 1980s as new laws were passed giving cable stations the right to import TV signals and the right of access to utility poles to string cables, and restricting cities' regulatory authority. More and more areas were wired — and prices began to soar. By 1991 there were more than 10,000 cable systems, and some 60 million homes received cable. (About two thirds of those homes could receive pay-cable channels, and half of those can order a pay-cable channel on demand.) Many cable systems carried seventy-five or more channels, and some were on the verge of moving to five times that number by digitally compressing the signals. Cable TV was a $20 billion-a-year industry.

It was also an industry steeped in controversy. Cable TV's prices and services had been regulated by the FCC until 1984, when the Reagan administration allowed it almost total freedom. After that, the average basic cable rate increased by 50 percent, to almost $20 a month, prompting a consumer outcry for re-regulation of the industry — a demand granted in 1992. The cable TV industry was also fighting an expensive political battle with the telephone companies, over who should be allowed to supply what information to the home, and with the broadcast television industry over whether or not cable systems should have to pay a retransmission charge for programs originated by the networks.

Cable was not the only alternative route into the house for TV. Starting in the early 1970s, individuals began to erect ten-foot diameter satellite dishes to pick up broadcasts intended for network affiliates or cable distributors. More than one hundred channels were available to the 1.2 million satellite dish owners in 1986, including a variety of not-meant-for-the-public raw footage being relayed between stations, and premium channels that cable subscribers had to pay for. In 1986 many broadcasters began to scramble their signals so that even satellite dish owners would have to pay to see their programs. This slowed down sales of satellite dishes, but by 1990 about 3 percent of American households were receiving TV directly from satellite.

New direct-broadcast satellite systems were proposed throughout the

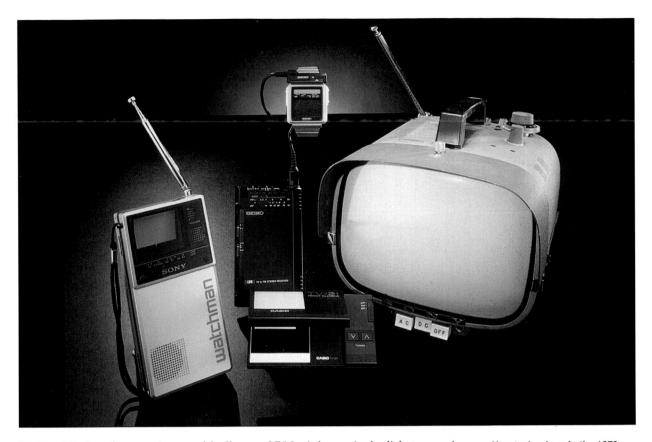

1980s. Higher frequencies would allow a $700 eighteen-inch dish to receive some 150 channels of TV anywhere in the U.S. One company proposed to begin broadcasting in 1994 and predicted some three million subscribers by the end of 1996.

New technology in the 1970s and 1980s allowed for bigger sets — and smaller sets.

Cable and satellite, joined by the VCR, or videocassette recorder, helped to bring about the second television revolution. (For more on the VCR, see BE-YOND TELEVISION.) Because of the vast multiplication of stations and networks that cable allowed, and the huge number of VCRs, new styles of TV programming developed. To the traditional forms of TV news, education, and entertainment were added MTV — music videos, twenty-four hours a day — twenty-four-hour news, both on Cable News Network (CNN, founded in 1980) and on C-SPAN; twenty-four-hour weather (the Weather Channel, founded in 1982); home shopping channels; all sports, all the time, on ESPN (founded in 1979); greater access to Spanish-language programming; and more. One effect of the explosion was the decline of the three networks. Network viewership, once more than 90 percent of all viewership, fell to less than two thirds of all viewing. In 1991 all three networks lost money, for the first time ever.

The new programming was, it has been argued, the first to take full advantage of the medium's potential. The introduction of the portable video camera had made possible an "underground" video art starting in the mid-1960s, and the introduction of the VCR and home video camera in the 1980s enabled consumers to produce their own TV programs. Music video became a new art form. The on-the-spot news reporting made possible by miniature hand-held cameras, and even by amateurs with their own cameras, anywhere and every-

Right, the Cable News Network control room in Atlanta, Georgia, and below, CNN reporter Peter Arnett on location in Baghdad, Iraq, during the Persian Gulf War. Cable News Network reporters use miniaturized satellite uplinks, satellite dishes small and light enough to take as luggage on an airplane. With this equipment, and with access to the satellite system already available, CNN can report back, live, from anywhere.

Cleared by
Iraqi Censors

Peter Arnett
CNN Reporting
Baghdad, Iraq

CNN's high point to date was its coverage of the Persian Gulf War. CNN producer Robert Wiener wrote in *Live from Baghdad* of the thrill of their coverage: "To broadcast, for the first time in history, live pictures to the entire world of a war in progress from behind enemy lines. Murrow would have loved it." But CNN , like the other American networks, failed to get through American censorship to cover the American troop buildup and movements. And overall, TV was not successful in relaying the facts of the war. Indeed, one study found that 16 percent of light TV viewers believed Kuwait was a democracy. Heavy viewers were more than twice as likely to hold that mistaken view. Yet because of its ubiquity, its ability to bring images from anywhere to everywhere, CNN has played an important role in opening closed borders. Just as years of propaganda, news, and advertisements broadcast over the Iron Curtain helped to bring about the end of Communism in eastern Europe, so might CNN have that effect elsewhere. Indian ambassador Abid Hussain spoke of its possibilities in helping to bring down the military government in Burma: "When you have a closed society, a repressive government, the only weapon you have is CNN ."

where, changed the nature of TV news. "Live" coverage had almost disappeared from television, in favor of tape and film; CNN brought it back. TV news got shorter, faster, and, many thought, meaner. (In the 1968 presidential campaign, the average "sound bite" was 42.5 seconds; by 1988 it had shrunk to less than 10 seconds.) Local news would fit twenty-five stories into a half hour, focusing mostly on crime. Programmers in every field kept their eyes on the overnight ratings, which seemed to rise with every violent story they broadcast.

Deregulation in the 1980s allowed more advertising and less public service programming, and television showed more violence and sex. And people watched more than ever before. In the early 1990s, 69 percent of the American public told pollsters that they got most of their information about the world from TV. Many children spent more time watching TV than doing anything else except sleeping. On any weekday evening in winter, one half of the American population was sitting in front of their television sets.

The question of what television did for people's lives was examined anew. While some critics emphasized that people interacted with television, and used it for their own ends, others worried about the effect of the estimated 2 million TV commercials an average person would see in his or her lifetime, or the impact on children of the estimated 8,000 murders and 100,000 other acts of violence they would see on TV by the age of twelve, or the stereotyped gender and racial images television portrays. Twelve percent of adults feel they are physically addicted to the set. Robert Kubey and Mihaly Csikszentmihalyi, psychologists who conducted lengthy interviews on when and why people watch TV, found that most people watch when they are depressed, and that, moreover, watching TV actually makes viewers feel more passive, bored, irritable, sad, and lonely.

Bill McKibben, in *The Age of Missing Information,* acknowledges the influence of television on the way we view the world: "Our society is moving steadily from natural sources of information toward electronic ones, from the mountain and the field toward the television." McKibben fears the changes that our dependence on television will bring, a loss of understanding and sympathy for the natural world; indeed, he finds that the transition "is very nearly complete." TV has triumphed.[14] And so it has, for television has redefined the way we look at the world, the way we look at our communities, even the way we look at ourselves. Meg Greenfield, writing in 1991, called TV the "real revolution in our time" because of the way it has provided us with "universally shared images."[15]

Everyone's list of those images will be slightly different, depending mostly on their age. But they overlap to a surprising extent. Our shared popular culture includes, perhaps, Elvis on "The Ed Sullivan Show," and the sets and hosts from "Jeopardy!" or "The Tonight Show." Images from TV also define our shared political history. The list might start with the Kefauver hearings, the 1951 congressional investigation of organized crime, and the army-McCarthy hearings a few years later. It might include political conventions, especially the 1968 Chicago Democratic Convention; scenes of reporters "on location" during the Vietnam War; space shots, especially the moon landing and the *Challenger* explosion; the murder of President Kennedy in Dallas; or the Rodney King beating. A different set of TV images defines the ideal of the American family. From the Waltons to the Huxtables of "The Cosby Show," television has told us what family life should be like. Television also defines how we think of the world. Whether the footage of the tanks rolling into Tiananmen Square, the young Germans atop the Berlin Wall, or Patriot missiles streaking upward to meet Scud missiles, we remember images, not ideologies.

These images won't last forever. New ones will replace some of them. But for better or worse, television images like these have come to form the common heritage of our culture. The television set has become the hearth, and watching television our primary national ritual.

FOR FURTHER READING

There are more books written about television than any other aspect of the Information Age. The standard history of television is Erik Barnouw's three-volume *History of Broadcasting in the United States* (1966–1970). A one-volume condensation is available: *Tube of Plenty: The Evolution of American Television*, rev. ed. (1990). Also useful is J. Fred MacDonald, *One Nation Under Television: The Rise and Decline of Network TV* (1990). Raymond Williams, *Television: Technology and Cultural Form* (1975), is a classic study. Roy Armes, *On Video* (1988), puts TV into its historical context and analyzes the philosophy of the video image. A good overall summary of how television fits into American mass communication is James L. Baughman, *The Republic of Mass Culture: Journalism, Filmmaking, and Broadcasting in America since 1941* (1992).

Historical statistics on TV as well as other media can be found in Christopher H. Sterling, *Electronic Media: A Guide to Trends in Broadcasting and Newer Technologies, 1920–1983* (1984).

There's an enormous amount of literature on TV programs, which I haven't discussed much here. See David Marc, *Democratic Vistas: Television in American Culture* (1984); and John Fiske, *Television Culture* (1987), an examination of what programming means, emphasizing that what's important is the way the viewer reads it. A good overall source is *Les Brown's Encyclopedia of Television*, rev. ed. (1992). A useful overview of television in the 1980s is Todd Gitlin, ed., *Watching Television: A Pantheon Guide to Popular Culture* (1986). Bill McKibben, *The Age of Missing Information* (1992), is the best summary of what's on TV in the early 1990s, as well as a profound reflection on what it all means.

The "prehistory" of television is found in Albert Abramson, *The History of Television, 1880–1941* (1987). The best simple explanation of how television works is John G. Truxal, *The Age of Electronic Messages* (1990), although the history here is not always accurate. The rise of cable television is discussed in William J. Donnelly, *The Confetti Generation: How the New Communications Technology Is Fragmenting America* (1986).

Who watches TV is a question of great interest to programmers and advertisers. A treasure-trove of information is Robert T. Bower, *The Changing Television Audience in America* (1985), which compares a series of major surveys about attitudes toward television from 1960 to 1980 and includes an extensive bibliography of surveys about TV. An analysis of the way TV influences children is Patricia Marks Greenfield, *Mind and Media: The Effects of Television, Video Games, and Computers* (1984). On women and TV, see Lynn Spigel and Denise Mann, eds., *Private Screenings: Television and the Female Consumer* (1992); and Andrea L. Press, *Women Watching Television: Gender, Class, and Generation in the American Television Experience* (1991). Similar topics are covered in Lynn Spigel, *Make Room for TV: Television and the Family Ideal in Postwar America* (1992). Cecelia Tichi, *Electronic Hearth: Creating an American Television Culture* (1991), is a fascinating study of the ways in which Americans have adopted TV, how they've talked about it, and how they've understood its place in society and culture.

NOTES

1. David Sarnoff, *Looking Ahead: The Papers of David Sarnoff* (1968), p. 88.

2. Rudolph Arnheim, "A Forecast of Television," *Intercine* (February 1935); reprinted in Rudolph Arnheim, *Film as Art* (1969), p. 161.

3. Quoted in Erik Barnouw, *Tube of Plenty: The Evolution of American Television*, rev. ed. (1990), p. 137.

4. Quoted in Neil Harris, "Color and Media: Some Comparisons and Speculations," in *Cultural Excursions: Marketing Appetites and Tastes in Modern America* (1990), p. 330.

5. Robert Lewis Shayon, "2,591 Years of 'Progress': Thales, Paley, and Sarnoff," *Saturday Review of Literature*, July 28, 1951: 26; quoted in Harris, "Color and Media," p. 332.

6. Arthur Hough, "Trials and Tribulations: Thirty Years of Sitcom," in *Understanding Television: Essays on Television as a Social and Cultural Force*, ed. Richard Adler (1981), p. 222.

7. Michael J. Arlen, *Living Room War* (1969), p. 268.

8. Archibald MacLeish, *Poetry and Experience*; quoted in William J. Donnelly, *The Confetti Generation: How the New Communications Technology Is Fragmenting America* (1986), p. 19.

9. Quoted in Barnouw, *Tube of Plenty*, p. 300.

10. Quoted in Bill McKibben, *The Age of Missing Information* (1992), pp. 204–205.

11. Quoted in Donnelly, *The Confetti Generation*, p. 31.

12. Marshall McLuhan, *Understanding Media* (1967), p. 334.

13. Marshall McLuhan and Quentin Fiore, *The Medium Is the Massage* (1969), p. 67.

14. McKibben, *The Age of Missing Information*, p. 10.

15. Meg Greenfield, "The Television Question," *Newsweek*, December 23, 1991: 74.

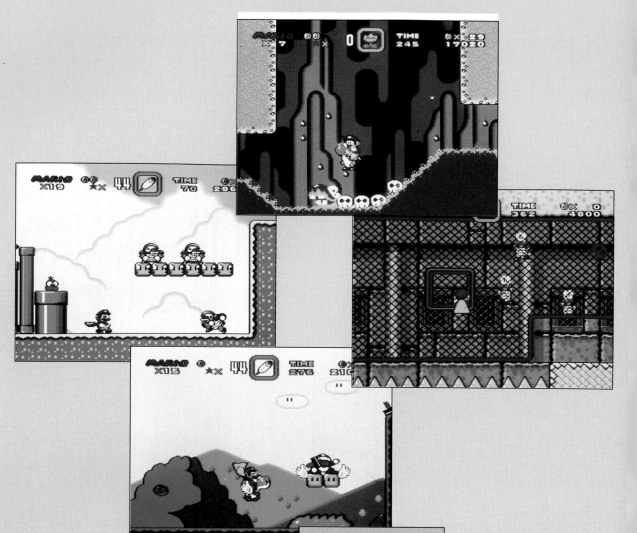

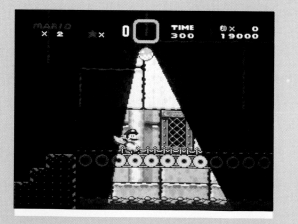

In the 1970s and 1980s there were many new ways of using the television set. You could tune in dozens of cable channels, or watch movies on the VCR, or hook up a Nintendo to play video games. People gained a new level of control over their video entertainment. They could watch what they wanted to watch when they wanted to watch it. With the video game, they could even control what happened on the screen.

ENTERTAINMENT
BEYOND TELEVISION

BY 1989, THERE WERE SOME 600 MILLION TELEVISION SETS in use, worldwide. Ninety-nine percent of American households had TVs. Most families had two or three. Americans purchased almost 25 million new television sets that year.

The television industry had changed drastically in its first fifty years. In 1950 very few imported radios or television sets were sold in the United States, a situation that was not to last long: in 1960 Japanese manufacturers had 31 percent of the American market for consumer electronics, and in 1975, 94 percent. Half of all black and white TVs sold in the United States were imported in 1970, and by 1981 all of them. Color TVs were not far behind. By 1976 one third of all color sets sold in the United States were imported. In 1968 there were eighteen American-owned producers of television sets; that number was down to six in 1980, and zero by 1992.

The technology had changed, too. A 1950s TV contained dozens of tubes, all of them wired together by hand. In the 1970s integrated circuits replaced some of the tubes, and by 1990 television sets were all solid-state, with larger screens, better color, and better picture quality. They were much more dependable than older sets. They picked up more channels — manufacturers assumed they would be attached to a cable or satellite connection — and some were able to show two pictures at once, or to reproduce stereo sound, or display closed captioning for the deaf.

But television technology was changing in more than just the details. Cable TV was one key change, making possible a vast new array of programs delivered to the home over wires. (See TELEVISION.) Just as important were changes in the technology that sat next to the TV set at home: the camcorder, the videocassette recorder, and the video game system. The TV set became interactive, not in the way that interactivity was originally conceived of — talking back to the studio — but rather by letting people add their own electronic boxes to the set, and use their TVs in new ways. VCRs and video games changed the way people used television.

And bigger changes were to come. Starting in the late 1980s governments began to consider the next generation of television: high-definition television, or HDTV. HDTV would be built to new standards, not standards determined in the 1940s, based on 1930s electronics technology. Some futurists suggested that HDTV would not just mean a clearer signal; the larger screen and finer detail, they suggested, would change the very nature of the experience. Watching TV would be more like going to the movies — or more like reality itself. That seems unlikely, an echo of the McLuhanesque notion that the medium is the message. (Much of what Marshall McLuhan had said about TV was based on its being a grainy, black and white picture.)

But the technology of HDTV may well have some major effects on the way we watch television, and the way we receive entertainment and information. The HDTV standard will be a digital standard, which means that the television set will not just receive and display pictures and sounds. Rather, the TV will itself be a powerful computer, a signal processor. The TV signal may be processed not only at the transmitting studio, but also at the set itself, by the viewer. TV, some futurists have suggested, may change more in the next few years than in its first half century.

VIDEO RECORDING

John Logie Baird, one of television's inventors, was the first to record video signals. As early as 1926 he recorded TV on 78-rpm records — a very crude image, to be sure, since the amount of information required to get a decent video image is more than 200 times the amount of information required to record sound. TV could be recorded on film, using a special camera called a kinescope recorder, a device occasionally used by the television networks to distribute programs and keep a record of their broadcasts. But magnetic tape, widely used for sound recording starting in the 1950s, was clearly superior to records or film, and several inventors tried to put video on tape.

The trick was finding ways to pack more information onto the tape. One way was to run the tape faster; another was to use multiple recording heads. Both of these schemes were tried in the early 1950s by engineers at the British Broadcasting Corporation and at RCA, but their systems were still unable to capture all of the information in the television signal. Ampex, an American company, made the key breakthrough in 1956: a rotating recording and playback head. The Ampex video recorder used two-inch-wide tape, with four video heads rotating at 250 revolutions per second; the tape moved at fifteen inches per second. The relative speed of the tape and the head was much, much faster than that of the stationary head used in earlier recorders, and so more information could be recorded. The machinery was large, expensive, and unreliable: at first, it was unable to play back videotape other than on the machine on which it had been recorded. The first Ampex machine, introduced in 1957, cost $45,000.

Ampex's technology, along with the next key breakthrough — the helical-scan recording head, invented at Phillips in 1959 — made video recording practical. Television networks and stations, which had been recording their programs with kinescopes, switched to videotape. This made it possible, among other things, for network affiliates to record network programs and play them back at different times. It also made for easier on-the-spot recording for news

The first broadcast via video-tape was a CBS news program in 1956. The tape was produced in New York, recorded on the Ampex videotape recorder at CBS Television City in Hollywood (the large box to the right in this picture), and replayed three hours later for West Coast viewers. Before long, all of the networks were using videotape to record their programs.

and investigative reporting. Videotape editing made possible "live" perfor-mances before studio audiences.

Shortly after the invention of videotape recording, several firms began to investigate the possibilities of videodisk recording. This made possible instant replay — a technique CBS used first, in 1965, during a football game — but also appeared to have potential for home use. People bought audio records; why not video records? At about the same time, video equipment producers began to in-vestigate the possibility of shrinking videotape recorders, reducing their price, and selling them for home use.

But the technology lagged behind the idea. The story of home video recording and playback is a complex one, a story of finding not only the right technologies but also the right marketing. Video engineers invented machines based on analogy with film, tape recorders, and records. The firms they worked for marketed them in even more diverse ways. Some were for playback only, some were intended to be rented, some sold, some to record off the air. It wasn't clear how people would use the machines; no one knew what the public might be willing to pay for. Most electronics manufacturers were convinced that there was money to be made in video recording, if only they could find the right tech-nology and the right market. Between 1965 and 1990 electronics firms intro-duced more than a dozen different consumer video systems.

The first home video devices were playback-only machines. CBS offi-cially announced its Electronic Video Recorder (EVR) system in 1967, demon-strated a monochrome player in October 1968, and promised a color version within a year. The EVR, which could play back fifty minutes of TV, was based on film technology. Inside was a film that was scanned by a device that transformed the optical image into a TV signal. The CBS recorder was aimed at the instruc-tional programming market, but it was far too expensive, and fifty minutes was

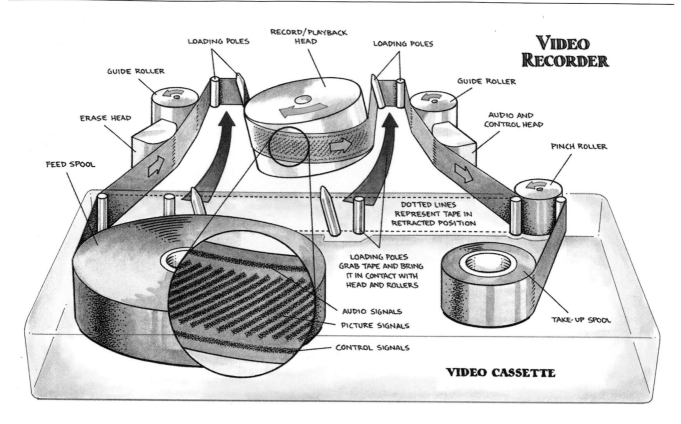

LOADING POLES
RECORD/PLAYBACK HEAD
LOADING POLES
VIDEO RECORDER
GUIDE ROLLER
GUIDE ROLLER
ERASE HEAD
AUDIO AND CONTROL HEAD
PINCH ROLLER
FEED SPOOL
DOTTED LINES REPRESENT TAPE IN RETRACTED POSITION
LOADING POLES GRAB TAPE AND BRING IT IN CONTACT WITH HEAD AND ROLLERS
AUDIO SIGNALS
PICTURE SIGNALS
TAKE-UP SPOOL
CONTROL SIGNALS
VIDEO CASSETTE

A VCR must record much more information than an audiotape recorder. The way to do this is to move the tape by the recording head much more quickly. In a VCR, the record/playback head is mounted at an angle to the tape and spins rapidly at the same time the tape moves. This records the signal in diagonal tracks across the tape, one track for each frame of the picture. The sound information and the synchronization signal that controls the pictures are recorded in two separate, linear tracks at the top and bottom of the tape.

too short for recording movies. It was never successful, and CBS stopped development in late 1971. Kodak announced a similar TV-playback system based on 8-mm film, but it was never released.

In 1968 several manufacturers introduced videotape recorders that used reel-to-reel tape, essentially consumer versions of professional equipment. These were cheaper than the Ampex device that Nieman Marcus had featured for $30,000 in 1962, but at prices up to $4,000, they were still too expensive for widespread use. A home videocassette system was introduced in 1968 by Playtape, Inc. The engineers at Playtape had developed a way of increasing the recording time of existing videotape technology. They sold the idea to Avco Manufacturing, which changed its name to Cartridge Television, Inc., and introduced a half-inch videotape cartridge under the brand name Cartivision in 1971. Cartivision was expensive — it came with its own specially modified TV — and it sacrificed quality for longer playing time. Cartivision decided that the main market was prerecorded videotapes, and set up a rental system. (To appease Hollywood's fears, the tapes could be rewound only by the supplier!) But the system was too expensive, and too few were sold to get it off the ground. Cartivision stopped development in 1973 and wrote the whole thing off at a $1 million loss, after selling only 6,000 machines.

RCA had been watching these introductions with great interest. Once the greatest innovator in the American electronics industry, it had introduced no major new products since color television, in the 1950s. In 1965 it started an extensive research program on home video, convinced that it would be the next boom market. Some estimates had RCA reaping half its sales from home video by 1990. Desperate to recapture its reputation for technological leadership, RCA pushed forward on a wide range of systems, including a videotape-based system called Magtape, and four kinds of videodisks: one that used an electromechanical needle in a groove, like a record; one that recorded the signal by changing capacitance in a recordlike groove, played by a sapphire needle; one that used a piezoelectric sensor that turned changing pressure into an electrical signal; and a laser system. RCA gave up on its Magtape videotape system in 1974, and devoted its research to disk systems.

After spending several hundred million dollars on research and development, RCA introduced its Selectavision VideoDisc in February 1981. RCA had taken a very conservative approach to the videodisk. Its system did not use a laser pickup; rather it was a mechanical system that depended on capacitance. A stylus riding in a groove sensed "pits" on the surface of the record, the depth of each pit encoding the information. This method promised to be cheaper and easier to produce — after all, no one had ever used a laser in a consumer product before. It also promised a profit from the sale of programming, mostly movies. But RCA had enormous problems in turning its research and development into production. The program stretched on and on, and RCA's investment grew far beyond what anyone had imagined. Producing the disks at a sufficiently low price proved difficult, and selling them even more problematic. Even with a $20 million advertising campaign, first-year sales of the players totaled only 100,000. When, after three years, only 550,000 had been sold, RCA decided to write off the whole business. It has been estimated that RCA lost $580 million on its videodisk project.

RCA's videodisk lost out to videotape. By the time Selectavision appeared on the market, there were already two consumer formats of VCR, as well as several competing videodisk systems. The most important videodisk was the Phillips system. Phillips had gone for the high end of the market with its laser-pickup videodisk, first demonstrated in 1972. The Phillips optical videodisk could do tricks that RCA's system would never be able to do. The user could select any one of 50,000 frames instantaneously, or play the disk forward or backward at any speed. It was an amazing technological feat — even if no one knew what to do with all of that capability! By the end of 1985 fewer than 500,000 videodisk players had been sold. These machines were just too expensive for general home use. They did find special-purpose niches, for example in video displays and in schools. But even by 1992, twenty years after its introduction, only about one tenth of all public schools had a videodisk player. (The videodisk player works much like a compact disk player; see RECORDED SOUND for details.)

Videotape proved to be the winning technology. While RCA had invested its time and money in the disk machine, Phillips and Sony had continued videotape development. The VCR was a descendant of Ampex's video recorder, but much reduced in size and cost, and with improved quality and length of tape. Akio Morita, founder of Sony, had insisted that home videotape recording was possible, and had driven his engineers to make it practicable. In 1969 Sony demonstrated a color VCR, and in 1972 put on the market a $1,300 VCR that used three-quarter-inch tape. This machine never took off as a consumer product but found wide use in education, and for use with portable news cameras. Phillips introduced its home video recorder in 1972; Sony introduced its Beta system in 1975. It was expensive at first; a tape deck and TV cost $2,300, and a tape that could record one hour of programming cost $15. JVC/Matsushita introduced its incompatible VHS (Video Home Service) system in 1976; its tape could record a longer program — three-hour tapes were thought essential, so that people could record entire football games — though at reduced quality.

The VCR was cheaper than the videodisk, and even more important, it could record. VCRs were introduced without software, with the expectation that VCR owners would record what they wanted off the TV set. (There was an enormous battle over the copyright issue, with both sides spending millions on lobbying. The Supreme Court finally ruled, in *Universal* v. *Sony* in 1984, that recording for personal use was legal.) The low price and endless availability of free programming turned out to be the winning combination. The VCR was in 400,000 homes by 1978. In 1983, 4.1 million VCRs were sold in the United States; in 1984 almost 8 million were sold. In 1985, 20 percent of homes had a VCR, and a typical VCR was used thirty times per month, 40 percent of that time for recording and 60 percent for playback. VCR owners, not surprisingly, watched more TV than people without a VCR. By 1990 three quarters of all homes in the United States had VCRs.

The VCR changed the way people used TV, initiating what media observer William J. Donnelly called "the age of personal choice television."[1] The VCR allowed "time shifting" — you could record soap operas while you were at work, say, or David Letterman to watch at breakfast. People felt this gave them control over their TV. A small amount of control, anyway: it let them fast-forward over the commercials, and reschedule programs to their own liking. Indeed, for all of the talk about "interactive" or two-way TV, the only truly successful interactive TV device was the "zapper," the remote control that became part of every TV and VCR in the 1980s. (The remote control was introduced in 1949, by Zenith.)

In addition to "time-shifting," the home VCR was put to use for watching prerecorded videotapes. Seven out of ten VCR owners rented cassettes, an average of thirty-five a year, in 1985. In that year the sale and rental of videocassettes brought in over $3 billion — about the same as ticket purchases in movie theaters. People who wanted to watch sexually explicit movies at home were among the first to buy VCRs. (Over half of all videocassette sales were of pornographic movies in the late 1970s, and even in 1985 more than 40 percent of VCR owners admitted that they used their VCRs to watch pornography. In 1989 the adult video industry's rentals and sales totaled almost $1 billion.) Over the course of the 1980s there was a vast increase in the number of tapes available, making possible a kind of "narrowcasting." Old movies were available from mail-order outlets. Movies from around the world were also available, often through ethnic food stores, and they served as an important tie to home for recent immigrants. In 1985, 22 million videocassettes were sold; in 1988 almost 80 million. (The average price had dropped from $30 to almost half that.) There was a video store in nearly every shopping center. Rentals of videocassettes increased from 1.2 billion in 1985 to twice that number, over 2.5 billion, in 1988.

The VCR had a rather different career outside the United States and the developed countries of the West. In many poor countries a TV and VCR were the first electrical appliances a family would buy. More than half the households in many developing countries own a VCR. More than 500 million have been sold worldwide. The VCR is used mostly, as in the West, for watching videotapes of domestic and Western movies and to time-shift TV shows, but also, in some places, for watching politically forbidden programs. It found wide use in countries with limited broadcasting, and in places where lax enforcement of piracy rules made tapes cheap. The spread of the VCR has been cited for the decline of cinema box-office takes in many countries.

The VCR has had an especially interesting career in the former Soviet Union. Access to Western television was closely controlled until the beginning of glasnost in the mid-1980s, and some Western radio and television broadcasting was jammed. But the VCR served as a way to get around the censors. In 1986 it was estimated that there were 300,000 VCRs in the Soviet Union. A new word was coined to describe clandestine audio- and videotape publishing — *magnitizdat* — a combination of *samizdat* (self-publication) and *magnetic*. In 1983 the smuggling of VCRs and the copying of Western videos was described as the Soviet Union's most vigorous black market. News came in, too, taped from Finnish or German television, and translated or subtitled in Russian. Light-

Video stores were suddenly everywhere in the 1980s.

weight video cameras also found subversive use, and amateur videotape was smuggled to Western broadcasters.

V. M. Chebrikov, head of the KGB, explained the problem from his point of view in 1986: "A new problem connected with the widespread proliferation of home video equipment . . . merits attention. This phenomenon, which in itself is good and progressive, is being used by some people for the propaganda of ideas which are alien to us, the cult of cruelty, violence and amorality. This activity must receive from the public a precise and uncompromising assessment. In our socialist society, just as on a well-tended field, there must be no weeds."[2] The Soviet authorities responded by cracking down on the video underground, and also by introducing their own VCR system, which was incompatible with Western systems. Before long, though, Russian magazines were publishing directions on how to modify the Soviet machines to play Western tapes, and a vast influx of Western movies and news broadcasts swept into the Soviet Union.

Back in the United States, the VCR was joined by a new piece of video technology, the camcorder. This was a combination videotape recorder and television camera, domesticated into an easy-to-use portable device. It was a technological tour de force, by the early 1990s a palm-sized camera that could store several hours of high-quality video on a tape about one third of an inch wide. The camcorder replaced 8-mm home movies. In 1990 about 3 million camcorders were sold. They could be found in 15 percent of American homes, up from only 5 percent in 1988. People carried them everywhere, documenting family activities of all sorts. One of the most popular television shows was "America's Funniest Home Videos," as homemade video found a place on the airwaves. Tape from home video cameras was used as evidence in some of the most notorious trials, and home videotapes of crimes, natural disasters, and accidents were broadcast on TV news programs and on "true crime" TV shows. Homemade, nonprofessional pornography won space away from professionally produced pornography in video stores. Suddenly, anyone could be a TV producer.

The VCR brought movies to television everywhere, and the camcorder added home movies to the mix. At the same time, cable channels brought an immense selection of other sorts of television programming into the home. The consumer of moving images had an overwhelming assortment to choose from — not necessarily more variety, but certainly more choices. He or she could take control of what appeared on the screen, or at least when it appeared. And there was more to come.

VIDEO GAMES

Marsha Kinder starts her book on the meaning of video games with a quote from her eight-year-old son: "A long time ago there were no toys and everyone was bored. Then they had TV but they were bored again. They wanted control. So they invented video games."[3] Donald Katz put the same idea another way in an article in *Esquire:* "Nintendo is like a '50s fantasy wedded with a '60s nightmare and '80s technology. It's about getting inside the television set and becoming one with it, being of it instead of outside looking in."[4]

Both of these analysts' history may be a bit simplified, but they seem absolutely on track in pointing to "control" as a key urge that leads to playing video games. Everyone wants to reach inside the TV and tell the characters on the screen what to do.

Video games happened almost as soon as there were computers capable of playing them. The first game was a computer ping-pong game, invented by William Higinbotham at the Brookhaven National Laboratory in 1958. He used an analog computer and a radar screen, but never patented the system: Brookhaven was not interested in games. "SpaceWar," the first digital computer game, was written at MIT by Steve Russell in 1962. Based on the "Lensmen" series of science-fiction stories by E. E. "Doc" Smith, it allowed players to take control of a spaceship, and blast away at an "enemy" ship. Other games followed at universities and computer centers all across the country. Most were shoot-'em-up space games, clever interactive graphics requiring quick reactions and good visual skills — basically video pinball, but without as much physical interaction with the game. It was great fun, so much so that in many places game playing was banned except at night; people couldn't get to the computer to do any serious work. (At MIT the rules for "SpaceWar" included the interesting idea that playing the game was lower priority than making new versions of it!)

Another sort of computer game was the "adventure" game, role-playing without pictures but with complicated scenarios in imaginary worlds. In these games you had to travel through a cave or dungeon, finding swords or magic potions; the computer responded to your directions according to the rules of the imaginary world that had been programmed into it.

The first home game system was Magnavox's Odyssey, based on a patent granted to Ralph Baer in 1970 for work he had started in 1966. Baer was an engineer at Sanders Associates, a defense contractor in Nashua, New Hampshire.

Video arcades sprung up everywhere in the early 1980s, a high-tech version of the pinball arcade. In the movie *Nightmares* (1983) a teenager plays so often that he's consumed by the machine and becomes part of the game.

He was looking for something to do with the television set other than, as he put it, "turn it on and off."[5] Baer's patent covered the basic idea of a ball-and-paddle game. Magnavox introduced the Odyssey in 1972. It sold for $99, and before long more than 100,000 were sold. Magnavox had granted licenses to over twenty companies by June 1974. It was cheap to make — in 1975 General Instrument offered a microchip for $5 that could operate six different games — and millions were sold. In 1976 there were more than seventy video game manufacturers.

Nolan Bushnell, who had discovered "SpaceWar" while at the University of Utah, and who had seen an early version of the Odyssey, decided that there was a market for video game machines in arcades. Along with fellow Ampex engineers Ted Dabney and Al Acorn, he introduced "Pong" in 1972. The next year, Bushnell founded Atari, to sell the game. He sold 100,000 copies in 1974; every bar and student lounge needed one. In 1980, 4 million home video game systems were sold; in 1982, 7 million. Over 16 percent of American households owned game systems, and in that year they bought more than 60 million video game cartridges. Americans spent $8 billion on video arcade games and $3 billion on home video game systems and cartridges in 1982 — more money than they spent on movies or music. Video games were blamed for the decline of the record industry. Then the market crashed. Suddenly you couldn't give the things away. In 1983 Atari lost $530 million, Mattel $200 million. Total sales of home video game systems in 1985 were only $100 million. The problem was that the games were exciting only when you first got them. After you figured them out, they were no fun.

Then came Nintendo. Nintendo, a Japanese toy company, introduced

Famicon — Family Computer — a video game system, in 1983, in Japan. In the next eighteen months 2.1 million of them were sold. The game entered the U.S. market in 1985, and by 1989 Nintendo controlled 80 percent of the market, which was back to the $3 billion level it had reached before the crash. Nintendo accounted for 20 percent of the entire U. S. toy market; twenty-five of the thirty top-selling toys in 1989 were video game–related. One in five homes had a Nintendo system. By 1991 there were 30 million Nintendo sets in the United States, more than all other computers put together.

One secret of Nintendo's success is a wide assortment of software, at the right levels of complexity. Much of the most popular software combines the graphic imagery and fast action of the first computer games with story lines based on the early adventure games. This means that there's not only shoot-'em-up excitement but also a narrative, and a continually increasing level of difficulty. Kids can play the same game for months. "Super Mario Brothers," introduced in September 1985, sold 2.5 million copies in the next four months. Some 50 million game cartridges are sold each year. Games such as "Super Mario Brothers" and "Sonic Hedgehog" come with lots of commercial tie-ins, everything from TV shows to clothing, "cereal systems," and toys. Several magazines with circulations of more than a million serve the craze.

Today, Nintendo and a handful of competitors dominate children's play, the most popular toys by far. They have little competition for the attention of boys between the ages of eight and fifteen. (Most players are boys: one survey found that 60 percent of Nintendo players are males between eight and fifteen; Nintendo itself claims that 50 percent of players are over eighteen, 36 percent female.) Nintendo and its competitors are the most widespread manifestation of the Information Age marriage of computers and television. Not only are they the most popular computers by far, they are the ones that people have the closest interactions with. One need only look at the sheer concentration on the face of a kid playing his Game Boy to know that the game's important to him. But why? There are as many interpretations as there are observers. *Newsweek* interpreted the Nintendo phenomenon as an expression of primitive maleness: Something in the games, the magazine suggested, "speaks to something primal and powerful in their bloody-minded little psyches, the warrior instinct that in another culture would have sent them out on the hunt or on the warpath."[6]

John Fiske, a student of popular culture, offers a political reason for the popularity of the games. Video arcades are popular among "subordinated males" (by class, race, or age) because, he suggests, they "can be used to think through, to rehearse in practice, the experiential gap between the masculine ideology of power and performance and social experience of powerlessness." Kids learn to beat the system, winning free plays. They can participate, changing the story, more than they can with TV. In the video arcade "the skill, performance, and self-esteem of the subordinate receive rewards and recognition that they never do in society."[7] (The same, it might be said, applies to computer hackers more generally; see SOFTWARE.)

Sherry Turkle considered video games in her analysis of computer hackers, *The Second Self,* a study of the personality of computer programmers. The games "are a window onto a new kind of intimacy with machines that is characteristic of the nascent computer culture. The special relationship that players form with video games has elements that are common to interactions with other kinds of computers. The holding power of video games, their almost hypnotic fascination, is computer holding power."[8] There has been no end of psychological and educational studies of video games. These studies often come down to one final concern: should parents worry when their kids play the games? Or are kids learning something valuable? Nolan Bushnell, the first video game millionaire, claimed not only that video games increase hand-eye coordination, but that they also inspire people to "experience the essential creativity they knew as children," and teach children problem-solving skills.[9]

Others disagree. The U. S. Surgeon General warned that the games are addictive and can lead to aberrant behavior in children. Researchers who analyzed typical story lines found that the games encourage values of masculine domination, violence, and consumerism. (Women rarely play active roles in the games.) Eugene F. Provenzo, Jr., who surveyed the many studies of video games, found contradictory results. His summary puts problems above benefits. Video games, he writes, allow children no room to construct their own fantasies. They "do little or nothing to help the child develop an inner culture, a sense of self, an awareness that while the world provides challenges and problems, resourcefulness and the use of one's imagination and knowledge of self are an important part of being able to confront those challenges. . . . Compared to the worlds of imagination provided by play with dolls and blocks, they ultimately represent impoverished cultural and sensory environments for the child."[10]

Other, more hopeful interpretations suggest that video games are a first, easy step to the world of computers, or that the games can help with the development of visual and spatial skills, or that they might have educational and therapeutic value. (If so, these writers suggest, girls should be playing the games, or they will fall behind on these vital Information Age skills.) The military found that video game–like trainers were good practice for pilots and tank drivers. Humorist P. J. O'Rourke suggested that the success of American soldiers operating "smart weapons" in the Persian Gulf War can be traced to these skills. He wrote in *Rolling Stone:* "[The soldiers] grew up in video arcades. This is the mother of all Mario Bros., the Gog and Magog of hacker networks, the devil's own personal core dump. And our soldiers have an absolutely intuitive, Donkey Kong–honed, gut-level understanding of the technology behind it."[11] (General Norman Schwarzkopf put attitudes like this in useful perspective when he reminded us that war "is not a Nintendo game.")[12]

Perhaps the most far reaching and interesting claim about video games is that they somehow represent the world of the future. Leonard Steinhorn, writing on the op-ed page of the *Washington Post* in 1992, suggested that video games (along with fast-cutting music videos and TV ads) define "a dynamic new cultural milieu": "Through video and computer games and all the fast-paced and disjointed videos on MTV, young Americans have been processing information in a way that makes little sense to the uninitiated, but is really the wave of the future. To them, ideas and information come visually, in images. . . . All those hours playing Nintendo are preparing them for a new age of interactive technology."[13] Steinhorn goes on to suggest that America's future strength will be based on the ability to manipulate images, to play with software. We shouldn't worry that the United States is falling behind in math and science, he says, for it's the kids who know how to play video games and watch TV who will lead us into the brave new world. This may be so; it's true that the American music, video, and movie businesses are larger than the Japanese electronics business. But it seems clear that the Information Age must mean more than just playing with images; it must also mean playing with ideas and information. A kid who plays Nintendo doesn't need to know anything about how the technology works; it might as well be magic.

But images, ideas, and information do overlap, more and more. Connect a computer to cable television and get interactive TV. Exploit the archives of movies and television programs to produce video games. Publish newspapers and magazines in interactive, on-line format. Use the telephone and cable TV wiring for computer communications. Connect a CD-ROM player to a computer and you've got the potential for interactive sound, graphics, text, and video. Add enough computer power and interactive virtual reality is a possibility, too. Firms in every segment of the information industry began to look for new ways to connect entertainment software with electronics hardware.

And so entertainment companies — TV networks, movie studios, record producers, and video game manufacturers — are merging with information companies, phone companies, cable TV providers, and computer and electronics manufacturers in a desperate search for synergy. Sony paid $3.4 billion for Columbia Pictures Entertainment in 1989. Matsushita, another Japanese electronics giant, purchased the movie studio MCA for $7 billion. The company that pushed this "digital convergence" furthest was Time Warner. Time, Inc., a publisher and pay-TV powerhouse, purchased Warner Communications, a music, cable television, and movie empire, to create Time Warner, the world's largest communications company, in 1989. Two years later Time Warner formed a joint-venture partnership with Toshiba and C. Itoh, Japanese electronics manufacturers, each of which invested $500 million for a few percent of the company. In 1993 Time Warner was also involved with joint ventures with phone company U S West, video game manufacturer Sega, cable TV powerhouse Tele-Communications, and software leader Microsoft, among others. Microsoft was already working with Intel, the leading chip manufacturer, and General Instruments, a major supplier of cable TV equipment.

All of these firms and many others are fighting for a foothold in what they are sure will be a brave new world of complementary technologies — where communications and information processing will merge, where software will sell hardware and hardware will sell software, where there's no easy way to draw a line between computers and television, video games and movies, or even, it seems to some, entertainment and information. Just as the businesses have converged, so have the technologies. Digital electronics has become a universal solvent. Some analysts predict that by the year 2000 the digital interactive multimedia industry may be worth $3 trillion.

HIGH-DEFINITION TELEVISION

The new uses of television were matched by proposals for a whole new kind of television. TV uses standards that were set in the 1940s, standards established at the very beginning of the electronics age. These standards were based on compromises necessitated by the crude state of the electronics art. Color standards, set in the 1950s, were made to fit into the black and white bandwidth. Electronics had come a long way since then, and starting in the 1980s, some manufacturers campaigned for the establishment of new standards.

This new standard would be called High-Definition Television, or HDTV. It would offer better resolution, approaching that of a 35-mm movie. Its screen would be wider rather than higher, to make video more realistic, or at least more like movies. Everyone could agree on the general shape of the end product, but there was no agreement at all on how to achieve it. Should the new TV signal be compatible with the old one? That would probably mean lower quality, but to do otherwise would make obsolete billions of dollars' worth of installed TV broadcasting and receiving equipment. Should the system be based on the assumption that TV would continue to be broadcast over the air, or should its designers assume that cable, or direct satellite broadcast, would soon make greater bandwidth possible? Cable TV operators assumed that it should be delivered by cable. Owners of TV stations assumed it should be broadcast. Entrepreneurs attempting to break into the TV broadcast market favored satellite.

There was a lot at stake in this decision. The HDTV business was predicted to be worth more than $100 billion by the year 2000. Most of the existing television business had been captured by Japanese manufacturers, and European and American manufacturers looked to the new standard as a way of getting back into the television industry. That made it hard to come up with a single worldwide standard, since no country wanted to adopt any other country's standard for fear of losing the business.

The Japanese were the first to propose a new HDTV standard, called MUSE. It uses thirty pictures (sixty fields) per second, 1,125 lines for each picture, and a width-to-height ratio of 16 to 9. This amount of information, though, requires a 12-MHz channel and therefore can't be transmitted in the bandwidth of an existing television channel. (The Japanese assumed that most HDTV broadcasts would be by cable or satellite, which would allow more spectrum space for each channel.) MUSE was turned down by the Europeans, who came up with their own standard. They formed Eureka, a group of some thirty firms and laboratories, and spent $1 billion between 1986 and 1990 to create a new HDTV standard called MAC, and an intermediate standard called PAL-plus, that would be compatible with existing European TVs, before deciding in 1992 that they had taken the wrong tack. Both the Japanese MUSE and the European MAC standards were analog technologies that doubled the vertical and horizontal resolution.

American firms were slow to get into HDTV, a tardiness that turned out to be an advantage. Whereas the European and Japanese standards were analog, by 1990, when the Americans were deciding on an HDTV standard, it was slowly becoming clear that digital was the way to go. Digital HDTV offered all sorts of new possibilities. American manufacturers could leapfrog over the Japanese and Europeans and take the lead. The original deadline for submission of HDTV standards was June 1, 1990; all of the proposals were analog until, on the last day, General Instrument submitted a digital system called Digicipher. The process was reopened, and a number of digital systems were proposed.

Standards for digital HDTV were still being formed in the early 1990s, with the regulatory environment and the technological possibilities both still in flux. The FCC was insisting that the new signal fit into the existing 6-MHz channels, even the channels left vacant because of interference problems. Broadcasters would be given a new channel, to simulcast both low- and high-definition TV. After fifteen years the old, NTSC-standard TV signals would be phased out, by which time everyone would have bought a new high-definition television set.

To make HDTV work, engineers are devising ways to make TV sets "smart." To fit in the available spectrum space, the signal must be compressed; a computer inside the TV would decompress it as it came in. By using compression cleverly, digital signals can take up much less bandwidth than analog signals. For example, bandwidth might be saved by transmitting those parts of the pictures that change more often, and having the TV set remember the parts where no action is taking place. Information-processing power at both the broadcasting and the receiving ends can substitute for bandwidth in between. If the signal is sufficiently compressed, it might even be sent over existing cable TV lines, or even — and this is something that phone companies would like — on existing telephone lines. Compressed digital video would allow movies on a CD, direct broadcast satellite, and hundreds of channels of cable television, even television on demand. (As might be expected, there is a political battle over who will deliver the new digital video, and how; see BEYOND TELEPHONES.)

The Advanced Television Test Center, in Alexandria, Virginia. Several firms proposed standards for high-definition television systems, and each was tested here for quality and for how much it interferes with television signals on adjacent channels, both over the air and on cable. The choice of the HDTV standard was made on technological, political, and economic grounds.

Perhaps the most radical approach to HDTV was proposed by George Gilder. Gilder suggests, in his *Life After Television* (1992), that new microelectronics technology would allow the "brains" to be put in the TV set, not the broadcasting studio: "Intelligence could move from the broadcast station into inexpensive home-based personal computers. The PC would eventually be able to manipulate video signals at the user's will, zooming in and out, performing replays, storing and even editing pictures."[14] A camera might broadcast a 360-degree image; the viewer would select the direction and magnification he or she wanted. This would require an enormously broad bandwidth, but nothing that couldn't be done with a fiber-optic cable to each home, or, perhaps, with the existing coaxial TV cable and advanced digital-signal processing to compress the signal.

In Gilder's vision the TV set would be not just a TV set but rather a "telecomputer" — "a personal computer adapted for video processing and connected by fiber-optic threads to other telecomputers all around the world." Gilder sees this decentralized system of television as intrinsically democratic. "The top-down television system," he writes, "is an alien and corrosive force in democratic capitalism," "a tool for tyrants," and predicts its demise. "In place of the broadcast pyramid, a peer network will emerge in which all the terminals will be smart — not mere television sets but interactive video receivers, processors, and transmitters." The new system will substitute "an endless feast of niches and specialties."[15]

Gilder's predictions are based on a strange combination of technological determinism, technological enthusiasm and libertarian politics. A more powerful force driving digital HDTV is the market. Television is the largest electronics market; a new television standard will mean a boom market, as well as new technologies. Digital HDTV, with its requirements for electronic memory, computer-processing power, and optical-fiber or satellite technology, promises to spur a host of building-block technologies. HDTV will, for example, require memories of at least 32 megabytes — much more than the average personal computer today. It will require microprocessors that just a few years ago would have been called supercomputers. Elizabeth Corcoran, writing in *Scientific American* in 1992, summed up the enthusiasm for the new technology: "HDTV looked like a stairway to equipment makers' heaven."[16]

FOR FURTHER READING

For an overview of the new video technologies, see William J. Donnelly, *The Confetti Generation: How the New Communications Technology Is Fragmenting America* (1986). On video recording, see Margaret B. W. Graham's fascinating *RCA and the VideoDisc: The Business of Research* (1986); and for how the machines are used, Mark R. Levy, ed., *The VCR Age: Home Video and Mass Communication* (1989). The story of the introduction of the VCR in the United States is told in James Lardner, *Fast Forward: Hollywood, the Japanese, and the VCR Wars* (1987).

On video games, see Eugene F. Provenzo, Jr., *Video Kids: Making Sense of Nintendo* (1991); John Fiske, *Understanding Popular Culture* (1989) and *Reading the Popular* (1989); and Marsha Kinder, *Playing with Power in Movies, Television, and Video Games: From Muppet Babies to Teenage Mutant Ninja Turtles* (1991).

On HDTV, a good technical overview is K. Blair Benson and Donald G. Fink, *HDTV — Advanced Television for the 1990s* (1991). For an imaginative view of what changes it might bring, see George Gilder, *Life After Television: The Coming Transformation of Media and American Life* (1992), an expansion of some of the ideas in his *Microcosm: The Quantum Revolution in Economics and Technology* (1989).

NOTES

1. William J. Donnelly, *The Confetti Generation: How the New Communications Technology Is Fragmenting America* (1986), p. 103.

2. Quoted in Douglas A. Boyd, "The Videocassette Recorder in the USSR and Soviet-Bloc Countries," in *The VCR Age: Home Video and Mass Communication,* ed. Mark R. Levy (1989), p. 257.

3. Marsha Kinder, *Playing with Power in Movies, Television, and Video Games: From Muppet Babies to Teenage Mutant Ninja Turtles* (1991), p. 1.

4. Quoted in Eugene F. Provenzo, Jr., *Video Kids: Making Sense of Nintendo* (1991), p. ix.

5. Quoted in Steve Bloom, "The First Golden Age," in *Digital Deli,* ed. Steve Ditlea (1984), p. 328.

6. Quoted in Kinder, *Playing with Power,* p. 103.

7. John Fiske, *Understanding Popular Culture* (1989), p. 139.

8. Sherry Turkle, *The Second Self: Computers and the Human Spirit* (1984), p. 66.

9. Nolan Bushnell, "Computers and Creative Play," in Ditlea, *Digital Deli,* p. 334.

10. Provenzo, *Video Kids,* pp. 95–97.

11. Quoted in John A. Barry, *Technobabble* (1991), p. 185.

12. *New York Times,* February 27, 1991; quoted in Kinder, *Playing with Power,* p. 171.

13. Leonard Steinhorn, "Whiz Kids in America," *Washington Post,* April 14, 1992, p. A21.

14. George Gilder, *Life After Television: The Coming Transformation of Media and American Life* (1992), p. 30.

15. Gilder, *Life After Television,* p. 50.

16. Elizabeth Corcoran, "Picture Perfect," *Scientific American* (February 1992): 96.

American industry depended on information processing machines and systems long before the invention of the computer. From new filing systems to new ways of organizing production, businesses found that making money required careful control not just of people and materials but also of information.

The computer is the most visible symbol of the new age of electronic information. Developed during World War II for military and scientific use, the computer rapidly became a key tool of American

INFORMATION

business. Billions of dollars were invested in hardware and software as the computer found uses everywhere. It crunched numbers, processed words, helped make decisions, managed work, and, in the form of the microprocessor, controlled everything from automobiles to household appliances.

The computer changed our lives and the way we thought about the world. In the 1960s computers became a symbol of the problems of modern society, of bureaucracy and authority. In the 1980s personal computers became a symbol of freedom and autonomy. The computer promised more efficient information processing and new ways to organize our lives and our society, bringing the potential for new freedom, but also for new forms of control. The computer even became a metaphor for the human mind, suggesting the possibilities of artificial intelligences. Science-fiction writers played off the computer to imagine new futures, and to define what it means to be human. The computer is a malleable machine, and the ways in which we use it reflect our hopes as well as our fears.

Both science and business depend on information processing. The need for calculations in science and technology was a driving force in the development of calculating machines. Businesses needed to process information to maintain control of their operations, and so businesses encouraged not just new technologies of information, but also new styles of organization that made information processing easier. Computers, invented during World War II, would fit very nicely into the culture of American science and business.

INFORMATION
BEFORE COMPUTERS

IN 1874 FRANK BALDWIN, INVENTOR OF AN IMPROVED calculator, tried to sell one to the Pennsylvania Railroad. He received this response from a manager: "If I could have had a machine like that a year ago, it would have been invaluable. I have had a series of tables prepared, giving rates on quantities from 1 to 2,000 pounds, carried from 1 to 550 miles, making over a million computations. Each sheet has been checked by seven different clerks, and I have just had them lithographed for distribution to the agents." Baldwin checked the figures with his calculator. He found dozens of errors and made the sale. The head of the freight division wrote him: "It does the work of at least three men with a certainty of correctness and greater rapidity. For Railroad Companies, calculating mileages and tonnages, it is, I consider, invaluable."[1]

Railroads, like other business firms, came to depend on mechanical calculators in the nineteenth and early twentieth centuries. Businesses used them to figure everything from freight costs to insurance rates to accounting, to determine what they were earning or losing. Scientists and engineers used similar machines to process data and to test theories, as well as for more practical applications such as calculating tides or preparing astronomical charts or analyzing structures.

But mechanical aids to computation were only a small part of the information processing revolution in the century or so before the invention of the computer. More important were new ways of organizing business so that information could be gathered and put to use. Information processing machines were designed to fit into the way businesses were run. When computers came along after World War II, they slipped easily into the standards and styles of business and science.

MECHANICAL CALCULATORS

The first calculators were tools for keeping track of numbers. The earliest may have been in ancient Babylon, where piles of stones that represented numbers evolved first into a system that had place values (ones, tens, and hun-

Frank Baldwin, a Connecticut inventor, patented this calculator in 1875. He had a hard time selling it at first — there was a great deal of competition — but after tinkering with it for years, he was finally successful.

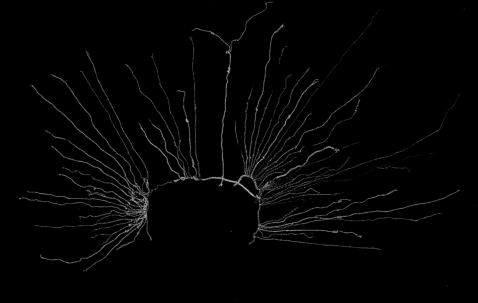

A *quipu,* an Incan calculating device used to keep track of numbers (taxes paid or censuses, for example). The shape of the knots in the hanging cords indicated the digit, the distance from the main cord indicated its place value.

dreds), and then into the abacus, a calculating device with movable counters, which saw wide use throughout the ancient world. Other early civilizations made use of knotted strings, such as the Inca *quipu,* the biblical "line of flax," or Chinese knotted cords, to keep track of numbers. The Hindu-Arabic system of arithmetic, with its zero and its place-value system, was introduced to Europe in the ninth century. Over the course of the next five hundred years, it replaced Roman numerals in Europe.

The earliest mathematical devices were the quadrant and the astrolabe, used in astronomy and navigation. The earliest known geared calculator is the Antikythera mechanism, a Greek calendrical device from the first century B.C. Its complex gearing showed (or predicted) the phases of the moon and the sun's passage through the zodiac. Similar geared calendar/astronomical clocks were made by Arabic scientists starting in the tenth century. Medieval Europe saw the invention and spread of clocks, including astronomical clocks that used complicated systems of gearing to show calendrical events.

In the seventeenth and eighteenth centuries scientists and instrument

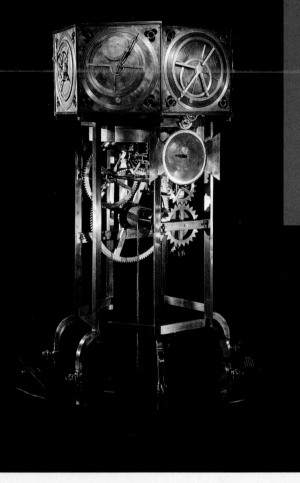

A replica of the clock Giovanni de Dondi built starting in 1348. It showed the positions of the planets and calculated the dates of eclipses and the movable feasts of the Catholic calendar.

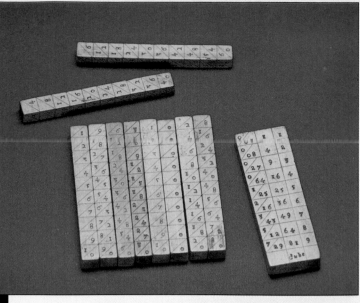

Napier's rods, a device to help with calculation, invented by John Napier in 1617.

makers invented a variety of tools to make calculation easier. These included charts and instruments for navigation — what was called "arithmetical sailing"— as well as general-purpose devices. Perhaps the first "adding machine" was John Napier's 1617 "rods," a device that allowed rapid multiplication and division. The slide rule, a mechanical system that used Napier's 1614 invention of logarithms to allow rapid division and multiplication, was invented by William Oughtred in 1621.

Mechanical devices using gears and levers followed. The first, known only from a picture, was a "calculating clock" invented by Wilhelm Schickard, a German mathematician and linguist, in 1623, to make astronomical calculation easier. This combined a mechanized version of Napier's rods with a mechanical adder. (The machine was lost, and became known only when Schickard's note to the astronomer Johannes Kepler about the machine was discovered in the 1930s.) In 1642 Blaise Pascal invented an adding machine to help his father, a tax collector, with his work. Charles Vion Dalibray, a friend of Pascal's, composed a sonnet celebrating the machine:

After your great intelligence, what is the point of having any?
  Calculation was the action of a reasonable man,
And now your inimitable skill
  Has given the power to the slowest of wits.[2]

Pascal sold few machines; they were expensive and not very practical. The next breakthrough in calculating machines, Gottfried Wilhelm von Leibnitz's 1685 stepped drum mechanism, added multiplication to the abilities of calculating machines. Like Pascal's machine, Leibnitz's machine was never commercially successful.

Not until the nineteenth century did calculating machines catch on. Scientists had the most complicated problems to solve, and computation was a major drag on scientific progress. L. F. Menabrea, a nineteenth-century Italian engineer, despaired that "many precious observations remain practically barren for the progress of the sciences, because there are not powers sufficient for comput-

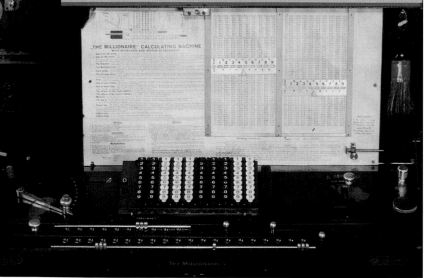

The Ferrell Tide Predictor, built in 1882, was used by the United States Coast Survey to produce tables of high and low tides. It works by adding together many of the component forces that produce tides to draw a line on paper that represents an approximation of the tide level at a given time and place.

"Millionaire" calculators like this one were used in insurance companies and for scientific computation from the 1890s through the 1920s, when they were replaced with easier-to-use calculating machines.

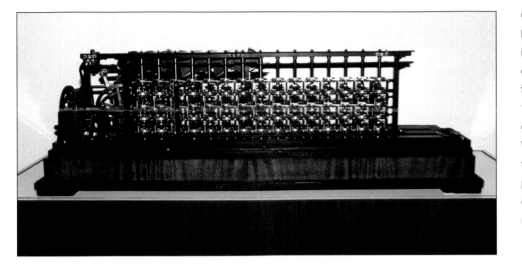

Georg and Edvard Scheutz built this calculating machine in Sweden in 1853. It was purchased by the Dudley Observatory in Albany, New York, in 1857, where it was used to produce astronomical tables. When the director of the observatory left in 1859 — fired in part because he spent $5,000 on the machine — it was never used again.

ing the results! And what discouragement does the perspective of a long and arid computation cast into the mind of a man of genius, who demands time exclusively for meditation, and who beholds it snatched from him by the material routine of operations!"[3]

There were several solutions to the problem. Many scientists hired "computers," people — in the United States, often women — whose job it was to undertake lengthy calculations. Scientists used numerical tables, calculated by the joint effort of dozens of people working as a team. (See SOFTWARE.) And they eagerly adopted new calculating machines.

Throughout the nineteenth century inventors developed faster and more accurate machines. Some were specially designed to solve certain problems, such as calculating tides or solving differential equations. Others were general-purpose calculators. By the end of the nineteenth century, calculating machines were common fixtures in scientific laboratories. Frederick Barnard, president of Columbia College, marveled at the machines: "To most persons the process of calculation involves a species of mental labor which is painful and irksome in the highest degree. . . . That this toil of pure intelligence — for such it certainly seems to be — can possibly be performed by an unconscious machine is a proposition which is received with incredulity; and even when visibly demonstrated to be true, is a phenomenon which is witnessed with unmingled astonishment.[4]

Even with the advances in calculators in the nineteenth century, scientists and businessmen continued to rely on general-purpose mathematical tables in their calculations. Several inventors tried to find new ways of making accurate tables. One of the most creative was Charles Babbage, an English gentleman scientist. In 1822 he began designing a mechanical calculator to print mathematical tables. He called his machine a difference engine. It was a Pascal calculator on steroids, an enormously complex device that used preprogrammed schemes of addition to compute each number in a table and print out the results. The British government supported the project, thinking that it would be useful for producing navigational tables. Despite more than £17,000 of government money spent on the machine, and more than ten years of work, it was never finished. (Swedish printer Georg Scheutz and his son Edvard, an engineer, did complete a machine based on Babbage's plan, in 1853.)

One reason why Babbage lost interest in the difference engine was that he had an even more extravagant idea, a device he called the analytical engine. He first conceived of the new machine in 1833, and worked on it until his death in 1871, producing thousands of pages of notes and hundreds of drawings and charts outlining its operation. The analytical engine, Babbage wrote, would not just add and subtract; it would be "a machine of the most general nature," able to calculate any formula given it.[5] It would be programmable using punch cards, and would have the ability to compare numbers and decide what operation to do next, depending on the result. Babbage's never-to-be built analytical engine was the first hint of the modern computer.

BUSINESS INFORMATION SYSTEMS

But long before the computer, businesses had come to depend on information processing — not just information machines but, much more important, information systems. Information is the lifeblood of business. Businesses need information to know what to buy or sell and what prices to pay or demand, and to keep track of employees, sales, and inventories. To do this, businesses must get information, process and analyze it to make it useful, and put it to use. And so businesses were responsible for the expansion of new forms of communication (see WORDS and TELEGRAPH) and new information processing technologies and systems.

In the eighteenth century a merchant or plantation owner got the information he needed through correspondence or conversation. He (almost all were men) kept his accounting records in leather-bound notebooks according to the double-entry method invented in Italy in the fifteenth century. He made decisions about buying and selling based on information he received from his contacts and knowledge based on his past experiences with the markets. These were traditional practices, not too different from those merchants had followed for centuries. But new systems of information processing were essential to the rise of big business. Business, in turn, was the main force behind the growth of the information infrastructure.

Adam Smith suggested in *The Wealth of Nations* (1776) that the "invisible hand" of markets guided production and sales decisions. But increasingly decisions were taking place inside business firms, not in the market between producers and consumers. The business historian Alfred Chandler has noted the rise of "the visible hand" of management in the second half of the nineteenth and first half of the twentieth centuries. The men (there were few women in management roles) who made these decisions needed the best information they could gather; their profits were on the line. They were willing to pay for the communications and information-gathering and processing bureaucracies that became the defining element of modern American business.

Managerial control depended on an array of information technologies and techniques: good records to keep track of labor and production; accounting to keep track of financial information and costs of production; and the increasing subdivision of work to make it possible for managers to direct the people who worked in the offices and factories. Firms hired bookkeepers, paymasters, clerks, and assistant managers to process information, act on it, and digest and concentrate it so that it would be easier for top managers to analyze. They did this not only to keep track of things — of orders, money, inventory — but also because of an increasing belief in the importance of orderliness and control.

Businessmen used these new systems, standards, and machines to improve their access to the information in their files and account books, and thus to understand and control their businesses better. Perhaps because the information was more accessible, managers began to use historical information about their business to make decisions about future activities. Cost accounting, used in very few businesses before the Civil War, found widespread use by the end of the nineteenth century. Managers used cost accounting to determine what each part of their operations cost, to get a sense of profits or losses on each product line. Standardized and uniform systems of accounting allowed comparison of information between companies. Managers used the new data to analyze past experience and project future possibilities.

The railroads led in managerial innovation. Railroad managers had to keep track of trains, passengers, cargo, and money over a large territory. They had to keep close control over operations, to get the best use out of their track and rolling stock, and to avoid collisions. The increasing speed of trains and size of railroad systems increased the pressure on management. Inadequate control of the railroads would mean more accidents and lower profits.

To overcome these problems, early railroad managers, many of them military men, developed new organizational systems to control labor and operations and new machines to help achieve that control. They realized that timely information in the hands of the people who had the authority to make decisions was the key to safety and financial success. Centralization of information and control, managers decided, was essential. Railroads were the first businesses to have midlevel managers. Clocks, watches, signals, rule books, and reports were the instruments of the new managerial hierarchy. A centrally controlled system of time keeping and signaling and improved communications helped keep trains in the right place at the right time.

Superintendent Daniel McCallum of the New York and Erie Railroad, a West Point–trained civil engineer and a stickler for order and control, went even further. To increase speed and safety on the Erie, he instituted in 1853 a new hierarchical system, based in part on a military model. He reorganized operations so that supervisors had control over their subordinates, but also kept their own managers informed of operations. He insisted that each employee wear a uniform with insignia that told at a glance what job each man held. This not only made the managers' jobs easier but also let the public know whom to go to with complaints or for information. (Not everyone was happy with the new idea; some attacked wearing uniforms as undemocratic.)

Most eighteenth-century merchants worked alone or in small offices. When Elijah Boardman, a textile merchant of New Milford, Connecticut, posed for his portrait in 1789, he was sure to include the materials he sold and the desk where he worked at his correspondence and bookkeeping.

A wreck on the Providence and Worcester Railroad, August 12, 1853. Public outrage over train wrecks in the 1840s and 1850s prompted railroads to establish new management structures to centralize information and control.

Railroad managers' first solution to their information problems was to make new rules. Carefully spelled out and strictly enforced procedures determined when a train moved, the distances between trains, and which train gave way when two trains met. Rule books included rules on everything from which trains had the right of way to how to check baggage.

This book recorded the rules of the Camden and Amboy Railroad in New Jersey in the 1840s.

McCallum was also very concerned with the collection of data. He wrote to the president of the railroad: "In my opinion a system of operations, to be efficient and successful, should be such as to give to the principal and responsible head of the running department a complete daily history of details in all their minutiae."[6] To do this, McCallum insisted on a series of daily and monthly reports. Managers analyzed these to determine twenty or more important statistical measures of the railroad's operations. The numbers allowed the top management of the railroad to make informed decisions. Before long, railroad managers across the country were following the Erie's lead, establishing managerial structures that facilitated the collection, processing, and use of information. By 1860 large railroads were employing forty to sixty salaried managers; by 1880 some employed several hundred.

The increasing complexity of railroad systems was also reflected in their accounting systems. Each railroad had offices full of clerks who kept records in file cabinets and specialized account books. Railroad accounting systems became increasingly interconnected. In 1867 the Master Car Builders Association established standards for the interchange of railroad cars. Railroads paid car owners a fee for the mileage a car traveled on their tracks, a system that created an enormous information interchange problem. Passenger receipts, too, required a complex bookkeeping system that could distribute the funds paid for trips that used the tracks of more than one railroad. The railroads operated one of the largest information processing systems in the country.

Manual methods of information processing, sophisticated though they were, couldn't deal with increasing traffic, and so the railroads eagerly adopted

In the early twentieth century, railroads found new ways of controlling the movement of trains on their tracks. The first picture (left) shows a mechanical system, circa 1915. By pulling the levers, the signalman set the switches and signals to guide trains onto the right track. The mechanism of the interlocker kept him from directing two trains onto the same track at the same time.

The second picture (below) shows an electromechanical system, circa 1930. The third (bottom left) shows a Centralized Traffic Control installed by the Union Pacific Railroad in 1948, with which one person could operate the signals and switches for many miles of track. The diagram at the top of the console indicates the position of the switches and signals and locations of the trains.

machines to help process information. Signaling was the first step. The first pole-mounted signals in the United States were used on the New Castle and French-town Railroad, in Delaware and Maryland, in 1832. Baskets suspended from pulleys were placed on poles about thirty feet high. A white basket told the engineer that the earlier train was on time, a black one that it was late and that he should wait. The signal was relayed down the line by spotters, who used telescopes to see the next pole.

Later in the 1830s more complicated mechanical signals conveyed more information about the state of the track and the location of other trains. One key invention was the "block system," a way of keeping trains from colliding by dividing the track into sections a few miles long, called blocks, and not allowing one train to enter a block until the previous one had left. The first block systems were manual, using telegraph messages to relay the status of each block to the signal men. The next step was to control the signals mechanically. Interlocking systems, invented in the 1850s, controlled both track switches and signals to allow only certain patterns of train movement. When supplemented by electrical systems that determined whether or not a train was in a block, the interlocking system became almost completely automatic. Interlocking systems were among the most complicated computing devices of their day.

In the 1920s Sedgwick N. Wight and other engineers at the General Railway Signal Company designed a system called Centralized Traffic Control (CTC), which coordinated the interlocking switch and signal operations for a long stretch of track. This was a revolution in railroad operations. Before CTC, operating trains was a project that required many people. A timetable established the schedule. A dispatcher wrote up and then telegraphed or telephoned exceptions to the schedule. Operators received orders and relayed them to each train crew. Special crews operated the switches. After CTC, a dispatcher at a central location determined where a train should go, and the mechanism set the switches and signals to make that happen. CTC reduced the number of employees needed, improved safety, and increased the capacity of track. In the 1950s the CTC mechanism was transistorized, and in the 1960s computers took over the job.

Many of the lessons learned by the railroads were applied to air-traffic control. A 1933 report suggested that "traffic densities at many of our airports have already reached a point where definite control, involving signaling equipment of various types and a carefully thought-out plan of traffic flow, is necessary."[7] At first, pilots objected to being told where they should fly, but the value of the system soon became obvious. In 1937, when plans were being put into place at several crowded airports, the government regulators used the railroads for historical perspective. "The rapid progress . . . in the last decade," said a report of the U.S. Department of Commerce, "compares favorably with the most modern and elaborate railroad 'block' system."[8] Air-traffic controllers used a complex system

Time clocks, introduced into factories in the 1890s, were both information-gathering devices and instruments of control.

of teletypes and clever mechanical devices to keep track of airplanes, a system that laid the groundwork for computerization in the 1950s. (See RADIO and COMPUTERS.)

Manufacturers, like railroads and airlines, needed information to control their operations. In the late nineteenth century the scale of manufacturing grew enormously. As technology made things move faster, and as the country grew, American society seemed to get more complicated, even out of control. New information systems were aimed at enforcing discipline on workers and markets, as well as taking care of business. Managers took responsibility for organization, reports, contracts, and accounting for labor, materials, sales, and profits, and for controlling operations and keeping track of them.

The managers of some firms tried to extend the reach of their information systems to their employees' every activity. Frederick Winslow Taylor was responsible for the theory behind the most far-reaching of

In process control industries like chemical plants and oil refineries, managers adopted a technological solution to the problems of control. They replaced the skilled individuals who checked temperatures and pressures and adjusted valves with mechanisms that did the work automatically. These machines — complicated mechanical devices that used vacuum, compressed air, or electricity to measure, record, and control — could be used in two ways. In some plants they were installed to extend the skills of the workers, who used them to monitor operations and to control and record what was happening. More commonly, managers installed these machines so that they replaced workers, reduced their responsibilities, or monitored their work. Sometimes they were installed so that only managers could see their readouts; managers then told the workers what to do. This all-conquering robot, built from process-control devices, starred in an advertising campaign for the Bristol Co. in the 1930s.

these attempts. He called his efforts to understand and quantify industrial work "scientific management." Taylor thought that if he could analyze the details of workers' motions, break each activity into carefully timed movements, and then tell the worker "the one best way" to do his work, he could greatly improve efficiency on the job. Not only that, but by understanding in detail what workers did, his system would give the boss greater control over his employees. "In the past," wrote Taylor in 1911, "the man has been first. In the future, the system must be first."[9]

Scientific managers used their time-study methods to figure out "the best way" to shovel, run a lathe, work on an assembly line, or type and file. (Some used photography to do this; see PICTURES.) For the most part, though, their efforts failed. Some workers revolted when scientific management was tried. More important was a fundamental flaw in the system. Scientific managers attempted to reduce vast amounts of knowledge to a few easily quantified bits of information. In part because of class prejudices, they underestimated the com-

Cash registers not only showed prices as they were added up and indicated total sales, but also kept a running total on a tape in a locked compartment inside the machine. The cash register kept sales-clerks honest.

plexity of industrial work. Scientific management never gained wide acceptance, but managers continued to find the idea of increasing their knowledge of and control over their subordinates' work appealing.

Merchants, too, found new ways to put information to use. The late nineteenth century saw a tremendous increase in the amount and variety of goods available for purchase. Inventors devoted enormous amounts of ingenuity to devices for keeping track of the flow of money and credit. One was the cash register, invented by James Ritty, a Dayton, Ohio, mechanic, in 1879. By the turn of the century a clever sales campaign had convinced most store owners that they needed cash registers. Some merchants reorganized their stores, breaking operations into specialized departments so they would be easier to manage. Others installed mechanical delivery systems, such as pneumatic tubes or wire-line carriers, to move paperwork and cash around the store, allowing them to centralize operations and keep control of the receipts.

More managerial control meant an ever-increasing load of paperwork. This in turn required improved filing systems (dozens of patented file systems came into use); preprinted forms to make sure that the right information would be collected, and would be easily accessible; improved control systems to keep track of work; and new machines such as time clocks, to keep track of hours worked by each employee, or for each project. Firms used information processing systems to improve internal controls and relations with other firms.

But all this technology wouldn't help if you couldn't find the papers you needed — if, as was traditional, they were kept in desk drawers, or bound with red tape and stored in boxes. The Woodruff file, invented in 1868, had a separate drawer for each subject, or each correspondent; it was the first major improvement in office filing. Office workers no longer needed to index each letter; filed in the proper place, it could easily be found. These filing systems gave way to the modern vertical file cabinet in the early twentieth century. The file cabinet was more than just hardware; it was a system. A textbook on filing insisted: "The definition of vertical filing . . . is — the bringing together, in one place, all correspondence to, from or about an individual, firm, place or subject, filed on edge . . . making for speed, accuracy and accessibility."[10] Business historian Jo-Anne Yates suggests that new filing systems were a key element of modern systematic management.

Insurance companies were among the most eager adopters of information processing technologies. They collected and stored information about each of their policyholders, and calculated estimates of life expectancy to ensure that they would be able to cover the costs of settling claims. Because it was easier to mechanize standardized, numerical measures of health than a doctor's com-

New information processing schemes changed all sorts of businesses, even racetrack gambling. Traditionally, bettors placed their bets with a bookie, who gave them whatever odds he thought fair. The marketplace enforced "fairness": the bettor could always go to another bookie if the odds were better.

In the late nineteenth century, racetracks developed an alternative: pari-mutuel betting. In pari-mutuel betting, the racetrack kept track of the amounts wagered on each horse and figured out the odds based on those amounts. This system required a lot of calculation, and

in the 1930s racetracks adopted new information processing technology to keep track of bets. Totalisator, or "tote" boards, continuously added the bets, calculated odds, and displayed them to bettors. These machines, based on telephone–switching technology, meant faster processing

and more honest operations. But many bettors thought that they had made gambling impersonal — that they had taken some of the excitement and some of the character out of it, made it too mathematical. Bookies kept a lot of their business.

In 1907 the Metropolitan Life Insurance Company built a new office building in New York City to house its office bureaucracy. The Metropolitan used every up-to-date technology. Most important of all was the filing system: some 20,000 file boxes held 20 million insurance applications, and there were 61 employees who did nothing but maintain these files. Also on file were 700,000 accounting books and 500,000 death certificates.

The Wooton desk, patented in 1874, represents the information processing needs of a small office. It is a one-man office, with room enough for one person to read, write, and file papers.

Office reformers hated desks like this, which seemed to encourage the hoarding of information. Frank Gilbreth, one of the most famous of the scientific managers, urged the businesses that hired him to do away with the desks. "You've got lots of stuff filed away in the pigeonholes that you can't find when you want it, and no one else can find it when you are away from the office. Clean it all out and empty the drawers, too. File it away in an information bureau, where anyone who needs it can get it when he needs it."

ments, insurance companies provided doctors with questionnaires to standardize examinations. They wanted to be able to use numbers — measurements — to describe an applicant's health, and so they were among the first to promote the use of instruments to analyze urine and measure height, weight, vision, blood pressure, and lung capacity. These numerical measures may not have been better predictors of health than the careful observations of a trained physician, but insurance companies were convinced of the value of numerical standards — perhaps because the technology to calculate based on numbers was available. Life insurance companies used this information not only to keep track of information about individuals, but also to calculate actuarial statistics that told them the probabilities of having to pay off on any particular person, and so allowed them to set rates. Actuaries eagerly adopted new calculating machines.

Whatever the business — transportation, manufacturing, marketing, or insurance — the key place where information was processed and communicated was the office. As the advantages of managerial control became clear, offices became larger and more structured. In 1900 there were about 900,000 clerical workers and 1.7 million managers in the United States. By 1920 there were some 3.4 million clerical workers — two thirds of them women — and 2.8 million

In 1869 Elizur Wright invented the "arithmeter" — a type of cylindrical slide rule — to speed up the more than 250,000 calculations per year his actuarial work required. Walter Wright, Elizur's son and first actuary of the New England Mutual Life Insurance Company, is shown using the machine in 1890.

Sears, Roebuck was the biggest retailer in the United States. In 1913, 10,000 men and women worked in Sears's Chicago plant. Each day they shipped 40,000 orders and answered as many as 90,000 letters. In that year, Sears shipped 26 million catalogs. This picture shows the data entry department, where 500 young women worked at special typewriter billing machines. They separated the items on the customer's order and wrote tickets for each of the different merchandise departments.

managers, 93 percent of them men. (Between 1870 and 1940 the fraction of Americans in clerical jobs jumped from 1 percent to 10 percent.) New information processing technology was put to use both in the office and in the field, changing the nature of the work that went on there.

Information processing techniques also found their way into the marketplace as a whole. Some businessmen used advances in communications and information processing in their attempts to dominate their marketplace. Trusts — several firms in one industry under the control of a single holding company — tried to control markets and prevent competition. Trade associations, while not going as far as trusts, distributed information about prices and production and set standards to help member firms. Manufacturers' associations regulated

The American Railway Association set standards to improve the flow of information among railroads. Standard interchange rules and standard procedures for the movements of trains, for example, made it easier for through-trains to proceed. Standard hazardous materials warning signs like this one helped improve safety; everyone could easily recognize the warning.

Stock exchanges are information processing machines, determining stock prices based on buyers' and sellers' beliefs about the value of businesses. By facilitating the buying and selling of stock — the trading of not only shares but also information about the companies represented by those shares — it lowered the cost of information, and thus increased the overall efficiency of the economy.

To do this, stock exchanges had to process huge amounts of information. In 1928 the New York Stock Exchange handled more than 3 million shares on a typical day, about 600 transactions per hour. The men and women who worked at the exchange used the latest communications and information processing systems to keep up with the paperwork.

markets. Sometimes this increased efficiency and safety and lowered prices; sometimes the exchange of information restricted entry into the market by smaller firms, and allowed trusts and associations to collude to raise prices.

The concentration of economic power in trusts, large firms, and trade associations provoked public outrage. As long as businesses had all the facts, they had the upper hand. To counteract their power, government agencies, including the Federal Trade Commission and the Interstate Commerce Commission, began to gather information, too. Information was power, and so the government got into the business of collecting data on a large scale. "Facts, and the exact expression of them, are what we seem to desire," one writer asserted in 1901.

"Would we convince the average American? It is best done by figures."[11] Information became essential not only to business but to government, too. Whoever had the best information could control the marketplace, or so it seemed.

TOWARD THE COMPUTER

The U.S. government gathered more facts than anyone else. By the 1880 Census, there had been so many questions added to the forms — over two hundred subjects were inquired into — that it took eight years to process and publish the data. There were even more questions on the 1890 Census, and so the Census Bureau redoubled its efforts to develop new information processing technology. After considering proposals that used color-coded ink on paper slips or color-coded cards, the Bureau of the Census selected new equipment designed by Herman Hollerith.

Hollerith was a young engineer who had worked at the Census Bureau in 1879, and then had gone on to other jobs, working on improved railroad brakes and as a patent examiner. But he continued to think about the Census Bureau's problems. In 1884 he applied for a patent on new technology for compiling statistics, and in the late 1880s received contracts from several states to use his machine to compile mortality statistics.

Hollerith's breakthrough was a punch card system that represented each person on a separate card. A hole punched in a particular place on the card signified a fact about an individual. An electric reader counted similar characteristics. Hollerith's machine could count the holes representing a particular group — say, people born in Norway — and it could also sort the cards so that the number of, say, Norwegian-born Americans over fifty years of age could be counted. The Census Bureau used ninety-six Hollerith machines to tabulate information on 80,000 people a day. The machine count was faster than the old system, but more expensive.

Large businesses quickly adopted punch card systems to automate some of their bookkeeping and filing. *Engineering,* a British journal, noted in 1902 that manual bookkeeping "would need the personal attention of someone of marked ability." "But when the data are punched on cards," the article continued, "the job can be put in the hands of a girl."[12] The new machines made the job not only easier but also faster, allowing ever more data to be processed.

Insurance companies found the new machines ideal: the Aetna Life and Casualty Company used Hollerith machines to compile mortality data

The first step in using the Hollerith machine was punching the cards (upper right). The cards were counted by placing them in a press and lowering the top of the press; where there were holes, pins descended into small cups of mercury, making an electrical contact and moving a counter (center). Tabulating machines had a similar sort of press, but this one sent an electrical signal to open the proper door in a card-holding device. The operator dropped the card in the open slot (upper left).

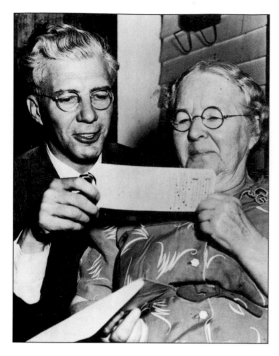

Social Security checks, starting with this first one in 1940, were punch cards.

starting in 1910. Railroads also began to use the machines in the early twentieth century. Using language that we wouldn't be surprised to find in a modern-day report on computerization, one railroad manager wrote in 1926: "Punch card systems are a proved means of economically producing facts and figures vital to operating a railroad intelligently, from which business records can be quickly and accurately classified and presented to the executives at the time they are needed in the form best suited to enable action."[13]

The U.S. government found an increasing number of uses for the machines. The army used hundreds of punch card machines during World War I to keep inventory and medical and psychological records. The War Industries Board, which controlled much of the economy during the war, did its accounting on them. Fifteen years later, New Dealers, drawing on the successful World War I experience of mobilizing and directing the economy, put punch card machinery to wide use.

By far the largest information processing job undertaken before World War II was the implementation of Social Security, in 1935. Information about the earnings of 26 million wage earners and the wages paid by 3 million employers was gathered, stored, and processed. The Social Security Administration used hundreds of pieces of punch card equipment. Even the checks, sent out starting in 1937, were punched cards.

Scientists found ways to extend punch card machines to make them more useful. Early Hollerith machines could just sort and count; by the 1930s advanced versions could do mathematical calculations — multiplication and even integration of differential equations — and complex tabulations in response to programs. Wallace Eckert's Watson Astronomical Computing Laboratory at Columbia University had the most advanced punch card machines. Eckert designed a "mechanical programmer" to control these machines as a unit. (See SOFTWARE.) He made the punch card machines sing. Scientists at Columbia used punch cards for calculations in astronomy as well as statistics, psychology, and engineering.

Punch card machines were one line of technology that would prefigure the modern computer. Machines built by scientists and engineers frustrated by the complexity of the calculations their work required were a second line. In the late 1920s and 1930s several scientists built calculating machines designed to solve specific problems. (Many of these machines were programmable; see SOFTWARE.) The machines made important technical contributions to what would become the main line of electronic computing. Just as important, they demonstrated the possibilities and potentials of rapid, programmable computation.

In 1927 Vannevar Bush, an MIT electrical engineer, invented the differential analyzer, a mechanical device to solve the complex equations that represented electrical power systems. Power grids were among the most complicated technical systems of the early twentieth century, and as they expanded, the mathematical tools engineers used to analyze them and predict their behavior lagged behind. The problems became too hard for slide rules, mathematical tables, and even miniature working models. It could take months to solve just one equation. The differential analyzer, an analog computer, could solve any problem that could be reduced to differential equations — everything from atomic structure to ballistics. About twenty of these large machines, expensive and complicated electromechanical devices, were built.

Howard Aiken, a physics instructor at Harvard University, took a different approach with his 1937 calculating machine. He connected a group of IBM accounting machines so that they could be directed by a strip of punched paper tape. His goal was to solve nonlinear differential equations. Under Aiken's direction IBM built the Automatic Sequence Controlled Calculator, popularly known as the Harvard Mark I. This machine was enormous: fifty-one feet long, eight feet high, and two feet deep, with some 750,000 parts. Almost as soon as the Mark I went into operation in May 1944, the navy put it to work calculating ballistics tables.

George Stibitz, an employee of Bell Laboratories, created a series of computers using electromagnetic telephone relays starting in 1937. Stibitz called his first device, which could add two binary digits together, the Model K, because he built it on his kitchen table. Bell Labs supported Stibitz's next model, which could carry out computations with complex numbers, calculations of the sort that frequently arise in telephone signal problems. (Claude Shannon, in his MIT master's thesis, had just shown that Boolean algebra could be used to design electrical switching circuits and that, vice versa, electrical switching circuits could perform Boolean operations: adding and subtracting binary information, performing logical comparisons, and storing numbers.) This machine, called the Complex Number Calculator, used some 450 telephone relays and ten telephone exchange crossbar switches, and could add, subtract, multiply, and divide complex numbers. It worked well, and was used from 1940 to 1949. Bell Laboratories used the Stibitz machine as the basis for several computers built for the military during World War II.

At about the same time Stibitz was building his machines, Konrad Zuse,

ANALOG AND DIGITAL

There are two basic sorts of calculating or computing devices. Analog devices use a continuous motion to represent some continuously varying value. Numbers might be stored as voltages, or as the turning of a wheel. A slide rule is an analog calculator. Digital devices, on the other hand, represent continuously varying values by their numerical equivalent. Most digital computers use a binary number system to represent values.

The differential analyzer at MIT, used to solve engineering and mathematical problems. The differential analyzer was an analog machine, representing numbers by the amount of rotation of a shaft. Gears served to multiply numbers. Differential gears did addition and subtraction. Integrators used the rotation of a sphere on a disk to sum up the area under the graph of a mathematical function.

The Harvard Mark I was the ultimate mechanical calculating machine. Designed using punch card technology, it used paper tape to enter instructions, punch cards to supply data, a set of seventy-two relay circuits that activated clutches to turn the wheels that carried out calculations, and electric typewriters to print results. It was used from 1944 until 1959. The people who worked on it didn't call it the Mark I, but "Bessy the Bessel engine." (The machine's specialty after the war was computing a type of mathematical equation called a Bessel function.)

a German aircraft engineer, was also devising a series of computing machines. His Z1, completed in 1938, used a system of sliding rods controlled by instructions punched on tape to perform binary arithmetic. Zuse's Z2 machine used electromechanical relays. His Z3 and Z4 machines were similar but larger. Zuse intended his machines for use in aircraft design, but he never received much support for them. They remained unknown to the engineers building computers in the United States and England in the 1940s.

Between 1939 and 1942 Iowa State College physics professor John V. Atanasoff and his graduate student Clifford Berry built a special-purpose electronic computer designed to solve systems of simultaneous equations of the sort found in physics problems. Solving these problems required many calculations, and so Atanasoff, after considering mechanical systems, turned to electronics, which would be faster. His computer (called the Atanasoff-Berry Computer, or ABC) used some 300 vacuum tubes as well as logic circuits, card readers to input data, and memory drums that stored information as electrical charges. Although never fully operational, it was a digital binary machine which demonstrated many principles of electronic digital computers, including electronic vacuum tube logic and regenerative memories. It was a single-purpose, not a general-purpose, computer. In 1973 the judge in the patent case that determined who invented the computer declared that the automatic electronic digital computer was derived from the ABC.[14] That conclusion seems incorrect; the ABC was not automatic. But the ABC was important, for it helped lead to the ENIAC, which was automatic, and to which most later computers can trace their heritage.

When World War II began, many of the engineers who had worked on these machines designed larger, more complex machines for the war effort. The machines built for the war would lead directly to the modern computer. World War II mobilized American science as never before. Scientists and engineers working as part of the crash project to develop radar laid the groundwork for solid-state electronics. (On the wartime effort in electronics, see RADIO.) Scientists working on the atomic bomb developed new calculating techniques. Scientists working on antiaircraft gun controls made important breakthroughs in automatic feedback devices. And scientists and engineers working on computing ballistics tables built machines that would lead directly to the computer.

The most important experiment in digital computation to come out of the war was the ENIAC, a machine designed to produce ballistics tables for artillery. In 1943 the U.S. Army's Ballistics Research Laboratory funded a proposal by the Moore School of the University of Pennsylvania for a general-purpose digital electronic computer. A team directed by John W. Mauchly and J. Presper Eckert designed and built ENIAC, the Electrical Numerical Integrator and Com-

George Stibitz built his Model K binary adder in 1937 out of spare telephone exchange parts. He called it the Model K because he built it in his kitchen. (This is a replica of the original.)

puter. Both Eckert and Mauchly had been frustrated by what they called "the calculator problem" — that science and engineering theory had become so difficult that it couldn't be applied because it required too much calculation — and jumped at the chance to build a general-purpose calculator.[15] The way to make calculations faster, Eckert decided, was to use electronic components (vacuum tubes, switched on and off at some 100,000 pulses per second) instead of mechanical or electromechanical components. Eckert remembered thinking, "Wires are cheaper than shafts and ball bearings and gears and things, and we ought to be sending [electronic] pulses" instead of using mechanical connections.[16] "The electronic computor [*sic*]," Mauchly wrote in a memo proposing the project, is "in every sense the electrical analogue of the mechanical adding, multiplying and dividing machines which are now manufactured for ordinary arithmetic purposes."[17] The army supported the project (it would cost some $500,000), and Mauchly, Eckert, and a team of engineers started work on the machine.

ENIAC was based on what Mauchly had learned from working on Bush's differential analyzer, what he saw in a visit to and correspondence with Atanasoff, and, more generally, on the organization of contemporary tabulating and calculating machines. It was completed in the fall of 1945, after the war had ended. Though originally intended to compute the paths of artillery shells, the machine was general purpose by design; it could solve all sorts of computational problems in fields such as nuclear physics, aerodynamics, and weather prediction. It was a general-purpose digital computer, programmable using plug wires and switches. The designers of the ENIAC would go on, after the war, to design and build programmable electronic digital computers.

Less is known about a second line of calculating machines developed during the war. Code breaking was, and is, a highly secretive business. It was also

The ENIAC was an enormous machine, thirty feet by fifty feet. It used some 18,000 vacuum tubes, 1,500 relays, had 6,000 switches, and hundreds of plugwires used for programming. It consumed 174,000 watts of power and weighed thirty tons. But it worked. ENIAC could compute 1,000 times faster than any existing device, adding 5,000 ten-digit numbers in one second.

Code-breaking bombes in a U.S. Naval Security Group Command building in Washington, D.C., during World War II. The women in this room ran some 120 bombes, each of which could simulate sixteen four-rotor "enigmas," the German coding devices. The bombes ran through the possible combinations of rotors, finding likely ones which were then sent to code breakers to try out. They could do this quickly enough to break the code before its daily change.

critically important to the Allied war effort. The German armed forces, especially the submarine fleet, depended on open radio communication for coordination. The Germans encoded messages with a sophisticated cipher machine called Enigma that could generate more than 100 trillion different cipher combinations. Because Enigma settings were changed regularly, the Germans were certain that the Allies could not break the code in time for any intercepted messages to be useful.

A group of Polish mathematicians devised a way of deciphering the code, and two teams of mathematicians and engineers, one in England and one in the United States, developed electromechanical systems to break the code quickly enough to be useful. In England a team under the leadership of T. H. Flowers, and advised by Alan Turing, developed a code-breaking machine called the Colossus. In the United States, the Naval Security Group developed machines called Bombes, based on the British design. (The name came from the Polish *bombas*, since the original mechanical machines ticked like bombs.) These machines were tours de force of electrical and mechanical engineering and mathematics. They proved essential to winning the war. But they remained classified after the war, and thus had less effect on the later development of computers than the better known ENIAC.

Other engineers and scientists worked on calculating and electronics problems during the war, too. Work on the atomic bomb, on radar and radar countermeasures, on aircraft simulators, and on antiaircraft-gun pointing mechanisms brought about breakthroughs in electronics and computation. After the war some of the engineers and scientists who had worked on these projects continued to work on computing technologies, developing the modern digital computer. That story is told in COMPUTERS.

FOR FURTHER READING

There are several excellent histories of computing machines that cover the period before computers. William Aspray, ed., *Computing before Computers* (1990), is excellent for the period before World War II. More technical is Michael R. Williams, *A History of Computing Technology* (1985), which covers all sorts of computers from early number systems to the IBM System/360. See also Stan Augarten, *Bit by Bit: An Illustrated History of Computers* (1984); Charles Eames and Ray Eames, *A Computer Perspective* (1973); Jon Palfremun and Doron Swade, *The Dream Machine: Exploring the Computer Age* (1992), based on the public television series that in the United States was called "The Machine That Changed the World"; and *Pictorial History of Digital Computing from the Smithsonian Institution* by Peggy Aldrich Kidwell and Paul Ceruzzi (1994), which describes many of the objects in the Smithsonian collections, giving not only information about their inventors and users but also details about how they work. The business of making and selling computing machines is detailed in James W. Cortada, *Before the Computer: IBM, Burroughs, and the Industry They Created, 1956–1965* (1993).

The second part of this chapter is based on the ideas outlined in Alfred Chandler, *The Visible Hand: The Management Revolution in American Business* (1977). His work has been extended to include more about the way in which information affected the structure of the business in JoAnne Yates, *Control through Communication: The Rise of System in American Management* (1989); and James R. Beniger, *The Control Revolution: Technological and Economic Origins of the Information Society* (1986).

On the technologies that led up to computers, see Paul Ceruzzi, *Reckoners: The Prehistory of the Digital Computer: From Relays to the Stored Program Concept, 1935–1945* (1983); and Herman H. Goldstine, *The Computer from Pascal to Von Neumann* (1972). The story of the punch card machine and its adoption is told in Geoffrey D. Austrian, *Herman Hollerith: Forgotten Giant of Information Processing* (1982). On Charles Babbage, the most interesting material is gathered in Philip Morrison and Emily Morrison, eds., *Charles Babbage and His Calculating Engines: Selected Writings by Charles Babbage and Others* (1961). See also the books in COMPUTERS; many include chapters on computing before computers.

The ways in which computing machines were put to use is found mostly in the journal literature. The best source on process control devices is Stuart Bennett, "'The Industrial Instrument — Master of Industry, Servant of Management': Automatic Control in the Process Industries," *Technology and Culture* (January 1991): 69–81. On the uses of calculating machines in science, see Peggy Aldrich Kidwell, "American Scientists and Calculating Machines — From Novelty to Commonplace," *Annals of the History of Computing*, 12, no. 1 (1990): 31–40. On the use of calculating machines in business, see Arthur L. Norberg, "High-Technology Calculation in the Early Twentieth Century: Punched Card Machinery in Business and Government," *Technology and Culture* (October 1990): 753–779.

NOTES

1. *An Interview with the Father of the Calculating Machine* (1919), pp. 7–8.

2. Jean Steinman, *Pascal* (1962), p. 32; quoted in Stan Augarten, *Bit by Bit: An Illustrated History of Computers* (1984), p. 28.

3. L. F. Menabrea, "Sketch of the Analytical Engine Invented by Charles Babbage"; reprinted in Philip Morrison and Emily Morrison, eds., *Charles Babbage and His Calculating Engines: Selected Writings by Charles Babbage and Others* (1961), p. 244.

4. Frederick Barnard, *Reports of Commissioners to Paris Universal Exposition;* quoted in Peggy Aldrich Kidwell, "American Scientists and Calculating Machines — From Novelty to Commonplace," *Annals of the History of Computing*, 12, no. 1 (1990): 33.

5. Charles Babbage, *Passages from the Life of a Philosopher;* reprinted in Morrison and Morrison, *Charles Babbage and His Calculating Engines*, p. 56.

6. Daniel J. McCallum, "Superintendent's Report," in *Annual Report of the New York and Erie Railroad Company for 1855 (1856);* reprinted in Alfred D. Chandler, Jr. and Richard S. Tedlow, *Coming of Managerial Capitalism: A Casebook on the History of American Economic Institutions* (1985), p. 202.

7. U.S. Department of Commerce, *Report of Committee on Airport Traffic Control* (1933), p. 4.

8. U.S. Department of Commerce, *The Federal Airways System* (1937), p. 16.

9. Frederick Winslow Taylor, *Principles of Scientific Management* (1911); quoted in James R. Beniger, *The Control Revolution: Technological and Economic Origins of the Information Society* (1986), p. 294.

10. David W. Duffield, comp., *Progressive Indexing and Filing for Schools* (1926), p. 12; quoted in JoAnne Yates, *Control through Communication: The Rise of System in American Management* (1989), p. 57.

11. Eugene White; quoted in Neil Harris, *The Land of Contrasts, 1880–1901* (1970), p. 9.

12. "The Mechanical Accountant," *Engineering,* December 26, 1902, pp. 840–841; quoted in Charles Eames and Ray Eames, *A Computer Perspective* (1973), p. 48.

13. "Railway Accounting with Punch Cards," *Railway Review,* September 4, 1926, pp.

353–354; quoted in Arthur L. Norberg, "Punched Card Machinery in Business and Government," *Technology and Culture* (October 1990): 766–767.

14. See Augarten, *Bit by Bit,* p. 223.

15. David Allison, interview with J. Presper Eckert, Smithsonian Institution Archives, Washington, D.C.

16. Allison, interview with Eckert.

17. Quoted in Augarten, *Bit by Bit,* p. 111.

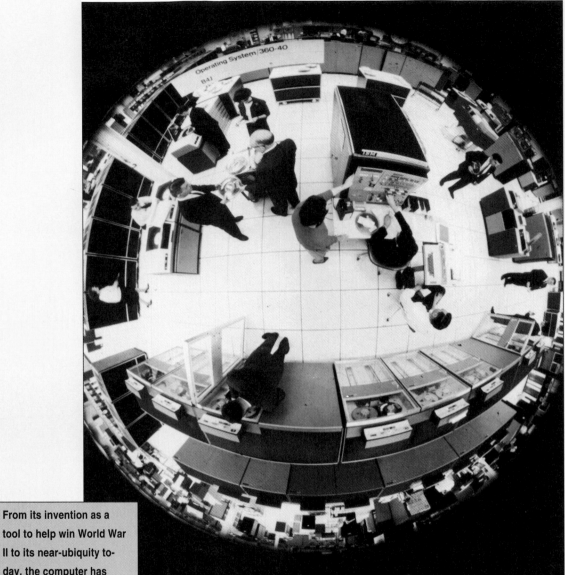

From its invention as a tool to help win World War II to its near-ubiquity today, the computer has been the focus of an incredible amount of research, development, and investment. Computers have become smaller, faster, cheaper, more convenient, and more powerful. They have been put to use in every part of the economy — indeed, in almost every part of our lives.

I N F O R M A T I O N
C O M P U T E R S

IN 1983 MARSHAL NIKOLAI OGARKOV, CHIEF OF THE
Soviet General Staff, told *New York Times* reporter Leslie Gelb that Russia would lose the cold war. He blamed it on the computer. Modern military power, he told Gelb, is based on technology, modern technology
is based on computers, and the Soviets lagged far behind the United
States in computers. Moreover, he said, the Russians would not be able to catch
up. The Soviet government was afraid to allow the use of computers to become
widespread, for fear that they would encourage a freer exchange of information,
and that an increased flow of information would help to undermine the state. In
the United States, by contrast, computers were everywhere, not only in military
systems but in offices, homes, and schools. Marshal Ogarkov thought that this
would give the United States an unbeatable superiority in any future war.

The story expresses well the ubiquity of computers and, even more, the
range of uses — science, entertainment, business, as well as military — their malleable nature allows. The freedom of communications they encourage, or permit, is a threat to a closed society such as the former Soviet Union, but they have
become a military necessity, increasing the effectiveness of hierarchical command
and control. Born in research during World War II, used first in war, then in
business, then in daily life, computers have become the defining technology of
the second half of the twentieth century. By 1992 there were some 70 million
computers in use in the United States, in every business, every field of science
and medicine, almost every aspect of life.

AFTER THE WAR

During World War II the military financed several high-speed calculating projects, including ENIAC, at the University of Pennsylvania, used by the
army for ballistics calculations, and the navy-supported Bombe, a code-breaking
machine. These machines, and others designed for scientific calculations before
and during the war, laid the technological basis for a new Computer Age. The
managerial style of American business would provide the social foundation for
the new machines. (See BEFORE COMPUTERS.)

311

The design John von Neumann outlined in his *First Draft of a Report on the EDVAC* (1945). The memory unit stored both data and instructions. The control unit, following the instructions in the memory, moved data between the arithmetic unit and the memory, and controlled the input and output.

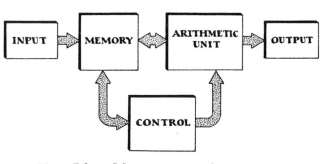

THE VON NEUMANN COMPUTER

At first computers were thought of as useful only for solving complicated mathematical problems, not as business machines; few of the computer's inventors thought that there would be a market for more than perhaps a dozen computers in all. But the military had learned the value of rapid calculation and was eager to continue supporting the development of faster computers. One of ENIAC's first calculations after its completion in late 1945 was a preliminary study to determine whether a hydrogen bomb was possible. Half a million punch cards of data were shipped to Philadelphia, and the ENIAC chewed away at them for almost six weeks before coming up with the answer that, yes, the bomb was not physically impossible — but there were flaws in the proposed design. Stanislaw Ulam, who was helping to design the bomb, recalled the reaction among the scientists at Los Alamos: "One could hardly exaggerate the psychological importance of this work and the influence of these results . . . on people in the Los Alamos laboratory. . . . I well remember the spirit of exploration, of belief in the possibility of getting trustworthy answers in the future . . . because of the existence of computing machines."[1]

John von Neumann, a Princeton mathematician, became the guiding spirit of the first generation of computers. Von Neumann had become, during the war, the country's most knowledgeable authority on computing. He had been an adviser to the scientists working on the atomic bomb, ballistics calculations, and operations research. He was also familiar with the work carried out by George Stibitz at Bell Laboratories, by the Astronomical Computing Bureau at Columbia University, and by Howard Aiken at Harvard. He was convinced of the enormous potential of computers, and he was eager to promote further research, design, and use. The basic design of postwar computers came out of his theories about how computers ought to work.

In 1946 von Neumann helped organize a groundbreaking series of lectures, "Theory and Techniques for Design of Electronic Digital Computers," at the Moore School of the University of Pennsylvania. The lecturers included Howard Aiken, J. Presper Eckert, Herman Goldstine, John Mauchly, and George Stibitz, as well as von Neumann — just about every expert in the field. Twenty organizations, including universities, private companies, and government agencies, sent representatives. Teachers and students at these lectures went on to become leading computer designers.

One of the key documents at these lectures was von Neumann's *First Draft of a Report on the EDVAC,* which he wrote (after discussion with Eckert, Mauchly, and Goldstine) in the first half of 1945. In it he outlined what would become the basic structure of digital computers, a structure that would serve as the model for most of the computers to follow. A computer, he wrote, should have five units:

- an arithmetic unit, to do calculations
- a central control unit, to tell the other parts what to do and when to do it
- a memory unit, to store both data and instructions — the so-called 'stored program technique,' which makes it possible for the computer to act on its instructions as data, an important breakthrough that made the machine much more flexible
- an input unit, for receiving instructions and data
- an output unit, to present results

The computer von Neumann outlined in this document would be a general-purpose machine, capable of solving any solvable problem. (See SOFTWARE.)

The *First Draft* caused hard feelings at the Moore School. Eckert and Mauchly thought von Neumann was claiming credit for their work, and feared that his publication would mean they would be unable to patent their ideas. (They were already fighting with the Moore School over patent rights.) The Moore School team broke up, and the principals, and many of the participants in the lecture series, began building their own computers.

By the late 1940s there were three main streams of computer development under way. Von Neumann was at work on his own machine, modified from the principles outlined in his report to allow some parallel processing — that is, the computer could work on several parts of a problem at one time. At MIT, Jay W. Forrester was designing a computer named Whirlwind that would operate in real time. And several computers based directly on the *First Draft* were under construction. Most of these projects were supported by the U.S. government, which by 1950 was spending about $17 million a year on computer research and development for improved guidance systems and atomic bombs, and an unknown additional amount on computers for electronic spying and code breaking. This funding propelled American leadership in the computer field.

Von Neumann's IAS computer (named after the Institute for Advanced Study in Princeton, where he had returned after the war) was optimized for scientific calculation. Completed in 1952 at a cost of several hundred thousand dollars, the IAS used 2,300 miniature vacuum tubes. It was built to do the massive calculations needed in meteorology, astronomy, hydrodynamics, and other fields of science, as well as the computation for designing atomic weapons, including the first hydrogen bomb. (Its first problem, for Los Alamos, took sixty days, twenty-four hours a day, to solve!) Numerical computation turned out to be of great value to many fields where the problems were too complex to be answered simply by solving equations. The existence of computers — and therefore of the possibility of carrying out lots of calculations quickly — opened up new fields to mathematical analysis.

The IAS, like most early computers, received its funding from the military and the Atomic Energy Commission, but few aspects of its design were classified. The project team issued a series of reports describing the logical design and also circulated working drawings. Computers based on the IAS machine were built at seventeen other research centers in the United States and in several other countries. These included the Johnniac, built at the Rand Corporation, the MANIAC at Los Alamos, and the ILLIAC at the University of Illinois. IBM based its first general-purpose computer, the 701 Defense Calculator, on the IAS.

While IAS-type machines dominated the field of scientific computers, which require fast processing for handling millions of calculations — "number crunching" — other approaches to computer design also emerged in the early 1950s as scientists worked to develop computers for a range of purposes. Whirlwind, built at MIT between 1945 and 1953, represented a different approach. Originally designed for use as an aircraft flight simulator for training pilots, it had to operate extremely quickly and process events in real time, as they happened. The first plans for Whirlwind called for it to be an analog computer; no one thought that digital computers could be made fast enough to operate in real time. But Jay Forrester, the chief engineer, learned about the EDVAC and decided to make his computer a stored-program, general-purpose digital computer. The Office of Naval Research supported Whirlwind, at a cost of about $1 million a year.

Whirlwind proved useful for all sorts of problems. In its first year it was used to study industrial production problems and oil reservoir depletion, to design magnetic storage systems, and to program digitally controlled machine tools. Whirlwind was even bigger than the ENIAC. At first it used electrostatic storage tubes like those in the IAS, but soon it added magnetic drum storage and a new invention, magnetic core memory. (Core memories store each digit — or bit — of a binary number in a tiny doughnut-shaped ring as a magnetic charge.

The Institute for Advanced Study computer broke new ground in computer design. The most powerful computer of its time, it was used mainly for scientific and hydrogen bomb research. It was one of the most elegantly designed of the early computers.

Core storage could be accessed quickly and was used for short-term storage.) Whirlwind used a cathode-ray tube (like a TV screen) for output and had many ways of receiving input.

In 1949, as the cold war heated up, Whirlwind was given a new mission, and a new sponsor. The air force decided that Whirlwind would be the prototype for a new system that would provide computerized electronic defense against the threat of Russian bombers armed with nuclear weapons. SAGE, as the new system was named (it stood for Semi-Automatic Ground Environment), would coordinate radar stations and direct airplanes to intercept incoming planes. SAGE consisted of twenty-three "direction centers," each with a SAGE computer that could track as many as 400 airplanes (it distinguished enemy planes from friendly ones by keeping track of flight plans).

Whirlwind and SAGE were breakthrough computers in almost every way. The SAGE computer used some 55,000 tubes and weighed 250 tons. SAGE had to handle many different tasks at the same time, sharing central processor time among them. It gathered information over telephone lines from as many as one hundred radar and observation stations, processing it and displaying it on some fifty cathode-ray tube screens. The "direction centers" were also linked by telephone lines. SAGE was an enormous project, requiring some six years of development and 7,000 person-years of programming. It cost some $61 billion. The phone bill alone was enormous, millions of dollars each month. SAGE represented not only new technology but a new vision of what military defense might be. This was the first time that a military strategy depended on a computer. SAGE, writes Paul Edwards, was "more than a weapons system: it was a dream, a myth, a metaphor for total defense."[2]

The third stream of computer development was based more directly on von Neumann's *First Draft*. The Manchester Mark I, at Manchester University in England, also drew on the work that had been done on the Colossus code-breaking machine. The first practical machine of this sort was the EDSAC (Elec-

SAGE operators communicated with the computer using a cathode-ray tube. They saw maps, like radar maps, on the screen; touching a point on the screen with a light pen could designate that aircraft as a target.

tronic Delay Storage Automatic Computer), in England, designed by Maurice Wilkes, and completed in June 1949. The EDVAC itself was completed at the University of Pennsylvania in 1952, and used at the Aberdeen Proving Grounds.

The engineers who had built the ENIAC at the University of Pennsylvania went into business for themselves, signing contracts with the Bureau of the Census and the National Bureau of Standards, and establishing the Eckert-Mauchly Computer Corporation in 1948. (One of the investors was American Totalisator, which owned the machines used to record betting and calculate odds at racetracks. The company, fearing that electronic tote machines might replace its electrical ones, decided to invest in the new technology!) The new firm's first computer was the BINAC (Binary Automatic Computer), designed for the Northrop Aircraft Company, and completed in late 1949. The BINAC was too small and slow to be of much use, but it served important experimental and marketing purposes, and helped make possible the firm's next computer, UNIVAC.

The UNIVAC I (the name stood for Universal Automatic Computer) was delivered to the Census Bureau in 1951. It weighed some 16,000 pounds, used 5,000 vacuum tubes, and could perform about 1,000 calculations per second. It was the first American commercial computer, as well as the first computer designed for business use. (Business computers like the UNIVAC processed data more slowly than the IAS-type machines, but were designed for fast input and output.) The first few sales were to government agencies, the A. C. Nielsen Company, and the Prudential Insurance Company. The first UNIVAC for business applications was installed at the General Electric Appliance Division, to do payroll, in 1954. By 1957 Remington-Rand (which had purchased the Eckert-Mauchly Computer Corporation in 1950) had sold forty-six machines.

Some computer pioneers thought it unlikely that computers, designed by mathematicians and for mathematicians, would be useful for business. Howard Aiken, the designer of the Mark I, wrote in 1956: "If it should ever turn out that the basic logics of a machine designed for the numerical solution of differential equations coincide with the logics of a machine intended to make bills for a department store, I would regard this as the most amazing coincidence I have ever encountered."[3] But the machine architecture von Neumann had designed was general purpose enough so that in fact the same machine could do both mathematics and department store billing. The key was the stored-program principle, high-speed input and output devices, especially punch cards, and the hundred-year history of business information processing. Computers fit well into the manual systems of billing, record keeping, and information processing that department stores and most other large businesses were already using. (See BEFORE COMPUTERS.)

By 1950 computers were becoming widely known. The first popular book on computers, Edmund C. Berkeley's *Giant Brains, or Machines That Think,* was published in 1949. Although Berkeley never used the word *computer,* preferring "mechanical brain," he recognized the broad interest in the machines. His book starts: "Recently there has been a good deal of news about strange giant machines that can handle information with vast speed and skill." The UNIVAC was the first computer to gain wide publicity, when it was featured on television predicting the outcome of the 1952 presidential election. "UNIVAC" became a generic term; it came to mean, to many people, "computer."

In the early 1950s many companies thought that there might be money to be made by selling computers to business. Not many computers: even in 1950 the total market seemed likely to be no larger than a few hundred machines. Approximately eighty companies entered the computer business in the early years. In 1955 commercial users purchased some 150 computers. Those selling computers included new firms such as the Eckert-Mauchly Computer Company; business equipment manufacturers such as Remington Rand; defense companies such as Bendix Aviation Corporation; and electronics companies such as General Electric.

Although IBM was late to enter the commercial computer market, it rapidly took the lead. Thomas Watson, Sr., president of the company, thought that computers would merely cut into the company's thriving punch card business, and so the company produced its first computer only when asked to do so by the Defense Department in 1951. The Defense Calculator, renamed the IBM 701 for marketing as a commercial product, rented for $15,000 a month. IBM produced nineteen of them. Twelve were delivered to corporations — eight went to aircraft manufacturers — four to government agencies, and three to universities.

In 1953 IBM announced its 650 computer, which soon became the most popular medium-sized computer in America. Rental cost was around

The IBM 650 was the first computer manufactured in large enough numbers to require organized production lines. More than 1,500 were sold between 1953 and 1968.

$3,000 a month. Users liked the 650's dependability, variety of programs, error-checking ability, and handling of input and output. The IBM 650 used about 500 vacuum tubes in its central processing unit. Because the IBM 650 was rented at deep discounts to universities, it became the machine around which the new discipline of computer science coalesced. By 1960 IBM dominated the computer market.

The keys to increased business use were lower prices and increased reliability. These came about as the technology of the computer improved, and, in particular, as tubes were replaced by transistors. The first generation of computers used tubes, their sockets linked together with hand-soldered wires. Transistors, invented at Bell Laboratories in 1947, found wide use in computers in the late 1950s. In 1963 computers used some $42 million of transistors, about one sixth of all transistors bought that year. (The transistor story is told in RADIO.)

In 1962 IBM decided to produce a computer that would appeal to both business users and scientists, and that would be usable over a broad range of computing needs. The System/360 family of computers, a series of six computers of different sizes, first put on sale in 1964, cost IBM over $5 billion to bring to market, including $500 million in research and development. It set a new standard for computing. The 360's sales were a surprise to everyone: over 1,000 a month were ordered.

These big IBM machines were used mostly in large businesses and government agencies, processing paperwork. The System/360 ensured IBM's leadership in the computer business, and set the style of business programming for years to come. It was joined by competitive families of machines from Honeywell, Burroughs, and a few other companies, and by "plug compatible" computers — ones that worked just like the IBM 360. Even Riad, a Russian company, made plug-compatible 360s.

DO NOT FOLD, SPINDLE, OR MUTILATE

By the early 1960s most large businesses, government agencies, and major universities had computers. They were used for keeping track of paperwork, for billing, and for large scientific experiments. In less than fifteen years the computer had gone from being a classified weapon of war to a common, if slightly forbidding, business and scientific appliance. In 1951 there had been ten computers in the whole country. By 1970 there were some 75,000.

The computer was the symbol of a new postwar world of science and business. The public had become used to seeing computers performing apparently miraculous feats. UNIVAC had predicted the 1952 election. Computers could play an almost unbeatable checkers game and a pretty good chess game. They were beginning to show up in the workplace, changing the way people did their jobs — the 1950s and early 1960s saw a huge debate over the effects of automation — and in the home, in the form of computer-processed billing statements. They had even begun to affect aspects of social and cultural life; computer dating was a fad in the mid-1960s. Though still well outside most people's experience, and still intimidating, complex machines, computers had begun to become part of everyday life.

In the 1960s grand predictions of the computer's capabilities and effects were everywhere. Even the words coined to describe the new age were impressive: it was to be the age of "intellectronics," or "synnoetics." The first use of the term "the Computer Age" came in 1962. Computers were a key part of the "go-go" economy of the 1960s; companies with names such as Intellectronics were everywhere. There were data to be processed, programs to be written, computers to be sold, fortunes to be made.

The political, military, and especially economic value of information brought with it an enormous enthusiasm for computerization. Arthur Miller, a thoughtful social critic, wrote in 1971:

> The new information technologies seem to have given birth to a new social virus — "data-mania." Its symptoms are shortness of breath and heart palpitations when contemplating a new computer application, a feeling of possessiveness about information and a deep resentment toward those who won't yield it, a delusion that all information handlers can walk on water, and a highly advanced case of astigmatism that prevents the affected victim from perceiving anything but the intrinsic value of data. . . . Too many information handlers seem to measure a man by the number of bits of storage capacity his dossier will occupy.[4]

But, as the sarcasm suggests, there was considerable disagreement over just how the new information technologies should be used. The two most controversial users were the military, and government and private data banks.

Robert McNamara, Secretary of Defense under President Kennedy, was an early sufferer from "data-mania." A great believer in systems analysis and operations research — mathematical methods for determining optimal ways to undertake military or business operations — he believed that everything could be quantified. It was this belief that helped bring the computer into government and business, and especially the military. The military used computers and mathematical theory to calculate everything from the optimal spacing of trucks in convoys to how often an infantryman should look out of his foxhole. The nuclear standoff with the Soviet Union and the war in Vietnam were thought of as problems that the computer would help solve. James Gibson wrote in his history of the Vietnam War that "The United States began to view political relationships with other countries in terms of concepts that have their origin in physical science, economics, and management."[5] One congressman complained that the technocrats who were running the Defense Department "believe we can settle all by a computer or a slide rule."[6] Hannah Arendt described the Pentagon decision-makers in *Crises of the Republic* in 1972: "They were not just intelligent, but prided themselves on being 'rational.'. . . They were eager to find formulas, preferably expressed in a pseudo-mathematical language, that would unify the most disparate phenomena with which reality presented them. . . . [They] did not *judge;* they calculated. . . . An utterly irrational confidence in the calculability of reality [became] the leit-motif of the decision making."[7] They were convinced that every problem could be solved by computer.

In the late 1960s the military sought a technological, computerized answer to the bloody morass of Vietnam. As a sign at a naval operations center in Vietnam put it: "Better killing through electronics."[8] The "electronic battlefield" was General William C. Westmoreland's vision. On the "battlefield of the future," he wrote in 1969, "enemy forces will be located, tracked, and targeted almost instantaneously through the use of data links, computer assisted intelligence evaluation, and automated fire control. [The army will be] built into and around the integrated area control system that exploits the advanced technology of communications, sensors, fire direction, and the required automatic data processing."[9] The military became the largest financial supporter of computers.

Civilian government agencies followed the military's lead. One of the main — and most controversial — uses was to create data banks, information about individual citizens. As society came to seem more complex, beliefs about the great value of information suggested that the more information government had, the better it could govern. An article in the *Nation* in 1968 suggested: "Government should be allowed to know a great deal more than it does about the community it was elected to serve. This requirement is essential if we want to see decisions made on the basis of fact. You cannot manage an advanced society, which is a vast, complex, interconnecting system, unless the facts are available."[10]

This was not a new idea. In the late nineteenth century the U.S. Census had begun to ask more and more questions — so many that it had been forced to turn to the new punch card machines just to keep up. (See BEFORE COMPUTERS.) One of the first civilian agencies to invest in computers, the Census Bureau used its expanding computer capacity to process data more quickly, and also to add many new questions to its questionnaires. Lots of these questions raised concerns about government intrusiveness and personal privacy. The 1970 Census came at a time of heightened distrust of government, and many people objected to questions they saw as racist, offensive, or unnecessary. Public protest eliminated questions on religion, handicaps, smoking, and union membership. But the Census Bureau used computers to make the data it collected more valuable than ever; government agencies employed them to assist in determining programs, and businesses to target markets and plan strategies.

The Internal Revenue Service also found computers useful. Computerization made it possible to exchange tax data with states; in 1969 some 45 million federal tax returns were made available on computer tape to state tax bureaus. Before long the IRS would use computers to match up the numbers submitted by taxpayers with electronic files submitted by employers and banks, making it possible, for the first time, to check data on a massive scale.

The Federal Bureau of Investigation turned eagerly to computers, too. In cooperation with state and local law enforcement agencies, it established in 1967 the National Crime Information Center (NCIC), a computerized database of information on wanted or missing persons, stolen property, and criminal histories. In 1969 some 40,000 items of information were received from local police agencies each day. Some 3,000 computer terminals all across the country were hooked to the FBI computer. The FBI also attempted to computerize its millions of fingerprint records, a dream that was not to be achieved for another twenty-five years.

Automated databases made the IRS and the FBI more efficient in their work. But the ease and rapidity with which information could be accessed raised issues of personal privacy. Their use by private individuals and army intelligence services was questioned, as was their abuse for political reasons against Vietnam War protesters. The data was occasionally shared with other government agencies. The Nixon White House, for example, tried to use it to cause trouble for its supposed "enemies." Moreover, FBI files were not always accurate, especially when arrest records, not only conviction records, were added. Because of the way the software was designed, it was almost impossible to correct errors. Hundreds of people were arrested mistakenly when "the computer" matched them with a wanted person.

The use of computers by the IRS and the FBI became a hot issue in the 1960s, when it became clear that by using computers, the government could keep track of everyone in the country. To some extent this had been true since the 1930s, when the Social Security bureaucracy had used thousands of file cabinets and millions of punch cards to keep track of payments and accounts. But with computers it was much easier. The debate heated up when the Bureau of the Budget proposed a National Data Center to centralize all of the government's databases. Critics hated the idea, raising objections about privacy, and the proposal was defeated. But government agencies continued to collect information, and more and more of it. People's uneasiness about the power of computers prompted the Privacy Act of 1974, which set safeguards against the misuse of federal records and some private sector records.

Private firms, too, built computerized databases. The ones that attracted the most opposition were those for credit tracking and information. The first private credit network, run by Credit Data Corporation (later TRW Credit Data), opened in California in 1965. By 1968 it had files on 20 million Americans. The company's database came from bank records, and was made available via computer terminals and phone lines to retailers and others who

The credit card wars were fought with data — not file cabinets of data but computerized data.

wanted information on purchasers or suppliers. Universal credit cards — Mastercharge (later MasterCard) and BankAmericard (later VISA) depended on computerized record keeping and, starting in the 1980s, on a nationwide telephone credit-checking system.

Mail-order firms, which had always built lists of customers, were quick to adopt the computer to expand their lists. By 1970 there were over 500 million names on mail-order lists, available for rent to anyone who wanted them. Combined with information on income — the IRS began to sell aggregate income statistics in the late 1960s — the lists made it easy to target potential customers. The possibilities for using the computer to make money seemed endless.

Whether the increasing size and use of databases brought about better and more efficient government or greater profits and fewer losses to business is hard to know. It certainly brought complaints about misuse of information, and charges of violation of privacy. "One big gossip column that is unforgiving, unforgetful, and from which there is no redemption, no erasure of early 'mistakes,'" Marshall McLuhan called these databases.[11] A

THE NEXT WAR WILL BE BETWEEN RIVAL CREDIT CARD FIRMS
© 1958, New York Herald Tribune Inc.

poem by Felicia Lamport, titled "DEPRIVACY," put the database debate in perspective:

> Although we feel unknown, ignored,
>   As unrecorded blanks,
> Take heart! Our vital selves are stored
>   In giant data banks,
>
> Our childhoods and maturities,
>   Efficiently compiled,
> Our stocks and insecurities,
>   All permanently filed,
>
> Our tastes and our proclivities,
>   In gross and in particular,
> Our incomes, our activities
>   Both extra- and curricular.
>
> And such will be our happy state
>   Until the day we die
> When we'll be snatched up by the great
>   Computer in the sky.[12]

Lamport's poem suggests the sorts of anxiety that greeted the computer. The 1960s fad of computer dating might be seen as an attempt to make the computer an object of fun — or at least a little more human. Computer jokes and stories were widespread. Some of these built on the fear of losing jobs to the computer. Others poked fun at the computer in an attempt to put it in its place: the computerized airplane pilot announcing, "Nothing can go wrong — go wrong — go wrong . . ." Computers running amok star in the movies *Red Alert* (1977) and *The Andromeda Strain* (1971). HAL, the neurotic computer in *2001: A Space Odyssey* (1968), takes over a spaceship bound for Jupiter, claiming it's for the good of the mission. In *Dr. Strangelove* (1964) a Soviet computer cannot be stopped from following its program to detonate the "Doomsday Machine," a nuclear bomb that will destroy the world.

To many people, the computer had come to represent everything that was wrong with modern life. It became a symbol of a bureaucratic society — an "IBM society," some called it — that had no room for individuality. The Computer Age was an era in which, wrote Michael Harrington, the computerized bureaucracy "folds, bends, spindles and mutilates individuals but keeps IBM cards immaculate."[13]

Computer punch cards, widely used for consumer bills, became a symbol of the computer, and the words "Do not fold, spindle, or mutilate," written on each card, became a symbol of alienation, fear of computers, and distaste for what they stood for: abstraction, oversimplification, and dehumanization. Punch cards were, it seemed, a two-dimensional portrait of people, human beings abstracted into numbers that machines could use. The cards came to represent a society where computers had become more important than people, and where people had to change their ways to suit the machines. People were dealing with one another not face to face but rather through the medium of the computer. All of the free-floating anxiety about technology, the information society, "Big Brotherism," and automation attached themselves to punch cards. The metaphorical ways in which punch cards were used reveals some of the reaction and resistance to the brave new information world.

Participants in the "Free Speech movement," the student protests at the University of California at Berkeley in the mid-1960s, unpacked the expression in all its metaphorical glory. The university administration used punch cards for class registration. Berkeley protesters in turn used punch cards as a metaphor for what was wrong with the "system." One participant in the movement wrote that the student in the "mass university of today" feels that it is "an overpowering, overtowering, impersonal, alien machine in which he is nothing but a cog going through pre-programmed motions" — what he called "the 'IBM' syndrome."[14] The punch cards stood for the university, and, of course, students began to fold, spindle, and mutilate them, burning them or punching new holes in them.

"Prisoner Number 6" on the 1960s TV show "The Prisoner" summed up the widespread reaction to the computerization of the world, of humanity: "I am not a number; I am a person." He summarized his stand against the "system" by saying, in the first episode: "I will not be pushed, filed, stamped, indexed, briefed, debriefed, or numbered. My life is my own."[15]

"I feel a sentimental attachment toward that particular button—it does the job I did when I first came here."

Cartoons and jokes expressed some of the widespread fear, anger, resentment — and wonder — of the computer.

COMPUTERS AT WORK

The first computers were installed in businesses in the 1950s, but the commercial market really took off in the next decade. In 1960 the value of installed computer equipment was about $1 billion, four times what it had been five years earlier. By 1965 the total was $6 billion. Businesses that handled many transactions — department stores, banks, insurance companies, airlines, and hospitals — invested heavily in the new technology.

In the 1960s the notion that America was becoming an information economy was commonplace. Kenneth Boulding spoke of an "organizational revolution." Daniel Bell wrote of the "end of ideology," Fritz Machlup of a "knowledge economy," John Kenneth Galbraith of the "new industrial state." In 1965 Thomas J. Watson, president of IBM, greeted the rise of the information economy and defined the changes: "From an industrial economy, in which most people work producing goods, through our present economy, producing services, we shall more and more become . . . a knowledge economy, with 50 percent or more of our work force involved in the production of information."[16]

And, indeed, the economy was changing. But it was starting off from a basic structure that allowed computers to enter easily. In 1950 more than 7 million clerical workers and 5 million managers used a vast array of machines for processing and communicating information and decisions. Offices were filled with telephones and typewriters, filing cabinets and punch card machines. The invention of bureaucracy and the machinery that supported it — the "visible hand" of management — was a key step in the formation of the Information Age. Computers and other electronic data machines would fit comfortably into the social and business structures that had been created, and then would begin to change them. Businesses already knew the value of information, and were accustomed to using information processing technologies. (See BEFORE COMPUTERS.)

Payroll and billing were the most common early computer applications. IBM sold many computers by promising that they could get the payroll done a day or two sooner than old-fashioned punch card systems. Insurance companies, long eager users of new information technologies, adopted the computer to keep track of accounts, moving records from thousands of file cabinets and millions of punch cards to reel after reel of magnetic tape. These computer applications did not bring about major changes in work, or in company organization. At first the computer fit nicely into their traditional ways, which had, after all, long been systematized and mechanized. IBM would roll out the punch card machines and roll in a computer, and business would continue much as before.

The computer promised to make information even more valuable: more accessible, easier to manipulate, more readily applicable to the problems at hand. And the computer would do all those things. It would also change the nature of work and the nature of business enterprises. Whether it would serve to increase productivity, to provide more goods and services to repay the investment in the technology, was another question — one that remains unresolved today.

The actual effects of most of these early computers were small. In the early 1960s McKinsey and Company, a consulting firm, found that eighteen of the twenty-seven companies it examined were not earning enough on their computers to cover their investment. Overall, the study found, American business was not seeing a return on its investment in computers. Often the problem was that companies had simply automated inefficient processes. The answer com-

Computers like the IBM 360 were given glassed-in rooms of their own, sometimes where the public could see them. Users were not allowed to actually approach the computer; they handed in their deck of punch cards to an operator. By the late 1960s, in part out of fear of sabotage by those who used computers as a symbol of the military-industrial complex, computer centers changed their look; they were hidden out of sight in blockhouse-type buildings.

Bar codes, which became popular in the 1970s, were the secret to much computerization. Norman Joseph Woodland and Bernard Silver received a patent on the idea in 1952, but it was years before it became practical. The first use was to identify railroad cars; tested in 1961 and adopted as a national standard in 1967, it was never very successful. In 1969 several factories adopted bar code systems to monitor the location of materials. But it was in the grocery industry, which adopted a standardized Universal Product Code in 1973, that bar codes finally found success. Bar codes soon became common in retailing and manufacturing. In 1981, the Department of Defense required bar codes on items sold to the military. Even the Post Office began to bar code letters.

It was at the grocery store that most people first saw bar codes. One percent of stores had them in 1978, 10 percent in 1981, and 33 percent in 1984. Bar code scanners, though very expensive, doubled the checkout speed in grocery stores, at the same time reducing errors by more than 75 percent. In exchange for the expensive equipment, the store gained a lot: the cost of running the checkout became lower, prices could easily be changed, and, most important, the information recorded by the computer could be used to track inventory and promotional campaigns. Many stores saved money by not marking prices on each item. In some states, consumer groups objected to the new system because of this.

puter firms came up with was "systems analysis," the systematic analysis of business processes, and ways to reorganize them to use computers better.

When businesses began to reorganize tasks around the new computers, the work people did changed, sometimes in dramatic ways. The story of the adoption of computers in the workplace is a complicated one. In the early 1960s many people thought that automation would be the savior of American industry, while others thought that it would mean the end of meaningful work for most people — indeed, perhaps the end of all work for anyone other than a few "cyberneticians." Some suggested that the obvious outcome of automation was unemployment. Jack Conway, director of the Industrial Union Department in the AFL-CIO, wrote in 1965: "The change occurring in the work force over the next decade will be of great magnitude. We will be confronted with unemployment problems so serious . . . we are going to have to abandon some of our old concepts."[17] Other analysts thought that the increased productivity would make America into a leisure society where people's main problem would be filling their three or four or five days a week off from work.

The results actually turned out to be more complex. For some workers, both blue collar and white, the new technology led to de-skilled, less interesting, and more fragmented jobs. Some secretaries became data-entry clerks; some skilled machinists became tenders of computer-controlled machine tools. The

The SABRE reservation system was one of the largest computer installations. It replaced a manual system (top) with first a Teletype system (center), and then video display units (bottom). SABRE was based on the breakthroughs of the SAGE system and as early as 1968 it was handling 100,000 calls per day. By computerizing their reservation systems, airlines were able to put the information they collected to use. They could continuously determine the demand for seats and change prices to match demand, making as many as 2 million changes some days. They could also keep track of miles flown, making frequent-flyer plans possible, and thus building customer loyalty.

machines took over their skills, decreased their autonomy, and increased their level of stress. Computers completely eliminated some office and manufacturing jobs, but far fewer than had been predicted. They did not, as some analysts had feared, "turn us all into $3.00 an hour clerks."[18]

Indeed, some workers fulfilled the opposite prediction, that the new machines would re-skill workers, and would improve working conditions. The management consultant Peter Drucker suggested in 1955 that "automation will upgrade the semi-skilled machine operator of today into a highly skilled and knowledgeable technician."[19] Business school studies of new technologies in the workplace in the 1960s suggested that automation had made jobs more complex, challenging, and mentally demanding. Some assembly-line workers had to learn computer skills; some machinists learned to program the computerized machine tools. The new technologies opened creative possibilities for these workers and changed their jobs, in some ways for the better. They gave workers a greater sense of control and responsibility, but increased the pressure on work-

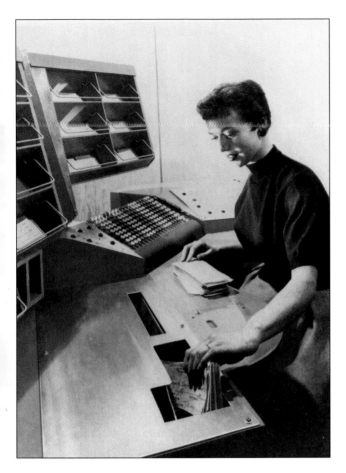

In 1952 bank workers processed some 8 billion checks. The job was monotonous, with employee turnover of almost 100 percent each year, and the number of checks was increasing rapidly. The American Bankers Association established a committee to determine how best to computerize check processing. The committee recommended many changes — changes typical of the way computers changed business practices.

To use computers effectively, banks had to standardize checks and check processing procedures and develop fast, easy, and accurate ways of putting computer-readable printing on checks — the "magnetic ink character recognition" numbers on every check today. To do this, they had to overcome skepticism about the uses of computers, opposition to the impersonal and standardized appearance of computer-readable checks (one reason punch card checks weren't chosen), and get a large number of banks and computer companies to agree to use a single system. ERMA (electronic recording method of accounting), the result of their work, started operation in December 1958. By the 1960s it was handling data from millions of accounts, tens of billions of checks a year. In 1967 ERMA and other similar systems were handling almost all the checks in the United States, replacing thousands of bookkeepers and check sorters.

ers and limited their interactions with their co-workers. One way or the other, the new machines changed almost everyone's job. By 1990 it seemed that there was a keyboard and a telephone at almost every workplace. Some 50 million Americans used computers in their work.

Clerical workers were among the first to feel the changes, for the computer's first business use was as a replacement for routine paperwork. The punch card machine was all these workers saw of the computer. They typed data gathered by other employees onto punch cards for entry into computers, or, after video display screens replaced keypunches and teletypes in the 1970s, sat at terminals typing in data. A 1961 analysis of office automation noted that computerization brought about a finer division of labor: increased specialization, with more routine and less interesting work. The computer took care of the complicated tasks, leaving just the simplest, most repetitive work for clerks. Data-entry personnel were almost all women, often African-American or Hispanic. Their skills were too specialized to offer much possibility of promotion.

In the 1980s data-entry clerks began to disappear. Some of their work was done automatically by tellers, retail clerks, and factory workers at terminals connected to the computer by phone lines. Mail-order operations combined the job of order taker and data-entry clerk. Bank tellers, working at computer terminals, did the work that had previously been done by punch card machine operators, and soon many tellers were themselves replaced by bank customers us-

In the 1957 movie *Desk Set,* an efficiency expert (played by Spencer Tracy) spars with an office researcher (played by Katharine Hepburn) over his plans to automate her job, replacing her with a computer named EMERAC — Emmy, for short.

ing automatic teller machines or the telephone to make their own transactions. Bar codes on many products allowed computers to keep track of inventory automatically. The computer collected information directly from the branch bank, the retail store — what had once been called the cash register now became the "point of sale terminal" — or the factory floor.

More skilled office workers soon saw the new technology changing their work, too. Expectations were high. The "paperless office" was always just around the corner, and computer salesmen promised vast increases in productivity. But while computers soon came to dominate office work, and changed white-collar jobs in a multitude of ways, the promise of increased productivity was never quite fulfilled. (See WORDS.)

Computers fit neatly into a long history of automating factory work, of using machines to increase productivity as well as to de-skill and control workers. American factory managers had been trying to automate and mechanize factory work as far back as the beginning of the nineteenth century. In the early twentieth century the assembly line and scientific management meant ever more simplified jobs, and reinforced managerial prerogatives. (See BEFORE COMPUTERS.) Norbert Wiener saw the connection clearly: "The notion of programming in the factory had already become familiar through the [scientific management] work of Taylor and the Gilbreths on time study," he wrote in 1954, "and was ready to be transferred to the machine."[20] The 1920s and 1930s brought in-

Charlie Chaplin caught in the wheels of progress, from his 1936 movie, *Modern Times*. The *New York Herald Tribune* review summarized the plot, and the problem: "The mechanized individual goes mad and proceeds to turn the factory into the madhouse that it really always has been."

creasing mechanization of factory work, and the use of "transfer machines," to carry work between machines. The word *automation* was coined in the 1940s by Delmar S. Harder, at Ford Motor Company, who saw it as a philosophy of manufacturing that included both mechanization and automatic transfer; he considered these technologies the first step on the road to the automatic factory.

In the 1960s and 1970s some managers believed that computer-aided automation would allow them to obtain ultimate control in the workplace, while increasing productivity. They viewed robots and other computerized machines as highly productive workers who never were sick, never took vacations, always followed orders, and, best of all, never joined a union. Some workers, by contrast, saw computerized machinery as competitors that would steal their jobs or, perhaps worse, take all of the skill and decision-making from their work. Visions of factories run entirely by robots filled corporate managers' dreams — and workers' nightmares.

The first computer to be applied to industrial work was the Whirlwind. In 1949 John T. Parsons, manager of a machine shop in Traverse City, Michigan, had developed a way to guide a milling machine (a machine tool that cuts metal in complex shapes) using punch cards. He turned to MIT's Servomechanisms Laboratory to improve his "cardamatic" system. The engineers working on the Whirlwind expanded Parson's fairly simple scheme into what became known as a numerically controlled machine tool. The first numerically controlled milling machine was operational in 1952, and the first commercially successful one — with a simpler programming language — in 1959. The air force had paid for this work, and one of the earliest uses for the Whirlwind-controlled milling machine was cutting metal into the complex curves of helicopter blades, aircraft wings, and other aircraft parts. This was work that had been done by a skilled

FIGHT AUTOMATION FALLOUT

WITH A SHORTER WORK WEEK

Some unions feared that automation would lead to widespread unemployment. The robot became a symbol not of progress but of economic problems.

machinist. The programmer captured the skills of the machinist and embodied them instead in the computer. Programmers, not machinists, decided what actions the machine should take. The machinist simply set up the machine and monitored it to see that nothing went wrong.

Numerical control machine tools seemed to promise not only increased productivity and accuracy but also increased managerial control. After all, if some of the skills and judgment of the machinist were captured in the computer that ran the tool, the machinist would have less power over his work. Indeed, no machinist would be needed at all, merely a machine tender. The Numerical Control Society wrote that one advantage of the new technology was that it put the decisions "in the hands of managerial and professional personnel rather than machine operators."[21] One manager at an automated factory stated his hopes, rather than reality, in an interview in *Life* magazine in 1963: "All [the worker] has to do is press the button to start the machine and then monitor it. All he has to know is what his machine looks like so he can find it when he comes to work."[22]

But numerical control was never as successful as its supporters thought it would be. Designed to meet air force requirements for extremely precise machining, numerical control was simply too complicated and too expensive for most machining jobs. Even after programming became easier (CNC, or computer numerical control, replaced NC, or numerical control), and microprocessors made machine tools "smarter," numerical control and its successor, computer numerical control, remained a difficult, underutilized art. As often as not, applications of the new technology failed. Machinists' skills proved more complex than managers had thought. It was twenty-five years before numerically controlled tools were generally adopted, and even in 1983 they represented fewer than 5 percent of the machine tools in use in the United States.

Computer-integrated manufacturing (CIM) was the ultimate dream of automation. CIM was the offspring of CAD (computer-aided design) and CAM (computer-aided manufacturing). The idea was that an engineer would design a device on a computer screen. The computer would then calculate the way it should be made and send those instructions electronically to the production machines, which would then make the part. The whole process would be untouched by human hands. This was done as early as 1965, in an experimental trial at Lockheed-Georgia. But CIM never really worked. It remains, as computer historian Paul Ceruzzi puts it, "little more than an acronym in the babel of computer programming systems."[23] (On computer-aided design, see PICTURES.)

When most people thought about computers in factories, what they had in mind was robots. There was a long history of science-fiction robots (see BEYOND COMPUTERS), and it seemed only a matter of time before robots would run factories. It seemed a short step from automatic assembly lines and computer-controlled machines to robots that replaced workers completely.

The first general-purpose patent on robots was issued in 1954 to George Devol. Devol sought to create "universal automation," or "unimation": a flexible manipulator that would take the place of unskilled workers, correcting what he called "a waste of manpower" on simple, boring jobs.[24] His patent combined a mechanical manipulator with a magnetic recording system, so that the manipulator could remember the path it should follow. Devol and the entrepreneur Joseph Engelberger joined forces to build robots based on Devol's patent. They established the first robot manufacturing firm, Unimation, and in 1958 produced their first robot. (Engelberger had decided to devote his life to building robots after reading Isaac Asimov's book of robot stories, *I, Robot.*)

General Motors bought the first Unimate in 1959. Few factories were eager to buy robots, though, in part because of their high price and limited utility, and in part out of fear of labor difficulties. (When Ford first introduced robots, they were called "universal transfer devices"; earlier machines called "robots" had been the victims of sabotage.) As the price decreased, though, robots increasingly found a place on assembly lines, especially in automobile plants, where they were used in dangerous, dirty jobs such as welding and painting.

The largest early order for the Unimate, the first successful industrial robot, was for the General Motors plant at Lordstown, Ohio. That plant was intended as the precursor of the new, roboticized factory. The managers at General Motors had decided that "robots and people can work together on assembly jobs," and, even more, "that they should be interchangeable."[25] General Motors bought robots that could fit easily into existing assembly lines.

But this vision, perhaps based on the science-fiction ideal of a robot, turned out to be exactly the wrong way to introduce robotics. Lordstown was to become famous, in the early 1970s, as an example of all that was wrong with modern automation: boring jobs, high absenteeism, workers turning to drugs and alcohol to escape meaningless jobs, even sabotage to get back at the machines that seemed to be controlling their lives. Norbert Wiener, creator of the science of cybernetics, had looked ahead with fear to the invention of "mechanical slaves," which, by competing with human labor, would turn people into slaves. It seemed as though Wiener's prediction had come true: toiling on the line next to robots, the workers in the factory had become robots themselves. Robots and workers had indeed become interchangeable, but not in the way that General Motors had hoped. Instead of robots taking on the skills and abilities of the workers, workers became more mechanical. Although their jobs often required increased skill, they experienced more stress and isolation. Studs Terkel,

The first numerical control machine tool, built at MIT using the Whirlwind computer in 1952. A numerical control machine tool system converts a written description of the part to be made — described in geometric terms of angles and distances — into a punched tape that contains a detailed description that controls each motion of the machine tool as it produces the final part.

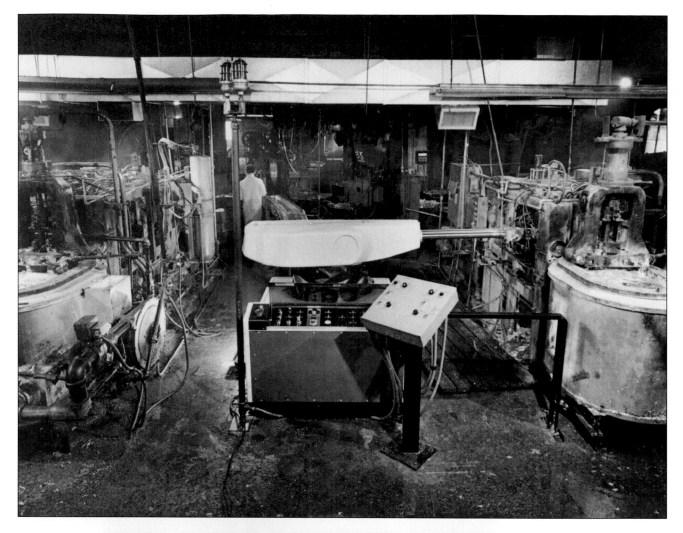

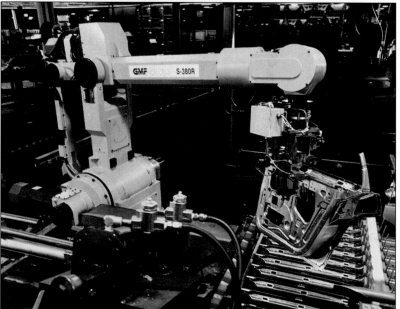

The Unimate (top) was the first industrial robot. It used hydraulic and pneumatic power and was controlled by an electromagnetic memory drum. It had no "intelligence" but simply repeated its programmed routines over and over.

The Cincinnati Milacron T3 robot (left; the name stands for "Tomorrow Tool Today") was the workhorse robot of the 1970s and early 1980s. It was designed to replace workers on existing production lines and so it was complex, with a wide range of motions possi-

interviewing people about their work, found that "for the many there is scarcely concealed discontent. . . . 'I'm a machine,' says the spot welder. . . . Blue collar and white call upon the identical phrase: 'I'm a robot.' "[26]

Still, the fantasy of the factory of the future survived. "Lights-out factories" was the new buzzword in the 1980s. *Newsweek* described the possibilities in a 1982 article: "Harnessing the computer's brainpower allows engineers and managers to control all phases of manufacturing — from the first design of a manufactured part on the CAD computer screen to the moment the part is shipped from the factory's loading dock to the customer." Sales of robots and other computerized manufacturing equipment topped $1 billion in 1982. In 1983 there were about 8,000 robots working in American industry, and everyone predicted an enormous boom. The payoff of these "computers, robots and a dazzling array of the latest manufacturing technology," *Newsweek* continued, "comes in improved productivity."[27]

But the prediction turned out to be false. Automation and robotics were much more difficult to achieve than anyone had thought. Work often required more skill and understanding than managers had imagined. Robots did get "sick"; they did not always follow orders; and they were not always as productive as the workers they replaced. Moreover, they were expensive. Managers could lay off workers when business was slow, but they had to pay the capital costs of the robots whether there was work for them or not.

Robotics never took off, and by the late 1980s most American robot builders were out of business. The vice president of the leading American robot builder told the *Wall Street Journal* in 1985, "This is a more complex business

ble, able to respond to vision and tactile sensors, and fully programmable, operated by a minicomputer. But this complexity was rarely used; most robots did routine jobs.

The GMFanuc S-380 robot, (right), a third-generation robot, differs from the T3 in its more advanced computer control and in its use of electric drive throughout. The S-380 was designed and manufactured for automotive spot welding application, though it was also used for material handling. Like almost all robots of the 1980s and 1990s, it was built in Japan.

than anybody thought it would be."[28] Automation for the sake of automation turned out to be expensive and not particularly profitable. Oftentimes, simple old-fashioned automation was cheaper and more reliable than robotics.

William Abernathy of the Harvard Business School, who studied the "productivity gap" between Japanese and American automobile manufacturers, discovered that the Japanese secret was not automation: it was their "'people' approach to manufacturing."[29] In the late 1980s American managers began to abandon their enthusiasm for automation, and to learn from the Japanese new ways to organize production. While robots do labor at some jobs previously done by people — especially dangerous or tedious work — and some parts are indeed designed on a computer screen and made by fully automated, computer-controlled machinery, these successes are unusual. Far more successful has been a different sort of manufacturing revolution. The adoption of Japanese-style manufacturing methods — just-in-time inventory, an emphasis on quality, and statistical methods of ensuring quality — has meant that many jobs require not less skill and responsibility but more ability to analyze and use information, and more authority, often the authority to stop production if quality lags. Information is spread across the hierarchy rather than being funneled to the top. Shoshana Zuboff's *In the Age of the Smart Machine,* the most penetrating study of computers in the workplace, calls this "informating" as opposed to automating, and suggests that it offers the opportunity to reshape work in a more humane as well as a more productive way.[30]

The fully automated train, with a computer replacing the driver, has been a long-time dream of transportation planners. Both the BART system in San Francisco and the Metro system in Washington, D.C., were designed to operate without drivers, but after accidents caused by computer problems, drivers were put aboard each train. Their main job is to open and close the doors; the trains are centrally controlled.

Many workers have come to use computers in their jobs, not lose their jobs to computers. Air-traffic controllers were among the first workers to use computers to increase their power at work. Chemical plants, paper mills, and other continuous-flow processes found that computers fit nicely into their operations, too. These computers replaced some workers but demanded new skills for those who remained. A spokesman for the Chemical Workers Union noted in 1963: "Frequently, the responsibility which a worker has is greater after automation. . . . He must correct errors that result in the process or on the part of the machine."[31] By the early 1990s, operators of most large materials processing plants, from steel mills to oil refineries, did most of their work sitting in front of computer terminals.

But many firms did use computers to de-skill their workers. Fast-food restaurants, eager to eliminate high-priced skilled labor and to keep quality and taste standardized, embraced computerization. In the 1980s McDonalds broke down all of the jobs in its kitchens to their basics, and then installed microprocessor-controlled timers to regulate the actions of the kitchen employees. At the front of the store, cash registers keep track of inventory and sales. They're directly connected to the master computer at the McDonald's headquarters, which in turn evaluates the performance of each store's manager. The manager's activities are determined in part by a computer which automatically predicts sales and calculates employee scheduling. As one manager put it in an interview with the writer Barbara Garson: "Basically, the computer manages the store."[32]

Steel mill operators do much of their work from control rooms like this, at Bethlehem Steel's Sparrow Point plant. The computer keeps track of the conditions at many points in the process.

COMPUTERS EVERYWHERE

In the early 1960s time-sharing, which made computers more easily accessible, became popular. A new electronics technology, integrated circuits, made possible smaller, more powerful computers, called minicomputers. And in the 1970s and 1980s the personal computer, based on a new kind of integrated circuit called the microprocessor, became a business, education, and hobbyist fad. The microprocessor found an astonishing range of uses, controlling everything from automobile brakes to sewing machines to the personal computer. Computers became ubiquitous.

Time-sharing was invented at MIT in the late 1950s. Until then, at most universities and corporations, users would submit their "job," a stack of punch cards, to the computer, and wait hours or days for results. After all, computers were large and expensive, and few businesses could afford their own. John Kemeny, one of the proponents of time-sharing, described the old way: "For the first two decades of the existence of high-speed computers, machines were so scarce and so expensive that man approached the computer the way an ancient Greek approached an oracle. A man submitted his request to the machine and then waited patiently until it was convenient for the machine to work out the problem. There was a certain degree of mysticism in the relationship, even to the extent that only specially selected acolytes were allowed to have direct communication with the computer."[33]

In a time-sharing system, by contrast, several users, at first a few, but by the late 1960s hundreds, were able to use the computer simultaneously, working at terminals connected to the machine. The trick to time-sharing was clever software that would switch quickly and invisibly among the users — fast enough that each could believe that he or she was the only one using the computer. In 1961 MIT's John McCarthy, one of the inventors of time-sharing, predicted that "computation may someday be organized as a public utility, just as the telephone is a public utility. We can envisage computing service companies whose subscribers are connected to them by telephone lines. Each subscriber needs to pay only for the capacity that he actually uses, but he has access to all the programming languages characteristic of a very large system."[34] This system was ideal for educational use, and universities were among the first to install time-sharing. Kemeny, who introduced time-sharing to Dartmouth College, wrote that it brought about "a fundamental change . . . in the relationship of man to computer. . . . It is only through this new development that a true symbiotic relationship between man and computer is possible."[35]

Time-sharing also allowed smaller firms to use computers, "buying time" on large machines and paying per minute of use. It dovetailed nicely with another new technology, the modem, which allowed computers to be used over the telephone. Time-sharing services provided terminals at businesses and schools, and hooked these terminals to their large computers via modems and telephone lines. The largest time-sharing firm was General Electric, which by 1968 served 50,000 customers from thirty-one time-sharing centers. Time-sharing meant an enormous expansion of computer use. By 1979 there were some 2 million cathode-ray tube terminals in use, most of them connected to time-

INTEGRATED CIRCUIT

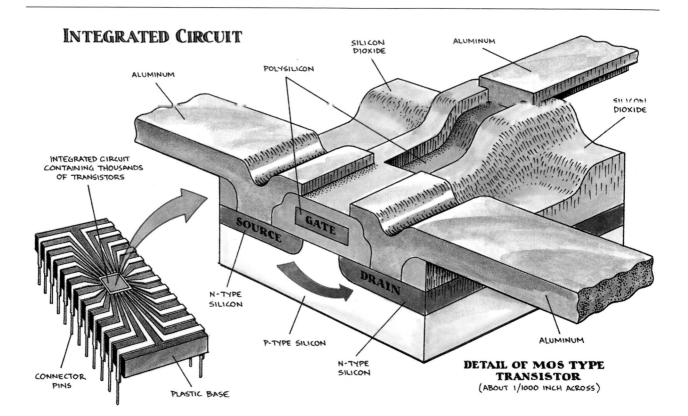

ALUMINUM

POLYSILICON

SILICON
DIOXIDE

ALUMINUM

SILICON
DIOXIDE

INTEGRATED CIRCUIT
CONTAINING THOUSANDS
OF TRANSISTORS

SOURCE

GATE

DRAIN

N-TYPE
SILICON

P-TYPE SILICON

N-TYPE
SILICON

ALUMINUM

CONNECTOR
PINS

PLASTIC BASE

**DETAIL OF MOS TYPE
TRANSISTOR**
(ABOUT 1/1000 INCH ACROSS)

An integrated circuit is a tiny piece of silicon onto which thousands or millions of electronic circuit elements are built by means of a series of optical and chemical processes. Transistors, diodes, resistors, and capacitors are created on the surface of the chip by adding "dopants" like phosphorus or boron, which change the way silicon reacts to currents; and by adding layers of metal and polysilicon conductors to connect electrically the elements in certain ways; and layers of insulating silicon dioxide, to separate areas where no electricity should flow.

The transistor in the drawing is a metal-oxide-semiconductor field effect transistor. It acts as a switch. When the gate is given a negative charge, it repels electrons in the substrate from it. The absence of these electrons means that no current can flow between the source and the drain; the switch is off. When a handful of transistors like this are connected in the right way, they can perform logical functions like AND, OR, and NOT, called "logic gates." When these gates, in turn, are connected in certain ways, they can store, add, and compare binary numbers. Decimal numbers, letters, sounds, and graphics can all be represented by binary numbers, and so an integrated circuit can store or process any kind of information.

shared computers. Time-sharing also made possible electronic mail, introduced in the late 1970s. (See BEYOND TELEPHONES.)

More powerful computers meant larger, more complex computers. By 1962 some computers had more than 200,000 individual electronic components — transistors, diodes, resistors, and capacitors — and connecting all of the components was becoming increasingly difficult. J. A. Morton, a vice president of

The PDP-8 (shown at right with its cover removed) found use everywhere. Programmers usually "talked" to the machine through a Teletype.

Bell Labs, outlined the problem in 1966: "Each element must be made, tested, packed, shipped, unpacked, retested, and interconnected one-at-a-time to produce a whole system. Each element and its connections must operate reliably if the system is to function as a whole. . . . The tyranny of large systems sets up a numbers barrier to future advances if we must rely on individual discrete components for producing large systems."[36] Integrated circuits, in which all the elements of an electronic circuit were contained on one chip of silicon, were the answer.

Jack Kilby of Texas Instruments was the first to patent an integrated circuit (IC) in 1959. This circuit was hand-wired; each separate element within the circuit was interconnected by hand. At Fairchild Semiconductor, Robert Noyce independently invented the IC, and went one step further; he invented the planar process, in which metal connections were evaporated directly onto the semiconductor surface. Constant innovation in integrated circuits made it possible to put more components onto a small piece of silicon, at first dozens, then hundreds, and by the early 1990s millions.

Integrated circuits found their first use in military programs: missiles, the antiballistic missile programs, cryptographic gear, and other projects where light weight, high reliability, and small size were important — and where cost was no object. In 1963 some 5 million ICs were made; in 1968 some 250 million. The average price had fallen by a factor of more than ten.

With increasing complexity — the number of components that could be put on a chip doubled almost every year — and lower price, integrated circuits found use everywhere. The space program was an important early user. The first consumer products were calculators and electronic watches, in the 1960s and 1970s. The first IC used in a household appliance was in an Oster blender in the early 1960s. Integrated circuits found their first computer use in memories; it was easy to replace magnetic core memories with the cheaper, smaller integrated circuit memories. Though not used in the IBM/360 computers of the early 1960s, integrated circuits were used in almost all later computers. In 1978 computer manufacturers purchased some $2.6 billion of integrated circuits, more than half of the total sold.

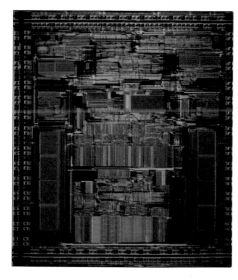

The microprocessor is a computer on a chip — a programmable integrated circuit that includes memory and logic circuits. It is a general-purpose device; it can do anything it is programmed to do. Instead of designing new chips for each application, all that is necessary is to write a program to direct the microprocessor and put that program into the chip's memory or onto a ROM (read only memory) chip next to the microprocessor. Intel's first advertisement for its 4004 microprocessor put the advantages in a nutshell: "The first system to bring you the power and flexibility of a dedicated general-purpose computer at low cost." Microprocessors are the most complex integrated circuits.

This Motorola 68040 microprocessor has more than one million transistors and other electronic elements in less than a square inch of silicon. On the left (below the clock unit in the upper left corner) are instruction caches and controllers. In the center, the two largest areas are the integer processing unit, top, and the floating point processing unit, bottom. On the right, below the bus controller (top right) are data caches.

And in the 1960s and 1970s a new kind of computer especially benefited from the integrated circuit technology. Minicomputers were designed to be used interactively, and were cheap enough to be used by one person at a time. Ken Olsen, an engineer on the Whirlwind, established Digital Equipment Corporation (DEC) in 1957 to build this sort of computer. DEC's first computer was the PDP-1, which cost $120,000 — about one tenth the price of an equivalent computer of the day. Scientists used the PDP-1 in their research. ITEK turned them into what it called Electronic Drafting Machines and sold them to engineering firms. Oil companies used them to control refineries. International Telephone and Telegraph used PDP-1's in its Teletype system, to collect, store, and forward messages. DEC sold forty-nine of the machines.

In 1965 DEC introduced the PDP-8, a wildly successful minicomputer — the "Model T of computing," as one of DEC's engineers put it.[37] The PDP-8 cost less than $20,000, and it opened the market for small computers even wider. About 50,000 were sold, finding applications everywhere from laboratories to factories to submarines to offices. A PDP-8 was even used to control the news display in Times Square. Its successor, the PDP-11, introduced in 1968, was cheaper and more powerful; more than 500,000 were sold. The minicomputer industry boomed. By 1971 some seventy-five firms were making minicomputers. As the minicomputers grew in power and size — the next step was the "supermini" — and as they became more powerful, they started to take business away from mainframe computers.

The more people thought of information as something to be managed, the more they found uses for computers. And there seemed an apparently infinite number of uses. The vast proliferation of small computers, along with timesharing, meant that computers, or computer terminals, were starting to become ubiquitous. Many people used a computer at work, or knew someone who did. But even as computers found their way into every aspect of the American economy, a new revolution was brewing. The very definition of computer was about to change as computers also found their way into everyday appliances of all sorts, and, before long, into a new kind of computer — the personal computer.

The key technological innovation that made the personal computer possible was the microprocessor, the computer on a chip. In the late 1960s several

Early personal computers. From left to right: the Altair, the Apple II, the Sinclair, and the Osborne. Each tried to appeal to a different segment of the market.

inventors had the idea of making general-purpose, programmable integrated circuits. Ted Hoff, an integrated circuit designer at Intel, was one. In 1969, in the midst of designing a complicated set of ICs for a calculator, he realized that there was a better way. Rather than designing a special-purpose integrated circuit for each job, it occurred to him that it might be possible to make a general-purpose, programmable integrated circuit, and write software to make it do whatever job was desired — to act as a calculator, a traffic light controller, whatever. Intel was the first to make a microprocessor.

Intel put its microprocessor, the 4004, on the market in June 1971, at a price of $200. An Intel ad claimed: "Announcing a new era of integrated electronics: A micro-programmable computer on a chip."[38] In 1972 Intel brought out the 8008, an 8-bit microprocessor, at a cost of $120. Designed originally for a "smart terminal," the 8008 was the first microprocessor powerful enough to run a personal computer. Intel sold millions. The 8080, introduced in 1974, was even more powerful. Every few years a new generation of computer chips would appear, each several times more powerful than the previous one. Microprocessors found two sorts of uses. They were embedded into other machines — everything from microwave ovens to calculators to automobiles — to control their operations, and they were used as computers themselves.

Automobiles were one of the first, and most widespread, machines to take advantage of "embedded" microprocessors. The most important use was the electronic engine-control computer. The engine-control computer receives reports from sensors that monitor speed, oxygen content, exhaust, and so on, decides the proper mixture of fuel and air, and then controls the fuel injectors to optimize power and fuel economy and minimize pollution. The 1977 Oldsmobile Toronado offered the first microprocessor-controlled engine. Its MISAR system controlled spark timing based on input signals from crankshaft position, manifold vacuum, coolant temperature, and reference timing. It improved fuel economy by about 10 percent. Antilock braking was the second widespread application of microelectronics, followed by a variety of less critical applications such as digital dashboards, adjustable suspension, electronically controlled transmission shifting and traction control, and computer-controlled four-wheel steering. For the most part, these microprocessors were hidden. Most people heard of them only when their auto mechanic told them that their car's "computer" needed replacing, and what was once a cheap and easy repair would now cost hundreds or even thousands of dollars. For some it meant a new kind of computerized hot-rodding, reprogramming engine-control computers for faster acceleration or greater top speed (and, usually, more pollution).

Microprocessors hidden in everyday objects were the largest part of the market, but microprocessors were better known when they powered PCs — personal computers. The microprocessor made the PC possible. It was the heart of the system, and, when connected to a video monitor for output, a keyboard for input, and a means of storing information — at first a tape recorder, then floppy disks, then hard disk drives — it became a computer. The first PCs were sold as kits, promoted in magazines for electronics hobbyists. The July 1974 issue of *Radio-Electronics* featured an article about the Mark-8, "your personal mini-computer," and 10,000 readers sent away for information; 2,500 bought circuit boards to build it.[39] But it was the Altair 8800, on the January 1975 cover of *Popular Electronics,* that really set off the boom. A company called MITS, in Albuquerque, sold the Altair for $395 as a kit and $495 assembled. Within three months some 4,000 people had ordered it.

Hundreds of tiny firms sprang up to make personal computers. At first only electronics hobbyists purchased them, people who were delighted to build computers that could do very little except blink lights. The first PCs were toys for people who like to play with electronic gadgets. They weren't of much use. But there were many people who did like to play with the new machines. One MITS executive told historian Steven Levy: "People were really caught up in this because they were giving computers to people who were so appreciative, and who wanted them so badly. It was a grand and glorious crusade."[40]

Personal computers began to find a niche. Computer languages were rewritten so they would run in the tiny memories of the new machines. Games were one key application, business programs such as spreadsheets and word processing others. Soon many other companies entered the market — Radio Shack, Commodore, and Apple among the most successful. The Apple II, introduced in 1977, was one of the best sellers. It had color graphics, which made games more appealing, and it used a floppy disk instead of a cassette tape, which made it easy to store information. Moreover, one of the most popular pieces of software of the day, VisiCalc, could run only on the Apple II. By the end of 1980, over 120,000 Apple IIs had been sold. In 1983 some 3.5 million personal computers were sold and the computer was *Time* magazine's "Man of the Year."

In 1981 IBM entered the personal computer market, establishing the IBM PC as a standard. IBM validated the PC business, and the market exploded. Some 35,000 IBM PCs sold the first year at a price starting at $1,365, and over a million in the next two years. The IBM PC's specifications were "open" — published and available to all — and before long hundreds of manufacturers were selling "IBM clones," computers that could run IBM PC-standard software.

Apple Computer's Macintosh, introduced in 1984, was IBM's most distinctive competitor in the PC market. Instead of using a "command line" interface that required users to memorize arcane instructions, the Macintosh used a mouse-and-windows interface. The user pointed out choices on the screen to tell the computer what to do. These instructions were, to some extent, standardized across applications; when you learned, say, a word processing program, some of that knowledge was applicable to a spreadsheet program, or a graphics program. Although the Mac was not an immediate success, its "appliance" approach made it a favorite with college students, people with home offices, and others who wanted an easy-to-operate computer. Its graphic interface made it especially useful to people interested in doing computer graphics and design. Improvements in the design and the development of desktop publishing software and hardware, especially the laser printer, eventually brought Apple success in the business market. (See WORDS.)

The Macintosh interface was not completely new. It followed in the graphics-oriented tradition pioneered by the Alto computer, developed at Xerox's Palo Alto Research Center in 1973. Larry Tesler, a researcher at Xerox PARC, recalled the problems that needed to be overcome: "We felt that this would be an opportunity to bring computing to everyone. . . . Remember, a computer at that time was thought of as something that was very forbidding, difficult, highly technological, you had to be a real expert and a doctorate to understand. That was kind of the public image. We somehow had to humanize computers and make them a common object that anyone could use."[41] The Alto, and then the Star, was Xerox PARC's answer. But the Alto was never commercialized, and the Star, introduced in 1981, cost $16,000. Apple's Lisa, introduced in 1983, was much cheaper — only $10,000 — but was still too expensive, and underpowered, and was never a commercial success. The Macintosh was the first successful personal computer to adopt the user-friendly interface pioneered at Xerox. (See SOFTWARE.)

Xerox PARC research also spawned another line of computers, called workstations. Like the Alto, they were designed to be on a network, and used the mouse-and-windows interface. One of the first commercially successful workstations was the SUN I, from Sun Microsystems, introduced in May 1982. Like the IBM PC, the SUN I was based on standard components and software. Unlike the PC, it had a high-powered microprocessor, lots of memory, a high-resolution display, and a mouse to select items on the screen, and it was designed to be used on a network, connected to other similar machines. Its software was based on AT&T's UNIX, which was widely available. (AT&T, unable to enter the computer market, had allowed its use without charge.) The SUN found wide popularity among engineers and scientists, who used its power to design circuits and structures, and to make the large number of calculations that the analysis of scientific data required.

By 1981 there were more than 2 million personal computers sitting on desks in offices and homes, by 1982, 5.5 million. Along with the expansion of the market came an explosion of rhetoric. Many early developers and users were afire with the idea that putting computer power in the hands of people in all walks of life would change the world. Christopher Evans, in his breathless book *The Micro Millennium* (1979), saw personal computers as bringing about the fall of communism, putting an end to war, transforming the Third World, reinvigorating capitalism, and doing away with the need to work more than a few hours a week. And that's just in his "short-term" category! Timothy Leary proclaimed personal computers the LSD of the 1980s.

Because the technology of the PC seemed to free individuals from the large corporate computers, some people thought that personal computers would help to break up large-scale companies and governments in favor of local and small-scale forms of power. Futurists such as Alvin Toffler suggested that the personal computer would make society less hierarchical and more fluid. George Gilder, in *Microcosm* (1989), mixed metaphor, politics, and economics in his

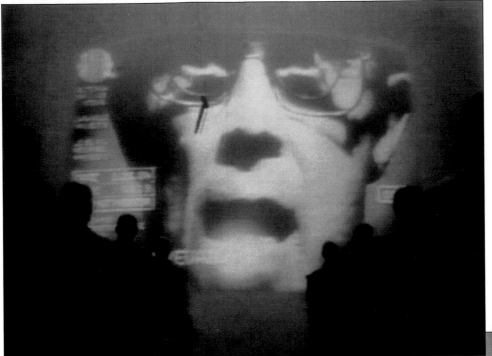

The utopian democratic ideas that so often accompanied — and were used to sell — new information machines were exemplified by a commercial for the Macintosh computer shown during the 1984 Super Bowl. The ad showed oppressed workers staring at a huge screen image of Big Brother. Into the hall bursts a woman, wearing a shirt with a Macintosh logo, who is being chased by police. She hurls a hammer through the screen and frees the workers from their daze. The ad suggested that the Macintosh would be the force that would deny the centralized control of information and humanity that George Orwell had predicted for that year.

claim that the "quantum era" of microcomputers and dispersed computer power demands an egalitarian entrepreneurial business structure, that small computers mean small companies, that large computer systems mean large bureaucracies. "Rather than pushing decisions up through the hierarchy," Gilder wrote, "the power of microelectronics pulls them remorselessly down to the individual."[42] Ted Nelson summed up the philosophy of the PC in the introduction to his underground manifesto *Computer Lib* (1974): "I want to see computers useful to individuals, and the sooner the better, without necessary complication or human servility being required. . . . COMPUTER POWER TO THE PEOPLE! DOWN WITH CYBERCRUD!"[43]

Langdon Winner describes the rhetoric of the personal computer revolution perfectly in "Mythinformation," an article that appeared in 1984:

> Books, articles, and media specials aimed at a popular audience are usually content to depict the dazzling multitude of technical innovations and social effects. Written as if by some universally accepted format, such accounts describe scores of new computer products and processes, announce the enormous dollar volume of the growing computer and communications industry, survey the expanding uses of computers in offices, factories, schools, and homes, and offer good news from research and development laboratories about the great promise of the next generation of computing devices. Along with this one reads of the many "impacts" that computerization is going to have on every sphere of life.

Like so many other information machines, personal computers inspired utopian ideas about community and freedom, economic advance and democracy. But, Winner continues, "even within the great tradition of optimistic technophilia, current dreams of a 'computer age' stand out as exaggerated and unrealistic."[44]

Fascinated with the idea of the PC, and the possibilities of "computer power to the people," personal computer enthusiasts overestimated the limited capabilities of the early machines. Even more important, they failed to recognize that technological revolutions generally reinforce the power structure in which they take place; they rarely overthrow it. It turned out not to matter whether the computer sat on your desk or in a distant computer center; what mattered was that your boss told you what to do with it. The excitement over the PC stemmed from a naïveté about technological change, a narrow focus on the wondrous new technology that left the business and social background blurred, and a confusion of metaphor with reality.

Millions of individuals and businesses, lured by the rhetoric, bought personal computers and found them of no use at all, or nothing but an expensive typewriter. Fantasies of computerizing recipes and other absurd home uses gave way to the realization that personal computers were not of much use to the average person. At work, early users of personal computers tended to be isolated from the information in the mainframe computer, hobbled by a slow processor and a meager amount of storage, and, in the beginning, by unsophisticated software.

But the PC could do more and more as it gained in computing power, as better software was written, and as intercomputer communications improved. The Intel 8008 which had powered the first personal computers was followed by a series of compatible microprocessors — the 8086, the 80286, and so on — and by a competing series of microprocessors from other firms, especially Motorola's 68000 family of chips. Each chip was many times more complex than the one before it; each promised a revolution in personal computing. (At least the ads for each new chip promised a revolution!) RISC (reduced instruction set computers) microprocessors, a new way of designing the computer's internal operations which became popular in the early 1990s, promised to allow the rate of increase to continue for many years to come.

The new microprocessors, dozens of times more powerful than those at the heart of early PCs, were accompanied by a vast increase in the amount of memory and storage space they could access. Prices continued to fall, and capability continued to increase. As PCs became "commodity" products, all more or less the same, fewer and fewer companies were able to compete successfully — a replay of what had happened in the radio industry some sixty years earlier. Rapid obsolescence, cheaper prices, and new uses meant the market could continue to grow. By 1992 some 65 million PCs were in use. But although increased power promised increased usefulness and increased ease of use, it seemed as if the ultimate promise of the PC was always a little further off, always a microprocessor generation away from being fulfilled.

But to those who needed it, the computer seemed a savior. Perhaps the most widely used software, after word processors, was the spreadsheet. (Spreadsheets model the operation of a project or firm in a matrix of interrelated numbers.) VisiCalc — the name comes from "visible calculation" — the first computer spreadsheet, was released in 1979. VisiCalc was a traditional ledger sheet, but with "intelligence"; the relationships among the cells were remembered by the computer so that a change in one entry would cause appropriate changes in others. Spreadsheets were an enormous hit, the first application that seemed to justify the purchase of a personal computer for office work. (Some 700,000 copies of VisiCalc were sold. Since it ran only on the Apple II, it was the main reason why so many people bought Apple computers.) In 1984 some 1 million spreadsheet programs were sold. More than any other software, they made the personal computer a success.

Spreadsheets were the office fad of the 1980s. Writer Steven Levy caught the spirit in his 1984 "A Spreadsheet Way of Knowledge":

> There are corporate executives, wholesalers, retailers, and small-business owners who talk about their business lives in two time periods: before and after the electronic spreadsheet. They cite prodigious gains in productivity. They speak of having a better handle on their businesses, of knowing more and planning better, or approaching their work more imaginatively. A virtual cult of the spreadsheet has formed, complete with gurus and initiates, detailed lore, arcane rituals — and an unshakable belief that the way the world works can be embodied in rows and columns of numbers and formulas.[45]

Many of the businessmen Levy talked to credit the spreadsheet with making possible the "entrepreneurial renaissance" of the 1980s. Levy suggests, though, that the ease of quantification that the spreadsheet allowed made businessmen tend to focus on "just the numbers," ignoring bigger issues. Or that the elegance of the spreadsheet — pure number, computer generated, *exact* — makes it easy to forget the shaky base of data on which it might be built. As Robert X. Cringely puts it in his very funny *Accidental Empires,* a history of the personal computer business: "PCs killed the office typewriter, made most secretaries obsolete, and made it possible for a 27-year-old M.B.A. with a PC, a spreadsheet program, and three pieces of questionable data to talk his bosses into looting the company pension plan and doing a leveraged buy out."[46]

Indeed, the most influential business book of the 1980s, Thomas J. Peters and Robert H. Waterman, Jr.'s, *In Search of Excellence,* makes the argument that managers' overdependence on analytic thought and quantitative analysis — a fascination with the numbers, as opposed to bigger questions of employees, production, and customers — was the main cause of America's failing competitiveness. It seems more than coincidental that a new philosophy of management that focused on the "bottom line" and the technical tool — the spreadsheet — found favor at the same time. The computer made it easy to manage "by the numbers," a policy that led to shortsighted decision-making and, many economists agree, the decline of American competitiveness in the 1980s.

Managerial work, especially midlevel managerial work, was targeted for reduction in many firms in the 1980s. In part this came about because of the increasing skill required for factory jobs; there was less need for a supervisor if the workers were responsible for their own performance. Middle managers were hit from above, too. Many midlevel executives had spent their time gathering and analyzing information, preparing it for their bosses. The computer made vast new amounts of information available, more readily than ever before, and made it easier to analyze. Executives could do the work themselves, and many middle managers found themselves out of a job. The new computer networks and computerized data analysis tools were in part to blame.

Computers also brought a variety of new health concerns to the white-collar workplace. In the late 1970s and early 1980s there were reports of radiation from computer monitors causing cataracts, miscarriages, and birth defects — reports that were never verified. Another scare swept computer users in the early 1990s, this time over nonionizing radiation. Repetitive stress injuries (RSI), muscular and skeletal injuries to the hand and wrist brought on by repetitive motions such as typing, were responsible for 56 percent of all workplace illnesses in 1990, some 185,000 workman's compensation claims. The costs of these injuries were estimated at as much as $20 billion a year.

Physical problems such as RSI and eye fatigue could usually be solved by improved ergonomics, redesigning the monitor, the keyboard, and the furniture, and with rules requiring workers to take occasional breaks from their work. Computer firms redesigned their monitors to produce much lower levels of radiation. Several localities passed laws regulating video display terminal (VDT) use. A few unions, including the Newspaper Guild, won contracts that provide for eye exams, eyeglass prescriptions, rest periods, and radiation testing.

Psychological problems connected with the monitoring of work also affected many users, often compounding physical problems. The computer made it easier than ever before to oversee workers. In 1984, according to one survey, 35 percent of video display operators had their productivity calculated by the computer. The computer counted keystrokes, measured break times, and used formulas to rate workers. At Northwest Orient Airlines, for example, data-entry workers were expected to type between 9,000 and 16,000 keystrokes per hour.

It was nothing new for typists to have their keystrokes monitored. Devices to count typewriter keystrokes had been around for many years. What was new was the accuracy (many systems measured workers' movements in units of 1/100,000 of an hour), the pervasiveness, and the immediacy (a supervisor could

Telephone operators used computerized switchboards which monitored their work. In 1984 telephone information operators were expected to answer each call in about one-half minute. Workers with a rating below 90 percent of that could be fired. The union protested this "firing by the numbers." James Irvine, a union official, put it this way in an interview with the *Washington Post*: "The whole world is changing and getting so computerized and dehumanized. It's important to have human beings, they ought not to be treated like an appendage to the goddamn computer."

see at a glance how each worker was doing). Also new, at some workplaces, was the complexity of the production measurements the computer allowed. Many workers were bewildered by the way their work was judged.

The new monitoring systems meant increased stress. The Post Office used computers to track the accuracy of mail sorters' work; less than 95 percent accuracy was grounds for firing. One mail sorter complained: "This computer is looking over your shoulder, watching you. It gets very stressful. . . . The supervisor knows everything about you, right in that machine."[47]

The early 1990s saw a new questioning of the value of computer systems — not just their cost to people in physical problems, job degradation, and job loss, but also their economic return. Economists added up the investment in information technology — about $1 trillion over the course of the 1980s, about one third of all corporate capital spending — and wondered what effect it had had. William Bowen, writing in *Fortune* in 1986, suggested that white-collar productivity grew more slowly after the introduction of computers than it had before. Citing figures compiled by Stephen S. Roach, an economist at Morgan Stanley, he reported that white-collar output per worker-hour had not changed between about 1970 and 1985, despite an enormous investment in computers in those years. Paul Strassman sums up the evidence in *The Information Payoff*: "The stagnant labor-productivity numbers simply show that even in America's two most automated service industries, there is no discernible effect on labor productivity as a result of extensive investments in computers."[48] "We see computers everywhere but in the productivity statistics," commented the Nobel Prize–winning economist Robert Solow.[49]

Part of the problem was the paradox of the incredible speed of improvement in computer technology: companies needed to make continuous new investment to stay up-to-date. But more important reasons could be found in the office itself. Some workers were spending more time learning how to use computers than they were worth. Other workers found they spent their time helping their co-workers with computers rather than doing their own work. (One 1992 study put the estimated cost of time lost from this kind of informal help at between $6,000 and $15,000 per PC, per year!) Or perhaps the computers were just not doing what needed to be done, or at least were not doing it any better than it had been done before. Or perhaps computers were increasing productivity, but it didn't show up in the figures. After all, white-collar productivity is notoriously hard to measure. During those same years, for example, government paperwork increased, requiring more white-collar work. (Perhaps there's a law of the computer here, that work expands to fill the processing capability!) And expectations are continually changing: people expect money to be available at ATMs twenty-four hours a day, or their loans to be processed in days, or to be able to make airline reservations or buy things over the phone at any hour of the day or night. Companies that don't keep up with the competition lose business, even if the computers they buy don't really increase productivity, or profits.

It's easy to document the misuse of computers, or computers' adding to inefficiency. Electronic mail can turn to electronic junk mail as workers distribute memos to everyone. One study found that secretaries spend about 4 percent of their time trying to get software to work, and estimated that 2 percent of the annual gross domestic product — almost $100 billion — is lost through people playing with their computers when they should be working. Standards of presentation have increased enormously. Documents once acceptable typewritten now have to look typeset.

But most important, computers had been put to work at the wrong jobs. Useless paperwork done by computer simply produces more useless paperwork. Badly managed jobs done by computer are still badly managed. It doesn't increase productivity. Some companies use computers to automate their problems, not to solve them. A 1992 editorial in *Business Week* called for "a corporate '12-step' program for technology sobriety," a rethinking of corporate goals and a close match of technology to those goals. "Without going back to the basics of corporate strategy and good management," *Business Week*'s editors wrote, "the addition of new technology can actually bollix things up, making them more complex, confusing and expensive."[50] Many companies buy new technology just because it's available, not because they need it. (*Business Week*'s advice was not all that different from that McKinsey and Company had given thirty years earlier!)

One computer advertisement raised the obvious question: "We've spent a trillion dollars. Are we having fun yet? . . . It's high noon on the cost justification trail. The bean counters are closing in. What's to be done?"[51] Some suggest that more technology, designed to fit the way businesses actually work, is the answer. Only 10 percent or so of workers use personal computers, they say. (People in the computer industry tend to take this line.) Others suggest that new, easier-to-use software might close the productivity gap. Jim Manzi, president and CEO of Lotus Development Corporation, suggests that networks, "groupware" (programs that allow people to solve problems together), and mobile computing, the hot new computer technologies of the 1990s (and ones his company is selling), will solve the productivity dilemma. Still others suggest that companies need to reorganize themselves to take advantage of computers. Economic historian Paul David says, based on historical analogy, that we just haven't waited long enough; productivity gains will show up eventually. But it seems that new ways of organizing work, of utilizing human skills, are at least as essential as new technologies.

By the early 1990s personal computers and workstations were powerful computers. In some ways they were the match of the minicomputers of just a decade earlier. Even more important, they were designed to be used as part of computer networks. The ideas of "distributed computing" — making use of computer power and storage anyplace on a network — and "client-server computing" — a combination of large and small computers hooked together so that each is used for what it does best — became new paradigms for computing. In many instances the mainframe computer with terminals gave way to a system of networked PCs and workstations, a process called downsizing. In 1991 the worldwide computer industry received more revenue from personal computers than all other computers put together. In 1992 more than 50 percent of companies were downsizing their computer systems.

Networks tying together many personal computers changed the nature of the computing environment in many businesses. An unanticipated result of the spread of computer networks designed for communications among computers was communications among people. By the early 1990s E-mail was widely believed to be a key computer application, and many firms sold products that allowed office workers to work jointly on projects. "Workgroup computing" and "groupware" became two of the hottest buzzwords in the computer business.

Networked personal computers and workstations could talk to one another, exchange files and mail, and, sometimes, share the work of processing data. It seemed that they would replace the time-sharing mainframe once and for all. Advanced systems allowed computers on the network to share work, speeding up the solution of complex problems. By 1990 there were more than 1 million local-area networks in operation. There were also networks that tied computers together around the world. (See BEYOND TELEPHONES.)

Large computers were changing, too. The traditional von Neumann idea of the computer was coming to an end. Parallel processing — dozens, even thousands of small computers, all hooked together to work on a problem — became a serious competitor to the biggest, most exotic supercomputers. Indeed, workstations and personal computers hooked up over high-speed networks to share the work of computation — "ensemble computing" — offered as much computer power as a large mainframe or supercomputer.

As computer technology changed, the computer industry changed, too. In 1992 the American computer industry was a $256 billion business. But it was a business in disarray. Downsizing was the rage. In 1987 mainframes, supercomputers, and midrange computers had represented about two thirds of the market. Just five years later those profitable computers accounted for less than half the market, personal computers the other half. Makers of large computers saw their machines beaten out by smaller computers. They were forced to go into competition with themselves, selling smaller, cheaper, and less profitable machines to the customers who had bought their larger, more expensive, more profitable models. Even IBM, which for years had forbidden "self-impact" to protect its mainframe market, at last succumbed. Facing a loss of some $5 billion in 1992, it broke itself into several small, competing businesses. *Business Week* described the computer industry as "an industry on the skids."[52]

The new demand for open systems — for published hardware and software specifications available for anyone to use — also meant changes. Since personal computers had become commodities, their manufacturers were forced to compete more on price and less on technological advantages. Proprietary operating systems for large computers began to give way to systems that were available to all, which meant that computer manufacturers couldn't compete on proprietary software. (See SOFTWARE.)

But even with all the problems of the industry, the product kept selling. There seemed no end to the number of ways computers could be useful, promising to solve yet another problem. Faster, more powerful computers, almost everyone believed, would find answers to problems faster. That was true, though, only as long as the problems were susceptible to computer solution. And more and more they were, for society had structured itself around the computer. Joseph Weizenbaum captured the close linkage between the computer and our bureaucratic, capitalist society in his seminal book, *Computer Power and Human Reason*: "The computer was not a prerequisite to the survival of modern society in the post-war period and beyond; its enthusiastic, uncritical embrace by the most 'progressive' elements of American government, business and industry quickly made it a resource essential to society's survival *in the form* that the computer itself had been instrumental in shaping."[53]

FOR FURTHER READING

See, in addition to the books listed in BEFORE COMPUTERS, these more narrowly focused books: William Aspray, *John von Neumann and the Origins of Modern Computing* (1990); Nancy Stern, *From ENIAC to UNIVAC: An Appraisal of the Eckert-Mauchly Computers* (1981); Kent C. Redmond and Thomas M. Smith, *Project Whirlwind: The History of a Pioneer Computer* (1980); N. Metropolis, J. Howlett, and Gian-Carlo Rota, eds., *A History of Computing in the Twentieth Century: A Collection of Essays* (1980); and Adele Goldberg, ed., *A History of Personal Workstations* (1988). Brian Randell, ed., *The Origins of Digital Computers,* 3d ed. (1982), is a collection of excerpts from important papers in the history of computers.

On integrated circuits, see T. R. Reid, *The Chip: How Two Americans Invented the Microchip and Launched a Revolution* (1984); Ernest Braun and Stuart Macdonald, *Revolution in Miniature: The History and Impact of Semiconductor Electronics,* 2d ed. (1982); Paul Forman, "Behind Quantum Electronics: National Security as a Basis for Physical Research in the United States, 1940–1960," *Historical Studies in the Physical Sciences* (1987): 149–229; and Alfonso Hernán Molina, *Social Basis of the Microelectronics Revolution* (1989).

On particular applications, useful books include Paul E. Ceruzzi, *Beyond the Limits: Flight Enters the Computer Age* (1989); on the introduction of numerical control machine tools, David Noble, *Forces of Production: A Social History of Industrial Automation* (1984); and for an opposing point of view, J. Francis Reintjes, *Numerical Control: Making a New Technology* (1991). On robots, see Isaac Asimov and Karen A. Frenkel, *Robots: Machines in Man's Image* (1985); and Peter B. Scott, *The Robotics Revolution: The Complete Guide* (1984). More generally, for computers in the factory, see Harley Shaiken, *Work Transformed: Automation and Labor in the Computer Age* (1985); Marjory Blumenthal and Jim Dray, "The Automated Factory: Vision and Reality," *Technology Review* (January 1985); and Shoshana Zuboff, *In the Age of the Smart Machine: The Future of Work and Power* (1988).

There's a large literature on computers and office work, including Diane Werneke, *Microelectronics and Office Jobs: The Impact of the Chip on Women's Employment* (1983); Richard W. Larson and David J. Zinney, *The White Collar Shuffle: Who Does What in Today's Computerized Workplace* (1990); and Barbara Garson, *The Electronic Sweatshop: How Computers Are Transforming the Office of the Future into the Factory of the Past* (1988). For an overview, see George Wybouw, *Office Automation and Productivity: Review of the Literature* (1986). For statistics, see H. Hartmann et al., *Computer Chips and Paper Clips: Technology and Women's Employment,* 2 vols. (1986–1987); and Steven Levy, "A Spreadsheet Way of Knowledge," in *Computers in the Human Context: Information Technology, Productivity, and People,* ed. Tom Forester (1989), pp. 318–326.

On computers in war, see Paul Dickson, *The Electronic Battlefield* (1976); and Les Levidow and Kevin Robins, eds., *Cyborg Worlds: The Military Information Society* (1989).

Not much has been written on the cultural response to the computer. See Paul Ceruzzi, "Computers and Expectations, 1935–1985," in *Imagining Tomorrow: History, Technology, and the American Future,* ed. Joseph J. Corn (1986), pp. 188–201; and Langdon Winner, "Mythinformation," in *The Whale and the Reactor: A Search for Limits in an Age of High Technology* (1986). See also the general books listed in the INTRODUCTION.

Collections of articles that provide an excellent overview of the issues and history are Tom Forester, ed., *Computers in the Human Context: Information Technology, Productiv-*

ity, and People (1989); and Tom Forester, ed., *High-Tech Society: The Story of the Information Technology Revolution* (1987).

NOTES

1. Quoted in William Aspray, *John von Neumann and the Origins of Modern Computing* (1990), p. 47.

2. Paul Edwards, "Closed World: Systems Discourse, Military Policy, and Post-World War II U.S. Historical Consciousness," in *Cyborg Worlds: The Military Information Society,* ed. Les Levidow and Kevin Robins (1989), p. 149.

3. Quoted in Paul Ceruzzi, "Computers and Expectations," in *Imagining Tomorrow: History, Technology, and the American Future,* ed. Joseph J. Corn (1986), p. 194.

4. Arthur R. Miller, *The Assault on Privacy* (1971), pp. 22–23 and 256.

5. James Gibson, *The Perfect War: The War We Couldn't Lose and How We Did* (1988), p. 14; quoted in Edwards, "Closed World," p. 153.

6. Walter A. McDougall, *The Heavens and the Earth: A Political History of the Space Age* (1985), p. 333.

7. Hannah Arendt, *Crises of the Republic* (1972), p. 11; quoted in Joseph Weizenbaum, *Computer Power and Human Reason: From Judgment to Calculation* (1976), p. 14.

8. Quoted in Paul Dickson, *The Electronic Battlefield* (1976), p. 76.

9. Quoted in Dickson, *Electronic Battlefield,* pp. 220–222.

10. J. Benn, "Where the Power Belongs," *Nation,* August 26, 1968, p. 36; quoted in Miller, *The Assault on Privacy,* p. 126.

11. Marshall McLuhan and Quentin Fiore, *The Medium Is the Message* (1967; reprint 1989), p. 12.

12. Quoted in Miller, *The Assault on Privacy,* frontispiece.

13. Michael Harrington, *Toward a Democratic Left* (1968), p. 144.

14. Hal Draper, *Berkeley: The New Student Revolt* (1965), p. 153.

15. Mathew White and Jaffer Ali, *The Official Prisoner Companion* (1988), pp. 9–11.

16. Quoted in Charles R. Walker, ed., *Technology, Industry, and Man: The Age of Acceleration* (1968), p. 298.

17. Quoted in Julius Rezler, *Automation and Industrial Labor* (1969), p. 22.

18. Quoted in Barbara Garson, *The Electronic Sweatshop: How Computers Are Transforming the Office of the Future into the Factory of the Past* (1988), p. 166.

19. Quoted in Rezler, *Automation and Industrial Labor,* p. 54.

20. Norbert Wiener, *The Human Use of Human Beings: Cybernetics and Society,* 2d ed. (1950; reprint 1988), p. 150.

21. Lamont J. Jenkins et al., "Getting More out of NC," *American Machinist* (October 1981): 185; quoted in Harley Shaiken, *Work Transformed: Automation and Labor in the Computer Age* (1985), p. 48.

22. Keith Wheeler, "Impact of Automation," *Life,* July 19, 1963, p. 68B.

23. Paul Ceruzzi, *Beyond the Limits: Flight Enters the Computer Age* (1989), p. 133.

24. George Devol, U.S. Patent 2,988,237, "Programmed Article Transfer"; quoted in Frederik L. Schodt, *Inside the Robot Kingdom: Japan, Mechatronics, and the Coming Robotopia* (1988), p. 31.

25. R. C. Becher and Robert Dewar, "Robot Trends at General Motors," *American Machinist* (August 1979): 71; quoted in Shaiken, *Work Transformed,* p. 173.

26. Studs Terkel, *Working* (1974), p. xi.

27. "The Factory of the Future," *Newsweek*, September 6, 1982, p. 59.

28. Quoted in Gregory Stricharchuk and Ralph E. Winter, "Second Thoughts," *Wall Street Journal*, September 16,1985, p. 18.

29. Quoted in Norman Gall, "It's Later Than We Think," *Forbes* (February 1981): 65.

30. Shoshana Zuboff, *In the Age of the Smart Machine: The Future of Work and Power* (1988), p. 10.

31. Quoted in Rezler, *Automation and Industrial Labor*, p. 22.

32. Quoted in Garson, *The Electronic Sweatshop*, p. 36.

33. John G. Kemeny, *Man and the Computer* (1972), p. 21.

34. John McCarthy, "Time-Sharing Computer Systems," in *Computers and the World of the Future*, ed. Martin Greenberger (1962), p. 236.

35. Kemeny, *Man and the Computer*, p. 21.

36. J. A. Morton, *International Science and Technology* (July 1966): 38; quoted in T. R. Reid, *The Chip: How Two Americans Invented the Microchip and Launched a Revolution* (1984), p. 18.

37. Bob Reed; quoted in *Digital at Work: Snapshots from the First Thirty-Five Years,* ed. Jamie Parker Pearson (1992), p. 84.

38. Intel advertisement, *Electronic News*, November 15, 1971; reprinted in Stan Augarten, *Bit by Bit: An Illustrated History of Computers* (1984), p. 264.

39. Augarten, *Bit by Bit*, p. 270.

40. Eddie Currie; quoted in Steven Levy, *Hackers: Heroes of the Computer Revolution* (1984), p. 226.

41. Quoted in Jon Palfremun and Doron Swade, *The Dream Machine: Exploring the Computer Age* (1992), p. 102.

42. George Gilder, *Microcosm: The Quantum Revolution in Economics and Technology* (1989), p. 352.

43. Quoted in Levy, *Hackers*, p. 175.

44. Langdon Winner, "Mythinformation," in *The Whale and the Reactor: A Search for Limits in an Age of High Technology* (1986), pp. 100 and 106.

45. Steven Levy, "A Spreadsheet Way of Knowledge," in *Computers in the Human Context: Information Technology, Productivity, and People*, ed. Tom Forester (1989), p. 319.

46. Robert X. Cringely, *Accidental Empires: How the Boys of Silicon Valley Make Their Millions, Battle Foreign Competition, and Still Can't Get a Date* (1992), p. 4.

47. Quoted in *Washington Post*, September 2, 1984, p. A1.

48. Paul Strassman, *The Information Payoff: The Transformation of Work in the Electronic Age* (1985), p. 163.

49. Quoted in Paul A. David, "The Dynamo and the Computer: An Historical Perspective on the Modern Productivity Paradox," *American Economic Review* (May 1990): 355.

50. "Curing a High Tech Hangover," and "The New Realism in Office Systems," *Business Week*, June 15, 1992, pp. 128 and 146.

51. Advertisement for Logical Operations in *MacWeek*, June 15, 1992, p. 52.

52. *Business Week*, November 23, 1992, p. 90.

53. Weizenbaum, *Computer Power and Human Reason*, pp. 28–29.

Software is the instructions that make a computer work. A computer programmer writes software that tells the computer exactly what to do, how to respond to data, and what answers to output. Programming a computer is an exacting task — much harder to do than the first computer designers thought it would be.

I N F O R M A T I O N
S O F T W A R E

I N 1792 THE FRENCH ENGINEER GASPARD CLAIR PRONY
was put in charge of drawing up a new set of mathematical tables. These
tables — logarithms and trigonometric tables used in astronomy, navigation, and engineering — were to be a monument to the new French
Republic, "a monument of calculation the most vast and imposing that
had ever been executed, or even conceived," a historian of mathematics wrote
in 1834.[1]

To undertake this task a system of division of labor was established. Six
eminent mathematicians determined the best formulas to use. Beneath them,
to carry out their decisions, were ten mathematicians, whose job it was to convert these formulas into simpler ones that required only addition and subtraction for calculation. These were then given to a group of one hundred
"computers" — that is, people who did calculations, which is what the term
originally meant, before the invention of the mechanical or electronic computer. These computers were organized in such a way that each one did a simple
piece of the problem and passed it on to another computer, who did the next.
The final result was recorded.

The job of the mathematicians at the top and intermediate levels was
programming: they turned the complicated problem into a simple set of calculations and operations that could be done sequentially by following the rules laid
out by the programmer.

Seventeen volumes of manuscript tables were calculated, though they
were never published. But the idea remained: to solve problems, break them
down into small pieces that could be carried out using simple procedures, and organize those procedures so that they could be done "without thinking." (The best
computers, Prony found, were those who knew only addition and subtraction!)

The idea of breaking mathematical problems into simple arithmetic
pieces, and then organizing the solution of those pieces so that they could be easily and quickly solved, had a natural application to computing devices. Charles Babbage, inventor of the Analytical Engine in the mid-nineteenth century, gave a good
bit of thought to how his machine might be given instructions. The Analytical Engine, properly programmed, wrote Ada Lovelace, an associate of Babbage's, "may
be described as being the material expression of any indefinite function of any de-

gree of generality and complexity." One simply needed to indicate on punch cards "the law of development of the particular function that may be under consideration." The cards would "compel the mechanism to act accordingly."[2]

PROGRAMMING BEFORE THE COMPUTER

Lovelace put well the problem that would face the designers of programmable calculators and computers: how to "compel the mechanism" to undertake the calculations for "any function." The first mechanical computers avoided the difficulty by being single-function machines, designed to undertake only one class of problem. Adding machines, and even the first punch card tabulators, were "hard-wired" to add, or tabulate, or whatever; they were not general-purpose but single-purpose. All of the "programming" was in the head of the person running them.

The first step toward programming was to redesign the "hard-wired" connections so that they might be easily changed. In this way machines could calculate a variety of problems, so long as all of them had the same basic format and followed the same procedures. In 1902 a simple plugboard was added to the Hollerith tabulating machine so that the "programmer" could decide which columns in the card should be added to which other columns. Railroad interlockers, devices that controlled railroad switches and signals, were "programmed" by bolting in new pieces to represent the configuration of the tracks that the interlocker was designed to control. (For more on these machines, see BEFORE COMPUTERS.)

Scientific calculating machines allowed for changes in variables, and some programmability. Tide-predicting machines, for example, could be set for different starting points and different locations, and would then carry out their calculations according to the preprogrammed mechanical scheme. Vannevar Bush's product integraph (invented in the mid-1920s) could integrate equations, that is, determine the area under a mathematical curve. But why not make the machine even more flexible? The next step was to build machines that allowed changes in their very setup, so that a much larger class of problems could be attacked. In the 1930s and early 1940s a series of general-purpose programmable machines were built. They were analog and digital, decimal and binary, mechanical, electromechanical, and — by the mid-1940s — electronic. (For more on all these machines, see COMPUTERS.)

The early computers were "programmable," but not without a lot of work. Wallace J. Eckert at Columbia University used what he called a mechanical programmer to connect and control a variety of IBM card punch machines. It consisted of a series of cams that controlled the machines; to change the "program," you would file a new nick in the cam. Bush's differential analyzer, started in 1930 at MIT, was "programmed" by rearranging gears and wheels and connecting rods, changing their sizes and configuration, as well as by setting dials and drawing graphs to represent new equations — a time-consuming process. Presper Eckert, who worked on the machine, recalled that to set it up, you had "to take lead hammers and set screwdrivers and go to work on it like an auto mechanic, for a couple of days."[3]

Programming like this was the bottleneck in using these machines, and engineers did their best to speed things up. During the war a second differential analyzer was built at MIT. This one used electronics to replace some of the mechanism, and punched paper tape readers from Teletype machines to tell the machine which shafts, adders, and integrators to connect and what initial conditions and constants to use. This machine was much more accurate, and could be set up to solve a problem in only five to fifteen minutes. Punch card machines also saw continuous improvement over the years as new devices were invented to sort, collate, compare, and calculate using punch cards. Scientists working at Los Alamos on the atomic bomb found even more complex ways to use punch card machines and calculators, setting them up as "a combination of the calculating machine and the factory assembly line . . . mass production married to numerical calculations."[4] In 1946 IBM introduced a "calculating punch" that could be programmed to undertake as many as a half dozen steps.

Punched paper tape, which had been used to record messages for Teletype (and which wasn't too different from the piano rolls for player pianos), was an obvious answer. If you could punch the data and the instructions on the tape, and have the machine reconfigure itself by reading the tape, it would speed things up enormously. Konrad Zuse, in Germany, developed a series of general-purpose computers — from the Z1 in 1938 to the Z4 in 1945 — that used binary numbers, and read both numbers and instructions from punched tape. The Z3, the first operational general-purpose program-controlled calculator, was completed in December 1941.

At Harvard, Howard H. Aiken proposed that a scientific calculator be built by linking together many calculators and using a "player piano" roll to control them. IBM agreed to assist, and in 1938 started building the Automatic Sequence Controlled Calculator, better known as the Mark I, the first automatic, general-purpose, program-controlled digital calculator. It was an electromechanical machine, built mostly out of tabulator parts, and programmed using paper tape. The tape, a few inches wide, with some two dozen holes in each line, controlled clutches that allowed wheels to turn. Data was entered using switches as well as paper tape; the tape indicated the location of the data, and the place where the results should be output.

The military found uses for all of these calculating devices when World War II began. Its major demand on these scientific calculators was for computing ballistics tables. These tables indicated what angle a gun should be fired at for a desired distance and altitude, given a number of factors such as wind speed and direction, air temperature and density, weight of shell and powder, and even the springiness of the ground the gun sat on. Each calculation required the solution of complex differential equations, approximately 750 multiplications, and took several hours of set-up and computation time on a differential analyzer — and each gun required thousands of calculations. The need for a high-speed programmable calculator was obvious. The ENIAC (Electronic Numerical Integrator and Computer), at the University of Pennsylvania, was the first answer.

It took about two days to program the ENIAC. To program it, first you'd set a few thousand switches to specify instructions, and then you'd plug in cables, a few hundred of them, to determine the order in which the instructions were to be executed. ENIAC wasn't easy to program, but ease of programming was not necessary for calculating ballistics tables. To change data, you'd feed in new punch cards; to change constants in an equation, you'd readjust switches. (There were 6,000 of them!) An ENIAC program was a wiring diagram.

ENIAC was fine for calculating ballistics tables — slow, but useful for problems that required only minor changes in a basic formula. But the war had brought new problems that required more complex mathematics, and greater flexibility. A programmable computer, not a calculator, seemed the answer. The basic design for such a machine was worked out by John von Neumann and the engineers who had built the ENIAC, Eckert and Mauchly, and presented in the *First Draft of a Report on the EDVAC*, in 1945.

The report on the EDVAC (Electronic Discrete Variable Automatic Computer) described something new: the stored-program computer. Instead of being entered on paper tape or by turning dials and connecting plugs, the instructions would be stored in the computer's memory — just like the data. That way the computer could modify its instructions as it went along. There would be a central control, which would make sure that one instruction was executed at a time, and that each instruction would be executed in the right order. To solve a problem, the computer's central processing unit followed the instructions to carry out a sequence of actions.

The theoretical foundations for this sort of machine had been laid a few years earlier, in a paper published by British mathematician Alan Turing. His "On Computable Numbers with an Application to the *Entscheidungs-problem*" (1937) had shown that an abstract universal computing machine could solve any problem that could be described according to the rules of algebra. The "Turing machine," as it came to be called — an imaginary machine, not a real one — was a tape-reading and tape-moving machine. It had an infinitely long tape, marked with a finite number of symbols. The machine could read one symbol at a time, and move the tape forward or backward depending on what it read. It could also print a new symbol, or erase an old one. After the war Turing applied his theoretical notions to a real computer.

In a lecture he gave to the London Mathematical Society in 1947, Alan Turing described how such a "universal" computer would work:

> Some years ago I . . . considered a type of machine which had a central mechanism, and an infinite memory which was contained on an infinite tape. . . . Machines such as the ACE [Automatic Computing Engine, which Turing designed] may be regarded as practical versions of this same type of machine. . . . We may say that the universal machine is one which, when supplied with the appropriate instructions, can be made to do any rule of thumb process. This feature is paralleled in digital computing machines such as the ACE. They are in fact practical versions of the universal machine. . . . When any particular problem has to be handled, the appropriate instructions for the computing process involved are stored in the memory of the ACE and it is then "set up" for carrying out that process.[5]

These instructions were what has come to be called *software*. They were part of the machine, but not part of its *hardware*, as the plug-wire configurations had been. (People began using the term software to make this distinction around 1950.) The idea of a central stored program was tried out on the ENIAC by Adele Goldstine and Richard Clippinger in 1948. The new language had, originally, fifty-one "orders" ("instructions," in modern computer jargon). It made the computer easier to program, but slowed it down greatly, and therefore didn't find wide use. As long as machine time was more valuable than the programmer's time, it made sense for the programmer, not the computer, to do the work of talking in the other's language. In June 1948 a small demonstration machine designed by Max Newman, the University of Manchester Mark I, ran the world's first stored program.

PROGRAMMING AND PROGRAMMERS

Some early computer designers thought that programming would not be difficult. Once the machines were built, and the mathematics of the problem had been carefully stated, they assumed that the instructions to the machine wouldn't require much thought. But von Neumann pointed out the difficulties. Programming, he wrote, "is not a mere question of translation (of a mathematical text into a code), but rather a question of providing a control scheme for a highly dynamical process, all parts of which may undergo repeated and relevant changes in the course of this process."[6] Just how hard it would be to make computer programs work came as a surprise to some computer pioneers. Maurice Wilkes, designer of the EDSAC, recalled: "It just had not occurred to me that there was going to be any difficulty about getting programs working. And it was with somewhat of a shock that I realized that for the rest of my life I was going to spend a good deal of my time finding mistakes that I had made myself in programs."[7]

The early computers were programmed in binary numbers. A line of a program for the Manchester Mark I, for example, was a row of sixteen binary digits, the first thirteen specifying the location in the memory of a piece of data or another instruction, the last three specifying the operation (addition, subtraction, moving, or whatever) to be done on it. Turing developed a "symbolic language" — close to what is today called an assembly language — which used some fifty short mnemonics that told that machine what to do, down to the details of where to store data. Assembly language was translated by the computer directly into machine code and then acted upon. The BINAC and UNIVAC used "Short Code," a system similar to Turing's symbolic language.

The need for higher-level languages, which would be easier to use, was clear. Alick Glennie, a programmer for the Manchester Mark I, described the problem, and the solution: "To make it easy one must make coding comprehensible. Present notations have many disadvantages; all are incomprehensible to the novice, they are all different (one for each machine) and they are never easy to read. It is quite difficult to decipher coded programmes even with notes and even if you yourself made the programme several months ago."[8] It was a *cri de coeur* that programmers would repeat many times. Software was hard to write, time-consuming, and expensive. The solution to this first "software crisis" would be new languages that were easier to use.

Grace Hopper, at Remington Rand, de-

Engineers had long talked of electrical systems having "bugs," or problems. When Grace Hopper, a programmer on the Harvard Mark II, found this moth jammed in a relay, she wrote in the log, "First actual case of bug being found." Fixing problems in computer hardware and software has come to be called "debugging."

Before time-sharing, programmers would punch their programs onto punch cards and submit the "deck" of cards to the computer operator. The programmer would return several hours later to pick up the results of the run, make whatever changes were necessary, and try again. Shown is a keypunch room at MIT in the early 1960s.

veloped the idea of a compiler in 1951. Her A-0 compiler for the UNIVAC translated the English-like phrases of a computer language into the binary code of the machine. But more important, it left some of the details to the computer. The programmer didn't need to worry, for instance, about exactly where the data was stored, or about retyping subroutines each time they were used. The computer kept track of those details; the programmer was able to refer to the data or subroutine by a name.

Perhaps the first high-level computer programming language, called Plankalkul, was invented by Konrad Zuse for his Z4 computer in 1945. (His work, though, was not widely known, and had no real effect on the later history of computer languages.) The MIT Whirlwind used the first practical compiler and high-level languages, invented by J. Halcombe Laning and Niel Zierler in 1953. It looked more like English than previous languages, and helped keep track of the details of where the data were, but it was too slow for everyday use: the machine ran at only one tenth its normal speed when the compiler was used! But the value of high level languages was clear. There would be a continuous development of computer languages, which would parallel the development of new computers, and new uses for computers.

The early 1950s saw many new computers, and with them many new languages. The IBM 704 was the first computer that had an easy-to-use, and widely used, high-level language. It was released in 1957 after several years of work led by John Backus and Cuthbert Hurd. This language was FORTRAN, short for "formula translation." Backus later described their aims: "One of our goals was to design a language which would make it possible for engineers and scientists to write programs for the 704. We also wanted to eliminate a lot of the bookkeeping and detailed, repetitive planning which hand coding involved."[9] FORTRAN, Backus wrote, "began with the recognition of a basic problem of economics: programming and debugging costs already exceeded the cost of running a program, and as computers became faster and cheaper this imbalance would become more and more intolerable."[10] FORTRAN, designed for scientific and engineering use, was soon joined by COBOL (common business-oriented language), for business applications. Both of these languages had semantic structures similar to spoken languages and used common words such as "run," "do," "read," and "print," which made them easier to learn and use.

The new high-level programming languages joined, but didn't replace, assembly language, which allowed more detailed control over the internal workings of the machine. Languages such as FORTRAN and COBOL had to be compiled, or turned into an assembly language program by a special program called a compiler. This tended to make them less efficient, and more wasteful of computer time and computer memory, a problem that became less critical as computers got cheaper. The new languages also had the advantage of being more or less machine-independent, or "portable": the same program, written in a high-level language, could be run on almost any computer, unlike assembly-language programs, which were limited to one kind of computer.

There was much debate about what sort of language programmers should use. Many programmers were opposed to languages such as FORTRAN. In 1962, at a symposium on the future of computers, Peter Elias of MIT argued that since computers would soon be speaking human languages, it was a waste of time to train programmers in computer languages. Others at the meeting thought that only by writing in machine code could the computer be made to go fast enough; there was an enormous fear of wasting the machine's time. Some programmers were afraid that high-level languages would result in a loss of some of their professional skills. Grace Hopper, one of the first programmers for the Mark I, suggested that this might not be a bad idea: "We should not only take away the programmer's freedom to allocate storage and time, we should also take away his freedom to arrange characters on cards and tapes. . . . Programmers are a very curious group. They arose very quickly, became a profession very rapidly, and were all too soon infected with a certain amount of resistance to change."[11] John McCarthy, an MIT professor of computer science, wrote that high-level languages "are not particularly easier to learn than machine code. Their purpose is to be more powerful, to permit an idea that can be expressed verbally in five minutes to be programmed in two weeks instead of six months, as is now required using straightforward machine languages."[12]

Computer languages created a new kind of job. In the late 1940s, telling the computer what to do became a separate task from building the computer, or fixing its electronics, or figuring out the problems for the computer to solve. Computer programmers wrote the code that told the computer what to do. (Indeed, before the word *programmer* came to this country from England, the people who programmed computers were called coders.) They first analyzed the problem (soon this would become the job of a specialist, a systems analyst), and then wrote the instructions that the computer would follow to solve it.

Many of the earliest programmers of the new computing machines were women with math and science backgrounds, often with Ph.D.'s in mathematics. When ENIAC first became operational, for example, its instruction manual and much of the early programming was done by Adele Goldstine. John Holberton was in charge of programming simpler problems; to assist him, six of the best computers — all women — were assigned to learn how to program the machine. Grace Hopper had been teaching mathematics at Vassar College when the navy sent her to Harvard to prepare coding for the Mark I.

Women were chosen as programmers for the early computers in part because there were few men available; military service and other war work made for labor scarcity. And women had traditionally had the job of "computer," that is, the person who did calculations for scientists, and so it seemed to make sense for them to take over the care and feeding of the new calculating machines. Women had also long been the keepers of office machines, and programming computers seemed, in some ways, to be a clerical sort of job.

In 1957 there were about 15,000 programmers in the United States. When IBM was looking to hire programmers, it ran advertisements suggesting that "those who enjoy playing chess or solving puzzles will find this work absorbing." (The *New Yorker* was sufficiently fascinated by the ad to send a re-porter to check out how "a profession we'd never heard of should have as many as fifteen thousand members.")[13]

Ten years later, in 1967, there were some 200,000 programmers in the United States, servicing some 35,000 computers, and there were continuing complaints about the "programmer shortage." Estimates were that the number of programmers needed by 1970 would be as high as 650,000. But whom to hire? It seemed impossible to figure out who would make a good programmer. The industry first hired mathematicians, then chess players, then those who liked solving mathematical puzzles. The industry began to use tests such as the PAT — the Programmer Aptitude Test, developed in 1955 — in hopes of find-ing good programmers. It was a test of "logical ability" and "abstract reasoning power." But even its originator, Walter McNamara, admitted in 1967, "We still don't know enough about what makes a person a good programmer."[14]

As the field expanded, men came to outnumber women. Historians Beth Parkhurst and Joan Richards, who analyzed the hiring of programmers in the 1950s and 1960s, showed that few women were hired to work at business programming. In the business world, programming was a prestigious, highly paid job, and so was mostly reserved for men. Women continued to be accept-ed as programmers in scientific and engineering fields, though, in part because programming was a comparatively low-status job in those fields. Overall, in 1967, 20 to 30 percent of programmers were women. "Girl programmers," a 1967 guide to careers in computer programming suggested, could do every bit as well as men. Even Miss USA 1964 became a computer programmer! It was the glamour job of the 1960s.

But while programming was glamorous, it was clearly a bottleneck in the increasingly important application of computers. By 1965 IBM was spend-ing as much to develop software as hardware. And as long as programming was an "art," it would remain hard to organize, hard to manage. Almost every ma-jor software project took much longer than predicted, and adding more pro-grammers often made progress slower, not faster.

Managers began to talk of a "software crisis." They came up with new schemes to improve programmers' productivity. The first step was to change the way programmers worked. One computer programmer remembered "the good old days": "I remember that in the fifties and early sixties I was a 'jack of all trades.' As a programmer I got to deal with the whole process. I would think through a problem, talk to the clients, write my own code, and operate the ma-chine."[15] But companies didn't like this. Programmers were difficult to control, often preferred to work strange hours, and didn't follow dress codes. Dick Bran-don, writing in 1970 on how to manage programmers, noted that "the normal employer-employee relationship, which in part depends on the fear of termina-tion or disciplinary action, does not exist. . . . It is not at all uncommon for a pro-grammer to threaten resignation, while simultaneously generating the type of undocumented programs that increase management's dependence on him. Thus he is in a position of strength from which he can (and in the aggregate, often does) use mild blackmail to achieve greater status, money, or dominance over management." Programmers, Brandon complained, were "excessively indepen-dent, egocentric, and slightly neurotic."[16]

This began to change as managers of information processing centers developed new ways to get around the artistic nature of the work, to make software writing closer to a production-line operation. Why not "software engineering," or "automatic programming"? It would be a goal of software managers for the next few decades, and many firms set to work to make software writing easier to control. An observer wrote in 1972: "The volume of work to be done is increasing, and wages less so. The romantic aura surrounding this inscrutable occupation is, if it ever really existed, beginning to fade. . . . Even the claim of programmers to be a special breed of professional employee has come to be disputed. Still more significant, authority over the freewheeling brotherhood of programmers is slipping into the paws of administrators and managers — who try to make the work of programmers planned, measurable, uniform and faceless."[17]

The first step was a division of labor. Starting in the 1960s, with the introduction of IBM's System/360, many firms no longer allowed programmers to enter the computer room. Instead, they handed their program to operators, who ran it for them and returned the results. In the 1960s systems analysis was established as a separate department. Systems analysts dealt with managers, to translate their desires into technical terms. The programmers became technicians, dealing only with the details. It was then easier to control them, to establish guidelines for their work. No end of productivity measurements were established: most of them, in the 1960s and 1970s, expected a programmer to produce about ten lines of code a day. (Curiously, this number didn't change much, even as languages became more powerful, and as new tools were developed to help make programming easier.)

The attempt to establish programming factories seemed to have succeeded in the 1970s. Programmers' salaries, which had increased steadily throughout the 1960s, leveled off. In 1971 the Department of Labor ruled that programmers were not "professionals," but that systems analysts were. Repeated attempts to institute certification programs failed, but so did most union efforts that tried to organize programmers. Programmers were "knowledge workers," but knowledge workers who worked within very narrowly established guidelines, and under close control.

As businesses came to depend on their computers, the amount they spent on them kept increasing. Some $5 billion was spent on new hardware in 1980, and some $1 billion on software. And software became increasingly expensive, in part because it was so labor-intensive. In 1977 the *Wall Street Journal* estimated that labor costs accounted for 75 percent of data-processing costs.[18] Aetna Insurance, for example, had 2,000 programmers on staff in 1983. One 1980 estimate suggested that many corporate users were spending $2 on software for every $1 on hardware. Software is expensive, in part because it's hard to get right. Some studies found that up to 50 percent of the total costs of software development were for debugging and quality control.[19] Fifty percent of the cost of U.S. military software, for example, is devoted to paperwork and documenting how the program operates, while actual writing of software accounts for less than 20 percent of the time and effort put into the project. (Current military standards require the creation of up to twenty different kinds of documentation for a program!)

There would be many attempts to make programming easier, less labor-intensive. One answer was the invention of application packages. To avoid the time and expense of programming a computer for each application, more and more computer users bought already written programs, or packages, that they could adapt to their needs. Application packages had their start in the 1960s, when programs for performing statistical analysis, or word processing, or scientific and engineering tests became available. By 1982 some 50 percent of software sold was in packages of this sort. When the personal computer became popular in the mid-1980s, the number of packages available increased dramatically. There was a packaged program for almost any purpose.

Another solution was computer-aided programming. If the computer was so smart, why couldn't it write the programs itself? One approach was to develop a "specification language." The programmer would outline the specifications, and the computer would write the program. This turned out to be almost as difficult as programming directly. More popular was what came to be called CASE — computer-aided software engineering. The idea was to have the computer help write the program.

A third solution was the idea of structured programming, invented by Edsger W. Dijkstra in the late 1960s. Dijkstra wanted to make programming rigorous, scientific. Software had not kept up with advances in hardware, and it was taking longer and longer to write the ever more complicated software projects business demanded. In 1968 Dijkstra demonstrated that unconditional jumps — "GO TO" statements — were not necessary, and moreover, that programs written without them were easier to follow. His principles were incorporated in the popular "structured programming" languages of the 1970s and 1980s, such as Pascal and ADA. A historian of programming, Philip Kraft, suggests that structured programming fit well with managerial attempts to increase control over programmers. Structured programming "made possible for the first time a genuine job-based fragmentation of labor in programming." For the first time, supervisors could actually read a program and figure out what it did.[20]

But even with all these efforts at getting around the labor-intensive, difficult-to-manage process of writing software, programmers remained essential. Today, there are about 1.7 million software engineers and professional programmers in the United States, and over 10 million worldwide. Yet still there is a constant concern with a software "backlog" and with a programmer shortage. Software writing has become a key part of American business, and it shows no signs of becoming less important.

Although most programmers worked on small pieces of big jobs under careful supervision, not all programmers fell into this category. At universities and at some small firms, "computer hackers" undertook prodigious programming projects, singlehandedly building computer systems that were often the most advanced of their day. These were one-man (almost all hackers were male) projects because the programs tended to be difficult or impossible for others to follow or to fix. (This was the exact opposite of the way in which large firms wanted software written.)

The first computer hackers, writes historian Steven Levy, were veterans of MIT's Tech Model Railroad Club. Once they discovered that the TX-0 computer was available late at night, many gave up on model railroading for computer hacking. They developed — first at MIT, then at other universities — their own code of ethics, and an astonishing prowess at computer programming, a skill built by programming round-the-clock and not doing much else. Joseph Weizenbaum, an MIT professor, described them in 1976:

> Wherever computer centers have become established . . . bright young men of disheveled appearance, often with sunken glowing eyes, can be seen sitting at computer consoles, their arms tensed and waiting to fire their fingers, already poised to strike, at the buttons and keys on which their attention seems to be as riveted as a gambler's on the rolling dice. When not so transfixed, they often sit at tables strewn with computer printouts over which they pore like possessed students of a cabalistic text. They work until they nearly drop, twenty, thirty hours at a time. . . . Their rumpled clothes, their unwashed and unshaven faces, and their uncombed hair all testify that they are oblivious to their bodies and to the world in which they move. They exist, at least when so engaged, only through and for the computers. These are computer bums, compulsive programmers.[21]

Unlike the engineer, who has to build in the real world, Weizenbaum explains, "the computer programmer . . . is a creator of universes for which he alone is the lawgiver." He is overwhelmed by his power to create a world, leading to what Weizenbaum calls "the compulsion to program." But the hacker is corrupted by his power. He revels in the complete control he has over his creation. The computer, writes Weizenbaum, "challenges his power, not his knowledge." His success "consists of his having shown the computer who its master is."[22] Weizenbaum reads the phenomenon of the computer hacker as a warning: the computer, like all science and technology, like any system detached from the reality of "authentic human experience," has "the power to sustain megalomaniac fantasies" — fantasies that may "fail catastrophically" when applied to the real world.[23]

Sherry Turkle, a psychologist who studied programmers, interprets hackers more sympathetically. Instead of using the computer as a tool, a means to an end, she suggests, for hackers, "the fascination is with the machine itself." Hackers "work for the joy of the process, not the product."[24] She accepts, to some extent, the hackers' defense: they are artists, not control-hungry fantasists.

The MIT hackers, and those who followed them, developed strong feelings about computers and programming, what might be called a hacker aesthetic. Critic Andrew Ross describes the hacker ethic as "libertarian and crypto-anarchist in its right-to-know principles and its advocacy of decentralized technology."[25] Steven Levy outlines its main tenets:

- Access to computers should be unlimited and total.
- All information should be free.
- Mistrust authority, promote decentralization.
- Hackers should be judged by their hacking.
- You can create art and beauty on a computer.
- Computers can change your life for the better.

Hackers became, as Levy subtitled his book, "the heroes of the computer revolution." But the hacker ethic — the hacker fantasy — was not to last. Even while the MIT hackers were establishing "a hacker Xanadu," in Levy's words, the rest of the world was becoming more dependent on solid, usable —

and boring — software.[26] (There would be a hacker revival when personal computers first became popular, in the early 1980s.) Even the term itself began to lose its original meaning, becoming shorthand not for someone who can make the computer sing, but for someone who uses the computer for antisocial or illegal purposes. Andrew Ross summarizes the hacker mystique of the 1980s: "On the one hand, this popular folk hero persona offered the romantic high profile of a maverick though nerdy cowboy whose fearless raids upon an impersonal 'system' were perceived as a welcome tonic in the gray age of technocratic routine. On the other hand, he was something of a juvenile technodeliquent who hadn't yet learned the difference between right and wrong."[27]

NEW LANGUAGES, NEW INTERFACES, NEW STANDARDS

As computers and their uses multiplied, hundreds of new computer languages were developed. Along with new hardware designs came new ideas about software. Some languages were written for special tasks, some intended for general-purpose use, some for specific machines, some for universal use. A look at a few of the languages of the 1960s shows the range.

In the mid-1960s John Kemeny and Thomas E. Kurtz of Dartmouth College developed a language intended to be easy to learn and use. FORTRAN, Kemeny wrote, had "extended computer usage from a handful of experts to thousands of scientific users." BASIC (beginners' all-purpose symbolic instruction code) would allow "millions of people" to write their own computer programs. "Profiting from years of experience with FORTRAN," Kemeny continued, "we designed a new language that was particularly easy for the layman to learn and that facilitated communication between man and machine."[28] Some 98 percent of all programs written using the Dartmouth computer system were in BASIC.

Programming languages like BASIC meant that students and others could use the computer without worrying too much about the details of how the computer worked. *The Whole Earth Epilog*, a stalwart of the counterculture, spoke for many when it encouraged people to learn to use computers: "For too long have computers been the center of a mystique and nowhere has this been more evident than in the languages with strange names . . . which frighten off those whose interest is not sufficient to sustain through months of study, page after miserable page of boring and incomprehensible jargon and math. Basic was developed so that 'people' could use computers easily."[29]

Many hackers objected that BASIC didn't allow the fullest use of the computer. A lot of them switched from Assembler to a new language called C, developed in 1969 by Dennis Ritchie at Bell Labs. C was designed by programmers for programmers. Ritchie's goal was to create a computer language that was good for computer science research and software development. C had many of the strengths of both assembly language and high-level language. It was designed for skilled users rather than novices. Over the next two decades C would spread widely, first throughout academia and then into business and government.

New languages were supplemented by new operating systems. The job of the operating system is to manage the computer's resources, control processing, and communicate with devices such as disks and printers. The first computers had no operating system; a skilled operator scheduled the work of the machine. But as computers became more complicated, in the 1950s, an operating system became necessary.

One of the first computers with a full-fledged operating system was IBM's STRETCH, built for the Los Alamos Scientific Laboratory in the mid-1950s. According to Fred Brooks, the designer of the machine, the most important new principle behind it "was the notion that a machine is run by an operating system, not by an operator. And we put in, for the first time, such things as an interruption mechanism, a timer, a supervisor mode, along with various other technical things that you must have to give an operating system control."[30] Before long, operating systems were an essential element of every computer, some of them programs with millions of lines of code, which controlled every aspect of the computer's activities. They are, computer scientist Douglas Comer suggests, "among the most complex objects created by mankind."[31]

One of the most important operating systems, UNIX, was designed by Ken Thompson and Dennis Ritchie at AT&T in the early 1970s. Because it was forbidden to enter the computer market, AT&T sold the program to universities for a nominal fee. Many students learned UNIX, and by 1983 there were more than 3,000 UNIX installations. UNIX was the first "open" standard, that is, anyone could use it. This was one reason why the federal government adopted it. But "standard" is a slippery word in the computer business. There are several competing versions of UNIX, each of them a "standard," as well as UNIX versions available from individual vendors, optimized for that vendor's computers.

Standards have been a key element in the history of computing. Until fairly recently each computer company had its own hardware and software standards, protected by patents, copyrights, or trade secrets. Programs written on one machine couldn't be used on another, often even if they were written in the same language. The first PCs, for example, were all slightly different, and the software for each of them was also slightly different. A Dick Francis mystery, *Twice Shy,* suggests why:

> "Yeah. Well, see, these computer firms are very awkward. All the smaller personal computers use BASIC, because it's the easiest language and also one of the best. But the firms making them all build in their own variations, so that if you record your programs from their machines, you can't run them on anyone else's. That keeps you faithful to them, in the future, because if you change to another make, all your tapes will be useless."
> "What a bore," I said.[32]

No one wanted to get stuck with a useless tape, and so there was an increasing push toward "open" — published — standards in both hardware and software. The IBM personal computer was an open standard, and the operating system that ran on it was open, too, for the most part. Open standards were tricky for manufacturers. On the one hand, an open system can be a commodity product, easily copied, and with low profit margins. On the other hand, if the rest of the industry follows the standard (as with the IBM PC), and the standard setter can innovate fast enough (which IBM did not), the standard can become a valuable product, since everyone else would have no choice but to follow.

Standards were especially important as the personal computer began to dominate the computer market in the 1980s. The PC brought about a revolution in the software business. Suddenly there was a huge new market, and at first, anyway, a simpler one. You could buy a PC for a few thousand dollars, sit at home and write software, and go into the software business. And thousands of people did. But since it was often easier to write a program than to distribute it, many programmers wrote "freeware," or "shareware" — programs that were distributed for free, to be paid for (on the honor system) if they were found to be useful. This fit nicely with the computer hackers' notion that information should be free.

Most early personal computers came equipped with BASIC, which was fine for programmers, or people who bought computers to learn about computers. But by far the larger market was people who were interested in using the computer to do a few specific tasks, especially business tasks such as financial analysis, word processing, or information storage and retrieval. Application software packages made programming for most of these users simply a matter of choosing the right program, loading it into the computer, and following the instructions.

The introduction of PCs made a new style of programming necessary. For the first time, the end user was dealing with the machine. The interface, or interaction, between the user and the computer became more and more important. While professional programmers might be willing to deal in obscure languages, people using computers to accomplish their jobs were not. More and more of the computer's processing power was devoted to making it easy for the user to talk to it. This was the culmination of a long trend in computer software. Computer languages from Assembler to FORTRAN to BASIC had developed so that the programmer could focus on solving the problem, not on dealing with the details of how the computer worked. The introduction of interactive computing, as early as the TX-0 and the Whirlwind, led to what would later be called the personal workstation. These computers allowed the user to react in "real time" to the machine, which meant a much more lively — and often more productive — use of the computer. Time-sharing, introduced in the early 1960s, also allowed this kind of interaction.

The visionary most responsible for the "modern" style of interactive, personal computing was Doug Engelbar. Engelbar was inspired by Vannevar Bush's ideas about information devices designed to improve the way people handled information. (See WORDS.) He decided that the right way to use the computer was as a machine to "augment" the human mind. He established the Augmentation Research Center (ARC) at the Stanford Research Institute, funded by the Department of Defense's Advanced Research Projects Agency. In 1968 Engelbar demonstrated to the Fall Joint Computer Conference in San Francisco new tools for dealing with computers: a mouse, a hypertext system, icons — what would essentially become, twenty years later, the Macintosh computer. ARC also established new ideas about "teleconferencing," electronic mail, and collaborative information processing tools.

The work Engelbar led at ARC was expanded at Xerox's Palo Alto Research Center. The focus at Xerox PARC was the "user interface." In 1972 researchers there demonstrated the Alto, an innovative machine which used a graphical user interface (GUI), bit-mapped displays with windows, icons, mouse,

The Xerox Alto was easy to use
— even for schoolchildren.

and pointers. (Some called this a WIMP interface. The name wasn't a coincidence; many programmers sneered at this attempt to make computers easier for nonexperts to use.) Moreover, it was electronically connected — networked — to other similar machines, and to printers. (See BEYOND TELEPHONES.) Much of the computing power was spent on the GUI, which made the machines expensive and slow, at least at first.

The first low-priced computer based on this work was the Macintosh. Soon similar interfaces were available for many workstations, and, in the late 1980s, for other personal computers. By the early 1990s, with the introduction of Windows for IBM-compatible personal computers, the idea of a graphical user interface was commonly accepted, and clearly the wave of the future.

THE ART OF SOFTWARE

Traditionally software developers hadn't had to worry about intellectual property law. Although the first computer programs were accepted for copyright in 1964, most programs were not copyrighted or patented, which would have meant making them public; companies just kept them secret. Not until 1980 was a Computer Software Copyright Act passed, which declared software to be a "literary work." After all, a program was a list of words on paper, not too different from a book. The Copyright Office expanded the coverage of copyright protection, by the late 1980s even allowing the logic of the program to be copyrighted. (Hardware, too, could sometimes be copyrighted, after the passage of the Semiconductor Protection Act of 1984, which protected the "masks," the drawings that determine the placement of the materials on the integrated circuit.)

In a 1986 court case copyright protection was extended to the "look and feel" of a computer program, the commands used to operate it, and the way it looked on the screen. Some of the largest software companies fought in court over copyright issues. Lotus Development Company won a suit against Paperback software because Paperback's spreadsheet program used the same commands as the Lotus 1-2-3. Apple Computer sued Microsoft and Hewlett-Packard for a user interface that looked a lot like Apple's.

How broadly a copyright could protect a program, where the exact details of the words weren't important — where there were other ways to accomplish the same effect — was a difficult issue. The idea of copyrighting user interfaces dismayed many, who pointed out that if it were applied to typewriters, every manufacturer would have to use a different keyboard layout; applied to automobiles, it would mean that each manufacturer would have to arrange the gas, brake, and clutch pedals differently, or perhaps only one would be allowed to use a wheel for steering!

Patent law as applied to software also changed over the course of the 1980s. Since processes other than those that transformed matter could not be patented, business methods, mathematical algorithms, and "mental steps" were traditionally beyond the reach of patent law. The turning point was a 1981 Supreme Court decision which suggested that the use of a computer program in a rubber-curing process did not make the process unpatentable. The first program to be patented was a data-retrieval program called SwiftAnswer, invented by Pal Asija, patented that same year. Over the next ten years, some 2,000 software patents were granted.

The point of patents and copyrights was to protect the creative work of engineers, to give them (or, much more commonly, the companies that employed them) a chance to profit from their efforts. But many people thought that allowing software to be copyrighted or patented was a bad idea, slowing down the progress of computer science. Patents were especially tricky: how could you draw the line between a clever new wrinkle and a patentable idea? How would a programmer know what had already been patented, and therefore could not be used without paying royalties? The League for Programming Freedom, an organization formed to fight software patents — "dedicated to bringing back the freedom to write programs" — summarized the problem: "This will turn software into a quagmire. Even an innovative program typically uses dozens of not-quite-new techniques and features, each of which might have been patented. Our ability to use each wrinkle will depend on luck, and if we are unlucky half the time, few programs will escape infringing a large number of patents. Navigating the maze of patents will be harder than writing software."[33] What it meant to copyright and patent the "look and feel" of a computer interface or the techniques of manipulating data within it were not easy questions for the courts to answer.

At the same time that the courts were worrying about the problems of protecting the intellectual property of computer programmers, the nature of software was changing. Where once each computer firm had its own operating system and its own languages, the 1980s saw the rise of open systems. Supported by a consortium of computer companies, and based on published standards, these systems freed computer users from being locked into the hardware made by one manufacturer. Open systems were portable; you could run software written for one computer on other brands of computer that used the same standard. It also meant that it was possible to connect a range of computers together, knowing that at some level they all spoke the same language.

One variation on openness was to make programs available for free. Richard Stallman, hailed by Steven Levy as "last of the hackers," was furious that the "hacker's ethic" was being violated by those who would profit from software. Treating software as private property, he wrote, slowed down the development of new software by making it necessary to start from scratch on each program; it couldn't build on earlier programs. Society would be better served, Stallman claimed, by free software.

He decided to rewrite some major pieces of software and make them available for free. His Free Software Foundation, "dedicated to eliminating restrictions on copying, redistribution, understanding, and modification of computer programs," released GNU, a free version of UNIX (the name stood for "GNU's not unix"), and free versions of many other commercial programs. These programs were not copyrighted; they were "copylefted," a word Stallman coined to indicate a program that could be used and distributed for free, but could not be sold without the continued right of the purchasers to distribute freely. Users had to be allowed to see and change the code.

But most firms were afraid of using this free software. Businesses had come to depend on software. A glitch could mean that business shut down — or worse. Software was used in running machinery of all sorts, from airplanes to x-ray machines. A failure could cause disaster. Almost every large system on which society came to depend had software at its heart. The phone system was nothing but a giant computer. The air-traffic control system was a feat of software writing. Most modern weapons systems depend on software. The size of some of these computer systems was enormous, millions upon millions of lines of code. The first space shuttle depended on about half a million lines of code. A telephone switch has some 2 million lines. The SSN-21 Sea Wolf attack submarine has a fire control system with more than 3 million. How can these be tested? How reliable are they?

As machines of all sorts came to depend on software, problems with software failures became more common. Some were merely annoying, like the computer that sent a bill for $0.00. Others were amusing, like the error that excluded Hartford, Connecticut, residents from federal grand juries for three years because the computer listed them all as being dead after a mistake pushed the *d* at the end of Hartford into a column where *D* stood for "Dead."

But some software bugs were more dangerous, truly deadly. An x-ray therapy machine built by Atomic Energy of Canada would, in very particular circumstances — maybe once every million uses, when just the right order of keys was tapped, in just the right timing — put out a full-power beam, enough to kill the patient it was supposed to cure. Two patients died before the error was fixed. An Airbus A320, one of the first "fly-by-wire" commercial airplanes, crashed when its pilot tried to push the plane beyond what the software would allow. A Saab-Scania Gripen jet fighter crash-landed because software incorrectly controlled pitch at low speeds. The space shuttle's first launch was delayed because of software problems caused by an attempt to get around other software problems: the five redundant computers that had to agree with one another, to make sure that they had given the right answer, didn't! A few "bugs" had the potential to cause even greater disaster, like the early-warning radar that confused a rising moon with an incoming missile.

Many "software errors" are actually user errors, or, more accurately, bad judgment in the human-software interface that results in mistakes being made in the *use* of the software. One of the hardest parts of designing computer systems is getting the interface right. Some three quarters of the "computer errors" found during *Apollo* space flights were, it turned out, errors in the way the programs were used. As Donald Norman writes in *The Psychology of Everyday Things,* computers, because they are so flexible, allow no end of possibilities for bad design. To overcome this, "the programmer [has] to develop an appropriate system for representing the actions to be performed, to find out what is possible, and then to discover what has happened — to make judicious use of feedback, of intelligent interpretation. There should be a natural dialog, a comfortable interaction between computer and user in which both parties cooperate to reach the desired solution."[34]

What happens when this isn't achieved can make the computer not only difficult to use but dangerous. One example: a rocket carrying a Strategic Defense Initiative experiment went off course and had to be destroyed after a technician accidentally hit the wrong key while loading software into the guidance system. He loaded ground-test software rather than flight software, and so the steering nozzles remained locked in place. A good interface design might have prevented this. A good user-computer interface is tricky. In an airplane, for example, the computer might be designed to do so much that the pilot loses the "feel" of the plane. Or it might not fail gracefully when problems arise, to allow the pilot to take over some of its functions. Or it might not respond well when the pilot tries to push the plane beyond what the software is designed to permit. Or the computer displays might be too complex, providing too much information, and overwhelming the pilot.

Perhaps the most widely noted software flaws were those that, on several occasions in June and July 1991, brought sections of AT&T's long-distance phone network to its knees. The problem was finally traced to a single error in one line of code. The software error meant that the overload-handling procedures of the telephone switches didn't work, and when other errors happened at a time of heavy telephone traffic, the switches shut down. Some 20 million customers lost their phone service for hours because of this bug. In 1990 and 1991 software problems were responsible for more than half the outages telephone customers experienced, affecting some 37 million telephone users.

The issue of software reliability had its fullest airing during the debate on the Strategic Missile Defense (Star Wars) system in the 1980s. The Star Wars system was estimated to require some 10 million lines of code. There was no way to test the whole thing (there's no way to show the absence of bugs), and it had to work the first time, or the hundreds of billions of dollars spent on it would be of no value. There was, finally, no way to answer the question of reliability until the system was used. The problem was sufficiently profound that some software experts suggested that software-based systems should not be used in situations where lives were at stake.

Software writing and testing is an art, not a science. In its half-century history software has become easier to write, more powerful, and more useful; it has also become increasingly important. Software is nearly ubiquitous, now, though it is still invisible. We rely on it every day, without thinking about it. But for all the effort that has gone into making programming easier, it remains the most difficult part of making the Information Age work.

FOR FURTHER READING

Many of the general histories listed in COMPUTERS discuss software. There are few general histories of software, including Jean Sammet, *Programming Languages: History and Fundamentals* (1969); and Richard L. Wexelblat, ed., *History of Programming Languages* (1981). The *Annals of the History of Computing* often carries articles on software history.

On the history of the management of computer programming, see Joan M. Greenbaum, *In the Name of Efficiency: Management Theory and Shopfloor Practice in Data-Processing Work* (1979); and Phillip Kraft, *Programmers and Managers: The Routinization of Computer Programming in the United States* (1977).

Computer hackers star in several books. See Steven Levy, *Hackers: Heroes of the Computer Revolution* (1984); and Andrew Ross, "Hacking Away at the Counterculture," in *Strange Weather: Culture, Science, and Technology in the Age of Limits* (1991).

For some interesting reflections on the uses of software, see Howard Rheingold, *Tools for Thought: The People and Ideas behind the Next Computer Revolution* (1985); and Raymond Kurzweil, *The Age of Intelligent Machines* (1990). For computer disasters, software theft, and other hot topics in computing today, see Tom Forester and Perry Morrison, *Computer Ethics: Cautionary Tales and Ethical Dilemmas in Computing* (1990); and Leonard Lee, *The Day the Phones Stopped: The Computer Crisis — The What and Why of It, and How We Can Beat It* (1991). A good general introduction to what programmers do is John Shore, *The Sachertorte Algorithm and Other Antidotes to Computer Anxiety* (1985).

NOTES

1. Dionysius Lardner, "Babbage's Calculating Engine," *Edinburgh Review* (July 1834); reprinted in *Charles Babbage and His Calculating Engines: Selected Writings by Charles Babbage and Others,* ed. Philip Morrison and Emily Morrison (1961), p. 174.

2. "Notes by the Translator [Ada Lovelace] to L. F. Menabrea, "Sketch of the Analytical Engine Invented by Charles Babbage"; reprinted in Morrison and Morrison, *Babbage and His Calculating Engines,* pp. 245–246.

3. David Allison, interview with J. Presper Eckert, Smithsonian Institution Archives, Washington, D.C.

4. James Gleick, *Genius: The Life and Science of Richard Feynman* (1992), p. 181.

5. Alan Turing, lecture to the London Mathematical Society, February 20, 1947; quoted in Andrew Hodges, *Alan Turing: The Enigma* (1983), pp. 318–320.

6. Quoted in William Aspray, *John von Neumann and the Origins of Modern Computing* (1990), p. 69.

7. Quoted in Raymond Kurzweil, *The Age of Intelligent Machines* (1990), p. 175.

8. A. E. Glennie, "The Automatic Coding of an Electronic Computer," unpublished paper, 1952, p. 2.

9. John Backus, "The History of FORTRAN, II, and III," *Annals of the History of Computing* (July 1979): 24.

10. John Backus, "Programming in America in the 1950s — Some Personal Impressions," in *A History of Computing in the Twentieth Century: A Collection of Essays,* ed. N. Metropolis, J. Howlett, and Gian-Carlo Rota (1980), pp. 130–131.

11. Grace Hopper, "General Discussion of G. W. Brown, 'A New Concept in Programming,'" in *Computers and the World of the Future,* ed. Martin Greenberger (1962), p. 283.

12. John McCarthy, "General Discussion of John R. Pierce, 'What Computers Should Be Doing,'" in Greenberger, *Computers and the World of the Future,* p. 315.

13. *New Yorker,* January 5, 1957, pp. 18–19; quoted in Mark Halpern, "On the Heels of the Pioneers," *Annals of the History of Computing,* 13, no. 1 (1991): 110.

14. I. J. Seligsohn, *Your Career in Computer Programming* (1967), p. 44.

15. Quoted in Joan M. Greenbaum, *In the Name of Efficiency: Management Theory and Shopfloor Practice in Data-Processing Work* (1979), p. 65.

16. Dick Brandon, "The Economics of Computer Programming," in *On the Management of Computer Programming,* ed. George F. Winwurm (1970), pp. 8 and 10–11.

17. A. P. Ershov, "Aesthetics and the Human Factor in Programming," *Communications of the ACM 15* (July 1972): 503; quoted in Greenbaum, *In the Name of Efficiency,* pp. 3–4.

18. *Wall Street Journal,* May 12, 1977, p. 40.

19. Caspar Jones, "Case's Missing Elements," *IEEE Spectrum* (June 1992): 38.

20. Philip Kraft, *Programmers and Managers* (1977), p. 58.

21. Joseph Weizenbaum, *Computer Power and Human Reason: From Judgment to Calculation* (1976), p. 116.

22. Weizenbaum, *Computer Power and Human Reason,* pp. 115–116 and p. 120.

23. Weizenbaum, *Computer Power and Human Reason,* pp. 130–131.

24. Sherry Turkle, *The Second Self: Computers and the Human Spirit* (1984), p. 201.

25. Andrew Ross, *Strange Weather: Culture, Science, and Technology in the Age of Limits* (1991), p. 84.

26. Steven Levy, *Hackers: Heroes of the Computer Revolution* (1984), pp. 40–45 and 49.

27. Ross, *Strange Weather*, p. 84.

28. John G. Kemeny, *Man and the Computer* (1972), p. 30.

29. Keith Britton, "Basic," in *The Whole Earth Epilog: Access to Tools* (1974), p. 704.

30. Quoted in Linda Runyan, "Forty Years on the Frontier," *Datamation,* March 15, 1991, p. 34.

31. Douglas Comer, *Operating System Design: The XINU Approach* (1984), p. 1.

32. Dick Francis, *Twice Shy* (1982), p. 35.

33. Quoted in *GNU's Bulletin* (June 1992).

34. Donald A. Norman, *The Psychology of Everyday Things* (1988), p. 231.

Why can't a machine be more like a person? Why can't computers think, be creative, live in the real world? Those are the basic questions that underlie the study of cybernetics, artificial intelligence, and robotics. They are questions that have their roots in ancient mythology, questions that have intrigued writers and scientists for the last two hundred years. Today, machines have been taught to simulate a few simple elements of human behavior. But our fantasies of intelligent machines still far surpass the reality.

INFORMATION
BEYOND COMPUTERS

IN THE LATE EIGHTEENTH CENTURY A CHESS-PLAYING robot won wide fame. The Turk, as the automaton, built by Baron Wolfgang von Kempelen in Presburg, Hungary, in 1769, was known, took on the most complicated game of all — and usually won. The machine toured Europe and America to great acclaim. Edgar Allan Poe, who saw the machine in Boston in the 1830s, wrote, "We find everywhere men of mechanical genius, of great general acuteness, and discriminative understanding, who make no scruple in pronouncing the Automaton . . . the most astonishing of the inventions of mankind." Several authors suggested that there must be a midget or a boy in the machine. Poe joined them in an 1836 article, in which he conclusively deduced that, as he put it, "the machine must be regulated *by mind.*"[1] "By mind." To Poe, that meant a person. The actual creation of machines that could think, that could even play and win a game of chess, was beyond the comprehension of the age.

But people wanted to believe that such an automaton could be built. There was a long mythology and history of artificial life. And while the actual creation of smart machines lagged far behind the fiction, it seemed — and to many still seems — only a matter of time before the technology catches up to the imagination. The myth of artificial, man-made life is found in many cultures. In Greek mythology, Hephaestus created golden mechanical women to help him in his smithy ("There is intelligence in their hearts, and there is speech in them / and strength, and from the immortal gods they have learned how to do things," sang Homer in the *Iliad*),[2] and built Talos, a giant warrior, to protect Crete. In Jewish tradition there is the story of the Golem, a mechanical servant that would protect the Jewish people in times of trouble. A famous Golem was supposedly created by Rabbi Loew of Prague to save the Jews of that city from a pogrom in 1580. Norbert Wiener, founder of the science of cybernetics, describes the Golem as "that figure of clay into which the Rabbi of Prague breathed life with the blasphemy of the Ineffable Name of God."[3] (Wiener wrote this after he had tried to breathe life into machines of his own.) In China, King Mu of the Chou Dynasty built a robot; in Japan there is the twelfth-century tale of the wizard Moronaka, who created several automata, some of which, unbeknownst to anyone, became leading politicians.

377

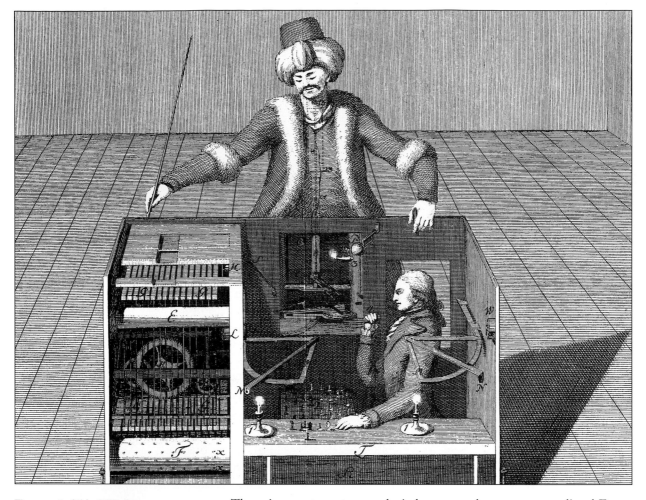

The secret of this 1769 chess-playing automaton was simple: an expert chess player was hidden inside.

There is an automaton myth tied, too, to almost every medieval European philosopher. Pope Sylvester II and Roger Bacon are both credited with having built brass heads to give them advice. Albertus Magnus, it was said, built a mechanical doorkeeper to greet visitors. Paracelsus and other sixteenth-century alchemists were thought to have aimed at creating "homunculi." The Faust legend of early modern Europe elaborates the idea of artificial life, and shows its dangers: Faust sells his soul for knowledge, including the knowledge of how to create life. In all these cultures the creation of artificial life was blasphemous — man playing God. But it stood also as an ultimate goal not only of these magician-scientists but also, in a metaphorical sense, of science and technology. It represents the striving for godlike knowledge and power. It is these myths that stand behind the attempts to make machines that act or think like people — and that tie the magical, divine heritage of knowledge to the scientists and engineers of the nineteenth and twentieth centuries.

THINKING MACHINES

Myth far surpassed possibility, of course. The first step on the path that would lead to thinking machines, let alone machines that were "alive," were machines to *help* people think. Abacuses, counting beads, mechanical calculators, and astronomical clocks made calculations easier, starting in ancient times, and gained wide use by the middle of the nineteenth century. (See BEFORE COMPUTERS.)

Machines to do "thinking" more complex than arithmetic came next. They built on a tradition of rules for deduction, called syllogisms, that stretched back to the ancient Greeks. The thirteenth-century philosopher Raymond Lull imagined a "universal language" he called the *Ars Magna* that would automatically find all "true" — that is, logical — propositions. In the seventeenth century, Leibniz hoped to find a way to reduce all argument to a simple set of procedures, and perhaps to embody these in a mechanical reasoner. Leibniz's work was the basis for the eighteenth- and nineteenth-century development of algebra and logic. The mathematicians George Peacock, William Hamilton, Hermann Grassmann, and George Boole found ways to express logical relationships in mathematical terms. In his *Mathematical Analysis of Logic* (1847), Boole suggested ways to generalize the ancient notion of the syllogism into a "logical calculus," a set of rules to make logical deductions.

Why not mechanize these rules? W. S. Jevons did just that. His "logical piano," built in 1869, used syllogistic reasoning to make deductions. There were several improvements in these machines over the next few decades. In the 1880s Allan Marquand, at Princeton, built a machine that displayed the implications of a set of logical propositions. He later designed (but never built) an electrical logic machine, based on suggestions from his former teacher, the philosopher Charles S. Peirce. None of these machines found any practical use. But they suggested the possibility that, someday, machines might emulate the human brain — or at least the logical part of the brain.

While scientists and mathematicians played with mechanical devices that "thought," mechanics and engineers were discovering more practical uses for such devices. Factory owners tried to find ways to substitute machines for troublesome skilled workers, to capture their skills — their ability to think and act — in machines. The most celebrated of these was Joseph Marie Jacquard's 1804 pattern-weaving loom. This loom used the pattern of holes punched onto wooden cards to control the lifting of each of the warp threads for each pass of the shuttle; the result was cloth with the preprogrammed picture woven into it. The

---

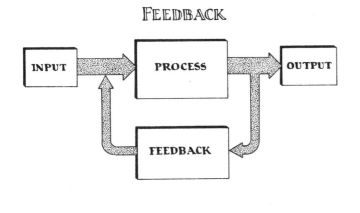

FEEDBACK

Feedback is an element in a control system which takes some portion of the output of a process and returns it to control the processing of the input. Feedback can be used to keep a system operating within predetermined boundaries. For example, a steam engine might drive a "governor," a feedback device that turns faster as the steam engine speeds up, and which in turn cuts the supply of steam to the engine, slowing it down. A household thermostat is a feedback device, measuring the output of heat and sending signals to turn down the heater when it reaches a predetermined temperature.

Jacquard loom resulted in the unemployment of many skilled weavers, and some smashed the new machines in an attempt to keep their jobs. But it was a practical success as well as an intellectual one. Not only did Jacquard get rich from his invention, but Charles Babbage adopted the punch card idea for his Analytical Engine, and punch cards found wide use in later calculating machines. (See BEFORE COMPUTERS.)

Most machines, even complex machines such as automata and the Jacquard loom, simply repeat the same procedures over and over; they are programmed. A key breakthrough toward making these machines "automatic" so that they could respond to changes in the world around them — toward making them "thinking" machines — was the invention of feedback control. Early examples can be found in ancient Greece: Hero of Alexandria designed devices that used feedback to control water levels. Medieval clocks used escapements to regulate the rate at which the spring or weight propelled the clock hands. Some temperature-regulating thermostats were designed in the sixteenth century. But not until the eighteenth century did feedback mechanisms come into wide use. Steam engines used feedback in their pressure regulators to keep them from exploding. Windmills used feedback to control their speed by furling sails so that they would not be destroyed by high winds. Most important was the feedback governor on steam engines, first used by James Watt. These devices controlled the amount of steam admitted to the cylinder so as to keep them at constant speed. They would eventually lead to automatic pilots in the 1920s, and automatic gun controls during World War II.

Feedback-controlled devices, combined with the increasing capabilities of ever-more complex calculators, suggested the potential for machines that would control their own actions to an unprecedented degree. What might self-controlling machines do? How might they be put to use, and what might they tell us about the nature of intelligence, or the nature of life itself? How might they change the world? These questions were addressed first as philosophy, then as entertainment, and then as science and technology.

MECHANICAL PEOPLE

The rationalist philosophers of the Enlightenment turned a cold eye on the workings of the body. René Descartes and Julien Offray de la Mettrie, among others, philosophized that animals were nothing but complex machines. Physical influences such as food, drugs, and fatigue affect the mind, they reasoned, and therefore it, too, must be physical. Modern science did its best to find mechanical explanations for biological phenomena. Why not think of the heart as a pump, muscles as engines, and digestion as chemistry? The brain, then, would be some sort of thinking machine. And if that was the case, why not build mechanical animals, even mechanical people? The eighteenth century saw a flowering of mechanical automata.

Perhaps the most famous was a mechanical duck created by the watchmaker Jacques de Vaucanson in 1738. It could walk, flap its wings, chew and swallow food, and even excrete. Other mechanics built brass and steel birds that sang, porcelain dolls that wrote and played the piano or the mandolin, and wind-up figures that walked, turned, and bowed. Whole gardens were filled with moving figures, driven by water power, performing a mechanical ballet. Automata not only reflected a widely held world view; they also were good fun, the ultimate challenge for a mechanic, and a grand entertainment for rich gentlemen and ladies.

An early seventeenth-century dog automaton. The dog's eyes move with each beat of the clock, and his jaw snaps each time the chime rings.

The historian Christine Woesler de Panafieu suggests that there was something more behind the eighteenth- and nineteenth-century fad for automata. She identifies the attempt to "create human beings mechanically" as "a masculine utopia." The point, she claims, was "to construct a controlled, stable, repetitive, rational, anti-mystical world by men themselves." Automata, de Panafieu argues, "serve to affirm masculine identity and to represent the male projection of femininity. . . . Female automata express the masculine ideal of women."[4] The creation of automata, she suggests, is an attempt to play God, the ultimate projection of power, an attempt to overcome a feeling of incompleteness that results from the exclusion of nature in men's world of science, and to control that world. The historian David Noble goes further in his provocative book *A World without Women*. The creation of automata, he suggests, represents men's striving to partake of a form of creation reserved for women: "maternal mimicry, an ersatz procreative effort to stimulate life."[5]

The advances of science and technology and the real-life successes of automatic machines in industry, as well as new questions about the nature of progress, reinvigorated the potential for automata in the nineteenth century. Once automata had been magical, or wind-up toys; now the possibilities began to seem real. Scientists and engineers could do wonders; why not create life itself? Just as ancient Greece had its stories of mechanical people, so too did the nineteenth century. But whereas mythology painted these mechanisms as helpmates, nineteenth-century fiction presented a more complicated picture.

The darker side of the modern mythology of man-made life starts with Mary Shelley's *Frankenstein* (1817), an allegory of creativity gone amok, of science overreaching the bounds of what is properly human knowledge, of man playing God. Dr. Frankenstein has read the writings of the alchemists, and devoted himself to understanding "the principle of life." It is, as he tells the story, "a bold question, and one which has ever been considered as a mystery; yet with how many things are we upon the brink of becoming acquainted, if cowardice or carelessness did not restrain our enquiries." After long work investigating "the corruption of death," Frankenstein succeeds in "discovering the cause of generation and life." He will play God, he decides: "A new species would bless me as its creator and source; many happy and excellent natures would owe their being to me."[6] But the creature Frankenstein brings to life is a monster who eventually turns on its creator and destroys him. Science overmasters the scientist. Hubris is rewarded with death.

A more optimistic version of the mythology can be found in a very popular American novel called *The Steam Man of the Prairies*, written by Edward S.

Steam Man, the mechanical super-hero of the nineteenth century, to the rescue. Edward S. Ellis's *Steam Man of the Prairies,* popular in the last third of the nineteenth century, spawned a whole series of Steam Man adventures.

Ellis's steam man was probably based in part on a real machine, a steam-powered man that walked and pulled a carriage. This peculiar creature was built by Zadoc P. Dederick, a mechanic in Newark, New Jersey, in 1868. Dederick's steam man got lots of publicity, for Americans were taken with technical ingenuity and with the notion of taming the power of steam. Although Dederick's steam man never worked very well and didn't last long, the novel it inspired would in turn inspire a long list of mechanical superheros.

Ellis, and published in 1868. This nineteenth-century superhero pulled a wagon in which its inventor and his friends rode, and went about the countryside chasing Indians, hunting buffalo, and generally serving as a literal incarnation of a deus ex machina by saving its creator from his own follies. Ellis sets up three categories of response to the steam man, reflecting generally held nineteenth-century ideas about race and technology. "Yankees" and Anglo-Saxon Americans generally understand the robot and are not afraid of it. Immigrants are curious, but most "gaze in stupid and speechless amazement." Indians are bewildered by the steam man; they think it is supernatural, and when they find it untended, their first response is to hit it in the stomach with a tomahawk. "Civilized" people, Ellis suggests, accept the new technology, and use it to their advantage.

Mechanical creatures reflect the hopes and fears of their times. Frankenstein's monster was to be a personal servant, but it turned on its master; science had overreached itself. The steam man, a mechanical hero, expressed an American faith in technology; the story ends with the steam man destroying itself to save its creator. The twentieth century, though, would see a new kind of mechanical monster. In the 1920s, with the rise of automated factories and an increased fear of technological unemployment, the myth of the man-machine found its modern expression in the economic arena.

The first modern robot story was Karel Čapek's *R.U.R.,* a play written in Czechoslovakia in 1920. "R.U.R." stands for Rossum's Universal Robots. Čapek's robots — he coined the word — are mechanical slaves who work in factories. But the robots bring problems in their wake. Men and women, deprived of their work, grow unhappy, and stop having children. But this problem seems minor when the next product of the robot factory, soldier robots, decide to stop killing one another, kill people instead, and unite to take over the world: "Robots of the world! We, the first union of Rossum's Universal Robots, declare man our enemy. . . . Robots of the world, you are ordered to exterminate the human race. . . . Preserve only the factories, railroads, machines, mines, and raw materials. Destroy everything else. Then return to work. Work must not cease."[7] People are superfluous to the robots, who want only to work, and to produce more robots. In the end, the robots learn to reproduce, starting a new race. The last remaining human, the chief engineer of the robot factory, blesses the first robot couple as the new Adam and Eve: "Life will not perish! Only we have perished."[8] *R.U.R.* ends on an ambiguous note of death and rebirth.

A complex image of the robot found its way into American popular cul-

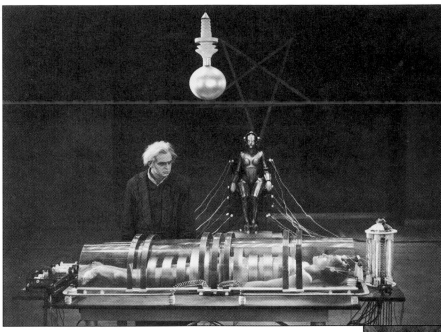

Fritz Lang's *Metropolis* (1927) was the first great robot movie. Set in the year 2000, it features a female robot to whom is transferred the spirit of Maria, leader of the oppressed masses. But the robot is evil, and incites the people to a revolt that destroys the city.

The evil robot, an old science-fiction tradition. This one appeared on the cover of *Astounding Science Fiction*, October 1953.

ture. The Steam Man of the Prairies was joined by a host of humanoid robots, from the tin man in *The Wizard of Oz* to the "metal giants" that captured the covers of the increasingly popular pulp science-fiction magazines of the 1920s and 1930s. But *R.U.R.* was popular, too, and the image of the robot taking jobs and life from American workers had a special resonance during the Great Depression. Some mechanical men were heroes, rescuing humanity from the mechanical men who were villains; robots, like technology more generally, were put to both good and evil uses.

The divided view of robots reflected Americans' split beliefs about technology. On the one hand, technology created unemployment, taking jobs from men and women who needed them. Technology had shown its fullest and most horrific potential during the First World War, when tanks — deadly mechanical robots — had seemed almost invincible on the battlefield. On the other hand, new technology was responsible for what seemed a never-ending increase in productivity. Automation meant that every middle-class American could afford a car. Robots showed up on labor union protest banners as a symbol of technological unemployment, but they also were prominent in corporate publicity, as a symbol of the importance of mechanization in the new world of consumer products. Robots became an apt, though contested, symbol of the power, promise, and problem of modern technology.

The most famous robot of the 1930s was found at the Westinghouse exhibition at the 1939 New York World's Fair. There, Elektro, the Moto-Man, and his mechanical dog, Sparko, held forth. Elektro's ancestor Willie Vocalite had been around since the late 1920s, appearing for Westinghouse (under a variety of names) wherever new technology was on display, from the inauguration of new airplane service to the introduction of a new refrigerator at a department

Elektro poses for the camera at the 1939 World's Fair. With him is Helen Bennett, director of the dish-washing contest at the Fair, and Bill "Bojangles" Robinson, the dancer.

store. Elektro, reads Westinghouse's World's Fair press release, was "designed to be a dramatic portrayal of the manner in which electrical devices . . . may be put to use to lighten the human load in industry and at the same time bring close tolerances, automatic counting and shut-offs as well as temperature regulation to the production line." The robot, people were told, would be useful, sometime in the not-too-far-distant future. Of course, Elektro was a fake. There was no interesting new technology here at all; inside Elektro and Sparko were nothing but gears and motors.

But the way the robots were presented is more interesting. Westinghouse used the robot as a symbol to sell the potential of high technology. The firm put out a series of press photographs showing Elektro in a variety of settings. In one, he is pictured with a group of midgets; in a second, with Bill "Bojangles" Robinson, the African American dancer. He's always accompanied by a woman, who holds his hand. All of the people he's shown with were, in the world of 1939, marginalized people — not considered quite fully human. They make the mechanical man look more human in contrast. His dog, Sparko, too, makes him seem more human, as does his smoking habit. "They may be just machines," reads one press release, "but they have electric personalities and give evidence of liking one another." Elektro was just one of the guys. The technological world of the future, according to Westinghouse, held no threat. There was no reason to be afraid of robots or, for that matter, any of the other marvels the future held.

Especially not the robots imagined by Isaac Asimov, starting in 1939. In that year Asimov began his series of robot stories — almost all of them about good robots, forbidden by the "Three Laws of Robotics" from causing people any trouble. Asimov established his rules in one of his earliest robot stories, "Runaround," published in 1942. They were repeated in many of dozens of robot stories Asimov would publish:

1. A robot may not injure a human being, or, through inaction, allow a human being to come to harm.

2. A robot must obey the orders given it by human beings except where such orders would conflict with the First Law.

3. A robot must protect its own existence as long as such protection does not conflict with the First or Second Law.

These laws would define the "good" science-fiction robot. Asimov later wrote: "I dealt with robots unemotionally — they were produced by engineers, they presented engineering problems that required solutions, and the solutions were found. The stories were rather convincing portrayals of a future technology and were not moral lessons. The robots were machines and not metaphors. As a result, the old-fashioned robot story was virtually killed in all science fiction stories above the comic-strip level."[9]

But not all science-fiction writers followed Asimov's suggestion that robots were simply machines. Some would continue to collapse the line between human and machine, populating their stories not with mechanical robots but with cyborgs and androids. The cyborg was part human, part machine, the android a biological robot so humanlike as to be almost indistinguishable from the real thing. The new stories would be based, in part, on new ideas about information, and about the possibilities of artificial life.

CYBERNETICS: REAL THINKING MACHINES

While science-fiction robots were becoming more realistic, if not always as "benevolent and useful" as Asimov hoped, the possibility of actually building thinking machines was becoming more real. With the invention of the computer and improvements in control engineering during World War II, scientists and engineers began to have the technology they would need to create thinking machines. They also had new sciences of information to call on. (See TELEPHONE.)

Three significant analyses of information appeared in 1948. Claude Shannon, at Bell Laboratories, wrote a classic paper in which he discussed ways to measure the information content of a message. John von Neumann delivered a seminal talk on automata theory. Norbert Wiener wrote *Cybernetics,* revealing a new science that focused on "the essential unity of the set of problems centering about communication, control, and statistical mechanics, whether in the machine or in living tissue."[10] Two years later Alan Turing asked the crucial question that would tie these subjects together: "Can machines think?"

Cybernetics looked as if it might be a grand synthetic theory that would lead to a new, deeper understanding of all of the fields that dealt with information, of thinking, of control. Von Neumann, writes Steve Joshua Heims, a historian of cybernetics, "wanted to link statistical mechanics, communication engineering, the theory of control mechanisms in machines, biology, *and also psychology and social science* by the common theme of 'communication.'"[11] "The unifying idea of these diverse disciplines," Von Neumann wrote, "is the MESSAGE, and not any special apparatus acting on messages."[12] Wiener's definition of cybernetics was as general as could be: "The theory of control in engineering, whether human or animal or mechanical, is a chapter in the theory of messages." This includes "not only the study of language but the study of messages as a means of controlling machinery and society, the development of computing machines and other such automata, certain reflections upon psychology and the nervous system, and a tentative new theory of scientific method."[13]

Although cybernetics would fall short of its grand goals, it received popular and scholarly acclaim. It was all the rage in the early 1950s. The reviews of Wiener's book are indicative of the excitement the field aroused. *The New York Times* called it "seminal . . . comparable in ultimate importance to . . . Galileo." The *Saturday Review of Literature* said: "It appears impossible for anyone seriously interested in our civilization to ignore this book. It is a 'must' book for those in every branch of science. . . . In addition, economists, politicians, statesmen, and businessmen cannot afford to overlook cybernetics and its tremendous, even terrifying implications."[14] Isaac Asimov wrote in 1957: "Cybernetics is not merely another branch of science. It is an Intellectual Revolution that rivals in importance the earlier Industrial Revolution."[15]

Cybernetics was the right science at the right time. Not only was the technology of computers finding new applications every day; the problems of bureacracy and organization were becoming ever more obvious, and cybernetics seemed a cure. Americans turned to a new science that might solve the problems of a society out of control. People eagerly read popular treatments of the field, books with names like *Thinking by Machine* and *Giant Brains, or Machines That Think*. People used the language of cybernetics in everyday talk — "feedback," "programmed," "system." And so almost every field was reconceived as dealing with information, one way or another. Information was central to human interactions, the cyberneticists claimed, the key to understanding not only machinery, but also business and society, and even life itself.

Cybernetics — the science of control — appeared to offer the solution to pressing economic, managerial, and political problems. A business, or an economy, run on cybernetic principles, maybe even run by computer, would not be authoritarian. It wouldn't depend on orders from the top, like communism or fascism. And it was not strictly free-market economics either, the system that had led to the depression. All that was needed, it seemed, was a free flow of information, and societies could be self-stabilizing. Not just the economy as a whole, but even individual factories might be run by cybernetic principles. "The next step in management . . . CYBERNETICS," reads a General Electric internal report: "It is the search for principles that govern the whole of a thing and the statement of those principles in some quantitative form that appears to lie at the heart of this attitude called Cybernetics. Those principles, so stated, will make more adequate and understandable communications between people, groups or even the controls within machines."[16] Information seemed to be the key to understanding, to bridging the gap between worker and manager, or consumer and business — indeed, the whole economic system.

The notion that computers could run businesses and the economy had enormous appeal to science-fiction writers. One of Isaac Asimov's robot stories, "The Evitable Conflict" (1950), describes the stable, prosperous world that computer control makes possible. "It no longer seemed so important whether the world was Adam Smith or Karl Marx. . . . The Earth's economy is stable, and will *remain* stable, because it is based upon the decisions of calculating machines that have the good of humanity at heart."[17] For Robert Heinlein, the computer that ran the economy was all that stood between order and chaos. In *Beyond this Horizon* (1942), one character asks: "What would happen if I took an ax and just smashed your little toy?" He's told that "it would result in a series of panics and booms of the most nineteenth-century type. . . . Carried to extreme, it could even result in warfare."[18]

Kurt Vonnegut parodied the notion. EPICAC, the master computer in *Player Piano,* figured out everything. It decided

> how many refrigerators, how many lamps, how many turbine-generators, how many hub caps, how many dinner plates, how many door knobs, how many rubber heels, how many television sets, how many pinochle decks —

how many everything America and her customers could have and how much they would cost. And it was EPICAC XIV who would decide for the coming years how many engineers and managers and research men and civil servants, and of what skills, would be needed in order to deliver the goods; and what I.Q. and aptitude levels would separate the useful men from the useless ones.[19]

Why such central control? Because people couldn't be trusted. They made a mess of things. EPICAC not only controlled output; it controlled demand as well. The common man made irrational decisions. As one of the characters in *Player Piano* puts it, "Used to be he'd buy on impulse, illogically, and industry would go nutty trying to figure out what he was going to buy next." And so computers took care of that problem: "Furnishings and equipment were replaced from time to time with newer models as [an individual] — or the payroll machines, rather — completed payments on the old ones."[20] But the cybernetic economy was not to be. "Panics and booms of the most nineteenth-century type" continued.

Cybernetics also promised to be the key to life itself. Why not apply the latest theory of control engineering to animals, or to people? In the 1950s there were many attempts to examine animals as machines, and the brain as an electrical device, as a computer. This approach built on work done by the physiologist Walter B. Cannon in the 1930s which used the notion of feedback to explain the way in which the body regulates itself. If life was nothing but a cybernetic process, then it shouldn't be too hard to build cybernetic machines that imitated living creatures. If the brain was but a machine, then it should be possible to produce animallike effects with simple cybernetic machines. The first was a "homeostat" designed by W. Ross Ashby in 1948. Ashby built on Walter Cannon's ideas about the way living organisms maintain their equilibrium — finding food when hungry and water when thirsty, sweating when hot, and so on. Ashby's 1952 book *Design for a Brain* described the homeostat as an electronic device that reacted to changes in its electrical inputs by adjusting its internal connections so as to neutralize the changes. (One author described it as "like a sleeping creature which when disturbed stirs and finds a comfortable position.")[21]

The most famous cybernetic robots were a pair of "mechanical tortoises" named Elmer and Elsie, designed by W. Grey Walter in England starting in 1948. These synthetic animals used simple circuits — two tubes, two sense organs, one for light and the other for touch, and two motors, one to crawl and the other to steer — cleverly connected so as to make the tortoises act in complex, "living" ways. They would go toward light until it got too bright, and then turn away. When their batteries got low, they would look for a bright light on which to "feed," then once "full," they would look for a soft light in which to sleep. "Although they possess only two sensory organs and two electronic nerve cells," Walter wrote in *Scientific American*, "they exhibit 'free will.'" Walter ended his description of his pet robots thus: "These machines are perhaps the simplest that can be said to resemble animals. Crude though they are, they give an eerie impression of purposefulness, independence, and spontaneity."[22] Cybernetics seemed to be on the verge of explaining life itself.

It was but a short step from understanding animals as mechanisms to thinking of people as mechanisms; from building robot animals to building robot people. It quickly became clear that cybernetics had a dark underside. It could come dangerously close to reducing human life to a simple mechanism, to nothing but information. Neuropsychiatrist Warren McCulloch wrote: "It is possible to look on Man himself as a product of . . . an evolutionary process of developing robots, begotten of simpler robots, back to the primordial slime; and I look upon his ethical conduct as something to be interpreted in terms of the circuit action of this Man in his environment — a Turing machine with only two feedbacks determined, a desire to play and a desire to win."[23] As Steve Heims writes in *The Cybernetics Group,* the ideals of most of the cyberneticists were not, at their core, humanistic. They neglected anything that couldn't be used in their attempt to turn behavior and society into "hard science." "The effort was always to give mathematical form, to simulate by a machine, or in other ways to resemble engineering when speaking of anything human, even the most personal feeling."[24] "Mechanistic metaphors for living," Heims continues, "belittling the subjective and the historical, may engender distasteful hypotheses about humans. Such hypotheses may be better suited for manipulation and control than they are for love and understanding."[25]

Indeed, Norbert Wiener was well aware of the problems with the cybernetic approach. A few years after *Cybernetics,* Wiener published a second book, *The Human Uses of Human Beings,* which raised profound questions about the possibilities of misusing the new science. Cybernetics, he said, would allow us to build machines that could run factories, putting both white- and blue-collar workers out of work. He feared the invention of "mechanical slaves," who, by competing with human labor, turn people into slaves themselves. He wrote, "It is perfectly clear that [automatic machines] will produce an unemployment situation, in comparison with which the present recession and even the depression of the thirties will seem a pleasant joke." He went on: "The new in-

Starting in the late 1940s, scientists and engineers interested in cybernetics created a menagerie of robot animals. W. Grey Walter designed "tortoises," which reacted to changes in light. Norbert Wiener built a two-function machine called both the Moth and the Bedbug; depending which way a switch was set, it was either attracted to or repelled from light. Claude Shannon, of information theory fame, designed a mouse that could run a maze. Squee the Squirrel, designed by Edmund C. Berkeley, ran around collecting tennis balls. The Johns Hopkins "Beast" of the early 1960s was most impressive: it wandered the halls looking for wall outlets and when it found one would plug itself in.

This picture shows two of Walter's "tortoises," Elmer and Elsie, responding to light and "reacting" to one another.

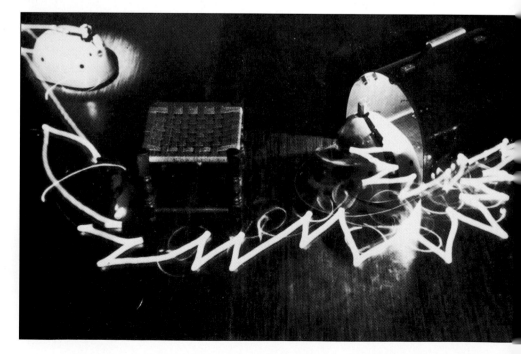

dustrial revolution is a two-edged sword. It may be used for the benefit of humanity . . . [or] it may also be used to destroy humanity, and if it is not used intelligently it can go very far in that direction."[26]

Indeed, computers based on the principles of cybernetics and its successor sciences would find use in the factory. They would also find use in the military, another fear of Wiener's. As would be the case with most computer technology, cybernetics and its stepchild, artificial intelligence, were to be supported by Defense Department dollars. The military saw in Elsie the Tortoise not a way of understanding the brain but rather the potential for the cybernetic soldier and the robotic tank. The smart weapon was to drive the development of smart machines.

ARTIFICIAL INTELLIGENCE

In 1950 Alan Turing proposed a way to determine whether or not a machine is intelligent. If a panel of judges can't tell the difference between the typed answers to questions given to a person and to a computer, then the computer passes the test. The "Turing test," as it came to be known, would remain a distant goal for the new field of artificial intelligence.

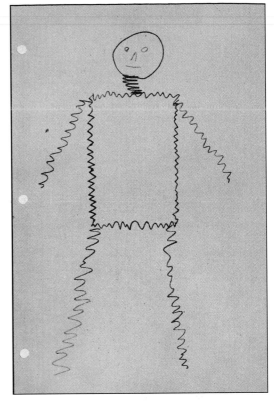

In 1959 the child psychologist Bruno Bettelheim published the story of "Joey the Mechanical Boy." Joey was an autistic child who thought of himself as a machine kept alive by other machines. Joey carried mechanical and electrical parts with him everywhere, and drew pictures of himself as a machine. Bettelheim suggests that Joey's hiding within a mechanical shell expressed our fears of machines and our dependence on them, taken to an extreme.

The first step toward artificial intelligence was machine translation of language. Language translation programs were heavily funded by the Defense Department, eager to translate Russian documents. These failed because the computer needed to understand not just sentence structure and vocabulary but *meaning*. The program had to *know* something about the situation being discussed. Models became important, both of language and of the subject matter. There were also attempts to program chess and checkers. As early as 1947, Arthur Samuels of IBM had written a checkers program that learned by varying the weights used in applying rules, and chess programs were written throughout the 1950s, which got to be pretty good. But it was clear that games weren't enough to gain computers more than a temporary fame, and a frivolous one at that.

Serious work on "intelligent machines" started in the 1950s. There were two basic approaches. As Seymour Papert, a pioneer in the field, puts it, there were two "daughter sciences" to cybernetics. One was based on the study of the brain, building on physiological theories to create "neural networks" that would learn as some believed the brain does, from scratch. The other abstracted further, building intelligent computer programs that included models of the world the program would learn about.

Neural nets built on early theoretical work by Warren McCullogh and Walter Pitts. In the early 1940s they proved that a sufficiently large number of neurons linked into a net could act as a "universal automaton," a machine that can solve any computable problem, given enough memory and time. Learning, to those who believed in neural nets, took place through changes in the connectivity and state of the neurons. Albert M. Uttley, Frank Rosenblatt, and others demonstrated that fairly simple neural nets — modeled by photocells and vacuum tubes — could be trained to recognize simple patterns, determining, say, whether a number was a 1 or a 0. They called these machines perceptrons and suggested that they were a "holistic" model of the brain. After some early successes, though, this school of thought lost out to artificial intelligence, a more rationalist, formal theory of symbol manipulation.

The modern history of artificial intelligence (AI) begins with the Dartmouth Summer Research Project on Artificial Intelligence in 1957. John McCarthy, who coined the term, was there, along with many of the researchers who would develop the field over the next few decades. Herbert Simon and Allen Newell, two of the key early players in artificial intelligence, outlined their goals: "We have begun to learn how to use computers to solve problems, where we do not have systematic and efficient computational algorithms. And we now know, at least in a limited area, not only how to program computers to perform such problem-solving activities successfully; we know also how to program computers to *learn* to do these things. . . . Intuition, insight, and learning are no longer exclusive possessions of human beings; any large high-speed computer can be programmed to exhibit them also."[27] It was a goal summed up in the first name for the field: cognitive simulation.

Many computer scientists made predictions that "smart" machines were just around the corner. "Within the very near future — much less than twenty-five years," Simon wrote in 1960, "we shall have the technical capability of substituting machines for any and all human functions in organizations. Within the same period, we shall have acquired an extensive and empirically tested theory of human cognitive processes and interaction with human emotions, attitudes, and values. . . . Duplicating the problem-solving and information-handling capabilities of the brain is not far off; it would be surprising if it were not accomplished within the next decade."[28]

Simon, like almost all of those who made predictions, did not foresee the difficulties that would face the field of artificial intelligence. It was not that they overestimated the increasing power of computers; it was rather that they underestimated the power, sophistication, and complexity of the brain. It was a flaw that stemmed, perhaps, from AI's cybernetic, nonhumanistic heritage. (It's revealing that one of the areas in which many artificial intelligence experts thought that computers would replace people was in the practice of psychiatry!)

The early 1960s saw the first use of a computer as a symbol-manipulating machine, not just a number-crunching engine. It also saw the first programs that depended not on algorithms — explicit instructions — but rather on "heuristics," general rules for solving problems. The first important breakthrough was Newell, Simon, and Clifford Shaw's 1960 General Problem Solver, a program that could solve logic puzzles. Other successes were programs that could do symbolic integration of differential equations, and could solve geometric analogy problems. Many experts in the field looked forward to programs with general intelligence, able to solve any problem.

Perhaps the best example of ways in which people overestimated the computer and underestimated the brain was Joseph Weizenbaum's 1966 ELIZA program. ELIZA — named after the character in George Bernard Shaw's *Pygmalion* — imitated a Rogerian therapist. It could carry on conversations, of a sort. If the user typed in "I hate my job," it could answer, "Why do you hate your job?" Given "I'm depressed," it might ask, "Are you often depressed?" Weizenbaum, who had intended the program to prove that no general solution to language understanding was possible — that language is understood only within contextual frameworks — was startled that many people thought he had solved the language-understanding problem. The computer didn't really know anything; it was following clever routines of playing with words. Most of the early AI programs, successful as they seemed, were capable of solving only the very narrow problems for which they were designed.

Unable to accomplish their original goals, AI researchers changed their direction, coming up with a new theory of intelligence that made a virtue of specificity. Marvin Minsky, the guru of artificial intelligence, defined intelligence as "a collection of indispensable categories, each rather complex: geometrical and mechanical properties of things and of space; uses and properties of a few thousand objects; hundreds of 'facts' about hundreds of people." In order for a machine "to behave with reasonable sensibility in ordinary situations," Minsky suggested, it had only to acquire "a hundred thousand elements of knowledge."[29]

The trick, then, was carefully to define "microworlds" that the computer could know all about, and come up with clever gimmicks that would allow the computer to "understand" these microworlds. Using this approach in the 1970s, artificial intelligence saw some of its most impressive successes. The best demonstration was one of the earliest: SHRDLU, a program written by Terry Winograd at MIT in 1970. SHRDLU "knew" all about an imaginary set of blocks and how to manipulate them, and how to parse language about those blocks. Winograd called it "a computer program which 'understands' language in a limited domain, by including a model of the subject being talked about as a context of discourse."[30] Unfortunately, it proved very hard to extend these microworlds. Winograd wrote later: "The AI programs of the late sixties and early seventies are much too literal. . . . This gives them a 'brittle' character, able to deal well with tightly specified areas of meaning in an artificially formal conversation. They are correspondingly weak in dealing with . . . less easily formalizable areas of knowledge."[31]

But less formalizable areas were where the money was. Starting in about 1975, expert systems — the new field was also known as knowledge engineering — promised to put artificial intelligence to practical use. The idea was to interview experts in an area, find out how to make judgments, and embody those judgments in "if-then" rules. A few hundred rules turned out to be all that was necessary. Almost never, according to Edward Feigenbaum, one of the originators of the field, "is an expert system larger than a few thousand pieces of knowledge. . . . Experts are often shocked and startled to find out that [their expertise] amounted to a few hundred rules."[32]

Expert systems had some success in medicine, spectrographic analysis, and even factory work — a computer was able to advise in the repairs of diesel locomotives and soup cookers — but they never got as good as the best experts. Intelligence always proved harder to simulate than researchers thought it would. The key thing learned from artificial intelligence, perhaps, is how *complex* intelligence really is. The big questions turn out to be easy. It's the common-sense questions that have so far proved an impossible task. Artificial intelligence, said a *Busi-*

Odex, a six-legged walking robot built by Odetics, Inc., in 1983.

ness Week writer in 1992, "has produced so much hype, so many dashed expectations, and even outright bankruptcies that software makers now shun the term."[33]

All of this has led to a resurgence of the old perceptrons, though in a new guise. The new model, called Parallel Distributed Processing, or connectionism, suggests that brains can indeed be modeled by multilayered networks of neuronlike elements that can train themselves, by experience, to learn. Advances in parallel computers — computers with many processors — have made it easier to model these systems, and they've met with some success. For example, a program called NETalk has taught itself to speak by comparing its attempts with what it was told words should sound like; after 50,000 iterations, the neural net was able to read aloud with about 95 percent accuracy.

But the jury is still out on which type of system is better. And both are very far from the human brain. It is estimated that the brain has approximately 100 billion neurons and 1,000 trillion synapses, and that the brain thinks at a rate of approximately 10 trillion bits per second. Its total memory is estimated at about 10,000 trillion bytes. Altogether, argues the mathematician Jacob T. Schwartz, from whose work these estimates are taken, it would require approximately 1 million trillion arithmetic operations per second to emulate the entire brain on a neuron-by-neuron basis. The biggest and fastest computers today have on the order of one millionth or one ten-millionth the capability of the brain, measured this (admittedly crude) way.

So the trick is to use that processing power cleverly. Consider a simple, common-sense skill such as walking. It shouldn't be too hard to design a walking robot. After all, there were lots of walking automata that simply used clever mechanical linkages to turn rotary motion into a walking motion. You can buy $5 wind-up toys that walk, after a fashion, based on these linkages. But for a robot to walk under computer control turns out to be a very difficult problem. (And this isn't even considering the at least equally difficult question of how the robot should figure out what path to take, another key problem.)

The first real walking robot was a "walking truck" designed by Ralph Mosher of General Electric in 1967. The Quadruped Transporter, which weighed 3,000 pounds and was eleven feet tall, had four independently movable hydraulic legs. But they weren't controlled by a computer. Rather, they were controlled by an operator in the robot's cabin. And it was very hard to control the machine — so hard, in fact, that the creature's creator was the only one who ever really learned to run it well.

Not until the late 1970s were computers put to work controlling walking machines. The first was designed at Ohio State University by Robert McGhee. It was a six-legged robot, so it could move slowly; it never had to balance because three legs were always on the ground. The computer solved the equations necessary to coordinate the eighteen motors that controlled the legs. A robot designed in 1984 at Odetics, Inc., called Odex, used the same principles, but clever mechanical design and a computer for each leg allowed it to move faster and with greater agility.

To go from six legs to two legs greatly increased the control problems. Two-legged robots have to balance, and balancing is tricky. Claude Shannon, the master of automatic control, showed one way the problem might be solved. In 1951 he built a cart that balanced a pendulum on a truck — a problem analogous to balancing on a single leg. But it took many years, until H. Miura and I. Shimoyama's actively balancing walking machine of 1980, before the control problems were solved. Their machine walked by constantly falling forward and then putting a leg out to catch itself. The first algorithmically controlled walking machine — actually a hopping machine — was built by Marc H. Raibert at Carnegie Mellon University in 1982. A few years later he extended his algorithms for a four-legged, and then a two-legged runner.

In the late 1980s a new breed of walking machine emerged. The Mobile Robot Group at MIT's Artificial Intelligence Laboratory, led by Rodney Brooks and Anita Flynn, designed a series of small robots that used emergent behaviors based on simple rules to walk and to figure out where to go. These robots, named Genghis and Attila, walked not by using complex algorithms, but rather by making use of communications between many small computers, each of which knew about a particular aspect of walking. Their movements were not "planned" but built on layers of simple techniques that called on other techniques as needed. For example, one computer knew about avoiding and following, another about moving legs, another about vision. When they were put together, the robot "learned" to walk, to find its way. These robots were not as smart as the insects they parodied, but they worked in a similar way.

In some ways the insect robots were more similar to cybernetic creatures like Elmer and Elsie than to the artificially intelligent, algorithm-controlled ro-

Many microprocessors, each good at a different aspect of walking, allow this miniature robot to get around. The motto of the Mobile Robot Group at MIT that built this robot was "Fast, cheap, and out of control."

bots like the Odex. These robots couldn't pass the Turing test — not even some sort of Turing test for insects — but they could behave, in some ways, like a not-too-bright insect. Their intelligence was limited, but it was useful — and real — in a way that earlier robotic intelligence was not. But it was not the stuff of science fiction. Science fiction had gone beyond smart machines to investigate how the line might be drawn — or erased — between people and machines.

FROM ROBOTS TO CYBORGS

As computers got "smarter" and robots got closer to being able to function in the real world — even if only at the insect level — they inspired a new wave of dreaming about the potential for smart machines and new forms of human-machine interaction. While most of the possibilities are still in the realm of fiction, the reality of humans and computers forming a union of some sort is clearly getting closer. Why bother to create artificial intelligence? Why not, instead, give machines human intelligence by somehow joining human brains and machines?

The idea of the cyborg (from "cybernetic organism") would serve science-fiction writers exploring the difference between people and machines. Science fiction would, in turn, give some computer scientists a goal, and a yardstick to measure their progress. The cyborg vision of people joining with machines would help define the changing relationships of nature, humanity, and machine. And most interestingly, the cyborg would come to be a metaphor for the redefinition of the distinction between human and machine, mind and body, male and female.

The cyborg appeared first in science fiction. The citizens of the thirty-second century in Samuel R. Delany's 1968 *Nova,* for example, all have sockets to plug themselves into computers and other machines. Arthur C. Clarke went one step further. Why not, he asked in his 1956 novel *The City and the Stars,* simply transfer the mind of the person into the machine? The story takes place millions of years in the future, in a civilization that has learned to extract the mind from the brain, but which somehow is still much taken with the language and philosophy of 1950s cybernetics. "The way in which information is stored is of no importance. All that matters is the information itself. It may be in the form of written words on paper, of varying magnetic fields, or patterns of electric charge. . . . Suffice it to say that long ago [men] were able to store themselves — or to be more precise, the disembodied patterns from which they could be called back into existence." As Marvin Minsky told *Newsweek* in 1980: "At some point people may even prefer to convert themselves into machines, because if they can transfer their intelligence into another embodiment, they might be able to live forever and continue developing."[34]

Hans Moravec, a computer scientist at Carnegie Mellon University, has developed this idea to its furthest extent. He predicts a "postbiological" future of "human thought freed from bondage to a mortal body." He describes a step-by-step, layer-by-layer transfer of the thoughts and feelings somewhere in the human brain to a new computer brain:

> The robot surgeon opens your brain case and places a hand on the brain's surface. This unusual hand bristles with microscopic machinery, and a cable connects it to the mobile computer at your side. Instruments in the hand

scan the first few millimeters of brain surface. High-resolution magnetic resonance measurements build a three-dimensional chemical map, while arrays of magnetic and electric antennas collect signals that are rapidly unraveled to reveal, moment to moment, the pulses flashing among the neurons. These measurements, added to a comprehensive understanding of human neural architecture, allow the surgeon to write a program that models the behavior of the uppermost layer of the scanned brain tissue.

The process continues until the entire brain is modeled in the computer, which is then connected "to a shiny new body of the style, color, and material of your choice." There are, Moravec writes, many advantages to this procedure. The mind can be sped up as new hardware becomes available. You can arrange for mind backups, just as we now make backups of computer disks, in case anything happens to your new body. You could have several copies of yourself made, if you desired, or you could have your mind combined with that of other "people," or, for that matter, other species. You could even be transmitted over a wire to travel at the speed of light. In a masterpiece of understatement, Moravec suggests that in this brave new world, "concepts of life, death, and identity will lose their present meaning." Those who do not like this vision he calls "human chauvinists."[35]

It's hard to know how to critique these ideas. Is it bad to be a human chauvinist? Is the distinction between person and computer important? In a book published some years before Moravec's, Joseph Weizenbaum gave one answer. Some applications of computers, Weizenbaum suggested, should just not be done; they are, he wrote, "simply obscene." "The proposal . . . that an animal's visual system and brain be coupled to computers, is an example. It represents an attack on life itself." The "very contemplation" of these ideas, he wrote, "ought to give rise to feelings of disgust in every civilized person."[36]

Science-fiction writers have contemplated these ideas for several decades now. Since the 1950s at least, science fiction has been populated by cyborgs. Unlike robots of the sort found in Isaac Asimov's stories, which are completely mechanical (which are, as he put it, engineering problems, "machines, not metaphors") cyborgs are a mixture of the human and the mechanical, and thus by their nature a metaphor for human-technological interactions. The line between human and nonhuman has come to be a major theme in science fiction, a way, writes critic Peter Fitting, "of embodying our contradictory hopes and fears about an increasingly mechanized world."[37] The hopes can be found in a variety of simple-minded wish-fulfillment stories in which people acquire the strength of machines when they take mechanical bodies, as in the 1970s TV shows "Six-Million-Dollar Man" and "Bionic Woman." But it's the fiction that expresses the fears which suggests a more profound critique of the nature of humanity, and our relationships with the machines we have built.

Philip K. Dick explored the potential of cybernetics in a series of robot stories beginning in 1952. His robots, unlike those in Asimov's stories, are rarely well behaved. Not only do they veer out of control, but as often as not they think of themselves as human. Dick erases the line between people and machines. In "The Little Movement," wind-up toys turn out to be aliens plotting to take over the earth. In "The Second Variety," robot weapons redesign themselves to look like children, or like wounded soldiers, to fool the human soldiers they are battling. And most complicated of all, in "Imposter," a scientist has (perhaps) been replaced by a robot and (perhaps) doesn't know it. A security agent explains to the scientist what has happened:

> "The robot was to destroy a particular human being and take his place. . . . Inside the robot was a U-Bomb. . . . The robot would live the life of the person he killed, entering into his usual activities, his job, his social life. He had been constructed to resemble that person. No one would know the difference. . . . That person whom the robot was to impersonate was Spence Olham."
>
> Olham stared down at his hands. "But I'm Olham!"[38]

Like so many of Dick's stories, "Imposter" switches perspectives dizzyingly. Not only is the reader never sure whether or not Olham is robot or human, but neither is he. Like the cyberneticists, Dick blurs the lines between the animate and the inanimate.

The plot in many science-fiction stories concerns trying to figure out who is machine and who is human, to better define what it means to be human. In Philip Dick's best-known work, *Do Androids Dream of Electric Sheep?* and the movie based on it, *Blade Runner,* four "replicants" — cyborgs — have escaped from the planets where they work and returned to Earth. The hero, Deckard, has to track them down. He succeeds in killing three of the four but because the replicants begin to show emotions, and realize the value of life — Deckard falls in love with a replicant, and is saved from death by her — they become more human and less machinelike. The same is true in the *Terminator* movies. The first cyborg, T-1, is a hostile mechanical cyborg with no emotions: it can't be reasoned with; it feels no pity, no fear. But T-2, exposed to human emotions, learns the value of human life, and begins to understand, and even display, emotions. A series of "Star Trek: The Next Generation" episodes about "the Borgs," an alien race that has no idea of individuality, plays out similar themes. The Borgs (cyborgs, of course) become more human when they are treated with friendship. By blurring the lines between human and machine, writers of cyborg stories define the nature of humanity, and often confirm human superiority over machines.

Another way of defining humanity is found in stories in which robots try their best to become human. Lester del Ray invented "Helen O'Loy," a female robot who watches too many soap operas on the "stereovisor" and falls in love with her creator. He resists at first, but finally marries her. "The neighbors never suspected they were anything but normal man and wife."[39] Love makes Helen O'Loy human. Love — more precisely, owning objects that speak of love — proves that "Data," the android on "Star Trek: The Next Generation," is human in the episode called "The Measure of a Man." A book, a cat, and, most important, a photograph of a woman he had sex with — these suggest he has emotions, and is more human than machine. Thus, he should be given the privileges of human rights, even though, as it turns out, he's not sure he really wants them.

In the 1980s "cyberpunk" fiction pushed the human-machine distinction in another direction. Indeed, the distinction no longer exists, and — most important — no longer matters. In William Gibson's novels there is no end of ways in which humans and machines might be joined; Fitting calls *Neuromancer* (1984) a "futuristic Sears catalogue of cyborg possibilities, of imaginative and perverse combinations of the machine and the organic. . . . The ability to distinguish between the human and the nonhuman is now meaningless."[40] The creatures that inhabit Gibson's fiction don't know whether they are machines or people. They don't even care.

Perhaps the most interesting analysis of cyborgs is found in recent feminist criticism. When the lines between people and machine are blurred, the distinction between maleness and femaleness can also become blurred; gender and sexuality are at the base of what it means to be human. This opens up new possibilities for examining the nature of gender differences. Feminist critic Constance Penley suggests that science-fiction films such as *The Man Who Fell to Earth* and *Blade Runner* make up for decreased sexual differences by exploring the difference between people and machines, or people and aliens. She writes: "The question of sexual difference — a difference whose answer is no longer 'self-evident' — is displaced onto the more remarkable difference between the human and the other."[41] Another critic, Janet Bergstrom, reads the differences the other way, suggesting that in movies where it's hard to tell androids from humans (like *Blade Runner*), sexual differences take on added importance.

The cyborg as metaphor has been pushed furthest by Donna Haraway. She suggests that women can use the idea of the cyborg to reimagine and retheorize women's position. Because of the liminal role of the cyborg, on the borders of humanity and nature, and without obvious gender, it opens up new possibilities for the relations between men, women, nature, and technology. In her 1985 "Manifesto for Cyborgs," Haraway argues that the cyborg is (or should be) the quintessential postmodern feminist figure. By melding nature and machine, female and male, art and science, it allows a new understanding of gender. Critic Judith Halberstam emphasizes the importance of the fading distinctions: "Because the blurred boundaries between mind and machine, body and machine, and human and nonhuman are the legacy of cybernetics, automated machines, in fact, provide new ground upon which to argue that gender and its representations are technological productions." The cyborg is flux: "The imperfect matches between gender and desire, sex and gender, and the body and technology can be accommodated within the automated cyborg, because it is always partial, part machine and part human; it is always becoming human or 'becoming woman.'"[42] A female cyborg can work from within, deceiving the dominant technological culture and seizing power for itself. "The machine," Haraway writes, "is not an *it* to be animated, worshipped, and dominated. The machine is us, our processes, an aspect of our embodiment. We can be responsible for machines; *they* do not dominate or threaten us. We are responsible for boundaries; we are they." Haraway celebrates the possibilities of the cyborg. "Though both are bound in the spiral dance," she concludes, "I would rather be a cyborg than a goddess."[43]

The cyborg, like the automaton, the science-fiction robot, and the intelligent computer, allows us all to project ourselves beyond the possibilities of the world of nature. In doing so, we might reimagine ourselves, free from the bounds of established definitions of humanity and human activities. The computer, born of war and bureaucracy, is, against all odds, a most malleable machine, a machine that we can shape as we please. Writers of science fiction and of feminist criticism have shown us how we might shape it, in our imagination. The task before us is to shape the future of computers to our needs and wants, in the real world.

FOR FURTHER READING

There are many illustrated books on robots in literature, including Harry M. Geduld and Ronald Gottesman, eds., *Robots Robots Robots* (1978), which includes reprints of important stories and articles; Jasia Reichardt, *Robots: Fact, Fiction, and Prediction* (1978); and John Cohen, *Human Robots in Myth and Science* (1966). For more interesting analysis, see Christine Woesler de Panafieu, "Automata — A Masculine Utopia," in *Nineteen Eighty-Four: Science between Utopia and Dystopia*, ed. Everett Mendelsohn and Helga Nowotny (1984), pp. 127–145.

There is a huge popular literature on artificial intelligence. The best historical overview is Daniel Crevier, *AI: The Tumultuous History of the Search for Artificial Intelligence* (1993). A good overview is the collection of articles in Stephen R. Graubard, *The Artificial Intelligence Debate: False Starts, Real Foundations* (1988). See also Pamela McCorduck, *Machines Who Think: A Personal Inquiry into the History and Prospects of Artificial Intelligence* (1979); and, for a skeptical view, Hubert L. Dreyfus and Stuart E. Dreyfus, *Mind over Machine: The Power of Human Intuition and Expertise in the Era of the Computer* (1986). Vernon Pratt, *Thinking Machines: The Evolution of Artificial Intelligence* (1987), gives an excellent historical overview. For an insider's point of view, see Raymond Kurzweil, *The Age of Intelligent Machines* (1990).

On robots, see Joseph Deken, *Silico Sapiens: The Fundamentals and Future of Robots* (1986); and Isaac Asimov and Karen A. Frenkel, *Robots: Machines in Man's Image* (1985). On cyborgs in science fiction, good sources are Thomas P. Dunn and Richard D. Erlich, eds., *The Mechanical God: Machines in Science Fiction* (1982); and Patricia S. Warrick, *The Cybernetic Imagination in Science Fiction* (1980). On the idea of the mind transplant, see Ed Regis, *Great Mambo Chicken and the Transhuman Condition: Science Slightly over the Edge* (1990); and Hans Moravec, *Mind Children: The Future of Robot and Human Intelligence* (1988). For an overview of the feminist critique of the possibilities of the cyborg, see Judith Halberstam, "Automating Gender: Postmodern Feminism in the Age of the Intelligent Machine," *Feminist Studies* (Fall 1991): 439–460.

NOTES

1. Edgar Allan Poe, "Maelzel's Chess-Player," *Southern Literary Messenger* (April 1836); reprinted in Harry M. Geduld and Ronald Gottesman, eds., *Robots Robots Robots* (1978), pp. 87 and 90.

2. Quoted in Pamela McCorduck, *Machines Who Think: A Personal Inquiry into the History and Prospects of Artificial Intelligence* (1979), p. 4.

3. Quoted in Harry M. Geduld, "Genesis II: The Evolution of Synthetic Man," in Geduld and Gottesman, *Robots Robots Robots*, p. 6.

4. Christine Woesler de Panafieu, "Automata: A Masculine Utopia," in *Nineteen Eighty-Four: Science between Utopia and Dystopia,* ed. Everett Mendelsohn and Helga Nowotny (1984), pp. 134–135.

5. David F. Noble, *A World without Women: The Christian Clerical Culture of Western Science* (1992), pp. 284–286.

6. Mary Shelley, *Frankenstein, or the Modern Prometheus* (1818); reprinted in Geduld and Gottesman, *Robots Robots Robots*, p. 45.

7. Karel Čapek, *R.U.R.*, in *Toward the Radical Center: A Karel Čapek Reader*, ed. and trans. Peter Kussi (1990), p. 76.

8. Čapek, *R.U.R.*, p. 109.

9. Isaac Asimov, "Introduction: The Robot Chronicles," in *Robot Visions* (1990), pp. 8–9.

10. Norbert Wiener, *Cybernetics, or Control and Communication in the Animal and the Machine* (1965), p. 11.

11. Steve Joshua Heims, *The Cybernetics Group* (1991), p. 22.

12. Quoted in Heims, *The Cybernetics Group*, p. 22.

13. Norbert Wiener, *The Human Use of Human Beings: Cybernetics and Society*, 2d ed. (1950; reprint 1988), pp. 15 and 16–17.

14. Reviews quoted in Wiener, *Cybernetics*, back cover.

15. Isaac Asimov, preface to Pierre de Latil, *Thinking by Machine: A Study of Cybernetics*, trans. Y. M. Golla (1957), p. viii.

16. General Electric Company, "The Next Step in Management: An Appraisal of CYBERNETICS" (1952), p. 180.

17. Isaac Asimov, "The Evitable Conflict," in *Robot Visions*, pp. 194–195.

18. Robert Heinlein, *Beyond This Horizon;* quoted in Michael Kurland, "Of God, Humans, and Machines: The Computer in Science Fiction," in *Digital Deli*, ed. Steve Ditlea (1984), p. 200.

19. Kurt Vonnegut, *Player Piano* (1952), p. 102.

20. Vonnegut, *Player Piano*, p. 143.

21. W. Grey Walter, "An Imitation of Life," *Scientific American* (May 1951): 43.

22. Walter, "An Imitation of Life," p. 42.

23. Warren McCulloch, *Embodiments of Mind* (1965), p. 157; quoted in Heims, *The Cybernetics Group*, p. 38.

24. Heims, *The Cybernetics Group*, p. 179.

25. Heims, *The Cybernetics Group*, p. 279.

26. Wiener, *Human Use of Human Beings*, p. 162.

27. Herbert A. Simon and Allen Newell, "Heuristic Problem Solving: The Next Advance in Operations Research," *Operations Research*, 6 (January-February 1958): 6.

28. H. A. Simon, "The Shape of Automation" (1960); quoted in Joseph Weizenbaum, *Computer Power and Human Reason* (1976), pp. 244–245.

29. Marvin Minsky, ed., *Semantic Information Processing* (1968), pp. 25–26; quoted in Hubert L. Dreyfus and Stuart E. Dreyfus, *Mind over Machine: The Power of Human Intuition and Expertise in the Era of the Computer* (1986), p. 68.

30. Terry Winograd, "A Procedural Model of Language Understanding," in *Computer Models of Thought and Language*, ed. Roger C. Schank and Kenneth Mark Colby (1973), p. 153.

31. Terry Winograd, "Artificial Intelligence and Language Comprehension," in *Artificial Intelligence and Language Comprehension* (1976), p. 9; quoted in Dreyfus and Dreyfus, *Mind over Machine*, p. 77.

32. Quoted in Jon Palfreman and Doron Swade, *The Dream Machine* (1991), p. 153.

33. Evan I. Schwartz, "Smart Programs Go to Work: How Applied-Intelligence Software Makes Decisions for the Real World," *Business Week*, March 2, 1992, pp. 97–105.

34. Quoted in Ed Regis, *Great Mambo Chicken and the Transhuman Condition: Science Slightly over the Edge* (1990), p. 150.

35. Hans Moravec, *Mind Children: The Future of Robot and Human Intelligence* (1988), pp. 109–110 and 115.

36. Weizenbaum, *Computer Power and Human Reason*, pp. 268–269.

37. Peter Fitting, "The Lessons of Cyberpunk," in *Technoculture*, ed. Constance Penley and Andrew Ross (1991), p. 301.

38. Philip K. Dick, "Imposter," in *Robots, Androids, and Mechanical Oddities,* ed. Patricia S. Warrick and Martin H. Greenberg (1984), p. 81.

39. Lester del Ray, "Helen O'Loy"; reprinted in Geduld and Gottesman, *Robots, Robots, Robots,* p. 222.

40. Fitting, "The Lessons of Cyberpunk," p. 302.

41. Constance Penley, "Time Travel, the Primal Scene, and the Critical Dystopia," in *Close Encounters: Film, Feminism, and Science Fiction,* ed. Constance Penley, Elisabeth Lyon, Lynn Spigel, and Janet Bergstrom (1991), p. 72.

42. Judith Halberstam, "Automating Gender: Postmodern Feminism in the Age of the Intelligent Machine," in *Feminist Studies* 17, no. 3 (Fall 1991): 439–440.

43. Donna J. Haraway, "Manifesto for Cyborgs: Science, Technology, and Socialist-Feminism in the Late Twentieth Century," in *Simians, Cyborgs, and Women: The Reinvention of Nature* (1991), pp. 180 and 181.

ILLUSTRATION CREDITS

P. xx: Courtesy Library of Congress. P. 3: © 1991 Mark Alan Stamaty. Courtesy Mark Alan Stamaty. P. 11: Courtesy of the General Research Division, New York Public Library, Astor, Lenox and Tilden Foundations. P. 14: Courtesy State Historical Society of Wisconsin (WHi (X3) 48225). P. 15: Courtesy Library of Congress. P. 18: Courtesy Lucille and Walter Rubin Collection. P. 20: Smithsonian photograph by Alfred Harrell. P. 25: Courtesy National Academy of Design. P. 26: Courtesy of the Boston Atheneum. P. 27: Courtesy of the American Antiquarian Society. P. 31: Photograph courtesy Museum of Modern Art Film Stills Archives. Copyright © 1932 by Universal City Studios, Inc. Permission courtesy of MCA Publishing Rights, a Division of MCA Inc. (bottom); Courtesy U.S. Information Agency (top). Pp. 32, 34: Courtesy Library of Congress. P. 35: Courtesy Dun and Bradstreet Company. P. 37: Courtesy private collection. P.38: Courtesy Xerox Corporation. P. 42: Los Angeles Times Photo (right); Smithsonian photograph by Richard Strauss (left). P. 50: Courtesy Lake County (IL) Museum/Curt Teich Postcard Archives. P. 53: Smithsonian photograph by Eric Long. P. 56: Courtesy Library of Congress (top and bottom). P. 57: Courtesy Library of Congress. P. 58: Smithsonian photograph by Eric Long. P. 59: Courtesy Photography Collections, University of Maryland, Baltimore County. P. 62: Courtesy Archives Center, National Museum of American History, Smithsonian Institution (bottom). P. 63: Courtesy of The MIT Museum. P. 64: Drawing by Jon Watson using StrataVision 3D, Courtesy of Strata, Inc. P. 65: Courtesy Intergraph Corporation. P. 66: Courtesy National Center for Supercomputer Applications. P. 67: Courtesy of Andrew Liebhold. P. 68: Courtesy of Mi Young Toh and Mark E. Molliver. P. 69: Courtesy Division of Medical Sciences, National Museum of American History, Smithsonian Institution. Pp. 74, 78, 80, 81: Smithsonian photographs by Alfred Harrell. P. 84: Courtesy Library of Congress. P. 85: Smithsonian photographs by Rick Vargas. Pp. 91, 96: Smithsonian photographs by Kevin Kornemann. P. 92: Smithsonian photograph by Eric Long. P. 94: Smithsonian photograph by Alfred Harrell. P. 95: Courtesy Library of Congress. P. 97: Courtesy Archives Center, National Museum of American History. Pp. 104, 109, 110 (bottom): Smithsonian photograph by Eric Long. P. 113: Courtesy National Archives. P. 114: Courtesy Archives Center, National Museum of American History, Smithsonian Institution (top); Smithsonian photograph by Eric Long (bottom). P. 115: Smithsonian photographs by Eric Long. P. 118: Courtesy Library of Congress. Pp. 120, 121: Smithsonian photographs by Alfred Harrell. P. 126: Courtesy Cook Collection, Valentine Museum. Pp. 128, 131, 133, 134, 136: Courtesy of AT&T Archives. P. 139: Copyright © by Universal City Studios, Inc. Courtesy of MCA Publishing Rights, a Division of MCA Inc. P. 146: Smithsonian photograph by Eric Long. P. 153: Courtesy of Prodigy Service Company. P. 155: Courtesy EDS. P. 156: Courtesy National Center for Supercomputing Applications. P. 166: Courtesy Library of Congress. P. 168: Smithsonian photograph by Alfred Harrell. P. 169: Courtesy U.S. Department of the Interior, National Park Service, Edison National Historic Site. Pp. 170, 171 (bottom), 173: Smithsonian photographs by Eric Long. P.180: Courtesy Library of Congress. P. 184: Smithsonian photograph by Damon Parrish. P. 187: Photograph by J. Lindy Pollard. P. 190: Courtesy Henry Chalfant/CityLore. P. 191: Photograph courtesy Photofest. Permission courtesy of New Line Cinema Corporation. © 1988 New Line Productions, Inc. All rights reserved. Photo by Greg Allen. P.192: Courtesy Mark of the Unicorn, Inc. P. 198: Courtesy Library of Congress. P. 200: Courtesy U.S. Department of the Interior, National Park Service, Edison National Historic Site. P. 203: Smithsonian photograph by Eric Long. Pp. 204, 205: Courtesy of Library of Congress. P. 206: Courtesy *International Musician*, American Federation of Musicians. P. 209: Courtesy of The Walt Disney Company. © The Walt Disney Company. P. 212: Courtesy Library of Congress. P. 218: Courtesy State Historical Society of Wisconsin(WHi [X3] 48229). P. 219: Courtesy Motorola Museum of Electronics. P. 220, 222: Courtesy Archives Center, National Museum of American History, Smithsonian Institution. P. 223: Smithsonian photograph by Eric Long (left). P. 224: Courtesy Archives Center, National Museum of American History, Smithsonian Institution (top); From the Collection of the University of Wisconsin-Madison Archives (bottom). P. 231: Courtesy Association of American Railroads (top). P. 235: Photograph courtesy Photofest. Copyright © 1960 Turner Entertainment Company. All rights reserved (bottom). P. 236: Photograph courtesy Museum of Modern Art Film Stills Archives. Permission courtesy of Paramount Pictures. "Handle With Care" copyright © 1977 by Paramount Pictures. All rights reserved. P. 242: Courtesy Motorola Museum of Electronics. P. 244: Courtesy Library of Congress. P. 248: Smithsonian photograph by Eric Long. P. 249: Courtesy Library of Congress. P 259: Smithsonian photograph by Eric Long. P. 260: Courtesy of CNN, Inc. © 1991 CNN, Inc. P. 264: Courtesy Nintendo of America, Inc., © Nintendo of America, Inc. P. 267: Courtesy Ampex Corporation. P. 271: Courtesy Erols, Inc. P. 273: Courtesy of The MIT Museum. P. 274: Photograph courtesy Photofest. Copyright © by Universal City Studios, Inc. Courtesy of MCA Publishing Rights, a Division of MCA, Inc. P. 279: Smithsonian photograph by Eric Long. P. 286: Smithsonian photographs by Rick Vargas. P. 287: Smithsonian photograph by Dane A. Penland (left); Smithsonian photograph by Rick Vargas (right). P. 288: Smithsonian photographs by Eric Long. P. 289: Smithsonian photograph by Rick Vargas. P. 291: Courtesy Metropolitan Museum of Art, Bequest of Susan W. Tyler. P. 292: Courtesy International Museum of Photography at George Eastman House (top); Smithsonian photograph by Kevin Kornemann (bottom). P. 296:

INDEX